SUSTAINED
by Eating,
CONSUMED
by Eating Right

SUSTAINED
by Eating,
CONSUMED
by Eating Right

REFLECTIONS, RHYMES, RANTS, AND RECIPES

ERIC L. BALL

excelsior editions

State University of New York Press
Albany, New York

Excerpts and paraphrases in chapter 19 from Eric L. Ball, "Greek Food after *Mousaka*: Cookbooks, 'Local' Culture, and the Cretan Diet," Journal of Modern Greek Studies 21 (1) (2003): 1–36, are courtesy of Johns Hopkins University Press.

Published by State University of New York Press, Albany

Excelsior Editions is an imprint of State University of New York Press

For information, contact State University of New York Press, Albany, NY
www.sunypress.edu

Production by Ryan Morris
Marketing by Kate McDonnell

Library of Congress Cataloging-in-Publication Data

Ball, Eric L., 1970–
  Sustained by eating, consumed by eating right : reflections, rhymes, rants, and recipes / Eric L. Ball.
       p. cm.
  Includes bibliographical references.
  ISBN 978-1-4384-4624-0 (pbk. : alk. paper) 1. Food habits—United States—Psychological aspects. 2. Nutrition—Social aspects—United States. 3. Ball, Eric L., 1970–   4. Suburban life—United States. 5. Vegetable gardening—United States. 6. Ball, Eric L., 1970—Travel—Greece. 7. Ball, Eric L., 1970—Travel—Europe. 8. Cooking, Greek. I. Title.
  GT2853.U5B35 2013
  394.1'2—dc23

                                                        2012017565

10 9 8 7 6 5 4 3 2 1

for all the new growth on our family trees

What do you believe you have already learned?
How do you decide that you have done so?
                    —Lee Herman and Alan Mandell,
                              From Teaching to Mentoring

The work that follows has been crafted out of my present recollection of experiences over many decades. Certain names, locations, products, organizations, and other identifying characteristics have been changed, and certain individuals/characters are composites or caricatures. Dialogue and events have been rearranged and re-created from memory, compressed or altered to convey something of what I recall having been said or having occurred, and in some cases fabricated altogether for the purpose of dramatizing the narrator's inner world of emotions and imaginings more accurately or succinctly.

This book is intended solely as a creative work and should not be construed as presenting or insinuating factual information, scientific knowledge, expertise, or advice regarding areas including but not limited to: health, medicine, psychology, nutrition, food quality, food safety, food manufacturing, food preparation, winemaking, botany, mycology, plant identification, mushroom identification, foraging, gardening, composting, biology, ecology, environmental science, agriculture, physics, journalism, business, economics, law, and theology. Nothing written herein should be interpreted as a substitute for the knowledge, proficiency, practices, guidance, care, or advice of credentialed and/or licensed experts in these areas.

Nevertheless, I sincerely hope readers will still discover something meaningful in the pages that follow.

Contents

Prologue: Report to Euphrosynos   1

1.   Salad Yard Rebellion   9

2.   Garden Soil, Psychological Dirt   17

3.   Hunting for Mushrooms and Total Freedom   31

4.   The Other Side of the Family   45

5.   Family Farmer Funeral   53

6.   I Get By with a Little Help from My Parents   61

7.   The Kid from the Country Goes Continental   69

8.   Meet the Parents   81

9.   Recipes   93

10.   Cheesy Coincidence   109

11.   Cretan Flesh, Cretan Spirit   119

12.   Impromptu Gatherings   133

13.   One Dream Ends, Another Begins   145

14.   Kitchen Apprentice   165

Contents

15.   Cooking Cretan in the United States   175

16.   Kitchen Apprentice Redux   197

17   Love of Hosting Others   211

18   The Vine, More than One Way   225

19   The End of Nostalgia   237

20   Birthdays, Inc.   255

21   Food and Health   265

22   Thanks, but No Thanks   285

23   Personal, Political, Environmental   299

24   Hot Tempers   313

Epilogue: "Happy Name Day, Euphrosynos"   325

Acknowledgments   333

Notes   335

Prologue: Report to Euphrosynos

I'm writing on my laptop, sitting on a barstool at our kitchen counter. No one else is around. I look up at you and the other "kitchen gods," as Sofia fondly dubs you. I see, hanging above the kitchen doorway, four color photocopies of paintings from art exhibition books that I glued to slightly larger pieces of thick, black foam board so they'd look like the icons I've seen for sale in Greece. One is by the Cretan-born Theotokopoulos ("El Greco") and depicts *The Last Supper*. Three are by various iconographers of the so-called Cretan school: another *Last Supper*, one showing *The Hospitality of Abraham*, and—my favorite—an icon of you, *Saint Euphrosynos the Cook*.

Jesus and Abraham look preoccupied with their companions and visitors, but you stand there alone gazing solemnly over the kitchen, where you frequently see me making something to eat, pouring a drink, emptying the dishwasher, or writing. I usually only notice you watching me when I'm by myself, without any conversations to follow, without even the quietest presence of another person to attract the compass needle of my consciousness.

To be honest, I know little about you—you were a Christian saint, your Name Day falls on September 11, you are known as "the cook"—so I feel free to imagine you as I wish. The way I figure it, you and I are two people who know something about cooking and who believe there are important connections between the sustenance of bodies and other supposedly higher matters, such as the sustenance of spirit. I like to imagine that you were a rebel saint who knew better than to turn your back on the material and the worldly in favor of the spiritual alone, but I haven't decided whether you knew better because you were a cook, or if you became a cook because you knew better.

Sometimes I look at your icon and feel inspired by the possibility that a society or a culture can juxtapose the words *saint* and *cook* for reasons other than to romanticize the unprotesting endurance of dedicated housewives or the patient resignation of especially dutiful grandmothers. Other times I'm reminded not to become overly nonchalant about my own cooking. And sometimes I even pretend to believe that you're keeping watch over my bread dough so that it will rise.

Above all, though, seeing your image there encourages me to believe that I'm hardly alone in holding a preoccupation with everyday food matters in such high esteem—What should I eat today? Who should I eat with? What ingredients should I cook with? How much should I pay for them?—and that my pre-occupation need not be mistaken for a mere hobby. It reminds me that the question of *eating right* is serious and important, and not only in the narrowest sense of good nutrition for personal health.

The question of eating *right*?

As someone who for half his life only sought to eat the tastiest food among whatever choices he happened to find right there in front of him, I sometimes find it difficult to believe that I'm so preoccupied with such a question.

For many vegetarians, eating right means something about doing right by nonhuman animals. For growing numbers of locavores, eating right is measured in food miles or carbon footprints. For believers, it has to do with such practices as keeping kosher or not eating meat on Fridays during Lent. But what about for someone like me who isn't persuaded by any such inherited custom or neatly packaged *ism* (vegetarian*ism*, locavor*ism*, etc.)? How can I be certain that I'm not just obsessed with *eating*? And how can I be consumed by eating right when I'm not entirely sure I even know what I mean by the word *right*?

(I'll gladly confess that I'm more than a little worried that what I'm writing here makes it appear as though I'm on a collision course with the second chapter of that *Introduction to Philosophy* textbook from my first year in college. Which reminds me: I should mention that, by now, I've read enough good books to know better than the freshman college student who thinks questions such as *What is right?* can be instantly disposed of by impatiently throwing up one's hands saying, "To each his own!" and "Everyone is entitled to their own opinion!" But I've also *taught* introductory philosophy enough times to suspect that hiding somewhere in the impatience of such freshman outbursts is the expression— inarticulate though it may be—of an intuitively grasped truth: no matter who we are, our own particular experiences and our thoughtful appraisals of those experiences matter.)

Plenty of other people interested in food and drink have written informative books about eating right. I may have occasion to mention a few at some point. But I want to try something different. Going against the grain of my professional training as a researcher, I want to pay close attention to my own experiences. Not because my experiences are representative of anyone else's. Certainly not because they are more valuable than anyone else's. But rather because I'm overcome with an unrelenting suspicion that by doing so I'll learn something valuable that I might not learn otherwise. This means I'll also have occasion to mention many of the dearest or most influential people in my life. In fact, when it comes to those individuals who have most significantly influenced my thinking about food, I'll have much to say.

In short, I want to try out the path of the memoirist for a while. I want to descend into memory to explore certain issues of the day from the vantage point of my own life. Still, not unlike those who argue against dredging the Hudson River for PCBs, I'm inclined to believe that some memories are best left undisturbed, so I plan to dig deep only when I sense that it's germane to the food- and drink-related topics at hand.

Considering how many human bodies on planet Earth go to bed hungry or die of malnutrition, and in spite of lofty assertions by certain intellectual-types that the unexamined meal is not worth eating, I believe that meditating at length about one's own everyday relationship to food and drink remains something of a luxury. History has not afforded this luxury to most people and therefore has rendered it that much more important for those of us who enjoy it not to squander it.

Should anyone care to *read* such a meditation? Part of me knows they shouldn't. That's why I, like Kazantzakis to Greco, am pretending to make my report to *you* instead of to an imagined audience of real human beings.[1] But another part of me realizes that while the particulars of my experiences may be unique to me—especially my dropping everything to go to Greece—making sense out of these particulars means putting them into appropriate contexts, and these contexts are hardly unique to me. Moreover, if I'm unable to make sense of them in a way that's meaningful to an audience of other people, then perhaps it means I'm not succeeding in making good sense of them after all. Even worse: perhaps it means I'm only justifying myself to myself on my own terms—and we're back to that solipsistic freshman who keeps insisting that everything is merely subjective.

I don't expect to report anything utterly remarkable or unprecedented. Any well-read American foodie who could see how Sofia and I have been living would tell you that in most respects there isn't much that's original about our everyday food lives: We have a vegetable garden—many suburban homeowners have a vegetable garden. We bake bread—many people bake bread. We eat wild greens—North America has lots of wild-plant and mushroom foragers. We buy olive oil in bulk—many people buy food in bulk. We shop at farmers' markets—more and more Americans are shopping at farmers' markets with each passing year. We make homemade organic beer—many people homebrew. We cook various international dishes—many Americans cook ethnic food.

If there's anything remarkable, it's probably just that we are engaged in so *many* food-related activities—especially considering that we both work full time and neither of us is employed in a culinary profession.

More abstractly, when it comes to our *convictions* about food and drink, I gather that Sofia and I are equally undistinguished next to people of academic backgrounds or political persuasions comparable with ours. We probably share most of the same values as many of our contemporaries who make efforts to take an informed approach to food. For instance, we care about relishing the immediate sensory pleasures of flavor, smell, texture, and presentation. We pay attention to issues regarding food safety. We try to maintain a healthy diet. We aim to keep our food-related expenses reasonable. We want to avoid hurting other people and therefore try steering clear of ecologically high-risk food practices and unfair and exploitative treatment of the people who raise, produce, distribute, or dispose of food.

Nevertheless, there are plenty of dedicated foodies who go to much greater lengths than we do to experience the widest possible range of food's sensory pleasures. There are environmentally minded individuals who do much more than we do to support ecologically low-risk food practices, just as there are many socially conscious citizens who are more unwavering in their activism and other forms of support for fair trade, farm workers' rights, and food co-ops. There's also a growing number of locavores who successfully seek to procure a higher percentage of their ingredients from within a short geographical range than we do.

I'll admit that some of my convictions about food and drink *are* rather uncommon, and unthinkable apart from my experiences with Greeks, especially when it comes to hospitality, getting together with friends or family or colleagues for a good time, and emphasizing more traditional styles of cooking over the latest trends. Well, maybe *unthinkable* is a slight exaggeration, since my convictions about these things might also have something to do with my upbringing in Upstate New York. I'm getting ahead of myself, though.

Something else that's remarkable, at least as far as I'm concerned, is that Sofia and I are doing these things in my old hometown—the very place that I, the fiercely independent oldest son, enthusiastically left behind more than fifteen years ago. A place where most individuals in one generation after another of my family seem perfectly content—sometimes downright proud—to continue living, but which I long ago decided had far too little to offer me in comparison with some other places I was discovering.

If you really want to hear about it, Sofia and I initially considered job-hunting in southern California, where Sofia's sister lives. Southern California's Mediterranean climate attracted me, especially when I imagined learning to grow lemons, oranges, and wine grapes. But I didn't like the idea of having to update our knowledge of wild-edible-plant foraging we'd just learned, based as it was on greens that grow in the northeast. And there was an allure to moving to a locale I was already familiar with. I considered the Adirondack Mountains and farther north—places where I'd enjoyed living during my undergraduate years, and which had the advantage of being close enough to visit my relatives but not *too* close. But I also worried that there in the far north even supermarkets might not carry the less common ingredients—parsley root, say, and pomegranates—that Sofia and I'd been taking for granted after having lived for a number of years in a major city in Ohio. I entertained the idea of places just below the Adirondacks, closer to my hometown, nearer to cities like Albany where Mediterranean and Asian markets sold many of the ingredients that Sofia and I regularly cooked with. Besides, after so many years of playing the role of the visitor from far away, part of me hoped that being "too close" to my relatives would make it more convenient for *them* to visit *us* on occasion.

Eventually, Sofia and I settled on job-hunting in something like a two-hundred-mile radius around my old hometown. Considering how difficult it was to find even one decent academic job in the region—especially fresh out of graduate school, and in the humanities and arts—we judged that we were incredibly fortunate when we both found tenure-track jobs in the same institution—just ten miles down the road from the house I grew up in!

Eight months later, the house adjacent to my parents' new house went up for sale. It was in a small development just a short walk from Grandma and Grandpa's old house, where my father's sister still lives. It was a bigger house than we needed. It would mean having to drive to and from the college. It would locate us farther away from some of the best grocery shopping in the region. And, it was built on a mere half-acre lot, much of which was already taken up by a new deck and a swimming pool, significantly limiting what we'd be able to do there in terms of growing some of our own food.

But we intuitively anticipated that this house's particular disadvantages would be made up for by the predictable and unpredictable benefits of our being right next door to my parents. If my brother's family visited my parents, they'd automatically be visiting us. If I needed to use a hacksaw, I could just walk next door and borrow one. There'd be twice as much room available, indoors and out, for large family gatherings.

There were other things we liked about the house as well. We liked the many windows. The kitchen was spacious and well laid out—I'd just have to get my father to help me do some minor renovations. I was confident—since I'd grown up in the area—that there wasn't any PCB contamination nearby. We liked that the house was new, since the romantic charm of an old building was much less important to us than good insulation, paint that wasn't peeling, and keeping the rodents outdoors. As Sofia and I weren't keen on moving again soon, a large house meant that it might remain spacious and comfortable for us and our visitors well into the future. Maybe when family or friends visited they'd take advantage of the pool, even if we didn't. When it came to food and drink, Sofia and I had always managed to make the most out of any apartment we lived in—surely we'd be able to make even more out of owning our own place.

We both knew that in certain respects it would've made more sense for us to settle down in a large city where we could take advantage of all the great grocery shopping and supplement it with a rooftop or community garden. Or, to buy ten acres out in the country with all the space we could ever desire for growing food away from prying eyes. But we didn't approve of the implication that America's sprawling suburbs could never be remade into places more hospitable to people with values like ours. What if more families gave the suburbs a makeover? Might it not help nudge along a gradual transformation—along more socially just, ecologically low-impact lines—in how North Americans organize and inhabit space?

Besides, I was eager to live where I knew I'd be surrounded again by some of this world's friendliest, most generous, and largely unpretentious people.

And so, ready to take our everyday life food-related activities to the next level, and filled with cautious optimism about doing so around the company of my family, Sofia and I tested our luck once more. We skipped the whole house-hunting ordeal, filled out a mortgage application, and made an offer.

Our life is well under way here, where questions about food and drink preoccupy me every day. Where I sit and write this report to you, Euphrosynos.

* 1 *

Salad Yard Rebellion

I get down on my knees. I place a large plastic bowl next to me in the grass, grab a handful of heart-shaped leaves with my left hand, and cut them off about an inch above the ground with the fishing knife my parents gave me for my thirteenth birthday. As with many other childhood things, I've taken this knife with me everywhere I've lived.

Twenty minutes later, I'm sitting on the edge of one of the hand-me-down plastic chairs on our back deck, sifting and trimming greens: chives and garlic chives, tender young leaves of dandelion and chicory, a stalk of celery's perennial cousin lovage, a handful of frog's belly leaves, a few sprigs of lemon balm and spearmint, and the heart-shaped leaves of the common blue violet. Everything I've collected is resting in large plastic bowls stacked up in another chair. I let the trimmings and debris fall from my hands into a bowl on the deck floor and toss the good leaves into another bowl sitting on the plastic patio table in front of me.

Our first salad of the calendar year is well on its way.

If somebody were to ask me in April what I think I should eat, I'd probably answer: "All the edible greenery I can scavenge from our own yard!"

When you live this far north, especially if you don't have a greenhouse, the duration of the annual-vegetable-garden harvest tends to be short. After the killing frosts of autumn, you settle in for the long winter and count in disbelief how many months will have to pass before your next homegrown tomatoes or zucchini will be ready.

Experienced gardeners know that supplementing annuals with perennials and planting cold-hardy vegetables like kale and leeks that can persist into winter are two good ways to extend the duration of the home-garden harvest. Around here, when it comes to perennials, rhubarb and asparagus rule the day. But Sofia and I only began vegetable gardening after we'd spent years foraging edible wild greens, so not only does our harvest season begin in April, asparagus and rhubarb are little more than punctuation on the wild-green sentences that are scribbled over different sections of our yard.

Many people who live around here love green salads. They also like saving money on food. They'd probably like to avoid some of the risks posed by pesticides and the dangerous strains of *E. coli* that occasionally show up on commercial salad greens. And, many of them would probably like to avoid the toil of conventional vegetable gardening (even though they appear to enjoy working hard on their lawns). So they'd probably benefit from experimenting with different kinds of yards around their houses, and with different kinds of salads in their kitchens.

When I was a child, I adamantly prophesized that, "When I grow up I'm not gonna have a lawn." My parents assigned mowing the lawn to my brother and me as our primary summer chore, and I detested it even more than dragging the wheelbarrow through snow to load up the downstairs porch with firewood for the wood-stove. We had a riding mower, so it wasn't physically demanding labor, just time-consuming and boring—though the invention of the walkman and just plain daydreaming about growing up to be a truck driver brought some relief. I didn't like the sound of lawn-mower engines, I didn't like the smell of freshly cut grass, and I was afraid of all those stones shooting out like bullets from the side of our old push-mower. I probably should've been tested for grass allergies, too.

The second or third day after we moved into our house, Sofia and I began transforming our half-acre lot with its conventional suburban grass monoculture into a cornucopia of plants that would increasingly provide us with safe, delicious, and healthful edible complements to the foods we buy.

We had only rudimentary knowledge and experience with growing plants, and, as newly hired college faculty who were busy trying to prove ourselves, we had limited spare time. So we never made an elaborate master plan the way some landscaping books recommend, but took things a little at a time—trying something out here, taking advantage of an opportunity that presented itself there—all the while learning from our experiences and from the books we were reading.

The violets in the salad I'm making are the result of having taken advantage of one such opportunity. My parents decided to remove all the violets that were spreading into their flowerbeds and asked if we wanted them. I removed the sod along the side of our garage and transplanted the violets in its place.

My parents also gave us a large bag of wildflower seeds that someone had given them, but that they never used. So I removed a four-foot strip of grass in front of the walk from our driveway to our front door and planted them there.

I stopped mowing most of the grass on the other side of the house, hoping to widen the buffer of shrubs and trees between our house and the house next door. Grubs soon destroyed most of that grass anyway, and then mullein—a typical visitor on poor, bare soil—appeared with its large, fuzzy leaves that make a flavorful herbal tea, now controversial because the plant might contain toxic coumarin and rotenone. (Note to self: Look for actual research regarding the toxicity of the dried leaves. Perhaps the concentration of these toxins is insignificant? Are the toxins even in the *leaves*?)

I'm relieved to know that Sofia and I aren't breaking any rules. I called our Town Hall the week we moved in and learned that there don't seem to be any ill-conceived local regulations regarding lawn care where we live. But I understand that the way we've been modifying our lawn still makes us rebels.

We aren't rebelling against our neighbors, but we *are* participating in the quiet rebellion against contemporary suburban landscaping norms in the United States, norms that were established in large measure by industries and special interest groups. (If you don't believe me, read *The Lawn: A History of an American Obsession.*[1]) Troubling evidence has been piling up that such landscaping norms are better for the pocketbooks of those who invest in lawn-chemical companies and support the squandering of fossil fuels than for the health and well-being of the people—not to mention other species—who live, or might someday live, on these lawns.

As far as I can tell, most of our neighborhood follows these norms as if they were a matter of self-evident aesthetic truth, or at least a good financial investment in terms of property values. I know what it's like to live in a place where rebelliousness is a celebrated aspect of local identity and cultural self-recognition, and this isn't such a place. Prudence therefore dictates that Sofia and I proceed cautiously as we reduce the expanse of grass out front, showing sufficient deference to the current aesthetic sensibilities of our neighbors. I think we're doing okay: the wildflowers are colorful and bright throughout much of the summer; the violets by the garage have filled out into a thick perennial border that doesn't grow too tall; and the mullein growing in the buffer-zone-in-progress, by virtue of some trees out front and the property line's angle to the road, isn't much visible to passersby. (It also doesn't hurt that my parents are friends with several other families in our development.)

I do mow the remaining grass in our front yard, but I use a manual rotary push-mower—the old-fashioned kind. This lets us avoid contributing to unnecessary fossil-fuel and noise pollution that conventional household lawn mowers bring to our neighborhood. Who knows, perhaps when neighbors go by and see me out front with my manual mower they genuinely wonder why I'm not using a gas-powered machine. If my lawn mower can provoke people to ask themselves a question then it's well worth my using it.

It's a couple weeks later and our early-spring raw salads have given way to boiled wild greens—especially dandelion or chicory dressed with olive oil and freshly squeezed lemon juice. Most of our dande- lions and chicory grow in the backyard, hidden from neighbors' view by fences and woods.

When we moved into the house, Sofia and I agreed—not knowing for sure if the previous owners had used any industrial herbicides, pesticides, or fertilizers the previous season—that for our own protection we'd abstain from eating anything that grew in the yard until the following year. (We didn't bother asking the previous owners about lawn chemicals, because even if they told us they hadn't used any I wouldn't have risked believing them. Just my own little paranoia.) After years of dreaming that Sofia and I would have our own little patch of earth from which to eat, it was difficult to wait another year before trying anything. We let most of the back- yard grow out for a season to see what edibles came up—slender nettles in a couple locations, black raspberries and dewberries along the back fence, a few purslane plants here and there, and, of course, dandelions. Along the new swimming pool, a large patch of lawn that had been reseeded just before we bought the house tempted us with a bumper crop of lamb's quarters—a delicious mild green that tastes outstanding when boiled and served with olive oil and freshly squeezed lemon juice. But since we'd read that lamb's quarters tend to accumulate unusually high quantities of nitrates when growing in artificially fertilized soils, we easily resisted.

While most of the backyard was growing unfettered, we also transplanted various wild edibles that we'd collected by foraging around town. In fact, Sofia and I had actually foraged some of these starter plants before we moved. Such was the case with the wild grape vines, cuttings of which we'd kept on the deck of our apartment in a jar of water in the weeks leading up to our move. We also had a pot of Greek spearmint from my friend Leonidas.

We transplanted many other greens foraged from around town. We found lots of yellow goat's beard, also known as oyster plant, growing in the unkempt flower beds around the parking lot of what would soon become our local supermarket. We located chicory growing in a big pile of gravel dumped behind the nearby hardware store. We got sheep sorrel from my parents' backyard. We happened upon colt's foot on a path along the river, and discovered lady's smock and wild carrots on the side of a nearby road. We found chickweed and wintercress in a field near the bridge to Hudson Falls.

We transplanted these in various locations throughout the backyard and waited to see what would happen the following year. Some, like the lady's smock, didn't come back. Others, like the wild carrots, quickly spread around the area we reserved for them. The goat's beard, a dandelion relative whose seeds are also carried in the breeze, came back far from where we'd planted it, but only where the habitat was just right—such as along the back edge of the garage where there was crushed stone, sand, and few other competing plants. The chicory came back but didn't spread much on its own, so the next year I gathered its seeds by hand, scattered them in pots, and then transplanted the seedlings in stony soil along the side fence.

My idea was to increase our chances of getting more wild edibles from the yard with each passing year, while continually decreasing the amount of physical labor it would involve for us to grow and harvest them. Transplanting wild perennials and vigorously self-seeding annuals was part of the strategy. Another part was letting things grow out so we could see what was already there, and then doing things that might coax them to spread. In addition to the stinging nettles, berries, and purslane, this eventually led to ground cherries near the back fence, common evening primrose in the stones by the house, shepherd's purse on the path out to the back gate, several patches of wild strawberries, wood sorrel, redroot amaranth, red clover, and a stand of staghorn sumac. We also tried to increase the diversity of minihabitats that our small backyard contained: compost piles, grassy areas, stony paths where I'd removed the sod, places where dry leaves tend to collect, places where pine needles land, and wood piles. Our hope was that more edibles would turn up wherever a minihabitat was favorable to their growth.

❈ ❈ ❈

I'm washing dandelions, my favorite green vegetable.

I fill up a large light-colored plastic bowl with water and then swish the dandelions around in it. I pull the dandelions out of the water in bunches and set them in a colander that is resting in another bowl to catch the dripping water. (When Sofia and I were graduate students, we were always on the lookout for utensils and other kitchen hardware that would make food preparation more efficient and economical. That's when we bought from a dollar-store several oversized plastic colanders and many huge plastic bowls—which, turned upside down, also make good covers for pies and cakes.) I repeat the whole process several times until I can see at the bottom of the *light* colored bowl that little or no more debris is coming off the leaves.

We love the flavor of dandelion greens so much that sometimes we save the water we boil them in, add earthy tea leaves (like *lao cha* or *pu-erh*), strain, and refrigerate.

Despite the assertions of far too many people who write about foraging, Sofia and I have yet to notice a correlation between a dandelion's bitterness and the time of year or its having flowered. For that matter, neither do we agree that dandelion palatability simply be correlated with bitterness, since many of the world's best-tasting foods and drinks are characteristically bitter—hoppy beer and black coffee come to mind. Sometimes when I'm trimming dandelions, I leave the flowers and flower stalks in with the leaves. Sometimes

I collect just the flowers for a special treat, like white sourdough bread subtly flavored with a cup or two of yellow dandelion petals.

Something else I've read: Many of the dandelions that are sold in supermarkets are not dandelions at all—they are a variety of domesticated chicory. Anyone who eats dandelions and chicories regularly will discover a significant difference in how they taste. To the tongue, "dandelion chicory" is no more dandelion than roasted chicory root is coffee.

The more varieties and quantities of wild greens Sofia and I manage to harvest from our yard, the more we enjoy being surprised by a little patch of this here or an unexpected shoot of that there. There's something exciting and artisanally improvisational about combining wild and cultivated plants. It's not just about eating weeds from our garden, but about continually readjusting the entire yard plan around whatever plants happen to come up, around encouraging certain things to grow by scattering wild seeds or creating minihabitats, and around the gradual evolution of our other outdoor needs, such as where we locate a compost pile or create a path through the yard.

It feels almost like we *and* the plants are deciding, in negotiations as it were, how to landscape this lot. As a result, Sofia's and my motivations for consuming wild greens now include a desire to be surprised, to reckon with the pleasantly unexpected, and to be delighted—and occasionally challenged, too—by the complexity of certain biological and ecological processes.

✳ 2 ✳

Garden Soil, Psychological Dirt

Sofia and I are eating lunch at a nearby coffee shop. I tell her that I ran into my father when he was out weeding their front yard and that he mentioned I could go get whatever compost there must be behind Grandpa's old shed—where Grandpa had dumped raked leaves and pine needles for decades and where my father has continued doing so ever since Grandpa passed away. I expect Sofia will be happy to get some additional compost for *her* garden rows.

We discuss whether it's worth the trouble—we don't have a truck and I don't want to ask my brother, who's usually quite busy, to help us with his. It dawns on us that the yard at Grandma and Grandpa's is going to waste. Aunt Patsy isn't doing anything with it. My father mows and maintains the grass because *somebody* has to. Why shouldn't Sofia and I expand our garden of domesticated vegetables by taking advantage of a second lot?

Our second year here we began teaching ourselves how to do this less-wild kind of gardening. We started with some of the basics—tomatoes, cucumbers, basil, zucchini, green beans, peas, carrots, peppers, radishes—which got Sofia increasingly passionate about gardening in general. Soon she was reading garden books and keeping meticulous records and notes about everything she was doing. It wasn't long before she was buying most of her seeds—mostly heirloom varieties—through the mail, starting seedlings under fluorescent lights by the kitchen windows as early as March, and saving many of her own seeds. Nowadays she also grows sweet potatoes, okra, corn, dill, cilantro, parsley, celery, cranberry beans, arugula, cabbage, brussels sprouts, lettuce, spinach, turnip, beets, celeriac, garlic, onions, leeks, tricolor amaranth, garland chrysanthemum, snow peas, various mustard greens, and pumpkins. We also put in a small patch of asparagus, transplanted some of Grandma's old rhubarb to our front yard, and created a thirty-foot row of fall-bearing raspberries that came from new neighbors up the road who wanted flowers in their yard instead of the raspberries.

❀ ❀ ❀

We continue sipping coffee. Sofia and I discuss the challenges of having an offsite garden. Neither of us expects to have the time or energy to check on it on a daily basis.

"What about shell beans?" Sofia suggests. "We could grow our whole year's supply, and we can let the beans dry on the plants."

I agree and suggest that after we harvest the beans in the fall we can plant garlic. "By covering the garlic beds with leaves and straw, we shouldn't need to do any watering the following spring or summer, except if there's a really dry spell. We can even throw in a few tomato plants so Aunt Patsy has something she can go out and pick for herself if she wants."

On the drive back home after lunch, Sofia and I stop off at my grandparents' old house to make sure Aunt Patsy won't mind our putting in a garden in the backyard, and so we can inspect the location of trees and sunlight.

Aunt Patsy doesn't seem to mind.

The three of us wander out back from the porch to take a closer look around the yard. I'm remembering clearly where Grandma and Grandpa used to have their vegetable garden, and where the big pine trees used to grow just north of it. It occurs to me that this was over *twenty* years ago. After I'd gone off to college, Grandpa had the pine trees taken down and transplanted spruce trees he'd dug up from my parents' friends' woods. For the first time, I'm noticing what and where these "new" trees are.

I know where the septic tank and leach field are located. I know where we'd need to leave room for a truck to make it from the gate over to the septic tank, and for Aunt Patsy to drive her car around to the hose so she can wash it.

I'm really only half-thinking about the garden, though, because I'm feeling overwhelmed just by being here. I'm disappointed that the pine trees and the fireplace I remember are long gone and that these new trees dominate the perimeter. It's frustrating to see Grandpa's garage, shed, and house looking somewhat dilapidated. At the same time, I'm exhilarated because so many other things are the same as they used to be. Grandpa's drawers of hand tools in the garage, his coffee cans filled with nails and screws, his shovels and pitchfork in the shed, and even the particular smell of the garage. I see Florence and Ormond's house out back—the one Grandpa had originally built for Aunt Patsy on the back of his lot when she got married—but I know that Florence and Ormond's son and daughter, who my brother and I always played with as kids, moved out of state long ago, and that Ormond has suffered a stroke. Grandpa's nephew Stanley's house across the road looks like it always did, but Stanley himself passed away a few weeks ago.

The three of us continue wandering around the yard, sometimes together, sometimes independently. Sofia doesn't look bothered in the least that it's taking me so long, for no apparent reason, to finish inspecting the situation. She doesn't seem taken aback by seeing this unexpected, less-hurried side of me.

I'm not even thinking about the garden anymore. I'm too distracted by everything else I see. So much looks the same, whispering to me that I *can* go back—that I *am* back. So much looks different—aging, decaying, falling apart, dead—reminding me that Sofia and I, too, are getting older, and that without children and living so far away from Sofia's sister and brother, we might be on a path leading to far more loneliness than maybe even someone like Aunt Patsy—divorced, without children, and living alone, but constantly visited by relatives, friends, and people from church—will ever experience.

We finally stop our pacing and scouting and confer about gardening options. Sofia and I conclude that there really isn't a good place for a garden unless we take down two small trees right behind the garage. This would open up the backyard completely and the garden would receive full sun, better than at our own house. One of the trees looks half dead and the other one is ugly. I mention my take on the situation and Aunt Patsy says she'd like to see those trees gone. Clearly she thinks they're an eyesore. She seems grateful that we might remove of them, but she tells me I'd better check with my father first to make sure he's okay with it.

Sofia and I head back to the car so we can leave. Aunt Patsy comes out to the driveway to see us off. I point out to Sofia the remnants of one of the birdhouses I built with Grandpa when I was twelve or thirteen. Aunt Patsy says, "Remember how your grandmother sat outside on the bench to make sure the bluejays wouldn't hurt that baby robin?" Turning more toward Sofia now, she adds, "There was a baby robin lying on the ground, and she sat outside on the bench for the *whole* day to make sure the bluejays wouldn't hurt it. Then she covered it with a box for the night. But when she came out the next morning she saw that the bluejays must've gotten it anyway. That's when we decided that *we* didn't like *bluejays* anymore."

Somewhat annoyed, I put the key into the ignition and start the car. Sure, I understand my grandmother's heartfelt urge to care for the weak or to protect the innocent—in this case, her favorite kind of bird, the kind she used to write poems about when she was in grammar school. When I was younger I loved this story. But nowadays I also see things I couldn't see when I was a child. Such as how my family can take what might otherwise be a meaningful and empathetic emotional response and turn it into an excuse for dividing whole categories of people or living things into the Good Guys and the Bad Guys. Such as how Aunt Patsy as a mere bystander can so eagerly become an ally to this kind of prejudice. Such as how some people in my family apparently think it's laudable to care for one random wild bird while effectively turning a blind eye to the suffering of so many random *people* who, perhaps through no fault of their own, could really benefit from more protection, care, and support. Then again, I know my grandmother did offer all the protection, care, and support to family and friends that any human being could ever reasonably be expected to—to Aunt Patsy, above all.

"Alright, we'll see you later, then," is all I can think to say before I finally close the car door and wave good-bye.

We arrive back home. I see my parents working in their front yard. I check with my father about taking down the trees and putting in the new garden. He's fine with it.

It's midnight. A yucky feeling about putting in the new garden is keeping me awake.

I keep trying to avoid thinking about why, mostly because I sense it'll make me feel even yuckier. But even without intentionally giving it any thought I'm pretty sure it has something to do with Grandma and Grandpa's house having been my home away from home when I was a child. Though only five miles away, to my young eyes it seemed like an entirely different world.

My parents built their house on a maple-strewn lot carved out of the country, surrounded by woods, clay cornfields, and few houses, on a coarsely paved town road with no dividing lines or posted speed limit. People called it the Hatchery Road because of the state-operated fish hatchery that was open during the earliest years of my life. On the half-mile bicycle ride over to look at the fish we only passed one other house. In the other direction we soon came to the end of the road where there were a number of older houses and a Methodist church, indications that Fortsville was once a noteworthy settlement, with a grist mill to boot. (So I've read, and it probably explains the old bottles, pails, and other pieces of rusted metal that my brother and I used to find on the bank of the mucky stream that ran along one side of our property—and the rainbow veneer on the water wherever it puddled.) In addition to the constants of a dog and numerous cats, we grew up with such pets as mallard ducks—living on our small fenced in pond that my father made by damming the stream, good for ice hockey and broom ball in the winters—white ducks, a goose, a rabbit, and on two separate occasions, a goat.

Grandma and Grandpa, on the other hand, lived on the outskirts of the nearby village of South Glens Falls. When they built their house it was among the first in their neighborhood, but by the time I was born, it had developed into a populous residential area. Cars went up and down the road all day long. The yard was full of pine trees and sandy soil. There wasn't the choir of tree frogs, bullfrogs, and crickets that on Hatchery Road drowned out the sound of the traffic on the Adirondack Northway on hot summer nights, just the occasional interjection of a pet parakeet or Chihuahua. At Grandma and Grandpa's house I could see the periodic flashes of light in the night sky that came from a tower at one of the local paper mills. At home all I could make out were the lights of the nearby prison.

I stayed overnight at Grandma and Grandpa's house as often as my parents would let me, and I always had loads of fun there.

When Grandpa was home, I might be out in the garage helping him fix up bicycles or building birdhouses, all the while listening to his many stories. He'd talk about his experiences in the Second World War, his favorite horse when he was a kid on the farm, and how much he paid for his first car—a used Model A Ford. He'd tell me stories about how he'd quit a job whenever it became too miserable, preferring to endure a pay cut for happier working conditions somewhere else. He'd speak about the corruption of local politicians and how the one politician he did trust was unable to make a real difference. He'd talk about the people he worked with down at the New York State highway maintenance garage—like Willie, who'd eat sardines and moldy bread and then have to stop the truck to get out and vomit on the side of the road. "Well everybody's different, you know," was his usual commentary on many of these stories. Sometimes, too, as he was lighting a cigarette he'd say, "Don't ever start smoking. It's an awful habit. I couldn't have been twelve when I started and now I can't stop."

If Grandpa was working, I might be outside playing with Florence and Ormond's kids, drawing pictures on giant pieces of newsprint, or playing the piano down cellar with my younger brother. Since Aunt Patsy lived there, too, having moved back in after her divorce, I might be listening to old '50s records with her, or playing cards with her and any other relatives who happened to stop by.

Grandma would always ask me what I wanted for dinner. This meant a difficult choice between her lasagna, and her beef with boiled potatoes, homemade gravy, and boiled carrots dressed with melted butter. The beef dish has remained the stuff of family lore because almost every time she made it she'd try to give visitors the most tender and best caramelized pieces of beef, but then sigh at the end of the meal saying, "Oh dear, I think I ended up with the best piece again." The beef was my brother's favorite, but whenever he wasn't staying there with me my first choice was lasagna.

If Grandma knew ahead of time I was coming up, she'd drop Grandpa off at work and keep the car. That way if she needed an ingredient she could run out to the Grand Union. That was another big difference from home. My parents did the grocery shopping once a week, usually right after church when we were already in town near the supermarkets. It was a veritable expedition, and my brother and I were expected to help carry the many bags of groceries from the car up to the kitchen before we could go out and play. Grandma kept a few shelves of pantry items down cellar, but living in town she could more readily go to the store for something she needed on the spur of the moment.

Grandma let me help her with the food whenever I wanted. I always helped shuck the corn on the cob they bought on the side of the Saratoga Road directly from the family who grew it. Grandma took me and her sister to pick strawberries for shortcake and sour cherries for pie at the fruit orchards over in Washington County. One year, I helped her and Aunt Patsy make so many pies to bring to my parents' house for Thanksgiving that there was one pie per person.

I loved Grandma's pies. Her rhubarb cream pie—made with her own rhubarb—and banana cream pie were big family hits. When I was in third grade, my class had a drawing contest for the design we'd use to decorate the classroom pumpkin. My pirate drawing won, and after Halloween I got to take the pumpkin home. So I asked Grandma if she'd make me a pumpkin pie. She not only made me the pie, but wrote me a poem telling the story of the contest, my pirate design, and my bringing her the pumpkin.

When I was in Junior High, I'd pass by Grandma and Grandpa's house every day on an afternoon school bus that went to the High School, where I'd change buses to go home. Once, when Grandma had made homemade rolls, she and Aunt Patsy used a giant sheet of newsprint to make a sign that said Rolls, and hung it on the garage door so I'd see it when I went by on the bus. Of course, I walked to their house instead of getting on the second bus to go home.

Aunt Patsy's living at Grandma and Grandpa's added to the menu of favorite foods I got to choose from whenever I stayed there—coffee cake for breakfast or potato salad for lunch out in the cool breeze on the screened-in porch. I also got to watch her make cakes—brightly colored, theme-based birthday and anniversary cakes, and elegant, multitiered wedding cakes—for family events or to sell. Sometimes she let me use the colored frostings to decorate an extra cake that we were keeping for ourselves. Aunt Patsy would also give me money to buy "pink candies" and "fudgicles" [sic] from the convenience store nearby.

I experienced many special foods and food projects with Grandma and Aunt Patsy. Breakfast cooked out on the fireplace. Homemade pizza parties. Baked grapefruit. In eighth grade, my social studies teacher gave us a homework assignment where we had to come up with a menu of dishes that used only ingredients that were available to the early American settlers. Grandma got out all her cookbooks and we looked through them for ideas. Going beyond what the assignment required, I ended up making an actual restaurant-style menu (for "The Silver Spoon"), decorated with food photos that Aunt Patsy and I cut out from magazines, and offering everything from a "hot corn mush cereal" to "Vermont-style baked beans"—water served free of charge.

Grandpa didn't cook, but he provided favorite foods nonetheless. If I was there on a Saturday morning he'd take me with him around town to garage sales (looking for tools), the dump (looking for old bicycle parts and anything else that looked useful), and a local bakery where we'd buy—"real cheap"—a brown-paper grocery bag stuffed full with cellophane bags of day-old donuts, crullers, cinnamon rolls, and other breakfast pastries. Grandma made her heavenly home-made donuts for us two or three times, but we usually just settled for the bakery items Grandpa bought. Donuts were one of Grandpa's favorite foods. Not that he was particular about what he ate, except that he wouldn't eat anything green—from cake frosting to spinach—permanently traumatized by having been fed a "green soup" by the Germans while he was a prisoner of war. Although the rest of us drank Adirondack Cola or "Peps" [sic] with our meals, Grandpa usually drank water, except on those Fridays when he and Grandma would take me to Long John Silvers and we'd both drink Dr. Pepper with our Fish 'n' More dinners—a special treat every time.

If my love of homemade foods began in childhood, so did my distaste for many industrial foods. The foods that I enjoyed at Grandma and Grandpa's, more often than not made from scratch, were quite different from what I was usually fed at home and at the homes of relatives of my parents' generation. Theirs was a generation given promises by the media, advertisers, government, and schools of freedom from the time-consuming drudgery, self-discipline, and difficult learning that homemade food supposedly entails.

It's not that I never ate food cooked from scratch at home. Some-times my mother would make homemade macaroni and cheese with real cheese, or cook roast beef or a roast pork. Sometimes she'd bake coarsely chopped tomatoes and onions with crumbled toast and plenty of butter in the oven. On holidays and other special occasions she'd slow-cook homemade spaghetti sauce, or she'd roast chicken, turkey, or ham and make mashed potatoes and homemade gravy. In the autumn we often went apple picking and she'd make pies and lots of applesauce. At Christmas, my brother and I would help my parents make dozens of different holiday cookies and fudge. For a couple years we even had a small vegetable garden. My mother learned how to turn the cucumbers into the bread 'n' butter pickles I preferred to supermarket dills, and with so much summer squash on hand, zucchini breads and zucchini cakes were like staples. One year we ate the eggs laid by our pet ducks.

But these foods were the exception, not the rule. More frequent were the frozen fish sticks or frozen french fries heated in the oven on a cookie sheet, applesauce from a jar, salad dressings in bottles, macaroni and cheese from a box, casseroles made with canned soup, canned spaghetti, canned fruit, and instant pudding with whipped topping. (I could go on.) Such were the everyday foods that I barely tolerated and only rarely enjoyed.

For some reason, I especially disliked industrial substitutes for more traditional foods, even when the latter were industrially manufactured. I liked whipped cream but not whipped topping. I loved butter but not margarine. I liked mayonnaise but thought a less-expensive substitute tasted gross. (I *think* I remember which brand it was, but now that a bunch of states have passed food libel laws, I'm too scared to exercise my freedom of speech.) I'll never be able to erase from my memory the time my mother's sister fed my cousins and me tuna fish sandwiches, and I didn't know she'd used that less-expensive substitute instead of mayonnaise until I took the first bite and almost gagged, but, then—too ashamed to say anything to her—forced myself to finish the sandwich.

My mother called me a fussy eater, though in hindsight I can't recall many foods made from scratch that I didn't like. It seems to me now that I appeared fussy because I didn't get along very well with most industrially manufactured foods or the semihomemade dishes that used them as ingredients.

*　*　*

Several days pass.

The yucky feeling goes away, but I haven't decided about the new garden.

Sofia and I have had so many garden chores in our own yard to take care of that we haven't had time to get back over to Aunt Patsy's. I've been quietly persuading myself that we don't *really* need an extra garden. I'm secretly hoping that Sofia has forgotten about it and won't remember again until it's too late in the season to plant shell beans. But I know it's more likely that she's just waiting for me to make up my mind, without giving me added pressure.

Something inside me starts nagging me to make a decision. I ask myself: Will putting in an extra garden cause more memories from childhood to resurface? Is it worth going through all this just for home-grown shell beans, more home-grown garlic, and seeing Aunt Patsy more often?

For the last decade or so of Grandpa's life, I found it increasingly difficult to stop by and visit him—*me*, the grandson who practically *lived* up there every chance I got. By the time I graduated from college, I'd experienced so many new things and found that so many of my beliefs, interests, and interpretations of the world had changed, that I felt like there was little or nothing left for Grandpa and me to do together or talk about. Whenever I'd visit, all I could think about was how uncomfortable it must've made him to sense this, and all I could feel was torn between pretending to be the same person I used to be so he'd be happy and just being myself—my *new* self.

Do I really think it's wise to start playing again in Grandma and Grandpa's backyard after all these years?

I surprise myself and tell Sofia that we should get to work on the new garden as soon as possible.

I load a tree saw and loppers into the car, plus my work gloves, a bicycle pump in case Grandpa's wheelbarrow needs air in the tire, our electric tiller, and two extension cords. Sofia adds whatever she needs. I drive us over.

We quickly saw down the two trees. As a big-city girl, Sofia has to take direction from country-boy me, but despite her small build and short height she provides all the help I need to get the trees down and cleaned up.

Aunt Patsy comes outside with her pet Chihuahua. She asks with genuine surprise, "How'd you get the trees down so *fast*? That was even faster than when they use those big . . . oh, what do you *call* those things? . . ." She makes some gestures meant to signify *chain saw*.

She lowers her voice and nods toward Florence and Ormond's house in the back. "I wish they'd take some of *their* trees down but *they* never will. All their leaves fall into my yard . . . but they *did* have the guy who cleaned their yard come pick up the leaves here, too, so that was nice of them."

I can't understand why autumn leaves in a yard are anything but wonderful, but I hold back my comment.

"When Stanley died, Dorothy finally had that tree in front of their house taken down. I always *told* them that their house looks better when you can see the whole thing, without that tree right there in the middle. Well, that [name of the owner of a local tree-care company] was a friend of Stanley's, and he came right over and took it down for her after the funeral."

I still don't comment.

Sofia trims the branches off the tree trunks and I use a hatchet to chop the stumps down flush with the ground. Aunt Patsy goes and sits on the screened-in porch to do her puzzles in the newspaper.

After a while I can just barely make out through the screen that she's talking with Cousin Dorothy, who's walked over from across the street. I haven't seen her in many years. Dorothy's silhouette waves to me enthusiastically and I wave back. Ormond comes outside and takes his routine walk—now with the aid of a cane—up and down the driveway, which runs adjacent to Aunt Patsy's backyard. He pauses, just like I remember him doing years ago, to observe the various plants and wildflowers growing along the way. I find myself being transported back to childhood again. I'm remembering Grandma's vegetable garden and old photographs of the flower gardens she had before I was born.

I go to the woodshed attached to the garage and pull out one of Grandpa's old homemade benches to put next to where our garden will be. I also see an old birdbath and some other decorations, but I resist the urge to do anything more to revive and beautify the backyard.

Sofia and I finish all the tree work. It's time to work on the garden itself. First we have to decide what it should look like. We go to the porch and Aunt Patsy gets us some paper. I know that whatever we decide to do, it shouldn't look too wild—Aunt Patsy is the one who's going to have to see it every day, not us. I know that the wide, slightly raised beds we've been using at home look nice. Still, I find myself enthusiastically suggesting that there are lots of different ways to lay out the garden. Before long I've got Sofia going along with me and, since she's the handiest when it comes to drawing, she's sketching out various circular shapes. I really like the idea of a circle. It strikes me as very decorative for a vegetable garden.

Sofia sketches two concentric circles with two perpendicular walking paths crossing through them. I ask Aunt Patsy what she thinks and she likes it. I'm delighted that it will look nice and that Aunt Patsy thinks it will, too, and I'm trying hard to avoid thinking about how inconvenient it'll be for us to make and tend. It takes me the better part of an hour to scrounge up some string and other implements and to scratch the pattern onto the ground.

Sofia and I spend the rest of the afternoon on the curvy rows, tilling the sod, mixing in compost-rich soil and leaves from out behind Grandpa's shed.

Days later, Sofia's seed order arrives in the mail and rain is in the forecast. We go over and plant. We cover everything with a layer of straw.

Two weeks go by.

One afternoon we stop by Aunt Patsy's to check on the garden. There's a terrible ruckus because a landscaping outfit is across the street at Dorothy's, taking down even more trees and sending the branches through the wood chipper parked on her front lawn.

Sofia and I walk out back to our new garden. We see that the shell beans (and the tomato plants for Aunt Patsy) are growing. I take an overview to get a sense of whether most of the beans have germinated. Sofia gets down on her knees and inspects many of the plants up close.

We're just about to leave when Aunt Patsy comes out the back door. "I've always *loved* watching them take trees down like that," she says. Then nodding toward Florence and Ormond's, she adds, "I wish *they*'d take some of their trees down but *they* never will."

This time I ask her why she wishes they'd take down their trees and she says she'd like to be able to see more sky. Then she repeats the thing about the leaves falling in her yard.

"Okay, then," I say, "See you later, I guess."

A few more days go by.

My mother calls while I'm cooking dinner: "I just wanted to let you know that Aunt Patsy just called all a mess and told me that last night Dorothy passed away."

※ 3 ※
Hunting for Mushrooms and Total Freedom

Sofia and I are driving across state to look for mushrooms.

Ever since we saw what we were 90 percent sure were two large morel mushrooms growing in our yard, we've been feeling like we're missing out because we've never learned to identify wild mushrooms. Morels seem easy to identify—provided you can find any—especially if you cut them open to make sure they aren't *Verpa* mushrooms, and you aren't talking about half-free morels. In many respects, though, wild mushrooms are more difficult to identify than wild plants, so we keep putting off learning enough about them to feel confident to try eating any.

We've dug out our mushroom foraging books again this spring. (My plan is to spend most of my time rereading about *poisonous* mushrooms—fundamental safety knowledge for all foragers.) Somehow I've managed to get myself to go along with Sofia's adventurous desire to attend a mushroom foraging event on the outskirts of Syracuse.

We're making a weekend of it. We're going to stay in Binghamton with my friend Leonidas, and the three of us will go to Syracuse from there. Then, when Sofia and I are coming back home from Binghamton, we'll stop to see my cousins who live near Oneonta.

Somewhere along I-88 I get to thinking about the mushroom hunting and how we'll be traipsing through who knows what kind of woods, and that we should've brought better footwear. I mention this to Sofia, adding, "Wouldn't it be great if we had the kind of tall black boots you see farmers wearing? I could also wear them whenever I collect black raspberries out back. And when we walk in the woods [near our house, where there's poison ivy], it'd be easy to rinse them off under the hose after, just in case." Sofia looks up from the sci fi novel she's reading—for some reason she doesn't get dizzy reading in the car—and tells me that we can go to the Agway in Binghamton because she's almost positive that they sell such boots. She goes back to reading. I take her word for it since she's the one who spends so much of her free time exploring all the nurseries and garden stores.

We arrive in Binghamton. I mention to Leonidas about going to Agway, and he suggests that he drive us to a local farm winery first, so I can buy the dandelion wine I've been eager to try. (Last year when we went they were all out.) Sofia looks glad that I'm up for it and that for a change we're not just going to spend the *whole* time watching Leonidas cook, eating, drinking, listening to Greek music, and talking.

We return to Leonidas's house with two bottles of dandelion wine and two pairs of tall black rubber boots for me and Sofia.

First thing the next morning, we drive to Syracuse for the mushroom event. We're among the earliest participants to arrive. So far it's mainly just the organizers standing around and having a cigarette and drinking black robusta coffee. One is dressed in blue jeans and plaid, and he's wearing a bandana on his head and has a mustache. Something about his overall appearance and demeanor makes him look like he's a bull rider by day and a stoner by night. Another is dressed in a mix of camouflage and plaid flannel. He appears smart and self-confident. He looks like someone who can rebuild an engine with his eyes shut and just as easily lecture you on the most intricate loopholes in local zoning laws or income tax rules. His eyes subtly betray that, like a wild animal, he never ceases quietly keeping track of everything going on and everyone else around him. I suppose it's no wonder, what with a bunch of total strangers like us coming onto his land.

Everyone is pleasant and welcoming but I remain acutely aware that Sofia, Leonidas, and I don't seem to fit in here. In fact I'm trying awfully hard to resist an unexpected but unmistakable urge to stereotype these guys as xenophobic, gun-toting, devil-may-care, self-sufficient, militia-joining, libertarian rednecks. I *know* this is unfair, but they seem sufficiently different from all the rural Upstaters I've known and trusted growing up that I'm grasping for anything that will help me ascertain who we're dealing with.

Sofia and Leonidas, by contrast, seem to be making themselves right at home.

More participants arrive—including quite a few other first-timers like us—and the mushroom hunt begins. Our leader, Plaid-and-Camouflage, gathers us together and explains good morel-spotting technique. He lectures us on how we should all spread out to about just over an arm's length from one another and proceed like a search party with each of us focusing on our immediate vicinity; how it's good to stop now and then and look in whatever direction is slightly uphill. He says the walking won't be difficult, but it won't be easy either.

We climb into the back of a pickup truck that takes us down the road to the place from where we'll work our way back through the woods on foot. The first thing we do is cross a No Trespassing sign, but since P&C presumably owns this land, I guess there's no reason for concern.

P&C goes ahead and keeps calling out loudly every so many seconds, "Come on everybody! Keep moving!"

Leonidas, recovering from a broken ankle, gives up within the first two minutes and says he'll walk back via the road.

I'm confused. First of all, the ground is terribly uneven, over-grown, and crisscrossed by one or more creeks, so I can't understand why we were told to space ourselves out evenly like a search party. Besides, even if it was somehow possible, P&C is moving ahead so quickly that I'm not sure we can keep up with him even if we stop paying *any* attention to where we're going, never mind trying to catch a glimpse of elusive morels.

After no more than five minutes of supposedly walking in a single direction, I'm almost certain we've turned around and are moving in a completely different direction. I usually pride myself on having a good sense of direction but I know that in the woods it's easy to lose it, so I make sure I keep tracking P&C's calls while always keeping Sofia in my field of vision. We're a group of twenty or twenty-five people, but now I only see two or three other people besides Sofia! I wonder if some of the other people who are significantly older than us—and who aren't wearing knee-high boots—can possibly keep up the pace in this terrain.

I'm starting to obsess about the fact that we've got *no* idea who any of these people are. We took it for granted that as an event that's been going on for years, there's nothing to worry about. But how do I know that it's a real event that's been going on for years? Just because it has a website? Anybody can just put up such a website.

One-third of my brain is paying attention to where I'm going and—amazingly—is trying to spot morels on occasion. Another third is vaguely recalling Hollywood thrillers with evildoers who lure their unsuspecting victims into the woods for who knows what kind of adventure that never leads anywhere good. The last third is trying to tell the second third that I'm totally overreacting simply because I'm not accustomed to trusting total strangers—never pick up a hitchhiker!—and that just because these total strangers have brought us into woods unknown to us, and that just because P&C seems more preoccupied with his smoke than with making sure our group isn't getting lost, and that just because this is *exactly* the kind of behavior you'd expect from some nut job bent on luring unsuspecting victims into the woods for a manhunt, doesn't mean I should go into a paranoid panic.

Whenever I manage to get close enough to Sofia to see how she's doing I notice that she looks like she's enjoying herself, largely indifferent to making sure we don't lag too far behind P&C's guiding calls, and looking all around for morels as she makes her way.

I gradually calm myself down but continue to maintain as my top priority staying on P&C's heels while keeping Sofia in sight. As I finally get closer to him I realize he's got a walkie-talkie and is in communication with another one of the organizers. I'm heartened to know that they're being more careful than I realized, but I'm also a little worried when P&C seems surprised that the other leader is so far behind us that when they try yelling to one another to check if they can hear each other without the walkie-talkies, they can't. But then I also figure the majority of participants who aren't keeping up with our cohort are probably alive and well and in the company of the second leader.

I'm further reassured by hearing P&C walkie-talkie-ing the other guy to ask if *they* are spotting any morels. When the other guy reports back that they aren't, P&C mentions that soon we'll all be coming to a spot where the morels are plentiful. As a forager I'm disappointed because now it feels like we're at an amusement park on some kind of mushroom-hunting ride. Nine-tenths of our racing through the woods isn't really about trying to find morels but a way to build suspense before arriving at the place we're being deliberately led to because the morels are already known to be there.

Still, I'm relieved overall because at least now I can make sense of our racing through the woods like this without resorting to doomsday scenarios. Better to be at an amusement park than hunted by sociopaths!

We arrive back where we started. I'm mostly calm but now I'm thinking that we shouldn't eat anything at the potluck that is about to begin—we don't know who *any* of these people are or anything about them. Even the organizers don't know anything about the newcomers (ourselves included), and who knows what food these people have brought. I know, it's not much different from going to a church potluck, except that it is. Since these people are interested in foraging for morels, they're already far more adventurous and unconventional about food than most people who bring a casserole to a church supper. Sure, there's always the risk of salmonella from Aunt So-and-so's chicken salad, but here there are people cooking with wild ingredients, including wild mushrooms. Some well-intentioned participant might've accidentally used a poisonous look-alike. Or worse, some wacko might *want* to poison people, for instance by using one of those deadly mushrooms I've read about whose initial symptoms can be delayed for *weeks*.

(It's not helping my paranoia any that my favorite foodie novel is about a sociopath who kills by cooking food containing deadly *Amanita* mushrooms for his unsuspecting victims.)

As I see everyone cheerfully lining up to eat I remind myself that the chance of something so dramatic happening here is negligible. And the last thing I want to do is offend somebody by acting like I don't trust the homemade food that they so generously volunteered to prepare and share. I see Leonidas getting in line for food. Sofia tells me she's on her way to get in line. I want to tell her that we shouldn't eat anything, but I don't want anyone to overhear me, and I continue wondering if maybe I'm being overly paranoid and should just let her go, maybe even join her. I finally wander my way down to the line as well. When I see that Sofia and Leonidas have filled their plates and are making their way to the picnic table, I drop out of line and go sit with them.

Part of me regrets not eating. Then, Sofia, excited about a dish with chanterelles, gives me some to try. I murmur something about not eating because of my stomach—a little white lie for the benefit of the other people sitting at the picnic table—but Sofia hasn't caught on and keeps insisting I try, so I finally give in and eat a forkful. Delicious! Of course as far as I know it's made from dried wild mushrooms from the supermarket.

Sofia finishes eating and we get in the car and head back to Leonidas's. I'm a little angry at Sofia because she insisted in front of other people that I try the mushrooms even though she knows I try to be super-super-super-cautious about wild mushrooms. But I also know I never really tried taking her aside at some point during the day to clue her in.

As we're driving, Leonidas tells us about his time talking with some of the regulars. He mentions that one of them said that they never used to have food but then people began volunteering to bring dishes and a potluck tradition evolved. He also mentions that she said that *she herself never eats the potluck food because she doesn't know who all these people are.*

Now I'm really pissed.

"What? You mean to say that one of the most experienced people there not only doesn't touch the stuff strangers bring, but she even *told* you that she doesn't, and you *still* went ahead and sampled *every single dish*? *And*, you didn't say a *word* to me or Sofia!"

Images of the regulars making sure to eat only one another's dishes play over and over in my mind.

By now I'm as convinced that we've eaten something deadly poisonous as I am that I'm being completely irrational by thinking such a thing. I try reasoning with myself in order to calm down, knowing that it never much works. What I really need is time and something else to take my mind off it.

We arrive back at Leonidas's. I keep saying things like, "It's too late now. No matter what happened there's nothing we can do about it so there isn't much point in my continuing to fret." It doesn't really help. I keep demanding that Sofia explain what she was thinking when she kept prodding me to try the potluck mushrooms. I keep asking Leonidas why he didn't pay any attention to the implicit warning he was given.

Luckily, after a quick snack, it's time to leave Binghamton and head to my cousins'.

Sofia and I are on our way to Oneonta. I keep having the same panicky thoughts again and again. For Sofia's sake, I mostly manage to keep them in my head.

As we turn onto the exit ramp, I'm hoping that visiting my cousins will be just the distraction I need to short-circuit my paranoia.

When I was a kid, Grandpa and Grandma often took me with them when they drove out to Oneonta to visit Grandma's niece Donna and her husband Danny. Donna and Danny probably came closer than anyone else in our family to participating in the counter-cultural spirit of the sixties and seventies. They also worked harder than almost anyone else I knew. Upon graduating from college with teaching degrees, but disenchanted by what *they* were taught, they decided they didn't want anything to do with the conventional education system and set out with plenty of why-not-be-creative and do-it-yourself attitude to pursue their own dreams from scratch. As college students, in part to save money and in part to be different, they'd already made the radical move of becoming vegetarians. (Whenever they came up to visit, Grandma would prepare macaroni and cheese, leaving out the cubed Spam.) For a while, they took on a variety of odd jobs and grew tomatoes to sell by the side of the road. Eventually they opened a local produce store aptly called Earthly Delights.

Knowing that Donna and Danny were likely to be preoccupied with tending to customers, unloading corn from the back of a pickup truck, or refilling tables with melons, Grandpa usually stopped in downtown Oneonta so we could eat lunch before heading over to Earthly Delights. Upon arriving at the store, I'd notice the hanging wooden signs—Corn, Peaches, Etc.—announcing the season's high-lights. They were lettered by Grandpa, who'd once taught himself paintbrush calligraphy from books and did freehand lettering of the local school buses and Jacobie's oil trucks.

On one of these childhood visits, Donna and Danny were able to make some time to get away from their ever-busy store to drive us out to the tranquil rural plot on the sloping hill where they were renting a place to live, and where they grew some of the produce they sold. I'd never before seen such a garden. Growing up I saw lots of cornfields on nearby dairy farms, and both Mom and Grandma had vegetable gardens in their backyards for tomatoes, zucchini, cucumbers, beans, and the like, small enough for one person to till by hand with a shovel in an hour or two. Donna and Danny's vegetable garden must've spread out over a half-acre or more. Their garden—and the fact that it was an integral part of their work—made a lasting impression on me. True to the title of a children's book they wrote, self-published, and self-distributed, it was indeed the Happy Garden.

Whenever it was time for us to come back home, Grandma and Grandpa would want to buy some fruits and vegetables, maybe some cider, from *Earthly Delights*. But it was always tricky. As discreetly as they might try making their way up to the cashier, by the time they got to the counter either Donna or Danny would have spotted them and run over to insist that their beloved aunt and uncle not pay. Grandpa would act annoyed and say, "You're gonna make us leave everything!" But there must've been some kind of compromise because we always ended up going back home with a bag or two.

The first couple years after Grandma died and I was in high school, Grandpa and I would drive out to visit Donna and Danny just the two of us. Since *Reader's Digest*, the Bible, *Funk and Wagnall's Encyclopedia*, and the *Post-Star* were about the only reading materials to be found in my parents' and most of my relatives' houses, my curiosity was piqued when, on one of our trips, I saw that my energetic cousins had several shelves full of books on such unlikely topics as atheism and anarcho-capitalism. "Maybe reading could be interesting after all?" I thought. I borrowed a couple, and they gave me some more for a graduation gift. By the time I went to college I was getting as hooked on philosophy as I was on computer programming and playing guitar.

Together with my friend Joe, I visited Donna and Danny at their trailer on the side of the hill for a couple days during winter break of my second year in college. Being vegetarian, Donna prepared a few dishes that were unusual for Joe and me. The only legumes I ever ate growing up were Grandma's baked beans (rarely) or side dishes of green beans or peas, so I was pleasantly surprised by the kidney beans when Donna served us so-called haystacks for lunch. I had no desire to become a vegetarian, yet being vegetarian even for a couple days was appealing—it felt intellectually alternative and wholesome—probably because I associated it with my cousins, whose idealistic alternative lifestyle and freedom-oriented politics I admired. It was the first time in my life I would've said I really liked beans.

❄   ❄   ❄

Because of the mushroom ordeal, I'm looking forward to seeing my cousins even more than usual. I can't wait to see their spring gardens. I just hope that the residues of my paranoia won't distract us from enjoying our visit.

We arrive, and although they're expecting us, Donna and Danny are nowhere to be seen in the store. An employee tells me they're working in one of their new fields. She explains to us how to get there and says that the walk over will be muddy, so Sofia and I go back to the car and put on our new boots for the second time today. We cross the road, head down the muddy path, and eventually come to a small field enclosed by deer fence.

I see Donna waving to us from inside the pickup and it soon becomes clear to me what's going on: They're covering rows of seedlings with landscaping fabric because of an impending frost. When I got up this morning I saw the frost advisory for our area on weather.com but forgot about it since most of what Sofia and I have growing at this point isn't frost tender.

Donna suggests that Sofia get behind the pickup and help to manage the unrolling of the fabric. I grab a handful of the plastic stakes from the box Danny is carrying and stake down my side of the fabric as he and I lay it down. My poison-mushroom anxiety is quickly cured by the light physical activity, being outdoors in a garden instead of chasing through the woods, helping to protect food plant seedlings, the excitement of dealing with an unexpected but impending minicatastrophe, and just being there with my nonstranger cousins.

We finish the job and Danny shows us around this new piece of property, then we walk back and tour the rest of their gardens and orchards. Donna asks us to point out any edible weeds we see growing, because she's interested in learning more about them. If only we lived closer, there'd be so much more about food we could all learn from each other.

When we get to the many matted rows of June strawberries that they'd already covered before we arrived, the late-afternoon gusts are so strong that the fabric is blowing off. We all work together to get it back on.

Sofia digs up a few of Donna's early-blooming daylilies to take home with us. We all sample some chive flowers at Sofia's suggestion, and I give Danny a horseradish root I brought from home so he can transplant it.

We wander into the store for ice cream and coffee. While Sofia is checking out all the ice cream flavors, Danny and I talk political theory, taking as our point of departure a book we'd both read.

When last we met, Danny lent me his copy of Joel Salatin's book, *Everything I Want to Do Is Illegal: War Stories from the Local Food Front*.[1] I already knew a little something about this "Christian-conservative-libertarian-environmentalist-lunatic farmer" from having read Michael Pollan's *The Omnivore's Dilemma*, [2] and I thought it would be interesting to read the book.

It's no wonder Danny liked reading *Illegal*. Salatin supplies many examples of absurd government regulation of farming and food that is most frequently detrimental to small farmers and the consumers who'd like to support them. Covering everything from salmonella to bird flu, government grants to organic, zoning to insurance, Salatin illustrates how laws and regulations are often stupidly constructed to support environmentally and socially irresponsible corporate farming at the expense of those who'd like to try out, or to support, smaller-scale initiatives that turn out to be safer, cleaner, and healthier.

Reading Salatin reminded me that many of the liberal critiques of the modern food system in the press and academia these days seem to suggest that all we need to do is to rectify the *lack* of some government regulation or another. Rarely do they acknowledge the many ways that government regulations are designed and implemented so as to support narrow special interests instead of protecting the general public. Salatin's book seems like a good antidote to this oversimplification. But when it comes to his recommendations to completely privatize education and get the government out of health care, and simply to *minimize* all government regulation of food and agriculture, I think he largely misses the political mark on what is needed for a better world, at least in the short run.

As we talk, I try pulling Danny in the same direction that I've moved since my undergraduate years when I was still persuaded by the capitalist-libertarian arguments he finds attractive. I'm troubled that although he and I continue to share a fundamental assumption about the value of total human freedom—we both define social justice in terms of an ideal of noncoercion—we've arrived at vastly different conclusions about what this entails. It's also interesting to me how, in spite of this divergence of conclusions, when it comes to living in the day-to-day world, we're often critical of the very same things, and we both seek to experiment with alternative ways of trying to live our own lives—sometimes in surprisingly similar ways.

Danny and I chat for no longer than about ten minutes, because

Sofia and I need to get back on the road if we want to check on our gardens before nightfall.

We're back on the road. With Sofia listening patiently, I take advantage of the driving time to try sorting through and further articulating the political ideas I was just talking about with Danny. Probably because I used to be thoroughly convinced of the same things myself, it bothers me that someone like Danny believes that freedom means an unregulated *capitalist* market, and that he thinks not voting in political elections is a way to avoid sponsoring coercion.

By the time we're approaching Albany, I'm getting talked out, but at last things are becoming clear to me. I think I've figured out a way I can sum up my political differences with Danny in terms of one basic disagreement.

It comes down to how property is defined. Noncoercion doesn't mean very much in the absence of a definition of property, since people acting freely usually involves more than just people—it also involves things. The ideal of total freedom is only meaningful once it's connected with a particular practice for defining possessions and property, and there are no god-given practices or definitions that settle the matter once and for all.

Danny, like so many anarcho-capitalists and procapitalist libertarians (not to mention many liberals and conservatives), seems to take for granted the practice of defining property that persists under state capitalism: my possession remains my property even when I pay you to use it to produce goods or services on the market. If you don't like it—even if you don't have anything of your own with which to produce goods or services on the market—then you shouldn't agree to use it. I'm automatically entitled to retain possession of it, and of the goods and services you help to produce with it.

This way of thinking about property is so familiar today that it feels more like a law of nature than a product of history. But it's really just *one* way to define property. It's not the worst way to define it, but it's probably not the best way either, if we really care about freedom. Moreover, as most everyone except procapitalist libertarians and some right-wingers would argue, the evidence suggests that allowing markets (using *this* definition of property) to operate unfettered by "democratic" governmental regulation significantly undermines the ideal of noncoercive human relations. It forces many hard-working people, finding themselves trapped in a pattern of lacking productive possessions of their own or living in fear that they'll end up falling into such a trap if they lose what few productive possessions they do own, to resign themselves to obeying the orders of one employer or another.

I, too, favor a free market unfettered by regulation, but if and only if that market assumes a better practice for defining possessions and property that is more compatible with noncoercion. Otherwise, unregulated markets are anything but *free* markets. A new definition of property might work like this: a possession remains your possession except when you cooperate with workers who use it to produce goods or services on the market—in which case the workers automatically join you in its coownership, and in coownership of the goods or services produced. With this definition, businesses with wageworkers would give way to businesses that are worker owned, like some of today's co-ops.

At any rate, my sense is that both "free" capitalist markets—especially in the absence of appropriate democratic government regulation—and state-socialist "economies" are highly coercive arrangements that keep too much wealth and power concentrated in the hands of a few at the bitter expense of the many.

I'm also unpersuaded by libertarian and anarcho-capitalist claims that nonparticipation in public institutions or state politics is a way to avoid sponsoring coercion, since dropping out of democratic government while remaining *in* the capitalist market probably winds up sponsoring greater coercion perpetrated on those who have the least wealth and access to power to protect themselves from it. Since, at least for the time being, innocence of coercion isn't an option for any of us, it seems we'd do better to ask how we can steer the uses of omnipresent coercion—in both governments and markets—in directions that more effectively protect the basic needs and well-being of all—which should include, I might add, the people of generations to come. As long as we're living in a capitalist democracy, I see no more reason to demonize enlightened participation in public and state institutions than to demonize employers simply because they hire wage employees—especially employers who work alongside their employees and who are trying their best to treat employees, customers, and the environment better than capitalist market forces alone (regulated or unregulated) would ever require.

I'm feeling pretty good about my analysis. But I'm also wary that the current definition of property feels so commonsensical to those of us who grew up with it that I might not ever manage to convince Danny to entertain the possibility that the ideal of total freedom isn't compatible with just any old definition of property, let alone to persuade him that it turns out to be incompatible with the capitalist definition that has so much currency.

I also feel guilty about wanting to persuade Danny of all people, without whose political provocations back when I was a teenager I might never have thought so hard about such matters.

Sofia and I are entering our neighborhood. Sofia notices broken branches in the road. We see some branches in my parents' front yard and even more in our own. We finally notice a poplar tree lying across the yard of our neighbor. Apparently the gusts of wind were even more powerful up here than at my cousins'.

Nightfall is upon us so Sofia and I rush to cover a couple small sections of the garden. It's easy because now we've learned from Donna and Danny about using landscape fabric as a blanket, and we happen to have a few rolls lying around.

I see my parents in their yard and they tell me about the neighbor's tree being blown down. Lots of smaller branches had landed in our yard, and our neighbor was kind enough to come over to pick them up and put them back into his yard.

It's ironic because I'm just about to go across the street and ask him if we can have his fallen tree trunk. Based on my observations in the woods near our house, I think if we lay the trunk of a dead poplar out back somewhere in the shade, edible wild oyster mushrooms might eventually grow on it.

4

The Other Side of the Family

Ben and Catherine are pulling into our driveway. They usually visit us two or three weekends a year.

Of my eight first cousins, all on my mother's side, only Ben doesn't live around here anymore. He and his wife Catherine live in her hometown almost three hours due south. Ben and I had a special connection when he was little—he'd always tell everybody that he was "my buddy"—so I'm not surprised that I've reconnected with him more than with all the rest of my cousins who live here in town.

Ben and Catherine crafted their entire wedding reception around the theme of wine. They used empty wine bottles as centerpieces and wine corks slit with a band saw to hold each person's place card. (They made sure my cork and the centerpiece at my table were from a Greek wine.) Their honeymoon was a tasting tour of California wineries.

As with most visits from the other side of the family, there'll be some serious drinking tonight.

As a child, I really felt like my mother's side of the family was the *other* side of the family. We turned right to head toward my father's parents, but left at the same intersection to get to Grandma and Grandpa Leclaire's. Turning right was the norm; turning left was something different, because we visited Grandma and Grandpa Leclaire so much less frequently.

Grandpa Leclaire was a discount-beer–drinking, pipe-smoking, self-employed plumber until the day he died. Because he was often working or on call, he was usually the most dressed-down person in the family, with his worn-out plumber's clothes and an old flat-cap. But whenever he'd dress up for church or to drop by a relative's house to play pinochle he'd dress up more than anyone ever would on my father's side. He'd even wear a tie. Grandma Leclaire, perhaps owing to medications for what used to be called manic-depression, was more aloof. It seemed like she'd spend hours on end without saying a word, rocking in a rocking chair and staring at the television.

Whenever my brother and I did stay overnight there, the next morning Grandma would fry eggs and make toast while Grandpa was reading the *Post-Star* or listening to the news on WWSC. Then, either the phone would ring and he'd be off to a job, or he'd drive over to what we in the family called the "barn." Before Grandpa bought it, the barn had served as a Laundromat or dry cleaners, and as a garage for car repair. Grandpa used it for storage and as a place to work. Old refrigerators, toilets, faucets, furnaces, sinks, and every imaginable shape and size of fitting, pipe, and ductwork were strewn inside and out. If he was taking me with him that day, I'd wander around the barn looking through all the junk for something fun to do, like collecting beer bottle caps off the floor. Sometimes he'd ask me to look around for a certain part he needed and I'd go on the hunt. I just didn't want to go up to the loft because the shaky old ladder-stairs without a railing terrified me.

There was nothing particularly culinary about Grandpa's work, but since he did a lot of jobs for local businesses, including restaurants and a locally owned supermarket, I caught some interesting glimpses into the professional world of food and drink that tickled my young imagination. I felt like a VIP whenever we went into Abbott's Corner Grill through the back door—directly into the kitchen—for take-out. I got to watch the locally legendary turkey clubs and fried chicken in the basket being made right before my eyes as Grandpa ordered and we both waited for what felt like forever because I was so hungry. Because of his work, Grandpa acquired food-related gadgets at home that I never saw anyone else have, such as a deli slicer and an electric meat grinder. Furniture, too, like the restaurant tables he had in his basement.

More than the foreign accents, the dress, the jobs, or the casual use of swear words, the most emblematic thing for me about the other side of the family was the presence of beer and liquor.

There was never any alcohol in my parents' house. Grandpa and Grandma and Aunt Patsy never touched the stuff or even allowed somebody onto their property with it—a stance not unlikely for people living just up the road from Clark's Corners, where in 1808 one of the nation's earliest temperance societies had convened, seeking "wholly to abstain from ardent spirits."[1] Grandpa told me stories about the drinking problems of his older sister's husband's (deceased before I was born). He also told a story about some of his fellow prisoners-of-war getting drunk while celebrating their liberation and accidently shooting each other during all the excitement. I don't think I ever saw an alcoholic beverage around *any* of my relatives on my father's Quaker, Methodist, and Christian Scientist side of the family.

Grandpa Leclaire, on the other hand, was a Roman-Catholic, French-Canadian immigrant who'd converted his entire basement into a place to drink, complete with a bar and six padded, swiveling barstools, a sink, and a full-sized "frigidaire" [*sic*] stocked with the "Canadian cheese" he'd bring back from his trips up north. In the back room he put a bar-sized pool table, and in the furnace room a urinal. I've heard that Grandpa played the fiddle before I was born and there was singing and dancing down there too. Whenever Grandma and Grandpa Leclaire babysat us, my brother and I would go downstairs to play pool, and when we got bored we'd "play bar" with one of us as the customer and the other as the bartender. We'd take out the glasses from under the bar and pretend to pour from the various bottles of vermouth or crème de menthe. We never considered sneaking an actual taste, though.

When any of our relatives came down from Ontario, their bilingual kitchen bustled. Grandpa did as much of the cooking as Grandma, and since one of his brothers owned a restaurant and used to be the head chef at the Queensbury Hotel, and another had his own catering business, the kitchen always filled up with many a willing cook. The elder generation would be sizzling up a storm while my parents, aunts, and uncles would be in the living room or downstairs watching hockey games on television, shooting pool, crocheting, or bottle-feeding my baby cousins. Uncles and great uncles—but never my father—sipped from cans or bottles of beer. Uncle Rich would invariably put a drop of beer on his finger for one of my little cousins to lick. I never did more than smell it, and the smell convinced me that I wasn't missing out on much.

The last family gathering at Grandpa Leclaire's house was immediately following his funeral. I was fifteen and it was the first family funeral I ever attended. I remember being struck by the way everyone seemed to cheer up a little as they ate and drank and talked at Grandpa's bar. I also remember the whisky. Before I was born, somebody gave Grandpa and Grandma Leclaire a bottle of Canadian Masterpiece whisky on the occasion of their twenty-fifth wedding anniversary. Grandpa announced that he was earmarking it for his own funeral, and it stayed in one of the cupboards behind the bar until that day. Then, just as Grandpa intended, my uncles took out the decorative box, removed the bottle, and poured out a round of shots.

❀ ❀ ❀

Ben and Catherine, in addition to being connoisseurs of wine and liquor, are foodies. Last fall when they visited us they mentioned that they'd eaten rose-flavored ice cream when they were in Paris traveling as chaperones for students at the school where Ben teaches. So I'm outdoors filling a colander with rose petals from the rose-bushes that are at either end of the row of violets along the side of the garage. My mother gave the roses to us after removing them from her flower gardens. She'd gotten them from my father's parents, who'd gotten them from their neighbors Florence and Ormond. I don't know much about roses, but a quick Internet search makes me think that they're *Rosa rugosa*.

I leave the rose petals in the kitchen and ask Ben and Catherine if they want to walk around the yard and see if we think of anything else special to cook with what's available so far this growing season.

Along the way I point out the ripe wild strawberries in case they want to pick some later on. I identify for them some of the more easily recognizable seedlings that Sofia has planted, but mostly I emphasize the perennial and wild plants that I'm primarily respon-sible for—the red raspberries and black raspberries that should be ready in a few weeks, various patches of chicory ("the wild ancestor of endive and radicchio," I explain), two short rows of Jerusalem artichokes we're trying for the first time ("rich in inulin, I've read," I mention).

"See all those white flowers? That's New Jersey tea."

This reminds me that Ben and Catherine live on just this side of the border with New Jersey, so I ask them if they know the Woody Allen joke about why New Yorkers are so depressed. ("Because up, having long been convinced that I'd never do such a thing. or the next few months I was like a child with a new toy, eager drink at parties with friends for the rush of intoxication. But ter feeling nauseated from drinking one too many beers, and as I came increasingly absorbed in my academic studies, my interest drinking faded away as quickly as it had appeared.

Though I eventually began drinking again, I didn't drink beer—not ntil my preconceptions about beer were transformed by tasting a ottle of good homebrew made by a friend of a friend in Ohio. Later, hen another home-brewer—a colleague from Scotland—ordered a eer I'd never heard of before, and which wasn't even listed on the enu of the pub we were at, Sofia and I followed suit, figuring he ust be in the know. We both became instant fans of Old Peculier.

For the next year, Sofia and I took a break from drinking wine n order to explore beer. We found plenty of information online nd learned of a store in nearby Albany that was selling almost very beer you could imagine a beer store carrying. We began trying verything from French *bières de garde* to German *doppelbocks*, from Belgian ales from the Rochefort brewery to maddeningly overhopped American brews. We started frequenting the local microbreweries n Glens Falls.

Then my brother learned to make beer. Within the year he talked me into making it. Then, as the next spring approached, he coaxed me into trying to grow hops. I just hoped I could grow enough for both of us.

※　※　※

Ben, Catherine, and I go back in the house so I can make the rose-petal ice cream. Ben and Catherine sit at the bar watching. I could steep-and-strain but today I just use the blender to pulverize the two big handfuls of collected rose petals in 1½ cups of unhomogenized cow's milk from a local creamery.

I separate three egg yolks from the whites, and add the whites to a small yogurt container that I keep in the freezer. The container holds just enough egg white for a single recipe of angel food cake. The eggs are from the farmers' market and the yolks look beautiful.

In a 3 quart saucepan I beat the yolks together with ¾ cup of sugar and whisk in the rosy milk. I add a tiny pinch of salt.

I heat up the liquid while stirring. When it reaches 170°F, I dunk

the light at the end of the tunnel is New Jersey.") Th
Catherine says Ben doesn't like Woody Allen. Trying to
of the comedian's whiney deliveries, I ask, "*Whyyyyee*
comedy is such a wonderful thing!"

I explain to them how I hadn't really noticed the Nev
growing the year before until after it had flowered, bu
to figure out from the three parallel veins in the leav
somewhat distinctive seed pod what it probably was, and
waiting until just recently for it to flower again so I cou
my hypothesis.

Next, I show them the beer hops. Of all the rhizomes I p
ground last year only one variety of aroma hops has surv
got it rigged to climb twine running up to the top of a pc
out of a young poplar tree. "I hope it won't snap off in
before the hops are ready. And here's two more plants grov
rhizomes that I just put in this spring. They won't grow tl
produce cones for beer brewing 'til next year. I still can'
that now *I'm* making *beer*."

For years I effortlessly followed in the teetotaler ste
father's side of the family. Even when I hosted drinking p
my friends in the dorms during my freshman year in college
drank myself. I'd boast, "If you don't drink the first one y
have to worry about drinking too many!" But the following
while living in a hotel in the Adirondack town where I was
for the Department of Transportation, I decided that perhar
being too close-minded, and that I ought to try to *appreciate* a
beverages, as distinct from using them like a drug. Since I wa:
the legal drinking age, I asked one of the carpenters on the
pick me up a couple inexpensive bottles. I kept them in the t
my car. I occasionally mixed vodka with supermarket orang
or rum with Coke—the only cocktails I imagined I knew f
make—and I sipped them for appreciation, even though I co
say I'd acquired a taste for them.

It wasn't until late autumn of my sophomore year that cur
finally got the best of me and I decided to get a buzz to see
all the fuss was about. Sitting at my dorm room desk, I k
mixing the rum I had leftover from the summer with cans of
I purposefully drank them up at a less-than-leisurely pace. I
buzz and it felt terrific. I went over to a friend's dorm room ar
we were sitting there chatting I finally let on that I was buzzing

the pan into a bowl of ice water and stir so as to cool down the custard quickly. As I'm stirring the custard I also gently rock the pan so the ice water keeps moving, which further speeds up the cooling process. My movements are almost involuntary because this is just an easier and smaller-scale version of what I've done dozens of times to chill the wort quickly when I'm making beer.

I add in 1½ cups of cream—which, since it's from the local creamery and has no other ingredients listed, is supposedly *just* cream. I cover the pan and put it in the fridge to chill. We decide that we'll churn it tomorrow morning.

Now it's time to make dinner.

I turn to Ben and Catherine and ask, "Should we open the first bottle of wine? Or do you want to start with homemade beer, made entirely from USDA organic ingredients that I ordered from an online co-op in California?"

☀ 5 ☀

Family Farmer Funeral

Sofia and I are out back pulling up a few heads of garlic so she can decide—by inspecting it for something or other—whether it's time to harvest.

Today is also Uncle Bud's funeral.

I can't believe that the last time I saw Uncle Bud was almost twenty years ago. At any rate, according to my mother—my source for most family news—it's been ages since Uncle Bud was Uncle Bud anyway, because of Alzheimer's. (Aunt Cloda, Grandma's sister, passed away over two decades ago in her fifties. I must've been in Junior High at the time. Aunt Cloda had become a Christian Scientist, so I don't know what she died from.)

My most vivid memories of Uncle Bud are of him sitting on the davenport at Grandma and Grandpa's house during a visit, his skin weathered to old cowhide, his movements muscular but stiff, and his speech raspy, high-pitched, evenly paced, and kind. I can't remember anyone really talking with him much except Grandpa. He wasn't only Grandma's sister's husband, he was also Grandpa's direct blood relative. In fact, if Uncle Bud's father or grandfather hadn't been put up for adoption, he and I would've had the same last name.

Uncle Bud and Aunt Cloda had a farm and I didn't see Uncle Bud all that often, probably owing to chores. During childhood, I gradually picked up on the difference between the chores that my brother and I did at home for an allowance and the chores of local farmers and their families. It was a distinction that was never more salient than when one of my elementary school classmates informed me that on Christmas morning she didn't just wake up and dash ecstatically into the living room to open presents and see what Santa

Claus left, because first there were cows to be milked, barns to be cleaned, and breakfasts to be made.

Grandpa grew up on a farm in the vicinity of Uncle Bud's, but as a teenager he abandoned it for the new freedoms offered by wage-labor in town. Grandpa's brothers and sister, too, all managed one way or another to get off the farm. So growing up I got the impression that Aunt Cloda and Uncle Bud represented a sweatier, more muscle-tiring past—they were *still* on the farm—the temporal prejudice reinforced by a spatial one—they *still* lived in Washington County, while most of the rest of us had managed to make it over into Saratoga and Warren Counties. This set the stage for guilt about such prejudices when I got older, especially when I realized that Aunt Cloda and Uncle Bud were about the only connection I ever had to the agricultural heritage on my father's side. This connection remains tangible today whenever I drive by their old house on the Argyle Road and speculate that some of my second or third cousins must live somewhere in Washington County.

❄   ❄   ❄

Sofia and I are checking out the garlic and making plans for curing it. I keep trying to make up my mind about whether I'll go to Uncle Bud's funeral. Thoughts are racing through my head. It would be easy not to go—I haven't seen my (second) cousins on that side, let alone their kids, in the many years since Grandpa's funeral. But I can't be sure that this means they won't notice my absence. What if they do? What if they interpret it as uncaring or even elitist? ("Mister Professor thinks he's too much of a big shot to bother with us.") Besides, I *like* my relatives and hardly ever get to see them, and the funeral provides an unusual opportunity to do so, albeit a sad one. For some reason, my brain also keeps returning to those childhood prejudices about farmers and thinking how ironic it is that now I—the brainy kid who went off and got so many college degrees—am one of the few people in our family who spends so much time tilling soil, pulling weeds, spreading straw, and harvesting food. (I do realize this is *not* farming.) I'm also thinking that a rather full week of college meetings begins tomorrow morning, that today we've got good weather for pulling garlic, and that I need to build some kind of rack in the garage on which to cure it. So I have good excuses to *not* go—except not really because this work will probably only take us a few hours.

I finally decide to go to the calling hours but not to stay for the funeral that will immediately follow, but I can't persuade Sofia to come with me. She wants to stay home to do miscellaneous garden work while I'm gone.

I go in the house and change my clothes. I put on my blue jeans and a black T-shirt, plus—given the solemnity of the occasion—a dress shirt—black—over the T-shirt. As I'm dressing I get to thinking that for the first time in years I won't feel anxious that I'm wearing jeans at a formal family occasion. Given Uncle Bud's agricultural background and the Washington County venue of the funeral, it seems likely that rural and working-class dress norms will not be as out-of-place as they seem to be at other family rituals I've attended where more suburban middle-class and middle-class-wannabe sensibilities predominate. But this makes me anxious about my standard footwear. My usual black leather shoes—which I reckon are the one saving grace of my attire on formal occasions when all my other relatives are dressed up—seem like they might come off as a bit pretentious in a world of blue jeans, sneakers, and brown leather work boots. Oh well . . .

As I'm getting out of the car at the funeral home, I get that butterflies-in-my-stomach feeling. I almost always feel this way when I know I'm about to interact with a bunch of strangers or near-strangers who know who *I* am, especially when I really want to interact in a way that they'll deem competent—but isn't quite the way I'm predisposed to interacting.

I enter the funeral home nervous as hell. Like a fugitive who tries to keep moving without drawing attention to himself by looking out of place, I proceed down the central hallway, passing several doors leading into various rooms with more people. I immediately luck out—twice. First, because I don't recognize anyone and no one recognizes me, meaning that all social interaction is avoided for the moment. Second, because when I arrive at the last door and instinctively head toward it—ta-da—there are not only my parents but also my mother's sister and her husband (Ben's parents!) all sitting in the far back rows of the main room where the (closed) casket is located. These superfamiliar faces put me at ease. Now I feel like I'm "here."

My parents are chatting with one of Uncle Bud's three kids, Manda—the one who is closest to my parents and to Aunt Patsy, and who I thus have occasion to bump into now and then. Once my mother tells her who I am—Manda doesn't recognize me with my long beard and disheveled hair—I offer her my condolences. As her face transforms from one that is viewing a stranger to one that is looking at *me*, I gather from her expression that she's genuinely happy to see me for the first time in quite a while. We exchange a few pleasantries before she gets called into the other room for something or another. I'm glad I showed up.

I look around and see Manda's younger sister Bizzy. I'm immediately struck by the fact that age is bringing out a resemblance to Aunt Cloda that I never noticed in years past, back when every now and then she and her husband Jack would pull into Grandma and Grandpa's driveway in their mud-caked first-generation Plymouth Duster. By now I'm feeling comfortable enough that I'm spontaneously able to head right over to Bizzy to offer my sympathies, after covering my beard and hair with my hands so she can recognize me. I'm on a roll. I even try to find something more to say. Since the only thing I know about Bizzy is that she works in a nursery (the kind with plants) practically just around the corner from our house, I say, "Hey, I didn't even know until like a year or two ago that you work right down the road from us! Sometimes Sofia goes there to buy seedlings." My enthusiastic small-talk provokes nothing but a distant stare into my eyes. For an instant I'm paralyzed by her lack of reaction. Am I remembering something wrong? Maybe she doesn't know where our house is? Does she even know who Sofia is? An instant later she's (re-?)introducing me to one of her sons, all grown up now, and our encounter concludes without further abnormality.

Manda's and Bizzy's brother Seth approaches from the front of the room. I remember well when I saw him last, when he came through the line offering condolences to my family at Grandpa's funeral. Even back then I hadn't seen him for about ten years, which was the case with most of the people who came through the condolences line that day, but I distinctly remember my interaction with him. The reason I remember it so well is because of how different his small talk was from everyone else's: "Ya workin'?" he asked me. It didn't matter whether it was something he said to people all the time or if he actually knew something about my actual predicament at the time. After decades of being asked generically *How ya doin'?* and *How's it goin'?* it was the first (and so far the last) time anyone ever said this kind of thing to me. I was struck by the unusualness, to be sure, but also by a vague intuition that there was something especially meaningful about this *particular* question. Before he continued on down the line I asked him back—probably working in a generic *How are you?* I can only remember one of the things he replied—"I quit drinkin'."

My father . . . no, my *mother* . . . well one of them—I can't remember which—quizzes Seth, "Do you know who *this* is?" and by the way Seth looks at me I can tell he doesn't recognize me. As fast as I can, I tell him who I am. (I mean, really, how can people in my family think that this kind of interrogation is *fun*, especially when the interrogated are the principally bereaved at a *funeral*?) Seth must be more stunned by the impromptu examination than anyone realizes because even after I tell him who I am and offer my condolences, I'm pretty sure from the look on his face that he still doesn't know who the heck he's talking to.

At any rate, I'm satisfied overall. I've done what I came to do in five minutes flat, so I think I should stick around for a little while longer and take my place on one of the metal folding chairs near my parents and Aunt Juliette and Uncle Rich.

Grandma and Aunt Cloda had one brother, Will. (Also a Christian Scientist—the first person in the family to convert, if I'm not mistaken—and the first to pass away in his fifties because he wouldn't go to a doctor.) He had two daughters—one is Donna of Earthly Delights—and a son, Ronny, who I rarely ever saw when I was growing up. Yet, sitting just on the other side of my father, here's Ronny, up from Binghamton for the funeral! I'm especially happy to see him given my ongoing connection with his sister and the fact that Binghamton is a place Sofia and I visit frequently because of my friend Leonidas. My father and Ronny are both renowned kidders, but either because it's a funeral (less likely), because they haven't seen each other in a while (more likely), or because Ronny has something weighing on his mind (that's where I'd put my money), conversation between the two of them seems unusually subdued.

My mother wanders in from the hallway with the surprising news she just heard from someone that Bizzy hasn't worked at the nursery near our house since last year.

Bizzy's husband Jack—I'm assuming they're still married—wanders in. He's perfectly recognizable, if a little more filled out than I remember him back in his twenties. (Wait, if Bizzy and Jack drove the Duster, who had the Mustang?) Jack's hair is neatly combed and he's dressed in a clean, pressed, light blue suit that's one or two sizes too small. I figure he either borrowed the suit from a friend or it's his one suit that he pulls out every few years for occasions like this. I'm serious. When I was a kid and one of my father's cousins would get married, he and Grandpa would dig deep into their closets to see if they had a suit that fit, sometimes trading with each other if one of them had lost weight and the other had gained since the last such event.

Now *I'm* at an age that I have to think about these weight issues, too, but, never mind—I'm getting ahead of myself again.

Back to my father and Ronny. After the recounting of various childhood pranks and the one that my father pulled on Ronny at his job a few years back, the two of them soon find their old groove. Their voices grow louder and their chuckling turns into all-out laughter. Is such behavior at calling hours normal here? Is it considered acceptable? Won't my other relatives feel offended? Or is it just me, because I've grow accustomed to different expectations?

I decide to distance myself from the whole scene and get up to take a look at the two poster boards of old photos that I notice are on display. Some date back to before I was born, and I strain to picture in my mind's eye from the old photos what Aunt Cloda and Uncle Bud must've looked like in 3-D when they were young. Other pictures are from weddings and various family events at which I was present. And there are a couple more recent ones from after I'd gone off to college and lost touch. I'm not sure when the aerial views of the farm were taken. Soon my mother joins me and points at the photos one by one trying to explain to me who's in them and where they were taken. (To appreciate the irony of this scene you need to know that my mother is well known in our family for her exceptionally unreliable memory—just ask my brother—whereas I'm often believed to possess a nearly photographic one—just ask my *mother*.) Time to slip away again. I wander back to my folding chair and sit for a little while longer, watching various people, mostly strangers to me, wander in and out to take a look at the photos or to stand solemnly at the casket.

I check my watch and realize it's getting close to the hour for the funeral to begin. The time has come for me to go back home to pull garlic, partly because I prefer to avoid the formal ceremony, and partly because Jack's attire has stirred up icky memories of the secondhand suits my mother bought for me when I was in high school, and that I'd wear to interviews for summer jobs, totally oblivious to how dorky many people must've thought I looked in them.

(Now I remember: it was Manda who had the Mustang, before she got remarried. I think.)

I get up and head toward the door. On the way out I pass Jack. I notice that, along with the light-blue suit, he's sporting his faded brown leather, probably steel-toe, work boots.

I arrive home. Sofia is ready for us to harvest the garlic. I change into my work clothes and get to work on a rack for curing garlic in the garage. I nail together four old two-by-fours into a simple frame, and then use the staple gun to connect an old piece of fence to it as a tabletop. I screw a couple of hooks into the garage wall that I can hang it from on one side, and prop up the other side with an old garbage can and some boxes. That ought to do the trick.

I change into my farmer boots and go into the garden to pull the garlic with Sofia. The phone rings. It's my mother: "I just wanted to let you know that Ronny followed us back home from the funeral and I was gonna make some sandwiches, so if you and Sofia want to come over you're more than welcome."

"We'll see . . . I doubt it . . . We gotta harvest our garlic today."

I go back out again and continue pulling up garlic as fast as I can. "Wait!" Sofia calls over to me. "You have to be careful not to bruise them."

"Don't worry, they come out easy from the sand."

"You should also check them for mold. If there's mold we're doomed, because we have to make sure we don't plant garlic in the same place for many years and we're already running out of space."

"Oh. [. . .] My mother called and asked if we wanna go over for sandwiches. You can meet Donna's brother Ronny."

"You can go if you want."

"I don't wanna go alone. Can't you come with me?"

✳ 6 ✳

I Get By with a Little Help
from My Parents

I'm standing in our backyard over a pile of limestone rocks from the same neighbors who gave us our raspberries. When they dug out the raspberries, they also dismantled the low rock wall that formed the border between their front lawn and the row of brambles along their fence. They're friends with my parents, and they asked my parents to ask us if we wanted the rocks, and we figured, "Why not?"

I've got an inkling that we can use them to beautify the front yard somehow. We've been making some good practical changes to the front yard lately but it's time that we pay a little more attention again to making sure things look more presentable to neighbors.

Back in the spring, I dug a trench between the row of wildflowers along the front walk and the vegetable garden bed, dumped in loads of newspapers and cardboard, and backfilled. Then I bought a long piece of gutter and added it at ground level to the outlet of the gutter from the roof of the house, so water would drain out into a large rock-filled hole and then seep into the adjacent paper-stuffed trench. I hoped concentrating lots of water near the vegetables we grow there might help compensate for the extra dryness of our soil-poor, sandy front yard. It's an inexpensive experiment since I only had to buy the one piece of gutter. And the extra exercise did me good.

Also in the spring, and after much deliberation, Sofia and I planted several fruit trees in the front yard. Sofia had talked with my cousin Danny about where he orders his fruit trees from and then began to read up on what's available. Sofia explained to me what she'd read in her catalogs about dwarf and semidwarf trees and convinced me that dwarf trees might be the solution to growing more fruit in our smallish front yard. I had my reservations about pruning, but an Internet search turned up some useful information from various states' Cooperative Extensions. Besides, I realized I could always take digital photos of the trees and e-mail them to Danny and he could probably tell me where I should make pruning cuts. Sofia read up on how to prepare and improve the soil before transplanting the trees—we should've begun the previous autumn but we did the best we could in the time we had. Two pears, a sour cherry, a three-on-one cherry, and one peach tree. I'm not planning on doing any chemical pest-control. We'll see if we ever get any fruit to eat.

Earlier this season I got annoyed when my father offered to mow our front yard for us with his gas-powered push mower. Our rotary mower wasn't able to cut down the somewhat taller stalks with seed heads that had popped up, and I hadn't gotten around to doing it with a hand-me-down tool from my parents. (I don't know what it's called, but you swing it back and forth and it cuts. As a kid I'd use it to bushwhack the many ferns in the woods behind our house only to be disappointed when they seemed to grow back again almost overnight.) I'm sure the seed heads must have looked ugly to my parents, at least to my mother, and since they were expecting relatives from Canada for a golf outing, I'll bet she was worried about being embarrassed.

"Oh, [my first name]!" was her reaction to seeing me plop the rhubarb from my grandparents' old house more-or-less randomly in the middle of the front yard, where it would get plenty of sun. (I was in a hurry.)

Sometimes she gets legalistic and tries persuading me that we have to do something about our yard because of the Association Rules of the development we belong to. "Landscaping must be consistent with the existing vegetation," is how the actual rule reads. So I remind her that she and my father have already violated some of the other rules themselves, but this just gets her going about how *their* violations are okay because they make their property look even better or make it safer. Anyway, there's a clause in the rules saying that if a violation goes uncontested for at least a year, then it can no longer be disputed. By now, except maybe for the ones about clotheslines and boats, most of the rules have been violated by one or more of us in the neighborhood for years. Never mind that the neighborhood got together and dissolved the Association before Sofia and I even moved in—I suppose so everyone could avoid paying the fees.

I'd describe my parents' yard but I can only describe what I have words for describing, and I remain ignorant of most of what they've got growing there. Various-colored daylilies, tiger lilies (not the daylily kind of tiger lilies), hostas, marigolds, and bee balm are about the only flowers I know how to identify out of the perhaps hundreds of varieties they have in their front and back yards. Many of them came from nearby nurseries, others from relatives or friends. Every fence, every wall of the house and garage and sunroom, and every walkway is bordered with flower gardens. A huge flower garden takes up something like the entire back third of the backyard, complete with stone walking paths, sitting benches, and evening lighting. There's a homemade swing set and a horseshoe pit; a gazebo on a stamped-concrete patio; a deck extending out from the sunroom large enough for a big glass patio table with chairs, a bench, and a porch swing under a rectangular, covered something-or-other. There's lush green grass everywhere.

In short, if you open the gate that my father made in our fence and enter their yard from ours, or our yard from theirs, the contrast won't go unnoticed. Images symbolic of "the two Americas, side-by-side," as a Canadian colleague put it to me last week after having visited us for a small Fourth of July cookout.

Speaking strictly in aesthetic terms now, a generous, pluralistic point of view would likely see each of our respective yards as beautiful in its own way, especially considering that each is a product of do-it-yourself, amateur landscaping.

But I'm sure from my parents' point of view, especially my mother's, our yard—like my new hairstyle—isn't clean-cut enough. It's got too many rough edges. The unkempt and the carefully organized intermingle too haphazardly. There are too many signs of a lack of attention to grooming. Some straightening-up is needed. Of course I'd disagree, but not entirely. I think Sofia and I have a vague sense of the kind of aesthetic outcome we're going for, but we have little more than a few primitive ideas about how to achieve it. We've resigned ourselves to discovering how to do it gradually, over the course of years of experimentation. This means that for the time being there are always some things about our yard that look unkempt even to us.

From my perspective, my parents' front yard is an unbelievable accomplishment of meticulous planning and upkeep, but one that ultimately falls short because it looks too much like it's trying to be an estate garden—without a sufficient command of actual estate-garden aesthetics—on a half-acre suburban lot. (I've got a lot of nerve saying this—if my parents didn't save money like crazy to put me through college, I'd never have been able to come up with a phrase like "without a sufficient command of actual estate-garden aesthetics.") If their yard is going to be *that* neat and controlled—with every line and edge clearly defined, each distinct color in its carefully planned-out place—it seems like all the components should be laid out in such a way as to provoke tranquility or a sense of balance or of vibrancy or of harmony or of welcoming or of intricacy or of *something* that visitors might enjoy having impressed upon them. All I can see is nervousness. A heart-shaped flower garden here and a circular outline of plants at the base of a tree there all look perfectly well-managed, but they don't seem to add up to anything. Yes, that's it: it's as if the *managementness* unintentionally eclipses any other more intriguing sense of beauty.

Maybe I exaggerate.

Mostly, however, I enjoy seeing their yard. Once I get past the nervous managementness of it all, I mostly see the bountiful love and attention they've given over to its creation and upkeep. And I don't think there are many people around here who—without any formal training whatsoever in landscaping or aesthetics—could pull off even half of what my mother has managed to accomplish through intuition, observation, and trial and error.

But I confess that when I see my mother looking oppressively exhausted, or hear my father over there from sunup to sundown pulling out dandelions from the lawn one at a time with a hand tool, I also worry that maybe they've allowed the gardens to get the best of them.

And I don't much like the underground sprinkler-system–watered, greener-than-green lawn.

Still, if my father is pulling up those dandelions one at a time because he's decided to cut back on the lawn chemicals after all the lecturing he's heard from me, how can I not admire that?

I open the gate and head out front. I walk around the grass surveying the situation. I'm thinking about using the limestone rocks to build a little wall or just make an outline somewhere. It's difficult for me to envision. When Sofia and I moved in, the front yard was just grass with a few trees near the edge by our other neighbors. Now there's the randomly placed rhubarb and a Rose of Sharon that my mother handed down to us. There's the garden row and wildflowers near the front walk. I see that I could use limestone to enclose both the rhubarb and the Rose of Sharon within a third-quarter-moon–shaped garden that would run up against the driveway. Or, I could make a curvy border that encloses them but then turns back out in the other direction to surround the area with the vegetable-garden row and the wildflowers.

I hear the storm door open next door. (Oddly, my father doesn't seem to oil it, which must be why I can hear it squeak. Maybe it's too high-pitched for him to hear now that he's getting older. But how is it that my mother hasn't asked him to do it?) Is she just letting the cat out? Nope, she's coming out. I walk next door, half-thinking that my mother will have a fair sense of what will look okay and half-thinking that if she knows I'm considering the aesthetics of the front yard, and that she even gets to have input into the design, she'll have less reason to object to the appearance of our front yard in the future.

I bring her back to our yard and tell her my two ideas. She says either one would look fine. She keeps looking around our yard.

Referring to the bushes at the corner where the front walk meets the driveway at the lamp post, she says, "You could even split those two bushes and line them along the edge of your driveway."

"You can do that?"

"Well, sure. Look how much they're overgrown. You can probably divide them into five or six bushes."

"How do you do that?"

"Wait. I'll get your father."

She goes back next door and I run in and summon Sofia from paying bills to come out to see what she thinks about all this.

My parents come back over. My father has his ax. I go get a shovel and the wheelbarrow. My mother gives directions about where and how much while my father does the digging. Once he's got the first bush out of the ground my mother calculates how many bushes we can fit along the driveway and tells him how many times to split the bush with the ax. My parents negotiate with one another about how many splits can feasibly be made and where the cuts should be done. My father starts splitting.

While he's doing that I dig new holes. It's sunny and hot and I realize we should get the roots back into the ground as quickly as possible. I mention something about the fact that we shouldn't be doing this kind of transplanting in August, but my mother says it should work fine as long as we keep watering the bushes every single day. No water is too much, especially since we're essentially transplanting into beach sand.

My mother shows me how wide and deep I should be digging.

Sofia brings out a few large buckets from the garage and fills them with water. She wants to keep the roots soaking in the water for as long as they're out of the ground.

My mother holds the first transplant in place and tells me how to backfill it. She has me shape the soil around the base like a bowl so that when we water it the water will collect and sink in instead of running off. My father goes and gets one of his shovels and starts digging another hole in the place my mother has marked.

I feel awful that my father is doing all this digging and axing, especially with his bad back. I can't really imagine making him stop, though, or at least I don't feel bad *enough* to make him stop.

Last year was worse: The cheap pine columns on our front porch had been splitting for a year or two. I couldn't tell, but my father was able to figure out that they were load bearing and needed to be replaced sooner rather than later. In other words, they were buckling. My brother gave me the name of a guy, and I left a message but after three weeks he never called back. My father came over on a Saturday morning and said it was bothering him so much that we hadn't managed to get it fixed yet that he wanted to do it himself. I already had plans to go hiking that day with a colleague, and Sofia had to finish revising an article for *Art Education* she had a deadline for, so we wouldn't even be able to help him. He kept insisting, so I went online and found some decent columns at a local lumber store, gave my father my credit card, and told him do whatever he wanted. Luckily I got back from hiking in time to help out with some of the more difficult parts that he never could've finished on his own, and even then he was the one swinging away the sledgehammer with all his might to prop up the porch overhang with temporary supports so the columns could be switched out. I didn't know which was worse: letting him do that kind of labor when I knew he had back problems or feeling pressured to do it myself when I didn't want to end up with my own back problems and was perfectly happy to wait for my brother's guy to call me back so I could hire *him* to do the job.

Today I'm doing more digging than I initially bargained for—and under a blazing sun, something that my Mediterranean experiences have conditioned me to avoid by choosing to work when it's cooler or when there's shade—but I guess I'm still my parents' son, because I'm handling it well enough. It seems a worthwhile price to pay for all the impromptu help we're getting, at any rate.

Within a couple hours we manage to get all the bushes dug up, split, transplanted, and watered. My mother keeps talking away about keeping them watered every single day. I'm bringing wheelbarrows full of the limestone rocks out front to make the outline enclosing the row of bushes, the Rose of Sharon, the rhubarb, the garden row, and the wildflowers.

"You could move your lilac bush over there," says my mother, pointing to the new area that has come into definition by the placement of the rocks.

"What lilac?" I ask. I don't even know what lilacs look like.

She points to the overgrown lilac between the front porch and the corner of the house. "You could split that, you know . . . Hon', you could split that lilac couldn't you?"

I call over to Sofia and ask her what she wants to do. My mother goes on and on with various ideas about where to put the lilac. We all wander around the yard trying to picture various scenarios my mother is describing.

Sofia and I confer and agree to put one lilac in the new garden area outlined by the rocks, and another out near the road on the other side of the driveway. I grab a shovel and dig around the lilac. I hit a big root and am getting ready to try cutting through it with a hard kick on the shovel, when somehow I get an emergency memo from my brain saying that it didn't quite feel like a root after all, and that I'm just a short stone's-throw away from the corner of the house where the gas, electric, and cable all come in. I throw down the shovel.

"Uh-oh," I say as I'm walking over to where my parents and Sofia are starting to prepare a hole for the first lilac, "I think I hit wires or something."

My father comes over and analyzes the situation. Luckily I didn't even scratch the tubing that encases the wires running to the house. My father digs around it and tells me how I can dig out the lilac without getting into trouble with the wires. I do my best to dig down and around it but I can't get it out of the ground. My father pulls it this way and that, telling me where I should be digging the shovel into the ground. It won't come out.

"Here, you come over here and pull it like this." He takes the shovel.

"Pull! Pull hard!" he directs me as he's pounding the shovel underground. At last the lilac comes free, and I pull it out as a load of dry sand falls from the roots.

My father splits the lilac and we begin transplanting. With the other bushes, we just dropped each one into its respective hole. With each lilac, my father rotates it around into various positions so Sofia can figure out which one looks the best before I backfill. My mother is watering the first lilac as we're transplanting the second. This second one looks a little funny no matter how it's turned. After it's in the ground and backfilled my father offers to bring over a stake so we can tie the second lilac to it, to train it, so it'll look a little nicer. Sofia and I take him up on it.

As I'm waiting for my father to come back, Sofia and my mother are on the other side of the yard talking more about the yard and garden. It never ceases to amaze me how Sofia can so easily—both in the sense of "not difficult" and "easygoing"—carry on non-small-talk conversations with my mother. It's certainly rare that I can.

I step out into the road to take in and admire our afternoon's accomplishments. It looks like an entirely new front yard. It certainly has a lot more character today than it did yesterday. Maybe I can move those hostas that I don't like from the back deck area to our newly outlined decorative garden. If I mix enough nonedibles in with the edibles, maybe the neighbors won't even notice how much food we're growing out front, or at least won't mind.

I try to remember what the lilac flowers look like and wonder whether they're edible. I tell myself not to forget to look it up after we go back in the house.

I'm also wondering how I'm going to deal with trimming all the grass that will inevitably grow in and around the new border of limestone rocks.

7

The Kid from the Country Goes Continental

Leonidas is visiting us for Labor Day weekend.

Early Saturday morning, the three of us go shopping. We check out the New-York–wine store in town and end up buying a bottle of Cabernet Franc from the Finger Lakes. At the farmers' market, finding ourselves in a decadent mood, we consider buying sausages. The vendor's signs claim that the sausages are "nitrate-free," but—as Leonidas always explains to the rest of us nonchemistry majors—nit*rates* aren't the most usual issue with cured meats, nit*rites* are. The kid selling for the farmers doesn't know anything about nitrates or nitrites but the official ingredient label on the actual sausage package mentions neither nitrates nor nitrites. We buy some.

Leonidas is one of the first Greeks I ever became friends with. I was majoring in math, and the math department had four faculty from Greece, some of the university's most charismatic lecturers. I should know—I took classes from all of them at some point. I'd sit in class imagining that these swarthy, articulate profs, who even in large lecture halls looked students right in the eyes, were simply the latest in a long line of Greek mathematicians dating back to Pythagoras and Euclid. I envisioned Greece as a sun- and sea-bathed paradise which for millennia had been giving birth to disproportionately large numbers of suave mathematicians who handled theorems and corollaries like the eighties Lakers handled a basketball. Professor Vlastos, the department chair, was so impressive in a lecture hall that starting on the second day of his Calculus 1 classes, students would spontaneously give him a round of applause the moment he came trotting in, sharply dressed, carrying only a cup of coffee, and livening up the room with his smug grin. As far as I could tell, we clapped not only because he was an impeccably lucid lecturer but because we were grateful that he proved by example that math-and-science types could be so damn cool.

The fall semester of my junior year I enrolled in a graduate-level algebra class, where I met a quick-thinking, energetic, and wide-smiling master's student named Penny who'd just arrived from the University of Crete to study under Vlastos. Sometimes Penny and I would talk when we ran into each other in the halls. I persuaded her to teach me some Greek words and phrases—"*Yasou, ti kaneis?*" "*Kala esee?*" "*Etsi ketsi.*" ("Hi, how are you?" "Fine, and you?" "So-so.")—and I'd practice them on her whenever we bumped into each other in the hall. Since I knew nothing of Crete and couldn't make any sense of how determined she was to avoid casual, easygoing social interactions with the opposite sex beyond what happens in classrooms and hallways, I kept trying to persuade her that we should do something together sometime. I had many female friends on campus, and not only Americans, so her resistance struck me as more than a little strange, but also intriguing. After many months, she gave into my pleading and invited me for a homemade lunch of Greek food to be followed immediately by bowling with her French and Dutch graduate student friends. As far as I could tell, there wasn't the slightest hint of flirtation.

After bowling, everyone was invited to stop by Leonidas's, who was house-sitting for two of the (married) Greek math faculty while they were back in Greece on sabbatical. Leonidas was a PhD candidate in chemical engineering who seemed to love music, eating, and just sitting around talking at least as much as I did, and he had an unrelenting, biting sense of humor that kept us all entertained. We sat in the living room talking and eating Leonidas's homemade baklava. I could hardly follow the conversations—what did I know of the European Community or Edith Piaf? But it was fun to watch Leonidas, every time someone said something tangentially music-related, dart into the other room and come back all proud that he had yet another cassette germane to the conversation. Leonidas's homemade baklava, just like the lunch Penny prepared earlier that day, was an extraordinary treat. I was enjoying homemade food at the university for the very first time—and a whole day of it at that—not because someone's parents or grandparents cooked for us, but because these Greek graduate students were themselves accustomed to preparing homemade food.

As it turned out, this was the first of many such gatherings over the next few months. Leonidas's place quickly became the evening and weekend hangout, the place to stop by for some coffee, conversation, and a homemade snack or dessert. Like many other male Mediterraneans of his generation, Leonidas learned to cook as a matter of necessity after coming to the United States for studies. There were no mothers, sisters, aunts, or wives around to do the cooking, restaurants were not affordable, and supermarket convenience foods were unacceptable substitutes for the homemade fare and other less-industrial flavors to which he was accustomed. Indeed, for all these budding researchers from—and soon-to-be-returning to—the metropolises of Continental Europe, a piece of baklava or a slice of *baba au rhum* made from scratch was a delicious way to feel a little closer to home during a stint in the St. Lawrence valley of northern New York. I suppose such items were the European equivalent of what I've heard Americans calling "comfort foods."

I must have clocked more hours hanging out with non–North Americans on that one day than in the whole rest of my life up to that point. Hindsight tells me that everybody there was probably wondering why this naive rural American kid was appended to their more cosmopolitan, graduate-level company, but I, like so many American tourists, delighted in all the benign cultural exotica: the large quantity of olive oil Penny used to dress the salad, the way everyone relaxed and enjoyed bowling without taking their skills too seriously or becoming competitive, the manner in which one leisurely activity just sort of spilled over into the next one, discussions in which ideologies like socialism and communism were not automatically equated with Pure Evil, sitting on leather couches on oriental rugs in my professors' living room, and just about *everything* about Leonidas—the music he played (in I don't know how many languages, but never in English), his marked accent, his unusually loud talking, his waving arms and other comically exaggerated mannerisms, the spanakopita (spinach pie) he served, but also the fact that he, an *engineer*, knew how to make this peculiar delicacy from scratch. Even the details of the spinach pie were enticingly exotic: the crispy paper-thin phyllo dough, the feta cheese (this was before feta had become so widely popular in the U.S.), and the fact that the spinach itself actually tasted good. My only experiences with spinach before then were watching Dad, and only Dad, eating a side dish of canned spinach doused with cider vinegar.

I was also struck by how different Leonidas was from other people I knew in terms of the way he treated his visitors. When gentle and soft-spoken Nicolaas arose from his chair and began picking up a few dishes, Leonidas boisterously waved his arms flaming in protest: "Sit down! Sit down! [...] Leave those plates alone!" But the Dutch mathematician just grinned and politely continued about his business. Leonidas, feigning outrage, bolted toward him, snatched the plates, and shouted: "I'm very serious! I don't pick up the dishes in your house, so please don't you pick up the dishes in mine!" The fact that he shouted ferociously at his guests in order to make them *more* comfortable struck me as more than a little unsettling, even though I'd seen Grandpa raise his voice in a restaurant to argue with Dad so he could treat his grandsons. But it was Leonidas's unrelenting insistence that his visitors not lift a finger that I found altogether alien.

Alien, but enticing. It resonated with my own secret distaste for picking up the dishes at someone else's house when I was a visitor. I never liked switching into chore mode during moments of relaxation and enjoyment. Besides, bringing things into a strange kitchen felt too much like going in and rearranging someone else's bedroom or bathroom. Sometimes I'd get anxious just wondering if I was really helping, just replacing one mess with a different mess, or interfering in some other way with my hosts' usual household order. What if I broke something? And nothing was worse than having one's genuine contentment suddenly overrun by pangs of guilt brought on by the thought that one's hosts might already be sitting there waiting for assistance, all the while thinking, "Is he *ever* going to help, or at least *offer*?"

What could be better for a visitor, I thought, than to be subjected to Leonidas's "no helping" mandate? Yet, this secret preference of mine was at odds with everything I (thought I) knew about the proper behavior of visitors. Growing up, I was led to believe that visitors should pitch in. Aunts and uncles would squeeze into the kitchen at Grandpa and Grandma's house after dinner to help wash and dry the dishes. At Mom and Dad's house, my cousins would bring their dirty plates back from the dining area to the sink after a meal. In fact, the higher regard in which someone was held in our family—the more generous but self-reliant, the more agreeable and unlikely to argue with others, the more they smiled, the less openly critical they were of people close to them—the more likely they were to lend a helping hand. From an early age I got the impression that visitors who didn't leap up to help with the dishes were deficient in character.

This inaugurated a conflict in me between my wish as a visitor to enjoy myself thoroughly, and a more general desire not to be judged by others—especially by virtual strangers—as deficient in character. Yet observing Leonidas approaching things in such a different way, I became convinced that my own ostensibly lazy or selfish desires as a visitor might be compatible with a workable model of hosting visitors after all, just not the model I learned growing up. The tacit philosophy of hosting I'd taken to be universally acknowledged by good people everywhere was put into a whole new light. I no longer felt compelled to accept it as a self-evident truth. I had no idea, though, how many more times my thoughts on this subject would evolve.

❊   ❊   ❊

It's sunny but not too hot, dry, with a light late-summer breeze. Sofia and I don't have a sunroom or a screened-in porch, and our back deck is really too sunny to sit on until late afternoon, so while the sausage is cooking in the oven we take a few of our hand-me-down plastic chairs and little plastic side-tables and put them in the shade of a large oak near the shed.

I slice up local sheep's-milk cheese and open the wine. Sofia makes a Greek salad.

I don't actually know the history of the salads that are known as "Greek salads" in the United States. Probably it has something to do with what Greek-immigrant-owned diners or restaurants served their customers years ago, as well as with the American stereotype of Greek food as built around spinach, feta, and olives.

I do know well the salads that many Greeks in Greece serve. Typical: Coarsely chopped cucumber and tomato and onion with plenty of olive oil and wine vinegar, some salt, and maybe some dried oregano. It's usually called a *horiatiki salata*, which can be translated as, among other things, "village salad," "villager salad," "country salad," "peasant salad," or "hick salad." Other ingredients can be added as well. Sure, these might be olives or feta or even spinach, but they could also be bell peppers or arugula or wild purslane.

Sofia makes the best *horiatiki salata*. She'll include anything from nasturtium leaves and buds, bronze-fennel tops (which taste like a cross of dill and the more widely known and more licorice-like bulb fennel), spearmint or lemon balm (thin strips cut with scissors), wild sheep sorrel, peppers sweet or hot, some young dandelion leaves, or wild purslane. Like snowflakes, no two Greek salads of Sofia's are quite alike.

Today she's just using tomatoes, cucumber, and olives, foregoing the raw onions that Leonidas doesn't like even *touching* his salad.

The irony isn't lost on me. Everything Leonidas ever says about food suggests that his food preferences have barely budged a centimeter since his childhood. Mine, on the other hand, started changing drastically pretty much the day I met Leonidas—*because* I met him.

A research fellowship funded by NASA let me stay on campus for the entire summer just after we met. It paid less than the summer jobs with the Department of Transportation (DOT) that I'd been taking on and, considering my tuition, it was definitely an issue, but being at the university meant that I could spend the summer lobbying for early graduation, early admission to the graduate program, and a graduate teaching assistantship—thus saving me my· entire senior year's worth of tuition and giving me a steady paycheck to boot. (Oh, and did I mention that it would give me more time to pursue Penny?)

On weekdays I worked on deriving my equations from the Navier-Stokes equations for fluid flow. The evenings and weekends I spent with Leonidas and Penny, and the Dutch and French graduate students of their posse. Leonidas often cooked dinner for Penny and me on weekdays and lunch, too, on weekends. My sense was that Leonidas and Penny hung out together a lot because they were both Greek, and that I was included because I was essentially alone as an undergraduate whose other undergraduate friends had all gone for the summer. Nicolaas, Pieter (also Dutch), Nicole (French), Jean (French), and others sometimes came as well, and they also took turns cooking their own feasts and inviting over the whole gang to enjoy. Leonidas called them "gastronomical orgies." After three years of not-too-awful university cafeteria food and two summers of yummy greasy diner food on a DOT expense account, I was now having homemade meals from scratch on a daily basis. The people I was eating them with were as sociable as my undergraduate friends, but also older, more widely traveled, fluently multilingual, and, as far as I could tell, encyclopedically knowledgeable.

One Saturday, Leonidas made some Greek dishes and invited a number of us over for lunch. He served red wine. I'd never tasted wine before, but in my mind it was symbolically a drink of sophistication, unlike the beer and liquor the other side of my family drank. Already titillated by the exotic good flavors of so many new foods, I eagerly anticipated the refined refreshment I was about to experience as I gazed at the dark red liquid gently hovering above the table in my stem glass. But the wine's dryness came as a sudden and unpleasant surprise, and the astringency made me feel like I was having my mouth vacuumed. I was secretly dismayed. Between the tantalizing color and wine's reputation I expected to enjoy it from the start. Apparently it would take a conscious effort on my part to acquire this new taste and to reach the point of appreciating and relishing it the way my new friends did. Whenever we took a trip that summer—whether it was to nearby Massena or as far away as Plattsburgh or Burlington, Vermont—Leonidas would stop at a wine shop and look for bargains on inexpensive reds from France, Spain, and Hungary. I picked up a few things, such as wine regions of France, and the differences between "table wine," "vin de pays," and "appellation d'origine contrôlée." It wasn't too long before I began to *enjoy* red wine with some of our meals.

Sometimes a group of us would go with Leonidas to Montreal for the day, the only real metropolis I'd ever visited. Our first stop was always the Greek neighborhood around Park Avenue, where a trip to the Greek bakery for a snack was the first order of business. Then we'd head downtown for shopping and tourism in the afternoon, followed by dinner at a Greek restaurant on Duluth Avenue. But first we'd drive over to a condominium to pick up a physics professor who lived in Montreal—another Greek whom Leonidas met through the math faculty. Then we'd pick up a bottle of wine for dinner, while Leonidas remarked—with younger naive me hanging onto his every word like an eager apprentice—that *apportez votre vin* was an indication that Montreal was more civilized than the United States. We'd wait in the line of to-be diners extending from the doorway all the way down the sidewalk. The food was mostly Greek and the menu mostly in French. We always started with a *pikilia* sampler plate of appetizers, some of which I recognized (like spanakopita), some that I didn't (like tzatziki), and some that I was afraid to try (like the fish-roe *taramosalata*). For my main course I usually had the souvlaki, recommended by Leonidas, and I always loved it. Dessert was Greek coffee, which Leonidas had already taught me how to drink at his house.

Once, we didn't go to the Greek place for dinner. We'd gone into the city with Pieter, Nicole, and Nicole's brother, who was visiting from France. Strolling around Old Montreal, the others noticed a French restaurant that caught their attention, so Leonidas and I went along with their proposal that we eat dinner there. Taking me aside at some point, Leonidas warned me that I shouldn't be surprised if we were still hungry after dinner even though we'd be paying more than usual. After dinner, as we continued wandering around the city looking for somewhere to have coffee and dessert, the two of us made sure we ended up at a place where we could get a little something extra to finish off our lingering hunger.

Driving back home that night, we saw the northern lights. It was my first time seeing them, and all I could think was, "This is really the life . . . living in a small campus town in New York's North Country, surrounded by sophisticated friends, and taking the occasional daytrip to a cosmopolitan city like Montreal. It doesn't get any better than this!"

Still, not returning the favor to Leonidas and the other Europeans by cooking something for them troubled me. Not only did I not have enough dishes and flatware to invite them over for a meal, but as graduate teaching assistants they would have felt uncomfortable visiting my on-campus apartment (covered by the NASA grant), because I shared it with three undergraduates who were *not* doing graduate-level work like I was.

I got another idea, though. I decided I'd wake up early one Saturday morning, make two loaves of Grandma's bread, and bring them to Leonidas's house for everyone to enjoy. I borrowed bread pans from Leonidas, purchased flour, shortening, and yeast at the supermarket, and spent the first half of the day baking. Back home, this bread had long been revered by my whole family as a special treat. It was only the second or third time I made it on my own since Grandma had died. When Grandma passed away—I was in high school—I asked Aunt Patsy for recipes of my favorite dishes, including Grandma's lasagna and her bread. I figured if I knew how to make them I could continue to eat them. Even though I knew that I'd only get to enjoy them once in a blue moon—or any other homemade food from scratch for that matter—I was content. In fact, realizing that this was more than my friends, my brother, and my generation of cousins could do, I was more than just content—I felt downright lucky. So I was a little hurt, but mostly just puzzled, when I discerned behind their outward shows of polite appreciation that neither Leonidas nor Penny was truly impressed by what I'd always taken to be the supreme example of a loaf of bread. I had no way of knowing yet that people in Greece had far more experience with eating a variety of homemade breads than the people in my family did, let alone that these Greeks' idea of good homemade bread involved crusty loaves with many more complex flavors than I'd ever experienced growing up.

As the second half of summer approached, Penny seemed like she was on the verge of giving in to my romantic interest. I noticed that her sprightly manner of interacting with me—the same way she interacted with all her friends—sometimes gave way to a serene moment together. She became less insistent about inviting other friends to tag along with us if we went bike riding or for a drive by the river. I finally worked up the courage (at a fast-food joint of all places) to tell her how I felt. "Try to forget about it," she insisted without trying to hide how naively she seemed to think I was behaving, "We are just friends. You shouldn't think about more than that."

I was initially dismayed, but Leonidas reminded me to pay more attention to her actions than to her words. My optimism grew. Being a math-and-science guy, I extrapolated from the subtle and gradual changes in her behavior—from the ostensible signs I thought I was getting from her—that she should eventually reveal her unequivocal romantic interest in me. But that she should probably do so about three days *after* her departure! Alas, this meant I had to wait for the fall semester when she returned from her trip back home to Crete to find out if I was right.

Meanwhile, Leonidas found out he had to move. The faculty whose house he was sitting were coming back to pack up their belongings to ship them home to Greece where they'd managed to secure academic appointments. Another math professor—a third Dutchman named Hans—asked Leonidas to apartment-sit for him while he (Hans) was in Europe for the rest of the summer. By this time I was only using my on-campus apartment for sleeping and showering, since I spent all the rest of my time either in my campus office or socializing with graduate students. Leonidas got Hans's permission to let me room with him.

As Leonidas's roommate, I quickly grew accustomed to a new life-style. This included chipping away at the only attitude I ever knew toward work. The first half of the summer I was treating my NASA fellowship like a nine-to-five job, going to my office every morning to work several hours, taking a short lunch break, and then working through the afternoon. Nobody was *making* me do this. My research faculty adviser only asked me to check in with him now and then about my progress. As a student I'd always worked more freely and flexibly to good effect, but knowing that I was getting paid to do applied math as a full-time *job* somehow made me think I should be putting in fixed hours like any other laborer. It certainly never occurred to me to wonder whether *I* was being exploited by a system that conditioned people like me to be grateful for being paid so little to do such specialized research valued by such powerful interests.

While staying at Hans's apartment, Leonidas and I would wake up, turn on the classical radio station from Ottawa, and leisurely cook a big breakfast, usually some kind of an omelet, salad, and bread leftover from the day before. After that, I'd put ingredients into the bread maker and set the timer so we'd have a new loaf waiting for us when we'd come back for dinner. We'd both go to our respective campus offices and work for a few hours. Later, maybe with some other friends, we'd meet up at the gym for racquetball or swimming, hot tub, and a sauna. Next, we'd work for two or three more hours. If the weather was good, some of us might meet by the Racquette River for a little afternoon canoeing. If not, I'd work on learning Greek from a book Leonidas had helped me find on one of our Montreal excursions. By early evening, Leonidas and I would take a quick trip to the grocery store, decide what to make for dinner, and buy whatever ingredients we needed.

These shopping trips turned out to be quite educational. Once, Leonidas told me we needed butter, so I went over to the cooler and selected a container of the brand I remembered Mom always bought. When he saw what I'd chosen he straightened up and looked sternly at me as though I should be ashamed for thinking I was college-educated, not to mention a straight-A math-and-science student.

He rattled off with ease (he *was* a Greek-speaking chemical engineer after all!) the difficult-to-pronounce ingredients and scornfully asked me how I could possibly think that this concoction was butter. The thrashing continued as he pointed out that the brand I'd chosen didn't even call itself "margarine," just "spread."

Every time we went shopping, Leonidas would stand in the aisle scrutinizing ingredient lists and explaining out loud what he was thinking. I, usually clueless regarding what all the fuss was about, would keep asking him to explain why he cared about these things. In time I learned that few tomato pastes listed "tomatoes" as their only ingredient, that many canned tunas come packed in "broth," and that many deli meats list sodium nitrite as an ingredient. I watched Leonidas compare labels and price tags, dismantling one supermarket advertising or pricing ploy after another. Since he easily memorized the prices of everything he was planning to buy, he always knew when a cashier—or, more precisely, when the automatic price that came up from the bar code—was in error. I was shocked to discover that almost every time there was such an error it was in the supermarket's favor.

Leonidas was in charge of the kitchen not only because he was a lot fussier than me about his likes and dislikes regarding even the most common ingredients and textures, but because he was the only one between us who knew how to make so many dishes from scratch. Green bean stew and chickpea soup. Spinach pie and cheese pie. Spaghetti with pesto, with tomato and ground beef sauce, or *alla carbonara*. Broiled ground beef patties. Chicken and potatoes in the oven. Pot roast with mushrooms. Pork souvlaki. Stuffed tomatoes. *Pastitsio*. Moussaka. Often, potatoes deep fried in olive oil. Always, either a tomato salad or green salad, and feta cheese. In a pinch we'd heat up a frozen pizza. Leonidas assigned me things that I could do to help prepare ingredients and, in the process, I began learning a lot more about cooking homemade foods, including such exotics as spinach pie and baklava.

From that summer on, home-cooked food prepared largely from scratch became the norm in my everyday life.

When the summer ended and Penny returned—and I had learned how to conjugate "to be" and "to have" in Greek, and how to pronounce difficult sounds like γ (gamma)—I found out that I was right about her romantic interest in me.

❄ ❄ ❄

Sofia, Leonidas, and I use plastic trays to carry the sausages, salad, cheese, and wine outdoors, along with small plates, forks, glasses, and some napkins. We see my father in his backyard and I call him over.

I nibble on the cheese and sip the wine. Then I try the sausage—not bad! I wash it down with more Cabernet Franc and realize that it tastes much better than I remember it tasting just a minute ago. *Much* better.

Sofia and Leonidas are making sounds of pleasant surprise about the food and drink. Leonidas says something about the pairing of wine and food, and I can tell from his unusually enthusiastic tone of voice that he's quite taken by the experience. He explains how when the food and wine are properly paired, both the food and the wine should taste better than each would've tasted if consumed unpaired.

I always thought food and wine pairing was mostly a matter of pretentiousness or of reinforcing certain customary habits or tastes. Now I'm wondering if there's more to it.

Our initial bout of eating and drinking winds down and I look up toward the parallel rows of the vegetable garden. In an ocean of green my eyes are drawn to a cloud of pink that is the Sweet William Catchfly that has come up on its own along one of the rows. God our backyard looks beautiful!

If only it sounded as good as it looks. Someone is running a gas-powered leaf-blower—at least that's what it sounds like—at one of the houses behind us. It's been going on for more than an hour. I can't figure out why—it's too early for autumn leaves.

The noise finally stops. I yell out as loudly and as sarcastically as I can muster on the spot, *"Thaaaank yooouuu!"*

✳ 8 ✳

Meet the Parents

Aunt Patsy calls early in the morning and tells me that she just read in the *Chronicle* that our town is going to hold its first-ever international food festival. She proceeds to read to me the section that describes all the foods they'll have, including Greek and Chinese, certain that I'll be interested. I know there's no point in trying to explain to her that a festival like this is actually intended to be enjoyable more for someone like *her* than for someone like me, and I try interrupting her before she can finish reading the whole article—not so much because waiting it out this one time is in itself so difficult, but because I instinctually worry that these calls will turn into a pattern. I'm hoping she'll take the hint.

"But they're gonna have *Greek*," she insists in a tone of voice that reveals how genuinely surprised she is that I'm not showing even the slightest interest.

We hang up and my mind is racing. Even if something of interest to me *was* going on around here, it's nearly impossible that my family would realize it *and* know about it before me. I've finally made peace with the fact that there aren't many things to do around here that interest me, so why can't I just enjoy it without my relatives calling me up all the time and telling me about events that not only don't interest me but at some level leave me feeling irked? By now shouldn't they get it? Does Aunt Patsy really think my interest in Greek food is like her interest in Elvis? What's she going to do next, give me a coffee mug with a picture of Greece on it for Christmas, the way she'd give my father a calendar with pictures of golf courses?

My relationship to Greek food is far too complex and personal to be reduced to festivals or coffee mugs!

The seeds of my passion for home-cooked foods were planted in childhood around people like Aunt Patsy. They germinated during my last year in college when I began hanging out with Greeks. But it wasn't until I traveled to the Greek island of Crete the following summer—just before Penny and I transferred to the University of Chicago—that they began to grow into a perennial devotion.

Despite having gone through more than our fair share of quarrels—or maybe not, considering how young and naive I was about relationships, never mind about relationships with someone from a culture so different from mine in ways I could hardly imagine, or even realize I should *try* to imagine—Penny invited me to visit her home and family for the entire summer. It was an invitation I was not about to refuse.

Traveling overseas was never something I'd given much thought to before then. A week before my trip, I stood hypnotized before the large map of the world that my college roommates and I had tacked up on the wall. As I examined Greece and Crete and the surrounding Mediterranean sea, it struck me how unlikely it was that in just days *I* would be on the other side of the planet, perhaps even swimming in that sea which had no reality for me except as a distinctive shape in geography books and as the setting of exotic, hard-to-memorize stories that high school history teachers told. Hanging out with Greeks and other Europeans may have made me feel like I was becoming more culturally cosmopolitan in terms of taste in food and music, but geographically speaking, I felt entirely—and somewhat defiantly—provincial.

I couldn't envision what it would feel like on an island being surrounded by tall, desolate mountains or tightly packed concrete houses. Growing up in northern New York, it never seriously crossed my mind that someday I'd actually find myself in such a far-off place. Twenty-one years old with a bachelor's degree and my compass on the world was the Adirondack Northway. North was the direction of familiar territories, storied landscapes, and countless memories. Even points just south of Exit 17 were a blur, including most of Saratoga Springs, just ten miles to the south of my house, and certainly Albany. Places south of Albany seemed as foreign, unreal, and almost as unreachable as Norway or Mozambique. I'd passed through New York City only twice—once on the way to Disney World by train for a family vacation, and another time on the way to Virginia by bus for a summertime academic institute. The farthest away from northern New York that I'd ever ventured more than once or twice was the outskirts of Oneonta—still in Upstate New York—to visit my cousins Donna and Danny at Earthly Delights.

Even if I preferred being farther up north, home for me meant the short stretch between Exits 17 and 19. That's where we lived. That's where all my grandparents and my parents' brothers and sisters lived. That's where many of my grandparents' brothers and sisters and their children's families lived.

Many points north of Exit 19 were homes away from home. Grandpa and Grandma used to take me camping at Lewey Lake, Brown Tract Pond, and Lake Eaton. My family stayed for various stretches of time in motels from Keene Valley to Lake Placid when Dad was assigned to the reconstruction of Route 73 for the 1980 Winter Olympics, and in cabins on Schroon Lake when he was assigned to the new bridge over the outlet into Schroon River. I'd been going to college in the St. Lawrence Valley for four years, and spent two summers living in a Keeseville motel and exploring the Champlain Valley when I worked for the DOT.

I knew almost every main road in the North Country, and just as many back roads. I went on day hikes, had favorite diners and restaurants, fishing spots, swimming holes, and inexpensive gas stations. I could point out geological phenomena, name mountains, imitate local accents, and knew how to sneak into costly tourist attractions. I was one of the few people of my generation or of Dad's generation who could show you in Whallonsburg where Grandma was born under the bridge (as she used to say), and take you up to visit her distant cousins just outside of Willsboro. And even farther north, across the border, beyond any firsthand experience of my own, were places like Limoges and Orléans, home to my French-Canadian roots, and to more aunts, uncles, and cousins than I could count.

But with almost a year of new foods, new friends, and a serious relationship under my belt, I was off to a Mediterranean island that would change my life in ways I could never have anticipated.

Upon arriving at the Irakleio airport in Crete, I saw Penny's father Manolis waiting for us with his *koboloi* beads in hand. When he embraced Penny tightly I was impressed by the look of relief he showed knowing that his daughter was back home. I'd never seen a father so solemnly happy to see his daughter. After warmly shaking hands with me, the teacher-agriculturalist with worn-out hands, a sturdy build, and uncharacteristically dark skin made his way over to the luggage belt insisting that he get our bags for us. Penny and her younger sister began talking up a storm in Greek and disappeared somewhere behind the crowds of travelers awaiting luggage. Manolis and I stood side-by-side at the luggage conveyer, effectively unable to communicate with each other. Recognizing a suitcase, I pointed and drew upon my infinitesimal Greek vocabulary— "Ένα, δύο, τρία, τέσσερα [One, two, three, *four*]"—to let him know which one to grab.

As we exited the building, I was almost blinded by the bright Mediterranean sun reflecting off the vehicles in the parking lot. Manolis and I put the suitcases into the bed of his small pickup truck, then Penny and I crowded into the Ibiza with her sister, who drove us to the family home, located in one of the oldest sections of the city. I was amazed when we turned off the main street along the picturesque harbor full of fishing boats into spaghetti-like streets barely wide enough for their supermini car; I couldn't believe ordinary people could drive there without hitting pedestrians or scraping up against the concrete buildings or old stone walls. I kept saying to Penny that I felt like somebody had just dropped me into a James Bond movie.

Penny's sister somehow squeezed the car into the extra width of street passing in front of their house. Manolis pulled in behind her and began unloading the suitcases as the rest of us headed up the stairs. As we entered the living room-slash-dining room from the stairwell, Penny's mother Eirini came gliding out of the kitchen. Bright and smiling, short and stout, she explained enthusiastically, "I am mother Penny's . . . I am mother Penny's." I was barely through the door and already I felt as welcome and at home as I did at Grandma and Grandpa's house when I was a child.

Soon Eirini was serving an early dinner, a meal that she'd planned to be restorative, but not too heavy on the stomach after a long flight. As the cacophony of scooters, motorcycles, and automobiles rushed in through the wide-open balcony windows and doors next to the dining table, out from the kitchen came chicken soup, tomato and cucumber salad, bread, feta, Manolis's homemade wine, and bottled spring water from the village of Zaros. "Come and eat. Come and eat," Eirini beckoned, in Greek, still smiling widely.

Eirini carried in the egg-lemon-thickened soup in wide bowls that made it easy for us to add pieces of the chicken, still on the bone, that she'd used to make the broth. The lemon's pleasant tang, the delicate grains of rice, and the soup's matte sheen were indeed lightly refreshing. The pronounced flavor of the chicken in the hot broth, seasoned simply with salt and pepper, was reinvigorating, as was that of the boiled and salted chicken. I never tasted so much chicken flavor in a chicken before. The lemon's flavor was a bright, unadulterated citrusy essence.

The salad was swimming in a glass plate of olive oil and home-made wine vinegar the color of bourbon. The tomatoes were green and red on the outside, but inside they were a juicy cherry, the best I tasted in over ten years, ever since the summer when my great uncle brought some up from his New Jersey garden to Grandpa Leclaire's and we sliced them onto pizzas. The cucumbers were sweetly scented and crispy without any chemical undertaste. Coarse sea salt sparkled on the tongue.

The crusty round loaf came from a nearby bakery and was cut into thick slices. The off-white crumb was unevenly spongy and perfectly moist, just salty enough to deliver generous flavor, and serving as a perfect contrast to the pungent slabs of feta.

I'd fully enjoyed many homemade Greek dishes over the previous year in the United States and Montreal—everything from spinach pie and moussaka to stuffed tomatoes, grape leaves, and grilled pork souvlaki. But Eirini's food, while quite similar overall, was on a whole other level. I kept praising the meal as we ate and drank, with Penny translating my comments to her parents. "This is *real* bread, *real* feta, *real* soup, *real* wine." It was the only way I could think of to explain that I'd enjoyed homemade dishes like these before, but only now realized just how good they could taste. The island's music, the dancing, the literature—these were tastes I'd acquire over time. But with Eirini's cooking it was love at first bite.

During my first meal in Crete, I also discovered that Penny hadn't said anything to her family about our being a couple. I'd just assumed they knew, and Penny never told me otherwise. But were they ever surprised when I turned and kissed Penny on the cheek.

Our second night there, Eirini prepared fish that Manolis had caught. One oversized *faggri*, head to tailfin, with long and narrow slices of potatoes, all oven-roasted in a huge round pan. I'd eaten my share of family-caught fish growing up—bullhead, rainbow trout, perch, smallmouth bass, pickerel, and more—miniatures by comparison to Manolis's. Sure, I'd seen the photographs of fishermen in the Adirondacks holding huge lake trout they'd caught, but I never saw one in person, let alone ate one. The huge chunks of this Mediterranean fish that slipped easily from the bone were more flaky and flavorful than I remembered any of our fish having been. The potatoes were variably crispy caramel on the outside, silky on the inside. We poured a shaken emulsion of lemon juice, olive oil, and dried Cretan oregano over the piles of fish meat we loaded onto our plates. I couldn't decide if I preferred the delicate white flesh better with or without the extra zing of *lemonolado*. Manolis and Eirini kept offering me the fish's head as Penny kept trying to explain to them that I'd never eat it. They even offered to extract the highly prized cheek meat for me to try, but I was not about to become so adventurous.

Loads of peeled, seeded, and grated tomatoes gave lunch on day three its color, and the color gave it its name, *kokkinisto*. On this particular occasion, Eirini had braised young beef with okra that had been soaking in freshly squeezed lemon juice. (By this time I'd surmised that lemon was to Cretans what soy sauce was to Chinese.) I never was a big fan of "beef stew" growing up, even homemade, but this braise was an altogether different dish. I think the flavor of the beef, together with the emphasis on flavorful acidity instead of on sweet vegetables like carrots, made it more to my liking. For dinner, Eirini served the household's staple omelet, thick as a frittata, made with thinly cut homemade french fries pan-fried in olive oil, and eggs with yolks as orange as ripe apricots.

Manolis and Eirini had been putting me up at night at a friend's nearby hotel (and, despite what Penny told me, were probably paying to do so). There wasn't extra room in their small city house for a visitor to sleep—something Penny kept telling me before we left the United States, but which I, with my experience with houses in Upstate New York, simply couldn't fathom until I saw it with my own eyes. Nevertheless, once her parents knew we were a couple, they decided that the arrangements should be changed. By the fourth day of my visit, they canceled the hotel reservations and turned over their very own bedroom to Penny and me. Eirini began sleeping on the living room couch, and Manolis would usually sleep at their house in the village, or sometimes on an old cot in the stairwell.

Two or three nights later, just after I'd fallen asleep, I awoke to the sound of the Ibiza driving off and then noticed Penny wasn't in the bed. I started thinking about whatever stupid thing I'd said or done that day to upset her again. I got up and found Penny's sister and asked her if she knew what was going on, but all she could tell me was that Penny needed to go to the village to talk to her father. I was sure she finally made up her mind that we should break up, and I grew nervous. When Penny returned a few hours later, together with Manolis, she explained to me that she was convinced that in Crete we simply couldn't go on being together casually like this for three whole months, and that she was prepared for us to get formally engaged. Boy was I surprised. *Pleasantly* surprised, of course.

Our engagement turned what was already likely to be a fun-filled summer into an extended celebration of sorts, packed with outings to tourist destinations, filled with midday trips to sunny beaches for a swim, and frequently interspersed with gatherings of Penny's family and friends.

Following Manolis's recommendation, I started reading the literature of Nikos Kazantzakis in English translation, and, the more of him I read, the richer I felt my experiences of the island were becoming. When I learned that El Greco was from Crete, I bought a book about him, and then another about the island's history. I also kept working on learning the language.

Penny, who enjoyed going on outings anyway, proudly showed me around her island—from ancient sites like Knossos and Gortyna to monasteries and nunneries, from archaeological and historical museums to distant beaches in East and South Crete. But I gradually realized that I was enjoying the touristy activities less than I was enjoying the more everyday things we often ended up doing. More than the beaches, I liked it when we'd go to the family's house in the village and visit Manolis's vineyard or Eirini's brother's gardens. Instead of museums, I preferred going to hear live Cretan music, and learning how to dance to it. I liked it when Penny and I would sip coffee at the local marina with Manolis more than when Penny and I would follow Penny's sister and friends to the latest trendy nightclubs and bars. Whenever there was an excursion during the day, the real joy for me was usually returning at night having built up an appetite, and then sitting down to a long, relaxing meal of

Eirini's home cooking and Manolis's homemade wine. Penny, by contrast, enjoyed the beaches and small-city nightlife as much as anything else and probably found me just a bit too much of an old country geezer for a twenty-something-year-old soon-to-be big-city grad student.

Penny's parents waited on us daily, doing everything they could to make my stay as enjoyable as possible. They prepared enormous quantities of delicious homemade food. Whenever we went out all together they wouldn't let me (or Penny) pay for anything—not restaurants, not museums, not even gas for the car. Every time I tried to insist otherwise—with images in mind of Dad and Grandpa quarreling about who was going to do the honors of paying a bill at a restaurant—Manolis would tell Penny to explain to me that he'd gladly let me pay for him when he visited us in the United States, which we all knew was highly unlikely. The most Penny's parents allowed me to do was to cook something for them. (I made a Chinese dish that I'd learned from my college roommate who was from Taiwan.)

Almost as if trying to live up to the Mediterranean stereotype, Eirini served huge quantities of carefully prepared food and always prodded us to eat more. The first time she brought out plates of moussaka for dinner, I couldn't believe it when I saw that each piece almost covered the entire dinner plate! She kept an especially close eye on how much I was eating, and no matter how much I ate, she always tried to get me to eat more. I jokingly called her the "food junta," referring to the dark days of the military dictatorship that they'd endured some twenty years earlier, and which Leonidas had talked to me about many times. This cracked Manolis up every time.

Eirini and Manolis went to formidable lengths whenever any visitor stopped by their house—always creating an atmosphere that was so warm and welcoming that impromptu visitors almost never declined to stay longer and often stayed for hours to eat, drink, talk, and smoke. Once in a while a full-blown celebration would erupt—the volume on the stereo would be turned up, the table pushed aside to make room for dancing, and the spring water bottles refilled with wine from the demijohn in the basement. Of course most visitors were not allowed, let alone expected, to help with the associated chores.

Everywhere Penny and I went—to an old friend's house or to an aunt's or a grandparent's—we were enthusiastically welcomed and treated and served. If we declined offers for a snack, coffee, a drink, or a full-blown impromptu homemade meal, our hosts would insist and cajole us into changing our minds with all their persuasive might. Without exception, the invitations felt sincere, and our hosts never did anything to make us feel like we might be intruding, that it wasn't a good time, that they had other more important things on their minds, or that they were too tired to serve and to please. Penny was untiringly vigilant about our not overindulging—which she judged primarily in terms of what was ethically appropriate according to local expectations about pride and honor, but erring on the side of the most demanding of such expectations—as receivers of all this generosity. She was just as vigilant about informing me when I should *not* say no to something, lest I seriously insult the offerer.

In Crete, I encountered the same kind of generous hosting that I'd first witnessed in the United States at Leonidas's and at Penny's apartments, but magnified and multiplied tenfold. The pleasure I experienced as a visitor in Crete was so great that it was an effortless decision for me to keep returning there with Penny during subsequent summers.

Such pleasurable experiences made me think that the Greek model of hosting visitors that I first experienced at Leonidas's was not only preferable to me *personally*, but an *objective* improvement on the American model I'd known. Both Greek and American models, I reasoned, seemed fair overall. In the American model, visitors were expected to pitch in every time, but then they got a lot of help when they were hosts. In the Greek model, people got a free ride when they were visitors, but paid the price when it was their turn to host. The two models divided up the work fairly, just differently. However, the way the Greek model divided up the chores created the potential for visitors to have a qualitatively different kind of experience. Released from the responsibility of helping their hosts, visitors could let go, to more thoroughly enjoy themselves, socialize, or celebrate. Feeling so carefree and cared for, visitors' hearts and spirits could reach heights they might not otherwise have reached, or have known existed.

Still, once we returned to the United States, I second-guessed myself on this argument. After all, I was in Crete with Penny as a temporary visitor and had little opportunity to return the favor. I became concerned that the overall fairness built into this extreme model of hosting in theory could not always exist in practice. Granted, it wasn't easy to think in terms of fairness anymore since our many Cretan hosts were so masterful at making us feel like there was nothing they'd rather do than to serve and please us. But I got to thinking more about the modest financial situations and sometimes borderline poverty of some of our most generous Cretan hosts. I felt guilty. This model of hosting had exposed its Achilles' heel.

Still, the pleasures it afforded and the enthusiasm of its practitioners were such that neither could I quite give up on it altogether. As graduate students, Penny and I worked on becoming more competent hosts ourselves in the same regard. (I was the one who needed the most work.) Even though we fit the University of Chicago stereotype of students without much of a social life, we had many opportunities to get together with friends and colleagues.

One evening in particular convinced me that we were improving and that someday I might be able to do Crete proud. Penny and I had attended a gathering put on by a club of Greek American students. As the organized festivities came to an end and everyone was leaving, Penny and I spontaneously invited three of the Greeks (from Greece) there—graduate students, our seniors, from the math department—back to our place "to drink a glass of wine." Upon entering the apartment, I put on some Greek music, got out drinks—including some of Manolis's homemade *tsikoudia* (grape pomace brandy)—and then Penny and I peeled potatoes, chopped onions, and put ground beef in the microwave to defrost. Whereas in the past we might've served the equivalent of a bowl of chips, that night we very quickly made from scratch *keftedes* (fried meatballs), fried potatoes, and other Greek *mezedes*, dividing our attention between the kitchen and our company in the living room until everything was plated and served up on the coffee table. Penny was especially skillful at the kind of fast-paced, competitive banter I noticed many Greeks seemed to enjoy, so much so that I think some of the non-Cretan male Greeks we knew found it very challenging—and thus intriguing—to try keeping up with her energy and wit. As the evening progressed, Dimitris leapt up and began dancing introspectively to the *zeimbekiko* music that played on the stereo. We clanked our glasses of *tsikoudia*, and more impromptu dancing followed. Even the somewhat reserved American friend who'd tagged along with Dimitris got up and gave it a try. And no one poked fun at him as he tried moving his body in ways that he probably believed were similar to the gestures of his more seasoned Greek friend. I think it was a rare moment when many of us felt like we'd been suddenly transported back from Hyde Park to Greece. For me, it also felt like a rite of passage, because I was actively participating with Penny in the creation of an atmosphere inspired by that which I'd experienced as a visitor in Crete.

Later that year, it occurred to me that, assuming reciprocal fairness really matters, it need not be conceptualized in terms of the same individuals—I host you so you host me. It could also be thought of as: I host you, you host someone else, they host someone else, and so on. I surmised that as long as visitors also became hosts for *somebody*, it would all sort of work out in the end. I was a visitor in Crete, but in Chicago Penny and I could strive to host friends and colleagues and never care one iota about whether they returned the favor. There was no need to calculate who gave or took more or less.

In subsequent years, whenever Penny was going on to her father about someone she thought was taking advantage of her parents, I'd hear Manolis replying back to her that "each person gives whatever they have," simultaneously urging virtuous generosity while pardoning the ungenerous by suggesting that their stinginess is all they have to give. His words reinforced my convictions about the objective superiority of a Cretan model of hosting. By refusing to be held captive to immediate calculations, the Greek model was more likely to encourage free-flowing sociability and conviviality. It discouraged friends from fussing over small change when treating one another, or over how many times they paid for your coffee or bummed a cigarette off you. It also meant that get-togethers, planned and unplanned alike, avoided rigid schedules—especially predetermined end times—so visitors would not have to preoccupy themselves with watching the clock and could participate wholeheartedly in generating the event's own rhythms and sense of time.

From each host according to their ability, to each visitor according to their need. Interpreting things this way constituted the next—but hardly the last—readjustment in my thinking on the subject.

❊   ❊   ❊

I sit for a while brooding over the phone call from Aunt Patsy about the local festival with Greek food. I remember how the last time she came over to our house she told me, "I like visiting you guys. It reminds me of how it used to be with Mom and Dad [i.e., my grandparents]."

I consider how good it felt to hear those words, and I wonder why I won't find a better way to receive her well-intentioned, impromptu phone calls.

✳ 9 ✳

Recipes

Sofia is improvising a snack with ingredients on hand: thinly sliced *prosciutto di Parma* wrapped around a piece of cucumber, a piece of sheep's milk feta, and some arugula. I jokingly call it *prosciutto sushi* even though there isn't any rice.

It's so delicious that I want to share some with my parents, so I put two on a teacup saucer and—as I often do—hop next door.

My mother hears the doorbell and comes to the front door. She takes the plate, asks what it is, and, this time, I tell her.

Then she continues, "I wanted to let you know that the Friday before Halloween Audrey is coming to stay for the weekend." (Audrey is one of my mother's first cousins who I've only recently met.) "She always says how much she loves your cooking so I thought I should let you know she's going to be here in case you wanted to make something."

I nod just to acknowledge that I've heard what she said but give no other indication of a response.

"Alright then," I say as I turn and am about to leave.

"Oh, wait!" My mother goes back in and gets washed plates from a previous such delivery. She also tries to give me a multipage "fun" quiz about music.

"No thanks, I'm not interested."

"It's from Steve," she insists enthusiastically.

"Yeah, well, it doesn't matter. I get spam e-mails with stuff like this all the time and I always just delete them. I'm not interested in these kinds of things. Sorry."

She gives up and I come back home.

The calm joy I felt watching Sofia make the snack is now largely replaced by frustration. As Sofia finishes wrapping with prosciutto and we both continue eating, I describe to her what happened and struggle to figure out a way to break the pattern of this kind of interaction.

"What about a canned response I can tell my mother in situations like this?"

[. . .]

"I can tell her something like: 'Okay, I'm not trying to hurt your feelings, I know you think I might be interested in something like this, but most likely I'm not. If I have time, I prefer to read or do other things that I choose. I feel bad [sic] to keep saying no like this because it seems to make you feel bad, but you shouldn't feel bad, it's just a matter of taste.'"

"That sounds good, but can you do it?"

"Probably not."

"Besides you're always bringing things over to them and they always accept them."

"That's true. So even if I could say it, what do I do if my mother responds: 'Yes, but you're always bringing things for us to eat, movies for us to watch, and stuff'?"

I try to think of ways to reply to such an objection. After all, having grown up around them, I often have good reasons to think I know some of the kinds of things they might enjoy. For example, I rarely recommend my favorite films to them, but films I think are up their alley—and the fact is that most of the ones I've recommended to them in recent years they went out and bought copies of after they rented them. Besides, my mother has learned to cook quite a few new ingredients and dishes I've shown her.

Sofia points out how every possible reply I can think of will either be misinterpreted by my mother or sound downright elitist.

"Well, isn't the point that she kept pushing me to take the quiz after I said no, not that she offered it in the first place? Maybe she just can't accept the asymmetry and remains determined to discover meaningful ways to connect with me, even though she knows I live in quite a different world from theirs?"

"That's what mothers do. My mother does the same thing."

"Ah, but maybe every time I bring food next door she's interpreting it as: 'He expects us to enjoy this because he knows so much about cooking. It's our duty to eat it, and to try to like it.' Whenever

I bring over a film or a book or something, she might be thinking: 'Our son wants us to know about this so let's not hurt his feelings and give it a chance.' Maybe *I've* been *encouraging* her to believe that we *all* think it's important to accept all these offers from each other as normal. Maybe she senses that this is a good way to improve the connection between us?"

"Maybe. You're her son."

"So maybe from now on *I* should frame whatever I offer *them* in a way that makes it explicit that it's more like an FYI: 'Here's something I thought you might like or which might benefit you, *if* you're interested.' Maybe I need to make sure they know I won't feel bad [I won't?] if I learn that they aren't interested in such things after all, that my feelings aren't at stake [they aren't?] in their accepting these spur-of-the-moment offerings."

Sofia concurs, and asks again, "But can you do it?"

The Friday before Halloween arrives. I call my mother to ask if they all want to come over for French onion soup—one of my mother's favorites. I hear her holding the phone away from her face and excitedly telling Audrey and my father that it's me asking if they want to come over for dinner. She says they'll come.

I put on a Cretan CD.

The only starch tonight will be bread, which I need to start making immediately. I worry that the bread will be too fresh for the soup but hope that toasting it'll make it work well enough. I'd rather take my chances than buy a loaf from the store.

From the refrigerator I remove the plate-covered soup bowl containing a blend of 1 cup of white flour and 1 cup of water that has soured, and I pour it into the bowl of the stand mixer. I put a cup of fresh water and a cup of fresh white flour into the bowl to replenish. I cover it and leave it off to the side on the counter—I'll put it back in the fridge tomorrow. I heat 1 cup of milk for 30 seconds in the microwave and add it to the stand mixer. I add 1 tablespoon of dry yeast (not instant) from a jar in the freezer and less than a palmful of kosher salt. I add a spoonful of thyme honey from Crete. I turn on the mixer with the dough hook for about 10 seconds for an initial mixing.

I take off the shelf two of the large tins—the kind Chinese egg roll snacks come in—filled with flour. Using the measuring cups that I store inside the tins with the flours, I measure out about 1½ cups of barley flour and 1½ cups of whole wheat flour and put them into the mixer bowl. I turn on the mixer just long enough to get everything more-or-less combined into a big gooey mass.

I start making the yogurt. Audrey raved about my yogurt the last time she was here, so I consider it a must tonight—as a dessert served with walnuts and honey. I take a small container of my last batch of yogurt out of the refrigerator so it can warm up a little. I pour a half gallon of cow's milk from the local creamery into a pot from Sofia's Thermos "Shuttle Chef"—a made-in-Japan thermal container that holds two cooking pots. I put a thermometer that my mother passed on to me years ago into the pot to monitor the temperature.

I turn on the stand mixer again briefly then shut it off when I see the dough suddenly change consistency and look somewhat smooth. I remove the bowl and the dough hook. I take a stiff plastic spatula down from the piece of scrap wood I hung on the wall with nails pounded partway into it for hooks. I scrape the rest of the dough into the bowl. I leave the spatula in the bowl, cover it with a shower cap, and put it off to the side on a table. I check the clock—the dough needs to ferment for about 3 hours.

As the milk gets warmer, I stir it with a flat-bottomed wooden utensil to keep it from sticking too much. When it reaches 180°F, I shut off the heat and move the pot with the probe thermometer still in it over onto a cooling rack on the counter.

I add water to a large pot and heat it on high to make broth. I add bony cuts of local beef that we've kept in our chest freezer. I go outdoors and cut some celery and pull up some carrots from the garden. I trim and wash them and drop them into the pot.

I give the slowly cooling milk a stir to keep a skin from forming.

I grab a few small onions and one head of garlic from the make-shift rack where they've been curing in the garage. I trim off the ends of the onions and the outer layers of skin before adding them. I also add the cloves of garlic without peeling them. I go down cellar to get some sprigs of thyme that I dried over the summer and toss them in.

I stir the cooling milk some more.

The broth comes to a boil and I turn down the heat so that it'll just barely simmer when covered. I wait a minute or two then cover.

When the temperature of the milk gets down to around 120°F, I carefully pour in the heading-toward-room-temperature yogurt as a starter culture, just a little at a time, stirring constantly with the other hand. When the yogurt is all in I cover the pot and put it into its Thermos. I check the clock to see what time it is—it'll need about 3 hours to get the way I want it.

I vacuum the living room, take everything off the dining table and wipe it clean, and I empty the food-scraps bowl into the compost bin outdoors.

I make a cup of coffee and drink it.

I already washed the placemats—hand-me-downs from my most recent dissertation adviser—and they're dangling from binder clips on a string along the edge of a homemade wooden shelf we use for pots and pans. I notice the placemats are dry, so I put them out.

I set the table, going back and forth between the table and Sofia's old particleboard bookshelf, which we outfitted for holding dishware with plenty of extra shelves and a piece of fabric hanging over the front from a dowel like a curtain from a rod.

I go back out to the garage and bring in as many onions as I can carry. Before I peel them I dump a container of cream into another bowl that fits the stand mixer, put on the whisk attachment, and whip it until the butter separates out. I pour it through a wire strainer over a bowl to catch the butter and drink up the strained-out buttermilk. I don't bother to rinse the butter. I put the butter and some olive oil into another large pot on the stove but don't turn it on yet.

It's time to continue the bread. I scoop some white flour onto the center of my breadboard—the one that Grandpa made for Grandma before I was born—scrape out the sticky dough onto the pile of flour, rub some flour onto my hands, and carefully try to pull some of the edges of the dough upward and toward the center, eventually flipping the whole thing over, and plopping it back into the bowl with the spatula and covering it with a shower cap for about 1 more hour.

I peel, rinse, and chop the many, many onions. As I'm chopping I turn on the burner with the butter and olive oil. When I'm done chopping I add them to the pot.

It's time to strain the yogurt. I take out two coffee filters, one that fits a cone from an old broken coffeemaker and another that fits the manual cone coffee brewer that Leonidas passed onto me when he found a job and moved to Binghamton. I place the filters in the cones and set them over two plastic yogurt containers I've saved. I ladle some yogurt into a third smaller container to save as a starter for a future batch and put it into the refrigerator. I ladle the rest into the coffee filters to strain out the whey.

I stir the onions.

I wash the pot I made the yogurt in so I don't have to waste space in the dishwasher.

I stir the onions.

I check on the broth and see the meat is about as tender as it's going to get and falling off the bones. I turn off the burner.

I stir the onions.

I use tongs to remove the hot pieces of meat to a bowl and cover it with an upside-down plate, thinking that the meat might dry out otherwise.

I keep stirring the onions, more frequently when they start to darken as they caramelize. Eventually I decide they're dark enough, add a large spoonful of white flour and stir for about another minute with the pot off the burner.

I pour the broth through a large strainer into the caramelized onions. I take an opened bottle of white wine out of the refrigerator and pour about 2-cups-worth into the soup. I move the soup back onto the burner.

I empty the contents of the strainer into the trash and wash the pot that I cooked the broth in.

Back to the bread. I take out a baking sheet and cover it with a sheet of parchment paper. I use the spatula to coax the dough out of the bowl as a single mass onto the pile of flour on the breadboard. I use a dough scraper to separate it into two pieces. I flour my hands and quickly shape each mass of dough into a loaf that I set onto the parchment paper. I scoop most of the flour left on the breadboard back into the flour container. I wash the stand mixer bowl, spatula, dough scraper, and breadboard. I turn on the oven to 425°F.

I pour salt into the soup directly from the kosher salt box, going on intuition and so making sure to err on the side of not-enough salt for now. I also grind in a lot of black pepper. I pour in some Armagnac. I partially cover the pot and leave it on medium-low heat.

The oven beeps because it's reached 425°F. I put in the baking sheet with the two loaves of bread on it and set the timer for 45 minutes. I also put a little hot water into a cup and throw it onto the bottom of the oven and quickly close the door again as it turns to steam—this is for achieving a better crust.

I take a wheel of local artisanal cow's milk cheese out of the refrigerator and cut off a fairly good–sized chunk. I put some parchment paper back over the cut part of the wheel and hold it on with a rubber band, then cover the whole thing in cling wrap and put it back into the fridge. I trim off the rind from the cut chunk, divide the chunk into smaller pieces, and run them through the food processor with the grater attachment. I lay out some baking sheets with parchment paper on them and make little circles of grated cheese.

I take a taste of the soup and add some more salt and pepper.

Once I've got the bread out of the oven, I put the baking sheets with the cheese circles under the broiler long enough for each circle to melt into a nice solid mass and just begin to get spots of brown color. I take the pans out of the oven and leave them on the counter.

I get out of the kitchen for a while so Sofia can wash and prepare the salad.

I transfer the strained yogurt to a glass container and put covers on the plastic containers with the whey. I put them all into the fridge.

I haven't been looking at any written recipes all this time.

My last year as an undergraduate I started becoming accustomed to cooking without the kind of written recipe I grew up with, and was on my way to learning a different kind of "recipe," though this isn't how I thought of it at the time. Eating and cooking with Leonidas, other European grad students, and my Taiwanese roommate Lee significantly weakened my reliance on written recipes. Sometimes through simple observation, other times by letting them make me their informal apprentice, I slowly acquired new insights into cooking techniques, strategies, and patterns.

This different kind of recipe frequently involved employing quantities that were intuitively discerned. Take the Chinese stir-fries that I learned from Lee. After cutting up fillets of meat—usually pork or chicken breast—into very thin slices, we'd marinate them in a bowl.

We'd pour on a little wine, some soy sauce, maybe a few drops of sesame oil, as well as loads of dry herbs and spices. After watching the procedure a few times and then doing it myself under Lee's supervision, I began to grow accustomed to measurements estimated by the feel of a bottle tipping in my hand and my perception of durations of time, by the weight and volume of an ingredient in my palm, and the sight of it in a bowl atop other ingredients. I was getting used to figuring quantities in terms of ratios among ingredients, instead of absolute target amounts—more meat meant more soy sauce; less meat meant less soy sauce. All other things being equal, a little too much soy sauce just meant cutting back some on the salt.

This kind of recipe was often a matter of combining and ordering particular techniques. To make bean stew, Leonidas began by gently sautéing an onion in olive oil, maybe some garlic. Then he added the beans, tomatoes, and seasonings. To make sauce for spaghetti he first sautéed chopped onion in olive oil, maybe some garlic, then browned the ground beef before adding tomatoes and seasonings. To make the filling for spinach pie his first step was to sauté onion in olive oil, maybe some garlic, and then to add the spinach and seasonings. Sautéing onions and garlic in oil, then building from there became a second-nature technique or step. Then there were variations. Lee stir-fried whole pieces of garlic and removed them from the really hot canola oil once they browned, and he chopped onions on a cutting board with his large-bladed Asian chef's knife. Penny cut up onions in her hand with a small knife. Leonidas didn't like pieces of onion and puréed his onions in a food processor. Where did a given technique begin and end? What was the difference between a technique and a variation? These were moot points inasmuch as I was picking up intersecting and overlapping patterns and clusters of techniques and variations gradually in an ad hoc fashion, depending on the kinds of dishes being learned, and from whom. I rarely conceived of them as techniques or variations per se. They were just things you did that worked and that you liked.

There could be more than one way to parse a whole recipe into parts. It was open to interpretation. And each part, in turn, could be apprehended as its own whole on a smaller scale: The dish was a sauté followed by a braise; the sauté was a chopping of the onion put into heated oil; the chopping was actually a peeling, a rinse, and then a chopping (or a halving, a peeling, and then a chopping).

The relationship between parts might be inescapably serial (one couldn't brown the meat *after* adding the braising liquid), or it could be open to parallelism (one could put the pasta water on to boil and then sauté the onions, or, one could put the water on to boil while the onions were sautéing). The ordering of certain steps might be whimsical or experimental, or it might be skillfully deduced on the spot in response to the particular circumstances. (Which burners on the stove are free? How much water am I boiling this time? Does the pot I want need to be cleaned first?) Somewhere in my brain, though certainly not consciously, parts and wholes, their necessary and contingent interrelationships with one another, as well as to those of other recipes, must've been getting inscribed onto an evolving, multidimensional map. Such a map would have looked dazzlingly complex if you could see it all at once drawn up on paper, but that's not how the mind used it, and so it actually felt quite simple in everyday practice.

A benefit of learning recipes of this sort was that it helped me understand more about their inner workings and how they might relate to other recipes. Sometimes learning this way wasn't immediately efficient, but I came to recognize certain long-term benefits arising out the challenges of learning recipes this way, especially when it came to my learning of many Greek dishes.

My primary inspiration for Greek recipes was Penny's mother's food. In Chicago, I tried approximating some of Eirini's meals based just on my memories from the previous summer of what they were like—dishes like her rice pilaf, meat stews, and chicken and potatoes in the oven. Granted, I was using sour cream instead of yogurt in my tzatziki, lemon juice from a bottle and chicken broth from dehydrated cubes in my *pilafi*, but at the time—and compared to most of my home-cooking before then—it tasted good to me.

Then there was Eirini's beef and onion stew—which I liked so much more than any American beef stews I'd ever tried. What I noticed about it initially, and took as the reason I preferred it, were the different ingredients: lots of onions and fresh tomato, nutmeg, cloves, no carrots, no potatoes.

Then, on my subsequent summer visit to Crete, I offered to make it at Penny's house for lunch to treat her family, including Penny's uncle, the butcher from whom we got the meat. Eirini was giving me a hand in the kitchen and there were moments when her facial expression betrayed bewilderment about what I was doing. I gradually sensed that something wasn't quite right about my stew, but I wasn't sure what. Eirini suggested that I uncover the pot and boil off some water—a *lot* of water actually. In time I realized that growing up I'd become accustomed to stews that were somewhat liquidy, even if the liquid was thickened with flour or excess starch released by the potatoes. Just *how* liquidy I never really noticed. Eirini's stews, by contrast, were not liquidy at all. They were more like pieces of meat and vegetables accompanied by a very oily sauce. However, given my attention to the different ingredients and flavors, I'd somehow never paid enough attention to the different consistency and style. For all the times I'd made my own version in Chicago, I somehow never realized how different mine was from Eirini's, maybe because I was in a different context—I didn't eat it with the same Cretan bread, didn't serve it in the same dishware, didn't eat it with the same people, and so forth. Focusing on the similarities between my stew and Eirini's—defined in terms of certain *differences* in ingredients from the ones I knew growing up—I thought I was making more or less the same recipe. Then, when I tried making it at her house in Crete, I began to sense a significant difference, even if I couldn't put my finger on it without Eirini's help. As a result, I learned another aspect of the recipe that I'd so far overlooked. In fact, I learned a technique that's used in many Greek and Cretan stews.

This wasn't the end of my learning about such stew recipes. Later, there were times when I'd happen to pass through the kitchen while Eirini was cooking a stew and I'd notice other details. For instance, I observed that she often took the meat out of the pot when it was ready, then added the vegetables (like green beans or cauliflower), and finally put everything back together again at the very end to serve. With so little water in the pot, the vegetables wouldn't have been submerged in the liquid if she'd left the meat in. I also noticed that she cooked the meat in stews at a relatively high temperature, with lots of intense bubbling going on, just the opposite of what I took for granted having grown up watching stews barely simmering, sometimes all day, in Mom's electric slow-cooker.

This wasn't the most efficient way I could have learned to replicate Eirini's beef-and-onion stew. But learning it this way meant that just how well I was approximating Eirini's recipe depended in large measure on the extent to which I'd observed or inferred the various techniques and ordering of techniques that characterized her way of making the recipe. I had to learn the patterns and variations. And, in order to learn these, I first had to become cognizant of them through observation, trial-and-error, hunches, inferences, and the occasional helping hand. With this particular stew, I was immediately aware of the dish's main ingredients and certain aspects of its flavor, but it took me much longer to observe important aspects of the texture and style of the liquid, and how to achieve these.

I tend to think learning dishes in this less efficient way helped me become a better home cook *overall,* in the long run. On the one hand, it meant that I was learning techniques that were part of other recipes, and therefore, implicitly, how different recipes were related. Moreover, it meant I was learning to become more aware of my own observational skills and knowledge of food in general. Indeed, once I discovered that for so long I hadn't observed something so "obvious" that was right under my nose all along—how watery my stew's liquid was compared to Eirini's—I realized how readily I could miss something right there in front of me. I became more aware of my own shortcomings as an observer. As a result, I learned not only to discipline myself to observe these things more carefully in the future, but also to keep in mind that no matter how intently I might *think* I'm making such observations, there could be things—important things that matter—that are continuing to escape my notice.

❄   ❄   ❄

I call next door to let my mother know when the food will be ready, but the phone is busy so I run over. It turns out Aunt Juliette is there and says she's about to leave. I know she'd like to come and tell her to join us. She says no, so I insist that she come or I'll feel insulted. She finally agrees to come. I go back home.

Any minute now, and everyone will be arriving at our house. I slice up and toast one whole loaf of bread. I put one slice into each soup bowl and another slice onto each plate. I adjust the seasoning of the soup one last time and then ladle it into the bowls over the toasted bread. I lay a circle of cheese over the top of each bowl. I put all the bowls onto baking sheets and put them under the broiler of the oven two at a time.

I take out a large jar of sauerkraut that I just put into the refrigerator a few days earlier—shredded cabbage from our garden sprinkled with a little salt and some whey leftover from making strained yogurt, fermented at room temperature for about a month. I put a large spoonful of sauerkraut onto each slice of toast (on the plates) and then cover the sauerkraut with some of the beef left over from the broth-making. I garnish each plate with a spoonful of mustard (that I made about six weeks ago) and a few early-spring grapevine tendrils (that I've preserved in Greek white-wine vinegar).

I hear the doorbell. Then I hear the door open and my father calling out, "Anybody home?"

Everyone comes in, the usual pleasantries are exchanged, and Sofia helps me get the food onto the table. When Audrey offers to help, I insist that we don't need her to do anything but sit down and get ready to eat.

After we dig in, that all-too-familiar moment comes when Audrey says—either as a mere compliment or as a genuine request—that I'll have to give her my recipe for the soup before she leaves.

Except in the rare instance that I've followed an actual written recipe—a recipe in the conventional sense that the requester means—I never know how to respond to this kind of thing without sounding either like someone who doesn't want to share what he's learned about cooking or like a culinary snob who thinks he's above the kind of recipe being asked for.

A few years ago when a fellow graduate student was dating an American who was a professional chef, and he asked her to ask me for the recipe for my chickpea soup—actually a simple traditional Greek recipe—I told her to tell him that for me such a dish was part of a larger culinary fabric of home cooking with its own place among other dishes in that fabric, not something to be pulled out and sewed onto a professional chef's repertoire. She seemed proud that I viewed this dish and the cuisine of her home nation this way and was perfectly glad to tell her boyfriend that I refused his request.

For years, whenever good friends or family would eat something they liked and ask me for the recipe—and somehow thinking it was reasonable to assume that I had "the" recipe for everything I made—I'd tell them that they'd have to come over and watch or help me make it. In fact, there's nothing I'd have loved more. I can't remember how many times I cooked at my parents' house when Sofia and I were visiting during a break, and I'd try to get them to watch so they could learn. One night we even took my parents to the supermarket to introduce them to all the vegetables they didn't know. Another time we drove them to Albany and showed them around Chinese markets (for greens and rice) and Indian markets (for spices, legumes, and rice).

Nowadays I usually just end up saying that I don't have a recipe in the conventional sense. I hate that it sounds so snobbish.

I do believe, of course, that there's always *some* kind of representation that guides the making of a dish, even if the maker isn't aware of it as instructions or as a recipe per se. Except for a purely whimsical conglomerating of ingredients and techniques, assuming such a thing is even possible, it seems to me that there's always a "recipe" of some sort.

But usually people are asking for the kind of recipe I grew up with—the kind written down in a cookbook or on a recipe card stored in a recipe box—beginning with a list of ingredients and their respective quantities followed by step-by-step instructions for what to do with them all.

I get it. Even as a child, I became aware of many of the advantages of this kind of recipe. Ingredients are typically straightforward: all-purpose flour is all-purpose flour; oregano is oregano; water is water. For any given recipe you just need to know what the ingredients are and make sure that you have them available.

Step-by-step instructions are mostly self-explanatory, though they might assume that one already knows not only what it means to "stir" or "mix," but also to "beat" (an egg) or "whip" (cream). In rare cases, a more advanced technique is called for. Grandma, a local leader in Home Demonstration and 4-H, showed me how to fork together flour and shortening for pie crust, test a cake's doneness with a toothpick, and even how to knead bread dough. For although Grandma's bread recipe listed exactly how many times to knead the dough, it didn't explain the precise motions of one's hands, or of the dough on the board. It didn't give any indication of how much pressure to put on the dough with each down-and-forward push of the palm.

Measuring ingredients is frequently overemphasized in these recipes. Grandma taught me to use a butter knife to level-off flour or sugar or shortening in a dry-measuring cup, and to squat down level with a liquid-measuring cup resting on the counter to look at the bottom of the thick line at the top of the liquid. By around age twelve—on my first try—I received a blue ribbon as a 4-H-er, demonstrating how to make a strawberry cow. Everybody was so proud that I'd learned the *right* way to measure. After all, not every cook was so dutiful. "You know Florence," Aunt Patsy would say, "She doesn't measure *anything* when *she* cooks. If a recipe calls for a cup of flour, she just does it by eye." I guess if Aunt Patsy—an Elvis fan—found Florence's taste for Italian opera a little too uptight, she also found the fact that Florence didn't measure ingredients just a little too libertine.

I guess it makes sense. Measurement and precision have often served as hallmarks of quality craftsmanship and moral distinction in my family. My great grandfather was a carpenter, and you couldn't build a good staircase or a solid roof if your tools and techniques weren't sharp. Grandma wouldn't have gotten very far playing Tchaikovsky on the piano if she hadn't practiced her scales and chords. Mom and Aunt Patsy follow precise patterns when they crochet. Even just tinkering with bicycles, Grandpa had to be able to adjust the spokes just right to get nice even rotation. Eye-levels, rulers, and plans drawn to scale were tools of the trade in Dad's work as a transportation engineer.

Culinary professionals know that precision is frequently more crucial for success in modern dessert-making than in other kinds of cooking. The wrong amount of baking powder and the cake will fall, and jelly will only be jelly if it's cooked to the right temperature. In my family, homemade sweets usually abound—cakes, pies, breads, fudge, and an astoundingly wide assortment of cookies—so there's yet one more reason for my relatives to consider careful measurement the hallmark of good work in the kitchen.

Growing up I also noticed how a strong reliance on conventional written recipes made it possible for us to enjoy the pleasures that derive from having a favorite dish come out almost exactly the same way every time. It also meant that the cook was essentially immune from anxiety that a dish wouldn't turn out well. On the downside, it meant we couldn't appreciate similar dishes made by other people with different recipes because we were so accustomed to our superlatively consistent versions. Grandma's lasagna was the *only* lasagna I really loved. Potato salads other than Aunt Patsy's or Mom's were letdowns.

Of course, for some dishes, too much of the same could become boring, so variations were allowed. Grandma would add pieces of sausage to the lasagna sauce, or Mom would leave the peas out of tuna macaroni salad. Usually these were more in the way of optional—but still precisely measured—versions, so I never imagined such departures to have anything in common with the allegedly wilder kitchen debauchery of someone like Florence.

Sometimes an equally good recipe for a well-liked dish would come our way from a friend or relative, and it would become part of the family repertoire, and the name of the person we got it from part of the dish's name on the recipe card—like "Donna's Bagels." In this way, Aunt Patsy ended up with more than one standard coffee cake. There was a recipe for apple pie with the usual crust, and another with a crust that didn't need rolling out with a rolling pin. Very rarely, a new recipe was judged to be superior to the family favorite, which would be forever deposed. Nothing ever toppled the reign of Grandma's Lasagna, although for a time (and "for a change"), we forewent the lasagna for "Dot's Spaghetti Pie," a recipe from one of Grandma's friends.

One downside to living by so much predictability was that when we *did* need to respond to contingencies or make unscripted changes and adaptations to foods, there was a lot of unnecessary anxiety. Aunt Patsy was notorious for this, fretting ad nauseam over the most insignificant of details—a small adaptation here because she didn't have quite enough of an ingredient, a minor adjustment there because the pan she normally used was already being used for something else. Even though her foods usually turned out just fine, every time it was the same story all over again, and listening to her fuss and sigh you'd've thought that the world was coming to an end. (No, Aunt Patsy, putting in a little more basil won't bring on Armageddon.)

❊   ❊   ❊

Sofia intercepts Audrey's request for my recipe, looking over at me and saying, "You probably don't even *have* a recipe, do you? Tell them your recipe for spinach pie."

"Uhhhm . . . 'Three hundred and seventy-five degrees for forty to fifty minutes.'"

Sofia explains how she thought it was interesting when she saw that this was the only thing I'd written down about how to make this dish in my three-ring binder of written recipes.

Everybody chuckles.

My father adds, with pretend sarcasm, "He even makes his own *mother* come over to watch him cook when she wants to learn how to make something."

Audrey says that it's just like that with her son-in-law and goes on to brag about his pizzas.

Thanks to Sofia, I'm off the hook.

✳ 10 ✳

Cheesy Coincidence

Back in September, Sofia and I went on the Washington County cheese tour so we could learn more about the farms, cheeses, and cheese makers in our area. But we didn't get to meet the cheese maker at the farm where we tasted the sheep's-milk cheese that was closest to what I remember eating in Crete, because he was in Italy. So I got his e-mail address from his mother and sent a message. When Andy and Dafne got back from Italy we set up a rendezvous at the farm to buy more cheese and so I could ask him about his male spring lambs for meat. It's for today at noon.

I'm driving in a different direction right now, though, because Sofia has a Feminist Studies faculty meeting she needs to attend. She and I both wish she was going to the farm with me, but knowing that I don't like calling people up to change appointments unless it's really unavoidable, she didn't try to persuade me to reschedule. One of the benefits of working in the same place is that Sofia and I can get by with just one car, but when something like this happens it means that one of us has to spend time driving the other to drop them off and pick them up. Sometimes we speculate about getting another vehicle—maybe a pickup truck, which would also be useful for certain gardening chores—so we don't have to negotiate with each other all the time about when we should come and go to the office. But I'm secretly glad she always manages to talk me out of it. And, besides, we can fit a bale of straw in the trunk of our Camry.

I drop Sofia off outside the door to our building. I put some Cretan music into the CD player and head back north to the farm. As I'm on my way out of Saratoga, I happen to glimpse a car turning into the same intersection as me from the opposite direction. I notice the lettering on the door of the car, which says, The Good Shepherd. The car belongs to a nearby assisted-living business.

I think to myself: That's weird. I never pay attention to things like this, especially when I'm driving. And here's this car that says *shepherd*, just as I'm on my way to a *sheep* farm, and while I'm listening to music by Psarantonis, who just happens to be from the same mountain village as a Cretan shepherd I used to know.

A few miles later I pass a commercial pickup truck going in the opposite direction, lettered with the last name Papadopoulos across the front lip of the hood. Probably not Cretan but certainly a Greek name, which you almost never see around these parts.

I'm giddy and a little freaked out. Knowing that the occasional clustering of coincidences in short spans of time are simply a fact of life (apparently well accounted for by the law of large numbers) just barely keeps me from believing that I'm fate's special project. I get to thinking about another coincidence—the fact that the moment I moved back to my hometown after so many years, goat's- and sheep's-milk cheese makers started popping up all over. When it comes to dairy, at least in my lifetime, this has always been cow country, and part of a cow's-milk nation. Most of the domestic "Greek" feta, suddenly so fashionable among Americans and ubiquitous in supermarkets, is even made with cow's milk, which is precisely one of the reasons why my Greek friends and I won't buy it. And even though feta is the unofficial national cheese of Greece, I mostly know Crete, where, sure, we ate some feta now and then, but much more frequently we ate cheeses like *kefalotyri*, *graviera*, *myzithra*, and *athotyro*. There was almost always part of a wheel of something in Eirini's fridge. Now there are all these people in neighboring Washington County who are making sheep's and goat's milk cheeses in bovine territory, and at least one of them is making cheeses that are close in flavor to my favorite Cretan cheeses.

I arrive at the farm. Andy and Dafne show me around and we trade stories about our experiences and some of our interests. The more detailed Andy gets about learning to make these cheeses in Tuscany—which is where Dafne is from—the more excited I see him getting about his experiences in Italy in general. The music. The food. The festivals. The gatherings of family, friends, and neighbors. I find out he's learning Italian. He takes out the accordion he's learning to play and runs through the song "Battagliero" that he's been working on.

Andy tells me that he and Dafne spend about half of each year living and working in Tuscany, and I suspect that for all his love of the farm and everything he's been accomplishing here with his cheeses, some part of him pines to be in Italy year round.

My suspicion is rooted in recognition, because the more times I visited Crete, always for months at a time, the more I fell in love with the idea of moving there—permanently.

The better I became at the language, the more I learned the music and the dances, the more accustomed I became to the flavors and the smells, the topography, and the kinds of emotions frequently expressed, the more I felt at home in Crete—and as a member of Penny's family. Many of the people I interacted with there were warmly sociable. There were constant opportunities to join in social activities that encouraged the expression of emotions, sometimes with near abandon. Somebody might argue with you sharply about your beliefs (and you were welcome to argue back) or criticize you openly for something you did, but rarely, it seemed to me, did people go out of their way to make you feel awkward or embarrassed simply because of who you were. I sensed that the predominance of lively, enthusiastic, and creative sociality, together with a widespread desire people had to connect with each other in times of joy and in times of sorrow, offered many opportunities—or perhaps the preconditions—for a kind of happiness and well-being that seemed unimaginable or out of reach to me before.

My passion for Crete quickly grew deeper.

This included a passion for the language. Early on in my learning of Greek, I made the decision to practice speaking with the particular pronunciation characteristic of the Malevizi region where Penny's family came from. (This led to a funny and awkward moment while I was auditing an introductory class on *ancient* Greek at the University of Chicago—when students stumbled through oral recitation with the made-up Erasmian pronunciation—and the professor called on me for the first time to read something aloud and I zipped through it with Cretan intonation and pronunciation.) By my second or third summer visit, after Penny and I visited Athens for a few days, getting off the ferry back in Irakleio and hearing Cretan intonation and pronunciation all around me, I was overcome by the sensation of having returned home.

My passion for Crete also included a passion for the music. As much as I continued to enjoy the music of Hatzidakis and Theodorakis that Leonidas had introduced me to, my love for Cretan music went much deeper. Just hearing the sound of a Cretan *lyra* stirred something within me, again with that sensation of home. The sound of a bouzouki was the sound of something Greek, but hearing a Cretan *lyra* was hearing something that felt like it was part of my core being. I sold my last remaining guitar to my friend Joe to get money to put toward a lyra. I had to learn to play. I just had to.

During my third summer visit, Penny's father dedicated his scant spare time to take me around Irakleio to various instrument makers and music stores. We shopped around for a few weeks. Then he asked the music teacher in his school for help, and she put a professional *lyra* performer and teacher on the case. But I couldn't wait any longer. Not yet accustomed to the tempos and rhythms of shopping for something like this in Crete, I ran out of patience. All by myself, I went to one of the musical instrument shops Manolis and I had visited, and bought the *lyra* that the eighty-something-year-old owner had shown us a few weeks earlier. Without Manolis there to help me, the owner managed to give me an inferior bow instead of the one he'd shown us before, and only gave me a receipt after I insisted—and even then, I later realized, only wrote down 10 percent of the actual price I paid. Lucky for me, Manolis took me back and shamed the guy into giving me the better bow. Manolis also asked the music teacher—who probably could have helped me find an even better *lyra* for the same price had I waited—to show me a few basics so I could get started. Back in Chicago, I spent much of my free time during the next academic year teaching myself how to play by listening to recordings of Cretan songs on my cassettes and CDs.

When I visited Grandpa on a short trip back to NY that winter, I realized that the mandolin he had bought a few years earlier was tuned in fifths like the *lyra*, and owing to my already playing another fretted instrument, discovered I was able to play several Cretan songs on it with hardly any effort. So Grandpa just gave me his mandolin! Although the *lyra* was the only musical instrument that could sing the sounds that were stirring in my soul, the fact that the mandolin was also a beloved traditional instrument in Crete, and

I could play it much more easily and better than the *lyra*, meant that I began to split my practice time between both instruments. Within a few months I was barely squeaking through a few *kontylies* on the *lyra* but on the mandolin I'd already learned how to play more than two CDs' worth of Cretan melodies.

I also became passionate about the traditional Cretan verse form known as the *mantinada*, comprised of two, rhyming, fifteen-syllable lines of iambic pentameter. I initially became interested in the *mantinada* on my first visit to Crete when I barely spoke any Greek. Penny's uncle Antonis had stopped by the house and, as he was on his way out the door, Eirini asked him to remind her of certain *mantinades* she liked that he'd come out with. (To "come out with" or "take out" a *mantinada* is how Cretans describe the act of composing a mantinada.) I sat at the table watching him tell narratives punctuated by a very stylized recitation of verses that were responses to whatever was happening in the narratives he was telling. Penny translated some of it to me to give me at least an inkling of what was going on. But what touched my heart was watching Antonis repeat the actual *mantinades*. The expressions on his face, the gestures of his arms and hands, the tone of his voice, the ways he articulated different words, the rise and fall of his pitch for emphasis—it was as though I was seeing someone communing with an invisible world of muses, or touched by some kind of divine grace—even though I could hardly understand a word. Antonis was always the most emotionally expressive among his siblings. As I watched him that day, it felt like I was witnessing something more human than human.

This transformed my understanding of the *mantinada* as merely the rhyming lyrics of traditional Cretan music. For the next few years, as I continued learning the language, I kept trying to come out with *mantinades* of my own. Sometimes it would take me a whole day to come out with just one. When I was a teaching assistant at the University of Chicago, required to sit in on every lecture of the professor whose students I was working with, I'd spend the entire class working a *mantinada* into shape. When I was waiting for the bus or walking alone to campus, I'd be thinking about a *mantinada* I was trying to come up with. I drove Penny crazy asking her to check my verses for errors.

In time, I came out with more than a hundred technically correct rhyming couplets, but they were hardly *mantinades*—though it would take a while for me to understand why. In fact, on my third summer visit to the island, I'd printed out every one of my "mantinades" and showed them to Penny's Uncle Antonis. Somehow he missed it when I told him that they were *my* creations—and so after he read through some of them he just stated coldly that, "These are childish." The frank criticism did me immeasurable good, though, because it made me understand that there must be even more to the *mantinada* than I so far realized.

Crete moved me in ways no other place I loved ever had. My second summer there Penny was driving her mother and me to their house in the village one evening. It was dusk. I'd been rereading Kazantzakis's *Freedom and Death*, this time in Greek. As we were making our way along one side of a Malevizian valley, I was staring passively out my door window at the landscape of mostly olive trees and vineyards rising up the other side of the valley and gradually giving way to the desolate mountains beyond. I was thinking about Kazantzakis's novel as Penny was skillfully but very respectfully negotiating with her mother in Greek about whatever latest motherly advice had just been dispensed. As it got just a little darker out, I saw the entire landscape wake up and start to . . . well . . . *dance*, yet somehow without visibly moving. I don't know how else to describe it. It was darker out but it felt like everything looked brighter. I was seeing both past and present, and sensing something at once human and nonhuman. I was overcome with powerful sensations of recognition, as though I'd just realized that I was a reincarnated Cretan, and the residue of an old Cretan soul somewhere inside me just became conscious that it was back in Crete.

The more passionate I became about Crete, the more I hated my life in Chicago.

It turned out I just wasn't into a lopsided life of intense specialization. As an undergrad, I dedicated much time, effort, and intuition to the mentally fascinating and frequently ineffably beautiful world of mathematical knowledge. Insofar as it intermeshed with the natural sciences as applied math, it was the closest thing I could imagine to an epistemological miracle. But I also continued learning and writing about such topics as ethics, politics, and aesthetics. It was Cauchy and Lebesgue one minute, Charles Ives and William James the next. But as a graduate student, my connections to the latter world were largely cut off, and I began to wonder if I cared more about what I was losing than what I was gaining from this sacrifice. Was I ever, or could I ever become, the kind of person who was sufficiently more interested in the Navier-Stokes equations than anything El Greco painted or Kazantzakis wrote? If not, how could I willingly dedicate myself to such a career, to such a life? If I was already less interested in working on my math than in studying my Greek, how could I hope to do original work, let alone significant research, in my field year after year after year?

I might have done away with such doubts by committing myself to finding a better balance between my connections to each world, but I had other issues, too. In fact, it was exactly my continuing fascination with ethical and political ideas that made me question further the path I was on. I found it increasingly necessary to question my own, and some of my colleagues', seeming lack of a sense of ethical or political responsibility when it came to our professional work in the sciences. I noticed that many of the published papers I'd studied acknowledged grant money from the armed forces. I observed that while many of us dutifully recycled at home, we never paused to deliberate what the environmental implications of our research projects might be. I felt like we were the brainy mercenaries of a network of dubious corporate and state interests, deceiving ourselves into believing that it was justifiable to wash our hands of such questions either because we were obviously working for the Good Guys, or because technically speaking we weren't the ones who *applied* our research to the real world. What naive ethical arguments for such complex thinkers!

Finally, on the level of everyday living, I felt like graduate-student life—or maybe just life in my particular academic department—was a matter of living in a subculture of psychological malaise and dulled emotions. In short, it was kind of depressing, even in the absence of any obvious reasons for being melancholic. I started asking myself: Why *choose* to live this way? Is this just boot camp for brains or my first real taste of the kind of life that typically follows? Either way, is it really worth it?

Meanwhile, Penny and I were getting into arguments on a far-too-regular basis, usually because of something I said or didn't say that to her mind betrayed my lack of devotion to her, or my putting my friends' or family's interests before hers. And there was also that time I brought her shame by asking her in front of other people if she was willing to split the cost of a CD I wanted to buy when I knew she liked it too. And another time while we were walking in the park and I insensitively admonished her for being upset about having to pay, as a foreign student, American income taxes.

Because of some administrative screw-ups, she already resented the university before we arrived, so it would've been difficult for me to look on the bright side of things even if I'd wanted to.

With each passing day, I identified more with the high-spirited Mediterraneans I'd hang out with in the summers, and I struggled to resist turning into yet another dispirited grad student. Penny and I gradually stopped participating in anything that might be intended to cultivate a sense of belonging with our peers or our department. We became friends with grad students from Greece in other departments, and tried finding little ways to cope—getting together with them for coffee or dinner, going downtown for shopping or a movie. At least with most of the Greek students, who came much closer to living up to her social and ethical expectations than most of our American classmates, Penny managed to keep up her usual energy, enthusiasm, sociality, and generosity. But even here there were more and more exceptions, especially when it came to those Greek students who—perhaps because they grew up in upper-middle-class Athens—weren't striving to live up to the same everyday social virtues to which she was accustomed to aspiring, and which she—and increasingly I—took as simply right and obviously true.

I struggled throughout the cold months to maintain summer Crete, not winter Chicago, as my lens on the world. But Chicago was a different world and nine months was a long time to pretend that one's real frame of reference was a Mediterranean island. There were times when Penny and I would get into such frustrating arguments that I'd panic over the possibility that she might not welcome me with her back to Crete the following summer. I became increasingly miserable and it showed. (Who walks around Hyde Park wearing his pants tucked inside tall black leather boots, taking more fashion cues from Cretan shepherd acquaintances twice his age than from his university peers?) On our next visit to Crete, Penny and I talked with her father about our trials in the windy city, and the apparent toll it was taking on our relationship. Manolis and I discussed the prospects of my finding a job in Greece and abandoning the PhD program. Penny remained heroically determined to finish her studies, but once we got back to Chicago that autumn, I sent out over a hundred bilingual résumés and cover letters to every U.S. business that had some kind of an office or operation in Greece. (I received not a single response.) Penny at last decided she needed some time away from both her studies and me. She took a leave of absence after the winter quarter and went back to Crete to try clearing her mind and getting back her usual energy and optimism. Soon after, I was more desperate than ever to move to Crete, and Penny—having become accustomed to certain things she preferred about her life in the United States—was surprised to find herself feeling somewhat like a stranger back home. Perhaps it was in a moment of weakness, then, that while speaking together on the telephone, she expressed her desire that I join her in Crete when I offered yet again to move there. She finally agreed that we should both leave Chicago behind forever; I would move to the island, and together we'd figure out something else we could do with our lives in a place where we felt at home. Maybe we'd finally get married.

After successfully completing the requirements for doctoral candidacy, I let each of my dissertation advisers assume that I was working closely with the other when in fact I was spending all my time expanding my Greek vocabulary by reading Dimaras's Greek literary history and Kazantzakis's novels—writing down new words on flash cards and practicing them all through the night. I decided to get my jet lag out of the way long before leaving, so I changed my clocks and lived on Greek time in Chicago. I'd get up at midnight local time, put on Cretan CDs or some classical music with Peter Van De Graaff on WFMT, and get to work on my Greek until after daybreak. I packed up everything I owned, had it loaded onto a ship for Greece, and bought a one-way plane ticket.

A week later I was walking around Irakleio, dropping off my résumé at all the larger English-language schools and U.K.-university-partnership programs. Within a few days, I secured my first teaching jobs. By the end of that summer—and after Penny came *this* close to breaking up with me for good because of a debacle involving flowers given to me by a female student—we were renting our own apartment kitty-corner to the cathedral of St. Minas, with a view to one of its clock towers from our balcony. The future was somewhat unclear, but I firmly believed with all my heart that I was in the right place.

※   ※   ※

I notice that Andy can get so carried away talking about Tuscany that he seems to lose track of the time. As happy as I am to be at his farm listening to him, especially hearing some of the ways our respective enthusiasm and interests seem to intersect, I decide I should leave so he can get back to work.

I'm about to go. He and Dafne give me a lot of cheese on top of what I've already bought. I'm dying to give them something, too. The only thing I can come up with is the Psarantonis CD I was listening to in the car. I don't know what Andy's taste in music is. I know that Psarantonis isn't an easily acquired taste for most Americans—not even for most Greeks. But it's the only thing I have here in the car.

At any rate, this isn't a matter of reciprocity. I recognize this feeling—the kind of thing I've only experienced since being influenced by Cretans. How can I describe it? I guess it's more like a strong desire to mark outwardly a personally meaningful event, however objectively small—to somehow symbolize the significance of the occasion so that it becomes *more* than just personally meaningful—grand even—and, at the same time, to express your delight at the other's (or others') unique and integral part in this.

Or, maybe this is just my after-the-fact attempt to describe something more primordial.

And since I only started experiencing this feeling after encountering Crete, there's probably yet another dimension to it, at least today: a desire to do something that will stamp this Upstate New York encounter as a Mediterranean one.

✳ 11 ✳

Cretan Flesh, Cretan Spirit

I awake from a December dream that I'm back in Irakleio again. My eyes are still closed.

I don't know how it is for other people, but in many of my dreams there's something like a parallel geography that is based on the geography of real life but never quite the same. In these dreams of being back in Crete, the geography is always incredibly detailed, especially in Irakleio, but every detail is slightly different from what it is in actuality . . . every street, every shop, every shop owner, the houses, the harbor, the city walls, the souvlaki joints and other fast-food places. Heading out into the mountains just west of Irakleio, beaches aren't quite where they should be, the roads aren't in quite the same places, the landscape is rockier, drier, and more desolate than in reality. After more than ten years of these dreams, sometimes it's easier for me to conjure up images of this parallel-universe Crete than of the actual island as I experienced it.

While I'm in one of these dreams I always feel an incredible sense of surprised relief: "I didn't think this was *possible*, but here I am again at last!" It's a lot like the occasional dream I have where I end up discovering that Grandma or Grandpa hasn't died after all, or has somehow returned from "death" after many years.

But when I'm in one of these dreams I also feel tension. The greater my joy, the more I sense that something isn't quite right, although I never understand exactly what that is until I'm awake again. In some dreams Penny wants me to move back to Crete, and the dream-me doesn't know I'm with Sofia now, but since my brain actually does know, I can sense something won't work. In other dreams, Manolis or Eirini might welcome me back but not Penny, or Penny might welcome me back but not Manolis or Eirini. Or I'll

119

be there talking to Manolis like in old times, but I'll be talking about things I've been doing in my life with Sofia. In other dreams, it's like Penny is no longer Penny but Sofia, and though dream-Sofia is happy to have me with her in Irakleio, the dream-me knows I can't live there because my job is here and there isn't any comparable job available for me there, and so I'm not sure what I can do.

I open my eyes. I'm stunned by the silence and spaciousness of the bedroom after the joyful hustle and bustle of life in dream-Irakleio. I decide to get up anyway.

There's never anything about food in these dreams, maybe because when I was living in Crete, food was mostly just one of the delights I could take for granted. Even with our own apartment—stocked with brand new kitchen appliances purchased for us by Eirini and Manolis on the occasion of our wedding—Penny and I continued eating most of our meals at the family home, walking there midafternoons for lunch and midevenings for dinner. Except on Monday nights, when we'd order out grilled chicken and stay in to watch *The X-Files*.

It wasn't long before I figured out that Eirini had been purposefully departing from her usual menu during our summer visits in prior years. During those visits, she'd prepared whatever dishes she thought Penny and I would enjoy the most, figuring that our suffering throughout the school year in Chicago warranted all she could do to help recharge our batteries, including concentrating a year's worth of the household's greatest eating pleasures into a span of three months. So what if it meant more expensive roasts and fewer lentils? Who cared if she exhausted herself making desserts like mille-feuille or *galaktoboureko* biweekly? What difference did it make if it meant eating Penny's favorite Easter *kokoretsi*—charcoal-fire spit-grilled lamb innards wrapped in intestine—in the middle of July?

All that mattered for Eirini was that such foods put smiles of genuine pleasure on our faces. But once our suffering in Chicago was over, Eirini followed her more usual pattern of meals. Lentils, chickpeas, and fava beans were more frequent. Sometimes she made green bean stews without any meat. We ate chicken more frequently than lamb. Everyone was expected to eat their share of the leftovers. Before Easter, she stopped using meats, and sometimes olive oil, in accordance with fasting rules of the Orthodox Church.

Manolis and Eirini often attributed the deliciousness of their foods to the fact that they were made with local produce, to the particular qualities of the Cretan weather and soil that resulted in flavorful produce, and to the less-industrial manner in which the meat and vegetables they usually bought were raised. To an extent, this must have been true: local village chickens really had tougher, darker, but more flavorful meat. Some goat and lamb, and the cheeses made from their milk, probably owed their special flavor to the fact that the animals were raised on the forage of mountain slopes. Manolis's fish were the freshest you could have short of eating them on the boat.

But Eirini's skills as a home cook also made a difference, not to mention the shopping savvy that enabled her to acquire some of the best ingredients available at the local markets. Eirini was as adept socially as she was generous as a cook and hostess. As much, maybe even more than Manolis, she befriended just about everyone she met with an almost naive politeness, sincere kindness, and genuine interest in their well-being, whether they were politically left, center, or right—though left-leaning herself. As if that wasn't enough, her connections with and advocacy for Cretan agriculture, as well as her kinship and friendly ties with many local producers, meant that she was regarded as someone who was in-the-know, especially when it came to her butcher, greengrocer, baker, and dairy supplier. She wasn't one to frequent the supermarket chains that were making inroads in the city. Why should she? The way she shopped, she could come home and tell you which village—sometimes even which family—raised the pig whose meat she just purchased. Would a butcher risk his reputation in the neighborhood by trying to pull a fast one on this well-respected couple with myriad local social ties? Highly unlikely.

Eirini also had to be credited for the extra work she put into foraging wild greens whenever she could. Sometimes when she went to the village, she'd come back to Irakleio with *radikia*, *stifnos*, or *glistrida*. Once, she learned of a good spot not far outside of Irakleio with lots of *stamnagathi* which, she said, was one of the most prized of all wild greens. She and a friend spent an entire morning collecting it. She came back in the early afternoon looking like she'd struck gold, with a large black garbage bag stuffed full. All the rest of the day she sat in the kitchen trimming the greens with a knife, letting the soil and unwanted scraps pile up on the marble floor around her. Salads of raw *stamnagathi* dressed with oil and vinegar were the highlight of the next several meals.

A distant cousin who'd been living for years in the United States and Athens, the son of Eirini's cousin, paid an unexpected visit and was promptly invited to come back later that evening with the rest of his family for a dinner that would include a salad of wild *stamnagathi*. The invitation itself was enough to light him up, but at the mention of *stamnagathi* he looked thoroughly overjoyed. All through the meal he and his wife made as much fuss over the salad as anything else. They said they probably hadn't eaten *stamnagathi* in over a decade and appeared visibly grateful that Eirini created this moment of reconnection for them.

"These cousins paid the terrible price of ambition," I kept thinking to myself during the meal. "They traded in the joys that Crete was already offering them for the mainstream temptations of the major metropolises." I sat there relieved that I'd seized the opportunity in my life to do just the opposite.

In time, I discovered that I loved certain foods—like yogurt and honey—that I never liked before. Once I allowed myself to be persuaded to try them, I realized that it was just the particular *versions* of these foods that I'd experienced back home that I didn't like. Eirini smartly handled my food preferences as she gradually assimilated me to many of the family's usual everyday ingredients, textures, and flavors. I'd claim not to like liver and other organs, so she'd make sure not to serve them to me when she made rabbit stew. But then they'd turn up in my bowl the next day in tiny little pieces when she used the leftover stew as the basis for a pilaf. By the time I'd catch on to what they were, it was too late—I'd have realized that their flavor didn't bother me after all. The first few times she made snails, she made them with a traditional pilaf of cracked wheat and tomato so I could eat the wheat with my snails removed. This ultimately made it easier to convince me to try a snail as we sat eating the cracked wheat, and I saw everyone else ecstatically scooping snails out of their shells while keeping an eye out to make sure that no one else got more snails than they did. Since I liked the cracked wheat that had been cooked with the snails, I finally decided to try a few. My lack of dexterity in pulling them out of their shells with the bent prong of a fork ended up becoming a greater deterrent to my eating them than the flavor, the texture, or the idea.

Try as she might, though, not all of Eirini's attempts were

successful in reforming my eating habits. When it came to boiled greens, I enjoyed sweet *vlita* from the first, but one taste of bitter *radikia* and I hardly touched them ever again. Tomato-and-onion or tomato-cucumber-and-onion salads were an important part of almost every meal. Yet, I rarely took more than a forkful or two. After every lunch and dinner, there was fresh fruit, but I'd usually eat it only when it was one of my absolute favorites and not messy or difficult to eat. I hardly ever touched figs. I never ate *lotos*. Apples and bananas bored me. With so many other foods to choose from that I loved, why persuade myself to acquire the more difficult new tastes and eating habits? "For your health!" Eirini insisted. But I was too young and fearless to pay any attention.

As time went by, Eirini found herself admonishing Manolis and me more frequently about our diet. Eirini insisted that, according to widespread dietary advice confirming the health benefits of a more traditional Cretan diet, we should eat legumes several times a week as our main course instead of so much meat and poultry. But Manolis and I took advantage of every possible opportunity—when he wasn't staying in the village doing chores or off fishing—to spend time together grilling meat over charcoal on the terrace. Once in a while we'd grill fish that he caught, occasionally a big chunk of lamb or a rabbit on a spit, and sometimes as frequently as once a week we'd grill thin-sliced fatty pork *pasetes* seasoned with just a little salt.

Our grilling was always leisurely. We'd drink Greek coffee that I'd brew in a *briki* set over the coals. We'd smoke a few cigarettes. Manolis would tell me stories—nostalgic reminiscences about years past, amusing anecdotes displaying the creative and clever way someone reacted or responded to a particular situation or high-lighting someone's character. He'd tell me about his plans to buy a small fishing boat with his retirement money. I'd tell him about what I was up to with my work or whatever I was scheming in order to find better work in the future. We'd trade thoughts on what we believed really mattered in life.

Some of his stories and reflections dealt with food and agriculture. Manolis came from a humble rural background. I was impressed that he never sought to cut himself off from his rural roots, despite having graduated from the teaching academy to become an elementary school teacher and principal, beloved by colleagues and students alike. He continued going to the village on a regular basis, usually alone, to work his tail off cultivating the olive groves and sultana vineyards inherited from Eirini's side of the family.

Whenever Manolis and I grilled meat, we also drank lots of wine. The first time I tasted Manolis's homemade wine was back in northern New York when I was an undergrad. When Penny returned from Crete at the end of the summer I'd been courting her, she brought with her a two-liter bottle filled from the old barrel in the shed under their house in the village. This wine wasn't red or white or rosé. It was amber. We opened it when Mom and Dad drove up to campus for a visit. A single summer of drinking Beaujolais and Côtes du Rhône with Leonidas hadn't prepared me for the potent, sourish, almost salty beverage in my glass that afternoon. It was too early to tell if I liked it—it was simply too different from anything I'd ever experienced.

The next summer when I visited Crete for the first time, we drank Manolis's wine with almost every meal, in rather large quantities whenever an evening evolved into a full-blown bout of singing, drinking, and dancing. Manolis not only made his own small quantities of wine, but used nothing but pressed grapes from his own vineyard, which he tended himself. No added sulfites, no added yeasts, no added water. He even pressed the grapes by stepping on them with his bare feet. I thought this was great, as was the fact that drinking significant quantities of it for hours on end never seemed to leave any of us feeling sick to our stomachs or hung over the next day—the ultimate proof of its purity, we believed.

Once I was living in Crete, my love affair with Manolis's amber wine really took off since it was available to enjoy year round. "Nectar," we called it, *agio nero* ("holy water"), and *amalago krasi* ("pure wine," using a Cretan idiomatic word for *pure*). I gradually realized how much better it tasted than much of the other Cretan homemade wine I'd tasted. I also began to notice that, if pushed on the matter, some of these other Cretans who said they didn't add anything to their wines would admit that in fact they did.

I increasingly used wine and spirit metaphors in my writing. I published an essay called "Water or Wine?" in an Irakleio newspaper, comparing my life in Upstate New York with my life in Crete, declaring that pure water was my symbol for the former and pure wine my symbol for the latter. If Manolis was home for dinner, sometimes we'd drink wine with the meal and then sit at the table

or out on the balcony sipping more, smoking cigarettes, and philosophizing about life.

At times I wondered if I was becoming an alcoholic, but given
how differently alcohol use and abuse were thought about in Crete
(compared with the U.S.), and given my suspicions about the scientific reliability of drinking guidelines coming out of a nation that
not so long ago produced temperance movements and prohibition,
I wasn't sure what criteria to take seriously. I observed that whenever the demijohn needed refilling from the barrel in the village we
simply wouldn't drink. I also noticed that the more I appreciated
Manolis's wine, the more infrequently I drank wine at weddings or
baptisms unless it happened to be especially good. Based on this, I
decided that I was becoming more of a homemade-wine connoisseur
than an alcoholic, albeit one who probably drank more heavily than
medical science would ever endorse.

Manolis had two barrels of homemade wine, a smaller one with
older wine that he was trying to save for the baptism of his first
grandchild, and another much larger one from which we usually
drank. As the larger barrel approached empty, he started rationing
what was left to make it last a little longer, interspersed with an
occasional demijohn drawn from the smaller barrel on special occasions. As the summer progressed, Manolis talked with me about his
plans for making new batches, and how he was looking forward to
my eager participation. He purchased several new plastic barrels to
use for the fermentation, and chatted with a local oenologist he was
acquainted with who reassured him—off the record, as it were—that
we'd almost be guaranteed good wine without professional techniques or commercial yeasts so long as we kept all the equipment
and barrels immaculately clean.

When the grapes ripened, Eirini, Manolis, Penny, and I packed our
bags and drove to the village. We got up at dawn the next morning.
Manolis, Penny, and I harvested enough grapes to make several
large barrels. Manolis drove them up to the sloped driveway of the
house, leaving them by the entrance to the shed located under the
house. He backed the tractor up to the shed door, and we covered
the wagon on the back with clean sheets of plastic. Manolis sanitized
the barrels, pails, and the other equipment.

We'd fill up a porous sack with bunches of grapes in the back
of the wagon, and Manolis would work the sack under his bare

feet to squeeze out the juice, folding the sack more and more times as the volume of grapes decreased. The driveway was sloped, so the juice readily ran down the plastic sheeting to one corner of the wagon where I'd catch it in a pail. As each pail filled, I'd replace it with another and dump the full pail into the large plastic barrels. I felt bad that Manolis was doing all the really hard labor pressing the grapes. I thought I should do my fair share even if he was ten times stronger than I was, and much less likely to slip and fall. But he just kept at it.

At the end of the day, we collected the *strafyla* (the grape pomace) to use later for distilling *tsikoudia*. We covered the top of the barrels with a fine fabric Manolis thought would keep out insects but allow the carbon dioxide to escape. Every couple days thereafter, Manolis went down and gave each barrel a good stir with a clean stick. Once the initial fermentation seemed complete, he closed up the plastic barrels and let them be. The plan was to transfer the wine—once we confirmed that it was indeed wine—to the wooden barrels the following spring or autumn.

When we opened up the first plastic barrel of white wine early that winter, it was cloudy and had a flavor that we knew wasn't quite right. I myself thought it tasted grape-musty but couldn't be sure. That winter we drank very sparingly from the old wine, and occasionally small amounts of the imperfect white. One evening the following spring, after Manolis had refilled the demijohn with the new white again, we realized that it was crystal clear and no longer tasted musty. It was potent and deliciously dry. We were surprised and relieved, and kept tasting it over and over. We'd speculate about what must have happened. My theory was that it had been too cold in the shed for the wine to finish fermenting, but that the spring warm-up had coaxed it the rest of the way. (But then, since the barrel was sealed, why weren't there any carbon dioxide bubbles in the wine? Perhaps it was because Manolis opened the barrel now and then to fill up the bottles for drinking?) Maybe it just needed more time for the dregs to settle? As amateurs, neither of us knew what really happened. But we knew we had plenty of good new wine to drink.

Neither the temperamental nature of winemaking nor what we thought was a close call with failure made me nostalgic for the guarantees of the cult of precision that I grew up with. On the contrary, I was touched that I'd learned a "recipe" that was at once so imprecise and so unforgivingly exact that when it succeeded the result could only be experienced as precious, priceless, potable art. And I was even more deeply moved that Manolis and I had at last collaborated in the making of the drink we so frequently relished consuming together.

Since it was essentially taboo to drink without eating, Manolis and I often extended our meat-eating beyond the meal proper. Eirini would pick up the table leaving just the platter of meat at the center of the table, and then she'd bring us a couple small clean plates. Manolis and I might pretend to compete over who got to eat another piece of *petsa*—the "skin"—or he'd pull a tiny piece of meat off a chunk left on the platter, and then say, "With this little piece here I'm good for two more glasses of wine!" I'd take another piece too and lift my tumbler of wine, tap it on the table saying, "εβίβα" (from the Italian *evviva*, I presume), and take another sip.

The fact that Manolis emphasized and explained his family's particular choices of foodstuffs not only in terms of flavor and nutrition, but also in terms of the environment, resonated with my own general worries about the environment, and endeared him to me more. He was frequently concerned about the ecological implications of modern food practices. A lifetime of tending grapes made him especially sensitive to the environmental warnings and ecological pronouncements he read about in the morning paper or heard on the evening news. He frequently reminded me that he'd observed firsthand how rampant pesticide use had led to an overall worsening in the pest populations in the village vineyards. Although he felt economically compelled to treat his raisin vineyards with what he thought were dangerous industrial chemicals, he'd explain to me his efforts to use the least amount he thought he could get away with without risking the harvest, and he spoke ill of Cretans he knew who sprayed willy-nilly or harvested produce before the sprays had worn off, at least according to their instructions. He'd also discuss the possibility of more sustainable organic techniques, hoping and wondering if he might someday find a viable and affordable alternative to the conventional practices he and his fellow agriculturalists had been steeped in.

Meanwhile, when it came to his own table, he tended fruit trees, several other varieties of grapes, and a vegetable garden—none of which he treated or sprayed, all of which were fertilized with composted manure. His mantra, especially when it came to the highly susceptible fruits, was that he'd gladly lose half his production to pests as long as he knew what he was eating. Manolis would also go to the trouble to collect and dry wild herbs from the outskirts of his paternal village, and would only serve the fish that he and his friends caught on their longlines. (I don't think I once tasted fish from the street seafood market that I walked through almost daily on my way to teach.) I shared in Manolis's disappointment that the city hadn't put more garbage bins down by the harbor to deter fishermen from throwing their trash into the sea, and in his anger that there were fishermen who didn't adhere to various environmental-protection measures governing the use of longlines and nets. Manolis also explained to me how he was finally getting around to fencing in a part of the field behind the family garden with a kind of chicken wire to see if he could trap in wild snails so he'd know what they were eating before we ate them. He also repeatedly discussed with me plans to fence in the family olive grove in order to raise truly free-range chickens for the family to consume. "You can grow anything you want in Crete," he'd say, unquestionably proud of the flavor, texture, and supposed health benefits of much of what grew on the island, cultivated and wild.

After grilling meat, family meals often evolved into occasions for improvising *mantinades*, especially once I began to understand the *mantinada* less as a miniature self-contained poem and more like the Cretan's stylized way of participating in a dialogue. Ours hovered around getting at what we thought the *spirit* of being Cretan meant. For Manolis, as for some other Cretans, the essence of what it meant to be Cretan ultimately boiled down to being a revolutionary.

Crete has been associated to the point of stereotype with unbridled passion for freedom and the fierce resistance and heroism it takes to achieve or maintain that freedom. In Greece and abroad, mention of Crete brings to mind unbelievable stories about Cretan peasants without weapons holding off German invaders in the Second World War, uprisings against Venetian and Ottoman rulers, and how the Cretans at the Arkadi monastery preferred to blow themselves up rather than to surrender to the Turks. With external conquerors less of an immediate threat by the late twentieth century, some Cretans were showing off their rebelliousness through such other activities as tax evasion, arguing with or deceiving the local police, shooting guns off in the air during festive gatherings, or taking pride in ignoring traffic regulations.[1]

But Manolis's focus on the revolutionary had little to do with these things. For him revolution was ultimately about the heart rebelling against the authority of the rational mind, heartless social conventions, and the inevitable decay of the physical body.

Once after dinner when we turned off the television and the two of us kept drinking wine and "philosophizing," Manolis took his copy of Kazantzakis's *Saviors of God* off the shelf and quoted passages employing mind-heart imagery.[2] Excited, he began improvising *mantinades* about the mind and heart. For instance:

Παλεύει η αντάρτισσα καρδιά σκλάβα ποτέ μη γίνει,
του λογισμού και κανενός, ελεύτερη να μείνει.

The rebel heart struggles never to become a slave
to thought or anyone else, to remain free.

To spur him on, I got out my mandolin and played modal melodies (*kontylies*) over which Cretans sing and sometimes improvise *mantinades*. After all, I had no such ability to improvise *mantinades*, and so could never respond in verse in the moment. I had to rely on my ability to connect and to influence the flow of improvisation through the music.

"No. No. I'm not saying any more [*mantinades*]," he responded, maybe feeling he wasn't really up to the challenge of more verse improvisation, especially solo improvisation. "I'm not saying any more, so there's no sense trying to coax me. I'm not saying. I'm not saying."

But the sound of the melodies I played was impossible for his heart to resist. He started clapping his hands above his head with the rhythm, clearly inspired. A few seconds later and he came out with another verse:

Παντέρμε νου προσπάθησε να εκφράσεις την καρδιά μου,
και βρες τσι λέξεις για να πεις τα φτερουγίσματά μου!

Poor old mind, try to express my heart,
and find the words to describe my flight [literally: "my flaps-of-the-
wing"]!

In characteristic Cretan fashion again, he clapped his hand on the table along with the music. He came out with more verses:

Είναι στιγμές που η καρδιά κατακτυπά να φύγει
και στου κορμιού τη φυλακή να μη ξαναγιαγείρει.

There are times when the heart races to leave
and never return to the prison of the body.

Εγέρασε το σώμα μου μα νιώθω νιος ακόμα
γιατί δεν καταδέχομαι να σέρνομαι στο χώμα.

My body got old but I still feel young
because I don't deign to crawl in the soil.

One after another the *mantinades* flowed. Eirini and Penny came rushing in from the kitchen concerned about disturbing the neighbors' kids during test season—Irakleio's houses are close to one another, and windows and balcony doors are frequently open in warm weather. They criticized Manolis for his loud singing, but he just responded with more verses:

Καλά περνώ και χαίρομαι που είμαι ο εαυτός μου,
οι άλλοι το τι σκέφτονται δεν βάζει ο λογισμός μου.

I have a good time and enjoy being myself,
I don't give a thought to what other people [literally: the others] think about it.

The more verses he came out with, the more high-spirited he became. I kept increasing the intensity of my mandolin playing. After about a half-hour of my cranking out melodies nonstop, he finally came out with this climactic one, before at last getting up from the table and heading to the balcony to smoke:

Θε μου, δε σε παρακαλώ, όχι για δεν αξίζεις,
αμοναχός μου θ' ανεβώ στα ουράνια που ορίζεις.

God, I don't beg you, not because you're unworthy,
All by myself I'll come up into the heavens that you command.

The evolution of the family meal into a prelude for Manolis to improvise *mantinades* to my musical accompaniment happened with increasing frequency. Instead of trying to impart his philosophy and advice to us in prose, he increasingly used *mantinades* to persuade us to notice some of the things that he thought really mattered.

The *mantinada* was central to the dialogue in which Manolis and I found ourselves. Whenever I'd written—*literally* written—a *mantinada* that I thought was good, I'd show it to him. I also made a point of saving dozens of the *mantinades* Manolis improvised from disappearing in the moment. Every so often I'd collect them together with whatever new ones I'd written and give them to him to read. He'd point out which he especially liked and which he considered imperfect. Sometimes he'd think up new-and-improved versions of the transcribed texts—occasionally preferring my suggestions about a word or phrase to his own. He'd memorize some favorites—including some of mine—and would sing them in future gatherings as a warm up before the wine and high spirits kicked in and he was ripe for full-blown improvisation.

By the time I'd been living in Crete for two years, I held in my hands the most tangible outcome of our dialogue—a small book collecting *mantinades* and other Cretan-inspired verse that I'd written, and a significant and evolving collection of what I considered Manolis's best oral improvisations, words I managed to keep from vanishing into the wine-soaked air. That I saved *mantinades* like these from disappearing, that I helped shape them, that they espoused a philosophy of Cretan life that he hoped could be spread to others, and that they were part of our ongoing dialogue—all led Manolis to insist that they were mine as much as they were his. In this sense, mine were his, too.

Collectively, our *mantinades* comprised the richest expression of the bond between a *petheros* and his only "son," between a born-again Cretan and his adopted *babas*.

※　※　※

I remember a *mantinada* Manolis came out with one night when it was just the two of us:

Πνεύμα το κρητικό κρασί να γίνει στην καρδιά μας,
στα ουράνια να πετάξουμε μακριά απ᾽ τα βάσανά μας.

Let Cretan wine become spirit in our heart,
so we can fly in the heavens far from our troubles.

I remember how when I transcribed it and showed it to him we ended up discussing it. As was often the case, we communicated through few words—ambiguous words open to lots of interpretation—and through our facial expressions and body language. I could tell there was an issue with his having said "*our* heart" and "*our* troubles" as opposed to just "my heart" and "my troubles." Neither of us came right out and said anything to the other about our respective troubles. We didn't even let on to one another whether we really *had* any troubles worthy of the name. I wasn't entirely sure, though, if the problem was the fact that, under the influence of wine, he'd let on about something (regarding himself or me) that he wished he hadn't, or if he just found the emphasis on troubles to be too unheroic, and perhaps problematic because I was young, idealistic, and essentially just starting my adult life. I offered a different verse, which he embraced as this *mantinada*'s "right" form from that moment on:

Πνεύμα το κρητικό κρασί να γίνει στην καρδιά μας,
στα ουράνια να πετάξουμε μαζί με τ' όνειρά μας.

Let Cretan wine become spirit in our heart,
so we can fly in the heavens together with our dreams.

12

Impromptu Gatherings

Sofia and I are at the rented hall of the American Legion with family and friends for Aunt Juliette's birthday bash. It's approaching 4:00 p.m., the party's scheduled end-time. It's evident to me that, between the drinks, the live Irish music, and the relatives who've come down from Canada as a surprise, people's spirits are ascending.

I discreetly check around to see if there are already plans for continuing the festivities. There aren't. I ask Sofia if it's okay to invite people back to our house, knowing that she never says no to me about things like this. She says she likes the idea and we spread the word.

I've been drinking, so I ask Sofia to take the car and buy some beer (which is what most people are drinking) to supplement the wine we already have at home. Labatt's and Guinness, since Aunt Juliette's side of the family is Canadian and Uncle Rich's side is Irish.

I ask Ben and Catherine to take me with them as everyone drives back to our house. I unlock the door and tell Ben and Catherine that they can find some music to put on while I head to the kitchen to get drinks ready and plan what to do about food. I end up making hot wings using chicken I've been saving in the freezer, potatoes fried in olive oil, and spaghetti with a creamy tomato-and-vodka sauce. Sofia roasts coarsely diced winter squash and shitãke mushrooms in the oven with lots of dried rosemary.

Several relatives, and some others I don't know, are sitting at the kitchen bar—drinking, talking, and seemingly enjoying just watching us do our thing in the kitchen. I can hear people in the other room laughing it up. I don't sense that anyone is preoccupied with dinner plans yet.

By the time everyone is getting hungry, some of the food comes out. Several people seem to enjoy trying what are for them our unusual dishes or ingredients. Uncle Rich's brother appears to be relishing a bottle of Cretan white wine that Sofia and I had picked up on our last trip down to Astoria in Queens. The compliments and gratitude about the food begin to flow. I respond, "Don't thank me. Thank the people of Crete."

I love this kind of impromptu gathering.

My earliest recollections of impromptu visits go back to the many occasions when I stayed overnight at Grandma and Grandpa's house. A car would pull into the driveway unexpectedly. Somebody would look out the dining room window and see who it was—a family friend, possibly, or relatives, maybe visiting from up north. Whatever else was going on in the house would come to a halt in deference to the newly arrived visitors, most of whom knew to come in by way of the back porch, through the kitchen. (Trick-or-treaters and the occasional unwelcome solicitor or proselytizer were about the only people I ever saw come up to the front door.) If it was time to eat, Grandma would set more places at the table. If it wasn't, she'd act as though everyone had already agreed to stay until it *was* time. Meanwhile, if there was homemade pie or cake or some cookies or ice cream—which there usually was—it would be served up right away. If it was later in the evening, chances are the visitors would be hoping to play pinochle, and out would come the deck of cards, sliced cheese, nuts, and soft drinks.

Another experience that left its mark on me happened during my sophomore year in college when I was sharing a dorm room with my best friend Joe. He and I had a long trip ahead of us through the Adirondacks to get back home for winter break. On a good day it was a three-hour drive, but on that particular day a storm was sifting a couple feet of snow all over northern New York. Most students just skipped classes and went home early, but Joe had a paper to turn in and I wanted to get back the results of a math test, so we didn't end up heading out until after four o'clock in the afternoon under an already darkening sky. Driving behind Joe's pickup through the mountain snow in my decade-old six-cylinder Mercury with the air vents open to keep the windows from fogging up was slow, cold, and stressful. Around seven o'clock in the evening we came upon the hamlet of Indian Lake and Joe called over to me on the CB radio asking if I wanted to stop by his Aunt Irma's house for a little break to warm up. He'd mentioned to me many times before that he had a great-aunt who lived there. "Sounds good to me," I replied.

I followed Joe down the side street, we pulled into the driveway, and Joe knocked on the back door as we both stood waiting on the snowy steps. Joe's Aunt Irma opened the door and, standing there in her slippers, beckoned us to come in out of the cold. Joe and I took off our damp, insulated, brown work boots, went into the living room, and sat down. As was our habit we analyzed the drive—which turns had been the slipperiest, where the roads had been plowed the best, and the pickup truck that pulled out in front of us in Tupper Lake without even looking. Joe's Aunt Irma came in from the kitchen with three cups of piping hot black tea and something that looked like a cylindrical banana bread or zucchini bread.

"It's hobo bread!" she said. "You bake it in a coffee can. I just made it this morning."

She sliced us some and we smothered it in butter. With all my attention on the driving I hadn't realized until that moment just how famished I was, and as the buttered hobo bread melted in my mouth I was reinvigorated. "Take more if you like it!" she urged. Then came more tea and we finished off the entire loaf. We rested a few more minutes and decided to get back on the road before it got any later. We thanked her and on our way out she reminded us to stop by any time we were passing through, day or night, and that she'd be sure to have hobo bread waiting for us in the freezer.

❊ ❊ ❊

Sofia's and my visitors have more or less finished eating. Spirits remain high. Almost without thinking I take out the two acoustic guitars I've ended up with—one is Sofia's and the other used to be my mother's. From all the stories I've heard, I know that my mother's cousin Gilbert (or, as my mother pronounces it, approximating the French-Canadian pronunciation as best she can, *Jeel-bye*) likes to sing and play at family gatherings. Gilbert says he can't play anything without his sheet music and that he doesn't have it with him. I play and sing a couple of American folk songs but no one else knows the words or is willing to jump in. Gilbert gradually recalls how to play, more or less, a Hank Williams tune and "Danny Boy."

As he's playing and singing, I'm straining to see if I can tell what chords he's playing and whether I can improvise a little something to accompany him. I'm not doing very well. Even though I know it isn't really possible, something inside me is bent on trying to push the evening to the same level of celebration as the gatherings around food, wine, and improvised music that repeatedly amazed me in Crete whenever they spontaneously erupted.

The most memorable such occasion began when Eirini's youngest and most comedic brother Mitsos, a woodworker, stopped by Eirini's and Manolis's for some reason—or maybe for no reason—on his way home from work. Penny and I were already there for dinner. Manolis poured Mitsos a glass of wine, and persuaded him to taste some of their nephew Vassilis's new sausage.

As the family sat talking and kidding around at the dining room table that filled much of the living room, I took out my mandolin. I gently picked the tune of a well-known, somewhat melancholic, somewhat yearning Cretan folk song that refers to the treachery of the sea. As I expected, Penny and Manolis quickly picked up on the melody and began singing along—"*Stsi Gramvousas t' akrotiri . . .*"—Penny in her smooth unembellished well-tempered soprano, Manolis in his tobacco-coated Byzantine high-mountain outpost chant.

A few minutes later, I picked the melody of another traditional song about desire that contains some classic Cretan metaphorical imagery and is a little more upbeat. I'd seen Manolis sing it enthusiastically on other occasions. This time even Mitsos sang along. As the song's single melody repeated over and over, everyone's singing grew louder and more passionate. By the end, Manolis was almost shouting the verses, "*Anathema to! kai to gaitani! . . .*"

Manolis, Mitsos, and I banged our glasses together and drank to each other's health. Everyone started talking and joking around again, in higher spirits than before.

I waited a few minutes and then quietly launched into one of the more popular *kontylies*. Manolis, distracted from the conversation, looked over at me with a buzzing smile, and in Cretan dialect pretended to admonish me, "You're trying to get me going again, aren't you?" Grinning downward, slightly rocking his head back and forth with the rhythm, his eyes closed, he soon came out with a new *mantinada*, singing it loud enough to get everyone else's attention too. It was about people having a good time together, and it subtly alluded to Mitsos's presence in a way that celebrated the fact that he was there with us and criticized that he wasn't there more often.

The mood continued picking up. Eirini knew where this was going and asked Manolis, "Should I call Antonis?" "I'll call him," Manolis replied. "You call Bigshot's kid," referring to Eirini's oldest brother's son. Eirini called cousin Alekos and then gave the phone to Manolis to call Antonis. Maria must have answered because I heard Manolis pick on her a little before asking her to get Antonis on the phone. After a short pause, Manolis, in Cretan dialect, ordered: "Listen!" and held up the phone so Antonis could hear the mandolin and the general raucous. The only other thing I heard Manolis say was, "Yes, at home."

Alekos came in with a bottle of his father's homemade wine, but Manolis promptly informed him that tonight we'd only be drinking *his* wine. Antonis had picked up some roasted chicken from a take-out joint on his way over. Penny got out some more small plates. Armed with a piece of chicken, cousin Vassilis's sausage, and a glass of Manolis's wine, everyone was sitting around the table talking and kidding around.

I started in with more *kontylies* on the mandolin. It wasn't long before the *mantinada* singing picked up again. Manolis and Antonis were both skilled mantinada improvisers, so the opportunity was ripe for some high-quality verse dueling.

Customarily after someone sings out the first half of the rhyming couplet, everyone else repeats it, in song. Then the second half is revealed. During the repetitions, Uncle Mitsos—true to his role as the youngest brother and family clown—kept cracking everybody up by changing the order of the words, intentionally messing up the iambic pentameter as well as the anticipation of the forthcoming rhyme.

Everyone's spirits continued to rise. Manolis and Antonis seemed to be getting faster and more elaborately creative in their responses to each other's *mantinades*. There were times I had a hard time keeping up the music because I was so astonished by their skillful improvisation, the likes of which I'd never before witnessed. It was exactly the kind of verse dueling that I'd read about so many times before but had never actually experienced. I kept thinking to myself, "I can't believe it . . . those accounts I read were *not* exaggerations. It really *can* happen like this!" Each might take a word or a phrase from the other's previous text and use it as a point of departure to challenge whatever had just been said. Or one might continue a metaphor or the imagery used by the other in a way that pushed the dialogue in a new direction, while simultaneously implying that the new direction was necessary because the other was going in a less significant direction, or had missed the real point of the previous verse.

Somehow I managed to keep the mandolin going. And I made sure to change up which mode I was playing in when I sensed there was a pause in the singing that called for some additional nonverbal oomph to sustain Manolis's or Antonis's improvisational velocity, or whenever I thought that a temporary climax in the thrusts and parries of the verse duel had been achieved, and a slight redirection of mood was called for to sustain interest.

Perhaps the highest point in the evening came when Manolis gradually nudged the flow of a duel's subject matter into the area of life and death. Soon his *mantinades* were referring to "the dead" and there was little question that everyone's mind was turning to the recent passing of Penny's (and Alekos's) grandfather (the father of Eirini, Mitsos, and Antonis). Eventually Manolis delivered an improvisational blow with a poignant *mantinada* which, still using metaphor, nevertheless expressed unequivocally how much he—a man whose own father was killed in the Second World War—loved his father-in-law like the father he never had.

Everyone burst into tears.

I stopped playing. There was crying and more wine drinking. Manolis, much quieter now, proceeded to tell a story illustrating "the grandfather's" peculiar wisdom that the rest of them had supposedly never picked up on. Then Antonis and Manolis got into a debate about what had really made the "grandfather" such a great man, and then they competed over who'd been the closest to him, and who'd understood him the best.

Everyone's spirits began to lighten. Manolis finally reminded us all that, "Life is for the living."

Eirini went into the kitchen and came back out with some more sausage, bread, and cheese. I put the mandolin in its case and put on a cassette of a famous Cretan singer of Manolis's generation. More cigarettes were lit. More discussions followed.

Alekos turned to me and declared with his usual masculine affect, now tempered by half-drunken sentimentality: "You're not American. You're a Kritikaros [their family's last name—on both Manolis's and Eirini's sides]!"

There were no words that I ever wanted to hear more.

But they were coming from Penny's cousin who I'd come to understand was one of those people who, like his father Bigshot, went around thinking he was special just because of the aristocratic renown of his family name, historically speaking.

I lifted my eyebrows and slowly tilted my head upward, a local equivalent of nodding "no."

Alekos insisted. "Yes, you're a *Kritikaros*! You're a *real* Kritikaros."

I struggled to find a way to respond, hoping to make a point. I wish I'd thought of responding with an old well-known *mantinada*, most famously sung in recent times by one of *Alekos's* favorite professional musicians:

Ο άντρας κάνει τη γενιά και όχι η γενιά τον άντρα,
σαν είναι ο τράγος δυνατός δεν τόνε στένει μάντρα.[1]

The man makes the family [in the larger kinship sense], not the family
   the man,
When the goat is strong, no pen holds him.

In the background, I could hear a different *mantinada* being sung on the cassette:

Η κάθε βιόλα στο μπαξέ έχει την ομορφιά τση,
Μ' απής την κόψεις χάνεται και αυτή και η μυρωδιά τση.[2]

Each flower in the garden has its own beauty
but when you pluck it [literally: cut it], both it and its aroma are lost.

As I struggled to find the right words to make a coherent retort to Alekos, I noticed Manolis raising his eyebrows. At first I thought he too was disagreeing with Alekos's comment, and I was dying to hear what he had to say. But then he burst out with a new *mantinada*, challenging the one that just played on the cassette:

Η βιόλα πού 'ναι στο βουνό με του μπαξέ δε μοιάζει,
για δεν την κόβει άνθρωπος και μένει η μυρωδιά τζη.

The flower on the mountain doesn't resemble that of the garden,
for no human plucks it and its aroma lasts.

Drawing on the conventional aesthetic code of his high-mountain Rethemniot heritage—which associates the highlands (and their shepherds) with strength and heroism and the lowlands (and their gardeners and agriculturalists) with weakness and corruption—Manolis invoked the mountain as a foil for the garden.[3] The recorded *mantinada* suggested that women are docile (waiting in the garden to be plucked) and lose their attractiveness once they marry or have sex—once they're "plucked." Giving the word *pluck* broader connotations and reversing the usual motif wherein men praise themselves for their plucks, Manolis's *mantinada* implied that the ideal woman is strong and independent—no one plucks her.

At this, the cassette player was promptly shut off, and I picked up the mandolin again. Manolis launched into one of his bursts of solo improvisation, coming out with one *mantinada* after another:

Τσι βιόλες δεν τσι κόβω εγώ, στη φύση τους να ζούνε,
στον κόσμο αυτό τον άχρωμο άρωμα να σκορπούνε.

I don't pick the flowers, let them live in their natural state,
to spread their scent in this colorless world.

Η βιόλα πού 'ναι στο μπαξέ, ο άνθρωπος την κάνει,
λιπάσματα και κοπριά συνέχεια της βάνει.

Humankind grows the flower in the garden,
constantly giving it fertilizers and manure.

I could see Antonis was enjoying Manolis's masterful use of metaphors but was also having difficulty finding his groove so he could join in and respond. Manolis kept going on his own as if there was no one else there to respond anyway:

Μα η βιόλα πού 'ναι στο βουνό ζεί μεσ' στο φυσικό τζη,
το άρωμα απού σκορπά είναι μόνο δικό τζη.

But the flower that's on the mountain lives in its natural habitat,
the aroma it spreads is all its own.

Then came one more without any obvious metaphors:

Βλέπω τη φύση και απορώ οι ανθρώποι πως μπορούνε,
να την παραβιάζονται, να τη λεηλατούνε.

I see nature and I wonder how people can
violate it and pillage it.

Taken aback, Antonis interrupted him—and *not* in verse as he
normally "should" have—"What, are you an *ecologist* now?" Though
accustomed to hearing Manolis speak about environmental issues
at the table, Antonis was caught completely off guard by this kind
of talk in a *mantinada*.

I was thrilled with Manolis's gradual movement from *mantinades*
that were "obviously" about women to one that was "obviously" a
comment on people's treatment of nature.

Since the *mantinades* leading up to the last one were also open
to ecological interpretations, in hindsight it was unclear whether
Manolis intended *any* of them to be about women or if he was
talking about the environment all along. Or, if he was doing both
simultaneously, and positing connections between the exploitation
of women and the exploitation of *mother* earth.

Manolis was revolutionizing the significance of invoking nature in
the *mantinada*. By playing with conventional Cretan codes for interpreting nature metaphors in his own *mantinades*, he was suggesting
a new way to interpret nature metaphors in *mantinades* in general.
In doing so, he implicitly remobilized for environmentalist purposes
a slew of *mantinades* by other Cretans for whom the environment
might have been the last thing on their minds. For example, one
could interpret the following *mantinada* as dealing with someone
unhappy about who they're with, or as a statement about the effects
of environmental degradation on other species:

Εγώ 'μαι κείνο το πουλί το παραπονεμένο,
Που χτίζει τη φωλίτσα του σε δέντρο μαραμένο.[4]

I'm that bird, the sorrowful one,
which builds its little nest in a withered tree.

Or this one either as a warning to a woman about her charms or love
life, or as a call for better environmental stewardship:

Αρχίζουν και μαραίνονται, στον κήπο σου οι βιόλες,
Άλλαξ' αν θες τον κηπουρό, πριν ξεραθούνε όλες.[5]

The flowers in your garden are starting to wither,
If you want, change gardeners before they all dry up.

Or this one as Cretan-dancing advice, or as a warning about modern
humanity's carbon "footprint":

Μην τη βαροπατείς τη γης, γιατί πονεί το χώμα,
Μα δε μπορεί να σου το πει γιατί δεν έχει στόμα.[6]

Don't stomp hard on the earth because the soil feels pain,
But it can't tell you so because it doesn't have a mouth.

The *mantinada* Manolis came to consider his favorite brought
together threads of his other *mantinades* with another beloved nature
metaphor: the Cretan wild goat, the *agrimi*—an animal often referred
to in modern literature by Cretan authors, a common figure of speech
in centuries-old Cretan folksongs that continue to be widely sung,
and nowadays *an endangered species*:

Αγρίμι, θέ μου, κάνε με, και στο τζουγκρί απάνω,
χορό να σέρνω τση καρδιάς ίσαμε να ποθάνω.

My god, turn me into a wild goat, and so on a ledge
I can lead a dance of the heart until I die.

We played and sang a little more, but the wine and the excitement
exhausted our creativity. We put on the cassette again and pushed
the table to one side of the room so we could do the traditional
dances that go with this music. In about another hour or so, we
males were wiped out, not to mention inebriated, so things began
to wind down. Penny and Eirini brought us out a big pot of herbal
tea made from cinnamon, cloves, and locally gathered chamomile,
thyme, savory, mint, and sage to help us come back down again.
Mitsos napped on the couch as the rest of us drank the tea and
continued talking. It was probably about 3 a.m. when Penny and I
walked back to our apartment to hit the sack.

All the next day while I was standing in the classroom teaching, I felt like I was floating on a cloud. Never before had I experienced such communal high spirits or collectively creative ecstasy. The emotional buzz lasted for days.

※ ※ ※

Everyone has left our house. Sofia and I are loading the dishwasher and she tells me that Catherine asked her more than once during the evening if we'd been planning all along to invite everyone over—which, of course, we hadn't. I take it that Catherine was surprised or impressed by our spur-of-the-moment efforts. Given how often Sofia and I did things like this back in Ohio, and having had so many opportunities to observe, learn from, and be inspired by truly masterful hosts of impromptu gatherings, it didn't cross my mind that we were doing anything particularly noteworthy. I'm reminded that living here we rarely experience this kind of impromptu visit and think I understand why it made an impression on Catherine.

I wonder how others without the benefit of experiences like ours—not to mention the years of learning as much as we could about food and cooking—might learn to do things like this. I remember how modestly Sofia and I started out, entertaining just a few people at a time, taking whatever we happened to know and gradually expanding from there. Perhaps as much as anything else, this prepared us for nights like tonight.

This, I suppose, and my stubborn conviction that such a practice is more valuable than ever in a world of precisely timed visits, mailed invitations, and thank-you cards.

13

One Dream Ends, Another Begins

I'm lying on the couch. Thoughts in my brain are whizzing around incoherently toward a power nap. I'm about to go completely under when my breathing becomes louder and irregular and makes enough noise to startle me back into lucidity.

I remember a Cretan *mantinada*:

Όταν κοιμάτ' ο δυστυχής να τον ξυπνάς δεν πρέπει,
Μην του ξορίζεις τη χαρά που στ' όνειρό του βλέπει.[1]

When the unhappy man is sleeping you shouldn't wake him up,
Don't send away the joy he sees in his dream.

It was a late-August midafternoon when I left my hotel room, went down the elevator, and entered the street. After living in Irakleio for more than two years, the wider streets and taller buildings of Athens might as well have been those of Montreal or Chicago. For the most part I found the scale of Irakleio's hustle and bustle comfortable and welcoming, but I instinctively shifted back into big-city mode as I walked several blocks to a Goody's, the major Greek hamburger chain that, in Crete, I'd never condescended to set foot in. I wanted a quick bite to eat, something fast, inexpensive, and easy to find. In a couple more days I'd have my plane ticket for the rest of my journey back to the United States, curse the hour.

As someone who worked at McDonald's in high school and was now fluent in Greek, I shouldn't have found it *more* difficult to order a hamburger in Greek at Goody's than thin-sliced *pasetes* from Manolis the butcher, strained yogurt from Kyria Vangelio, or a medium-sweet iced coffee with milk from a coffee bar.

"Χάμ-μπουρ-γκερ," I syllabified to myself as I waited in line staring at the menu board. "Should I suppress my Cretan accent when I order?" I deliberated, *"Ham-bur-ger or ham-bur-jer?"*

When I got back to my hotel room, I wolfed down the burgers followed by an unfortunately milkless, room-temperature *frape* from a single-serving non-Nescafé-brand packet that I bought from the kiosk on the corner. I pushed play on my walkman and let my brain sink into an ocean of tunes played by the Cretan masters. I sat up in bed, grabbed my pen and pad, and came out with some new rhymes:

Θα φύγω, βιόλα, απ' τον μπαξέ, ξέσπασε καταιγίδα,
κι ο μισεμός μου σού 'μεινε μια τελευταία ελπίδα.

I will leave the garden, my flower, a storm has broken,
and my departure remains for you one last hope.

Βαστώ την Κρήτη μέσα μου, κιαν φύγει το κορμί μου,
όσο μακριά κιανέ πετώ, θα πάρω αυτή μαζί μου.

I hold Crete within me, and even if my body leaves,
however far away I might fly, I'll take her with me.

Then I lay down and brooded over the fact that all my efforts to come and live in Crete had been in vain.

It was only a little more than two years earlier that I'd migrated to Crete from the United States, but it felt like half a lifetime.

Perhaps it was because I'd become accustomed to inhabiting a different language. Or, maybe it was because it felt like I'd experienced much more life in the last two years than I ever had in the United States over a similar stretch of time. I'd learned how to find and rent an apartment through networking and word-of-mouth. I'd figured out how to hold down teaching jobs without legal authorization to work. I'd picked up techniques for negotiating my wages with clever school owners. I'd built up a regular sideline of teaching English and SAT and GRE preparation out of our apartment. I'd witnessed the passing of Penny's grandfather, and joined Penny's mother at the cemetery when she exhumed and washed with wine the bones of the aunt who'd raised her. I'd attended numerous weddings and baptisms of family and friends. I'd stayed in the hospital one night with a nasty virus. I'd written essays in Greek and *mantinades* that were published by a local paper. I'd played Cretan tunes on my mandolin live on the radio. I'd befriended the well-known head cantor at St. Minas and sometimes slipped into church services just to hear him chanting. For Easter, two years in a row, I'd sat through hours of Holy Week liturgies while following the texts along word-for-word. I'd read or reread every one of Kazantzakis's novels in Greek, and I'd taught his *Spiritual Exercises* in one of my classes. I'd witnessed a major national election and was there for the passing of such larger-than-life figures as politician Andreas Papandreou and actress Aliki Vougiouklaki. I'd gotten into arguments with politically active locals over the pros and cons of capitalism and communism. I'd met nationally famous musicians Domna Samiou and Loudovikos of Anoyeia. I'd learned how to tie a vineyard and harvest grapes. I'd started playing the card game *prefa*. I'd written a small book in Greek with my own *mantinades*. I'd started smoking more regularly than in Chicago, and had changed my brand from Camel to Karelia Lights to Marlboro to Assos sketos. My mannerisms, my hairstyle, and my style of clothing had all changed, too. I'd gone through the entire wedding process—from arguments about which furniture to get for our apartment to choosing the right church, from making difficult decisions about the list of invitees to hosting my parents and brother for a week. At the wedding itself, I'd not only danced (Cretan dances, of course), but also sat in for a while on the mandolin with the professional musicians, singing my own *mantinades*.

Uncle Antonis called me "the phenomenon" because he couldn't believe that I'd taken up not only the language, but also Cretan mandolin, the *mantinada*, Cretan dances, and certain patterns of thinking and expression. I often chalked up the extent of people's impressions of me to enthusiastic exaggeration. But there was one time when I was sitting in the office of a local newspaper with the editor and he showed a draft of some verses I'd written to some other Cretan who happened to come into the office. The editor asked him if he knew who wrote them without letting on that it was me. The guy said, "An *old*-time Cretan." The editor told him that it was actually written by an American, which only provoked disbelief. As the editor insisted it was true, the guy actually got angry because he thought it was some kind of a mean joke. This was the same editor who wrote a short piece about me after attending Penny's and my wedding, titling his column in the paper that day, "The 'Cretan.'"

I'd eagerly adopted many, but not all, Cretan norms. I still held onto many aspects of my earlier American self. I consciously viewed my beliefs and my identity as matters of ongoing inquiry and debate. When I wrote personal essays for the newspaper, I usually tried coming to terms with my New York past and my Cretan present in relation to one another, judiciously bringing the significance of both places into my narratives.

When people visited Manolis and Eirini's house, they'd often ask, "How is it possible?" "How do you explain this?" I always thought the explanation was simple: Whenever I have a passion for something I dive in and work hard at it, and of all the things I'd ever had a passion for, this was the most powerful and complex.

But Manolis would always reply to them: "It's because in Crete he found himself."

As I looked out the hotel window, the streets of Athens made it seem like it was just another day of the week going by, but I felt sure the universe was in a holding pattern. I'd never been prepared to confront the mounting evidence that Penny and I were incapable of making our relationship work, no matter how much we wanted to make it work, and no matter how hard we tried to make it work. Not even in those fleeting moments when I should have realized that the evidence was incontrovertible, moments when the thought crossed my mind—but whose existence I refused to acknowledge to myself, let alone to anyone else, yet which Penny was able to discern—that I might be so afraid of breaking up because I'd lose the family and place to which I felt so attached. The only way out of this relationship was for it to be driven to a point of irreparable collapse.

I was just lucky that Manolis had the fortitude—in between his busy late-summer agricultural chores—not only to do everything his daughter depended on him for in a time of such emotional crisis, but to take every necessary precaution to keep me from completely falling apart, to facilitate the fastest and least painful separation possible, and to help me to get safely and comfortably on my way back to New York from Irakleio (while serving as a witness to my departure to reassure Penny that I was really gone). After we shared a final smoke together at the airport, he handed me the rest of his pack, stood up, and squeezed my hand with tears in his eyes. He took three heavy steps, turned around, lifting his open hands, shaking his head, protesting, "Όχι έτσι!" ("Not like this!") Liar life had already deprived him of his father. Now it was taking away his only son. He turned and walked away, forever.

I sat on the bed of the hotel room in Athens in shock. I kept asking myself, "Were my seven years with Penny *really* over this time?" "How would I endure losing every connection to a family I so loved and who so loved me?" "How would I stand living again in a place where Greek isn't the language people speak, where there aren't words like *logos* and *pnevma* rolling off the tongues of the people around me at the same time that they're being typeset on the pages of everything from Plato to the New Testament and *The Last Temptation of Christ*? How would I bear living again in a place where *wine* usually means something that comes from a store, in a bottle?"

Living in Crete, I'd realized that I felt less afraid of dying and remained calmer around certain dangers than when I was living in the United States. But leaving Crete wasn't a matter of death or danger—I was losing the very context that was fueling my newfound courage.

I tried digging deep for strength, reminding myself of certain old-time *mantinades* that Manolis and I liked and sang together often:

Το να πονείς και να το λες, αυτός δεν είναι πόνος,
Αξία έχει να πονείς και να το ξέρεις μόνος.[2]

To feel pain and to say so, that isn't pain,
There's value in feeling pain and being the only one who knows it.

Χαίρομ' απού 'μαι κρητικός κι όπου σταθώ το λέω,
Με μαντινάδες τραγουδώ, με μαντινάδες κλαίω.[3]

I'm proud that I'm Cretan, and wherever I am I say so,
With *mantinades* I sing, with *mantinades* I weep.

Although I was leaving Crete, I comforted myself by vowing not to leave behind the virtues I'd learned there. Faced suddenly with severe geographic, cultural, and familial dislocation, I was no longer in a position to take into reciprocal consideration both my New York and Cretan selves. I vowed to remain thoroughly Cretan regardless of how I might be perceived by other people. If at some level I knew this was an impossible task, I also kept in mind that for Kazantzakis, the ultimate command—the ultimate *Cretan* command—was not, "Reach as far as you can," but rather, "Reach as far as you cannot!"[4]

I don't remember much about the flights back. I recall feeling even more depressed upon seeing the gray skies—the first I'd seen in months, and the first I'd seen during summer in years—as we landed in New York. I hadn't gotten up even once on the Rome-JFK flight, so when the time came to get up, my knees were so stiff that I had difficulty straightening my legs. I remember explaining to the customs officials why one of my two suitcases was filled with nothing but containers of dried wild herbs, and I got annoyed when I realized that the puritanical American airport didn't offer any place indoors to smoke.

From JFK I flew to Syracuse, where Leonidas was waiting to pick me up. He was still living up north. He'd finished his PhD and several postdocs after that, but no job had turned up for glass-science expert. He was living on the last leg of his savings, sending out résumés and taking dead-end calls from headhunters. I'd called him before leaving Irakleio, explained what was happening, and asked if I could stay with him for a while. I found it inconceivable that I'd go back to the United States and *not* stay with a Greek, and Leonidas was not only the only Greek friend I had still living in the United States, he was the best Greek friend I'd ever had there. He'd aged visibly since the last time I saw him, but not as much as I had in the past few weeks.

I was in no great hurry to visit my family—which is why I flew to Syracuse and had Leonidas pick me up—but when I woke up the next morning, I was seized by a strong desire to visit them. Leonidas, who was focusing all his energy on catering to my apparent emotional fragility, didn't make a single comment along the lines that I should have just flown from JFK to Albany and then have him come pick me up from my parents' house, saving him the extra trek to Syracuse. We just got in his car and headed south.

Following roads I'd driven countless times before, everything looked strange. There was green vegetation everywhere, and tall trees coming right up to the side of the road, even overhanging it. I felt like I'd drown in so much green. We passed road signs with the names of hamlets and route numbers that I used to know like any self-respecting northern New Yorkers from a family with three generations of DOTers, but now they seemed vaguely familiar at best. Sometimes I'd have to remind myself that we were actually passing through my old stomping grounds—some of the very places I'd mentioned in my essays in Crete and which I *thought* I was picturing in my mind's eye while I was writing about them. I thought to myself more than once that I never would've believed—if I hadn't experienced it myself—that a person could be so shocked by what should've been very familiar.

When we pulled into my parents' driveway, the house where I grew up, I saw my father outside grilling lunch on the gas grill. My heart sank.

There was something about Crete, and perhaps my own brain, that made ordinary things, people, and events in the everyday world seem larger than life. And there was always this contradiction—every joy was accompanied by a little sadness and every tragedy by a little hope; fun was taken seriously, serious matters with a dash of playfulness. For me, visiting home was yet another scene in the epic tragedy that my life had now become, albeit tinged with the joy that I'd get to see my parents for the first time in over a year. Yet, the sight of my father at the grill and the expression on both of my parents' faces looked to me like they signified the kind of *unmixed* joy-without-solemnity that I'd've expected to see if I was coming home from college for spring break. The spectacle of supermarket steaks being gas-grilled on the grassy lawn was clawing at the myriad memories I had of Manolis and me grilling *pasetes* over homemade charcoal on the terrace, drinking bitter Greek coffee, and talking about life over a smoke.

"Έτσι ψήνουνε στα κάρβουνα εδώ;" ("That's the way they cook on charcoal here?"), I thought to myself sarcastically. "Άντε, μην είσαι κακός . . ." ("Come on, don't be mean . . ."), I then reproached.

In between my cigarettes, Leonidas and I spent the weekend trying to unravel for my parents the rationale—from a Greek point of view—behind the divorce and my decision to come back to the United States. But what I remember most about the weekend was when I was sitting out back with Leonidas, and then my father—genuinely concerned for his son's welfare—came out and asked me if I "really needed those cigarettes." I don't know if I even responded to him. All I could think was, *"Αυτό σε νοιάζει τώρα;"* ("*That's* what matters to you right now?"). Penny had tried to get me to quit for years, and I'd made many failed attempts to do so. But in my current situation nothing could've been less important to me. Of course, part of me knew that from certain points of view in the United States, a cigarette—or an alcoholic beverage, or an atheist, or a communist—was as much cause for worry as Satan himself, but this only made the comment more aggravating.

Back up north, the autumn was a roller coaster of nothing-much-left-to-lose, devil-may-care freedom one moment and I-have-no-future misery the next. Within a month, I began to appreciate that I was finally free of the pressure I always felt to not behave in ways that might upset Penny. Truly free: I knew there was no chance of winning her back this time—not even a viable way to consider trying. But I couldn't pay any real attention to this feeling on the few occasions when it managed to poke its way through to my consciousness in the form of an actual realization, because I was far too overwhelmed by the trauma of what I'd lost, and by my determination to figure out what I could do about it.

Leonidas didn't have a roommate, so the second bedroom was mine. We put some foam chair cushions on the floor covered with a sheet for a bed. My father had given me a laptop computer left over from an old construction job that I could use for writing. I had my walkman and Cretan cassettes to beam me back to Irakleio whenever I wanted. I had a couple hundred bucks from some old savings bonds I'd cashed in. I had my credit card bill—for my flight back and shipping home my belongings—paid off by my parents. I had some cartons of the cheapest cigarettes I could find at an Akwesasne gas station. Leonidas was there to listen to me analyze the past and my current predicament. When things got really bad I'd do things like put out a cigarette on my arm or think about scratching myself with a knife. Being back near my undergraduate campus—in fact in the same apartment complex where Penny had lived, and with a view to the house where Penny and I used to visit Leonidas that first summer while he was house-sitting—I was also surrounded by material reminders of my pre-Cretan past. My old math department kindly offered me an opportunity, which I declined, to finish my PhD.

There I was again, after all those years, back to eating the fifteen or twenty main dishes that Leonidas usually cooked almost always the same way. Our first night back from my parents', Leonidas suggested we open a bottle of red wine with dinner. I agreed, of course, though after years and gallons of Manolis's homemade nectar, all I could think was, "How can we call *this* wine? Even the poorest Cretan villager has access to better wine than this!" Still, I figured, some wine was better than no wine. Considering we were both unemployed, I had no money, and we weren't in Crete, I knew how fortunate I was to have even that.

I was generally miserable, but one day when I walked to campus to meet Leonidas, there was a moment when I was overwhelmed by the sheer beauty of the surroundings—pure blue sky, the sun lighting up the rustling leaves that were beginning to show autumn colors. My misery was no match for it and for a short moment I felt good. As soon as I realized that I'd spontaneously felt good, I realized that I hadn't completely died on the inside, and that some part of me yearned for happiness, regardless of my conscious judgment of the circumstances.

Leonidas introduced me to his newest posse of graduate students and postdocs, mostly northern Europeans. Leonidas and I effectively appointed ourselves to be this Euro-gang's hot-blooded Mediterranean representatives, wielding—or, I hope in retrospect, *feigning* to wield—our own reverse elitism toward the ostensibly elitist and cold-blooded Continental northerners. On weekdays, Leonidas and I usually woke up, took our showers, packed up tomato-and-feta salads, and met the gang on campus for lunch. Wearing my everyday outfits from Crete—black shirts, black pants or blue jeans, a black sports jacket, and black leather shoes—I always looked overdressed.

After a couple months, I went back to wearing T-shirts. Then I shaved my mustache. Part of me was sad to see these outward signs of my Cretan self go, but I also told myself that these were, in the end, superficial things, and that I just needed to remain determined not to let local norms peer-pressure me into abandoning the customary *virtues* I came to value highly in Crete, and which I took to be the hallmarks of Cretan civilization at its best.

At first it wasn't quite as difficult as I'd anticipated. Staying with Leonidas my first five months back, he and I often reinforced for one another our convictions about hospitality being the highest aspiration of quintessential Greeks and true Cretans. The fact that he was allowing me—homeless, jobless, and penniless—to crash at his apartment even though his own savings had almost run out was in itself a remarkable instance of such hospitality. And, as if that weren't enough, between what little money he had in the bank and my eventual small contributions in the form of food stamps, we managed to have friends over for drinks, snacks, desserts, and sometimes entire dinners.

Every week, Leonidas would go online to request videos of various artsy films from a nearby university. I'd go with him to pick them up. He'd e-mail his gang of friends announcing the week's picks and invite them to stop by Friday evening for coffee, tea, or drinks, desserts or snacks, and one or two films. Conventionally, this meant that I—a longtime friend and fellow "Greek" who was living in his apartment—would be temporarily considered more host than guest, and I'd help out with making the coffee. On such occasions, I invariably paid more attention to the status of everyone's glasses, cups, and plates than to the films or conversations. Like an all-too-attentive restaurant server, the moment I saw something was empty I rushed over to refill and to offer something else, proud to show off to those northerners how attentively hospitable we Greeks were.

Leonidas's food-shopping rituals were as elaborate and critically minded as ever. He made a weekly trip to the next town north for delicious loaves of bread from a small bakery. Once, we were shopping for eggs at the supermarket in the next town and he noticed that the sale sign on a dozen eggs advertised a price that was two cents lower than what came up on the register. He argued with the cashier and then with the manager, demanding that they either change the price in the register or change the sign. The manager, visibly annoyed, insisted that Leonidas just take two pennies (which the manager pulled out of his own pocket), and didn't seem to understand that his foreign-accented customer was trying to fight the man, not for the money. Leonidas finally gave up, took the two pennies on principle, and we left. Watching the argument unfold, I couldn't decide whether Leonidas was courageous for keeping up the fight against corporate dishonesty or if he was dishonoring himself as a Greek for making a fuss over small change in public.

To my delight—and to Leonidas's dismay, since he was usually my ride—the gang enjoyed frequenting the local bars. On a Friday night,

I was sitting in a crowded bar with Fritz, Alain, and Leonidas, who was frowning and covering his ears because of the loud music. The rest of the gang showed up, accompanied by the moody mechanical engineering grad student from Japan I'd met the week before. Already buzzing a little, I jumped up and invited her down to the lower level where all the dancing was. Though I always danced Cretan and Greek dances in Greece, I never used to dance in the United States, especially in public. But now living the nightlife without many inhibitions, I never gave it a second thought. Not even when I was dancing a bizarre hybrid of American, Greek, and Cretan moves, or smashing an empty beer bottle on the floor, which, at any other time of my life, would've been paralyzingly embarrassing. Emiko and I must have danced for over two hours. I told Leonidas he could go home and that I'd find some other way back. The special on pitchers of Canadian beer helped keep me going and as I was dancing I thought to myself, "This isn't wine and we aren't dancing *pentozalis*, but it's probably the next best thing, considering where I am."

Before closing time, I saw the wiry monsieur Alain out of the corner of my eye going at a stocky local kid who looked like he and his friends were up to no good. I was confident that Alain wasn't the type to *start* such trouble. Uncharacteristically, and without thinking, I leapt between them. As I tried keeping them apart, I yelled to Alain—who was in the United States on a student visa—not to risk getting into a big hassle over a couple dumb kids. As things were on the brink of getting out of hand, the bouncers arrived and everyone involved was escorted outside.

There'd indeed been mischief because a number of people, including Emiko, discovered their keys had been stolen. Emiko didn't think she could get into the house she was renting without them, and her roommate was in Europe, so I invited her back to Leonidas's apartment for the night, and told her we could deal with the problem in the morning. Naturally, she was apprehensive. But she eventually took comfort in knowing that Leonidas was a friend of colleagues she trusted. We had to walk back to Leonidas's since her car keys were gone, too, but that gave us a better chance to talk than when we were in the bar.

We explained to Leonidas what happened, and I gave Emiko my "bed" and said I could sleep on the other floor cushions in the living room. Leonidas and I continued to chat in the living room. I must've been going on like a fisherman who just caught the big one because Leonidas seemed very anxious and kept warning me that I'd better *stay* in the living room.

The next morning Leonidas made breakfast for everyone and then drove Emiko and me all around town. We stopped at the bar to check the lost-and-found. We stopped at the police station. No luck. We went to the car dealership and began the process of getting new keys for Emiko's car. We went to the house Emiko was renting and figured out a way in through the Bilco doors to the basement, up a stepladder, and through a hole in the floor. There must have been issues between her, the absentee roommate, and their landlord, because she didn't want to tell the landlord about the key so she could get a new one. As the day went by, the quiet and melancholic Emiko began to show her surprise that two virtual strangers were spending so much time and effort helping her out. Leonidas was trying to live up to his Greek virtues. I was too, but I also knew that it might help me score some points. It must have worked because soon my affair with Emiko began.

For the rest of the autumn, I spent my days at Leonidas's and my nights at Emiko's. Determined that I'd return to Greece eventually, I used the days to work on a plan. Professor Vlastos made some phone calls to help my chances of getting a math-teaching job in Athens, but nothing panned out in the short run. My humanities friends from the University of Chicago—now back in Greece—recommended that I go for a PhD in Modern Greek Studies. As reluctant as I was to relive the lopsided life of graduate school, it wasn't an idea I could easily dismiss. Such a degree would be a great stepping-stone for moving back to Greece on my own, and if I got stuck in the United States, at least I'd be living and working within a world of Modern Greek. I used interlibrary loan (I was allowed to as an alumnus) to get my hands on books by scholars in the field. The books spoke much more directly to my own experiences with reading, writing, and aesthetics in Greece than I ever imagined any book could, and I caught my first real glimpses of an interdisciplinary world of critical and cultural theory that I didn't even know existed. I wrote a statement of intent outlining a research project about Crete and applied to the Modern Greek program at Ohio State.

Meanwhile, I was determined to do whatever it took to ensure the continuation of my time up north with Emiko. Leonidas was almost out of money, so I went on welfare and applied for adjunct teaching jobs in the local universities and substitute-teaching jobs at the local schools. I got a few gigs substitute teaching—annoying because the calls would come in only an hour or two after I'd gone to sleep—but it gave Leonidas and me a few more much-needed dollars.

Emiko was working in mechanical engineering but seemed to care more about environmental issues, and I wondered what it might be like if we stayed together for the long term. She might find an engineering-related job focused on helping the environment while I taught part-time and wrote—much as I'd been doing in Irakleio. Emiko's apparent antisocial demeanor bothered me, but I convinced myself that her love of nature and concern for the environment sort of made up for it. I was in awe of her determination to live modestly—even by graduate-student-salary standards—and of the lengths she went to in order to minimize her individual impact on the environment. Before I met her, it had never crossed my mind to recycle the cardboard tube from toilet paper, or a box from spaghetti after removing the plastic film from its little window. Truth be told, when I thought about how many plastic bottles of spring water a family in Irakleio might go through in a week without any place to recycle them—not to mention all the large-scale industrial and fossil-fuel pollution going on in the world—I wondered if it was more than a little naive to think these kinds of things mattered. In time, though, I realized that, if nothing else, it mattered in terms of practicing vigilance about the potential environmental consequences of the ways we choose to live our lives in a world that mostly encourages us not to.

Still, there were plenty of reasons why I should've been more skeptical about our being together, not least of which was the fact that Emiko was constantly declaring that she was as unsure about wanting a future with me in it as I was about my future in general. After spending winter break back home, she concluded that we should break up.

A few nights later, I heard strange cracking noises in the distance, and tossed and turned half asleep, barely conscious that I was feeling colder and colder under the blanket of my makeshift bed. Such was life in the far north, and while I'd have given anything to be back in the Mediterranean, I'd already begun to reassimilate to winter weather. When I fully awoke that morning, I realized we'd lost power and heat during the night. I pulled back the curtain and saw thick blankets of ice draped over everything, and realized that the sounds I heard during the night were tree branches snapping under the weight. I called across the hall to Leonidas and told him to look outside. We weren't all that concerned until Leonidas turned on his battery-powered radio and discovered that there were almost no stations on the air. He finally got North Country Public Radio which, according to whoever was speaking, was relying on a generator and looking for volunteers to get fuel over to them to keep it going. This was not like any freezing rain I'd ever experienced before.

My immediate thought was that we get out of there as soon as possible and avoid the many inconveniences that seemed headed our way. I told Leonidas that we could drive down to my parents' house for a few days, but he ignored me. He had no intentions of driving with all that ice. "I'll drive your car if you want," I implored. "Better to take all day getting there than be stuck here," I urged. "Come on . . . the longer we wait the worse it'll be, we'll just drive really really slow," I begged. Leonidas didn't budge.

Once I resigned myself to the fact that we weren't going anywhere, we went to the kitchen and tried to figure out what to do about food. We tried unsuccessfully to cook eggs in a fondue pot over a small flame. Leonidas, not much concerned with anything but feeling cold, put on some coats and got back into bed with some extra blankets. I ignored all the warnings on the radio and walked downtown to see what was happening, with plans to buy snacks and other supplies to get us through a day without heat or electricity.

Though it was less than a mile to get downtown it took me forever. Apart from there being ice on everything, fallen branches and fallen wires were scattered all over the ground. As I walked, I kept checking all around to make sure I wasn't about to walk under something that could fall on me. I went into Stewart's. It was rather dark, the shelves were half empty, and customers were everywhere. I picked up some bags of potato chips and a few other things, and got into the long line to pay—cash only, of course.

I got back to the apartment and Leonidas filled me in on everything he'd learned from the radio. The storm was causing problems as far away as Montreal, although the worst of it was in our vicinity. The National Guard was coming in. Shelters were being set up on campus and there were calls for volunteers. The radio station was rationing its generator fuel, coming on the air only periodically with updates.

Then it dawned on me that Emiko's cordless phone wouldn't work with the power out. I picked up the phone and dialed her at her new apartment across town. Nothing. Emiko was a loner, and as far as I knew, what few acquaintances she did have were probably not even back from winter break, and even if they were, I doubted they'd think about checking on her. I decided I'd walk across town again to her apartment, and bring her one of Leonidas's extra telephones. Leonidas, trying to remain the voice of reason, insisted that I not go. It wasn't so much the dangerous weather, but the fact that I'd probably end up back with Emiko, and again be distracted from getting my future into some kind of order. As I was going out the door, he told me that it was *his* phone and that I didn't have permission to take it. "Try and stop me!" I told him, and headed down the foyer stairway.

Sure enough, Emiko and I got back together again that very afternoon. The power came back on in her little apartment, and as far as I could tell it was the *only* place that had power for miles in every direction. While much of the rest of town began migrating to the campus shelter, I just stayed with Emiko.

After a few days, the supermarket near Leonidas's apartment—still without power—was allowing the public in to buy food, having employees with flashlights accompany customers, and accepting only cash. Leonidas, Emiko, and I spent the whole afternoon walking there, shopping, and walking back. Leonidas stayed for dinner, and I made a version of Greek-style green-bean stew using frozen green beans and canned tomato paste. It hit the spot. It was one of the only Greek meals I'd cooked since leaving Crete, and—in the midst of a shivering State of Emergency—it was indeed comfort food. Most of the town was without power. Hoards of people were eating at the shelter, where other people I knew from campus were volunteering and pitching in as a matter of civic duty. (I know this because we walked over one day to check it out.) I felt a little guilty that we were sitting in a warm apartment, enjoying a hot home-cooked meal. But I also felt like the electricity in Emiko's apartment—of all places!—was a gift from the gods, perhaps a way of apologizing for sending an ice storm my way the very first winter I'd come back to the cold north from my Mediterranean paradise.

After the ice storm, I moved into Emiko's apartment and imagined that she and I might stay together. I broke down and bought a pair of black, insulated work boots, my first work boots since I was an undergrad. I walked around the icy town applying for jobs at places like the hardware store, the drug store, and the gas station mini-mart across from the apartment. Welfare regulations required me to pay back my food stamps with volunteer work, so I went up to the campus hoping to find something I could volunteer to do there. I lucked out and was also offered a part-time job tutoring and teaching for state- and federally funded programs for college students belonging to various marginalized ethnic and socioeconomic groups. They'd been looking for someone who could do exactly the kinds of things I was well prepared for: tutoring calculus, differential equations, and statistics, as well as GRE preparation, and assisting students with preparing applications for graduate school in the sciences. With the new job, I soon got off welfare and had a steady paycheck to cover my share of the food and gas, if not the rent and other old debts.

Emiko liked to eat, and, like me, didn't like prefab foods from supermarkets. She cooked a lot of stir-fries, usually with lots of vegetables, to go on pasta. Sometimes she used a lot of chili peppers, making dishes so spicy that I'd feel a tingle all down my body followed by a floating sensation. She also used ingredients that were completely new to me, like coconut milk and curry paste. She seemed mostly to enjoy Mediterranean and various Asian—though not Japanese—flavors. When she needed Asian ingredients we'd get up early Saturday morning to buy directly from the tractor-trailer that supplied one of the local Chinese restaurants.

Soon, Leonidas received a job offer downstate and prepared to move. I received a phone call from Ohio. Not only was I accepted by the program, I had a great shot at being awarded a fellowship for the first year and wouldn't even need to teach for my pittance. Who would have imagined that there were graduate programs able and willing to take chances on such nontraditional students like me? (I *was* officially a mathematician, after all, and had literally *no* formal training in anything related to Greece or literature.) Within the hour, all uncertainty and ambivalence about my short-term future evaporated. Clarity, direction, organization, and purpose came rushing back to my mind for the first time since I'd left Irakleio. I went to the store and bought ingredients to make an approximation of Greek gyros. I took the Pet Shop Boys CD out of the stereo and put on Cretan music. I made the gyros, wrapped them in aluminum foil, and headed up to the campus to find Emiko for lunch and tell her my news.

Neither of us was prepared to break up, but I made it clear that in six months I'd be going to Ohio and that our long-term future together looked uncertain at best. If we broke up right then, my plan was to go downstate with Leonidas and hang out with him until the fall. Otherwise, I'd stay with Emiko and keep working until I moved to Ohio. Either way, I'd spend much of my free time studying literary theory, reading more Greek literature, and—why not?—start in again on learning ancient Greek. I preferred to stay with Emiko, but having indicated to her my uncertainty about our future, I was also prepared to leave. I was moved, then, when upon returning from a day trip with Leonidas to Montreal, I discovered Emiko had spent the afternoon rearranging the furniture in her little apartment, turning part of the bedroom space into a study area just for me.

After Leonidas settled into his new digs and spring arrived, Emiko and I decided to drive down to Binghamton for a weekend visit. While we were there, we went to the huge bookstore. Leonidas went to check out the Greek cookbooks, not expecting to find anything but the usual touristy, feebly Americanized, recipe collections. I, seeking to do my duty as a proper guardian of Greekness abroad, followed him and was prepared to gawk and criticize right along with him. We discovered a book called *The Food and Wine of Greece* by Diane Kochilas. Its choice of dishes was surprisingly familiar and many of the recipes appeared relatively accurate to our own experiences with food in Greece. We then proceeded to subject the book to one of our more specific litmus tests: Did the baklava recipe say to sprinkle water on top so the phyllo won't curl when it bakes? It did!

Staying with Emiko, who wasn't nearly as fussy about her food as Leonidas was, I'd been cooking somewhat regularly for the first time since Chicago. So Leonidas bought a Kochilas cookbook for me, calling it an early birthday present. Back at his apartment, the three of us sat reading on the old seat cushions on the floor. While Emiko looked through some fashion magazines, Leonidas and I began reading our respective copies of Kochilas. Seeing the names of different recipes brought back memories of various foods from Crete that I hadn't thought about in many months. I grabbed a pencil and made lists on the blank pages, trying to remember off the top of my head every dish that I ever saw in Crete. I began recalling the Greek names of fruits, greens, and other ingredients, getting a little rush every time I remembered a culinary word that I hadn't heard or thought about for a while. I filled with wonder as I recalled ingredients in Greek whose names in English I didn't even know.

After we returned back north to Emiko's, I felt energized by a potent desire to make and eat more of the dishes I remembered from Crete.

As I cooked, I began to relish every step of the process. Gestures felt saturated with meaning, transporting me back to the island. Like Eirini, I'd hold the onion in one hand and a small knife in the other as I cut it directly into the pot, instead of chopping it on a cutting board. Also like Eirini, I'd grate tomatoes on a box grater for stews. In Chicago, I'd used lemon juice from a plastic lemon, but now I'd squeeze fresh lemons by hand. Cooking was bringing out the Crete within me and giving it wings to soar in North America.

A handful of simple utensils, some pots and pans, and the right ingredients in the refrigerator transformed the antiquated kitchenette in Emiko's apartment into the kitchen of an old Cretan mountain villager. In fact the entire complex of aging white apartment buildings was transformed into the quarters of a rural Cretan village. Now whenever I swept the apartment, I'd also go out and sweep the front steps and surrounding area the way I remembered seeing people in Crete doing. When I went to get the mail, I'd stop and have a cigarette with the student from Palestine whose apartment was by the mailboxes. Khalid started leaving his apartment door open whenever he was around, and then he put some furniture outside, protected from the rain by the deck to the second floor apartments. He and some of his other international-student friends began hanging out there on a regular basis, and it was as if we had our own village *kafeneio*. Khalid and I would take turns making Greek (or Arabic or Turkish or . . .) coffee for everybody. One sunny Saturday I got up and prepared a pot full of braised chicken and lettuce in a dill-flavored egg-lemon sauce along with Cretan-style french fries and brought out plates of it to everybody. While I was cooking, and even while I carried out the plates, it felt almost like I was an actor in a play who'd learned to embody the "part" of Eirini.

One day, Emiko and I took Khalid to his five-hour prelicensing course in another remote village. Driving back, we stopped to eat at an out-of-the-way diner. Northern New York accents were more pronounced here than near campus. The servers were friendly and informal, but not in the annoying Hi-I'm-John-and-I'm-going-to-be-your-server-this-evening way that they were in the newfangled corporate restaurants my parents would take me to whenever I went down for a visit. A charbroiled cheeseburger wasn't exactly the grilled lamb chops doused with lemon I would have ordered in an off-the-beaten-path *psistaria* in the mountains of Crete, but it still hit the spot. Looking out the window I saw more pickups than sedans in the parking lot. Some of the customers smelled of dairy farm.

As I sat in the diner, awash in sensations taking me back to my childhood and adolescent years in northern New York, an overall feeling of deep-rooted familiarity tempered my realization that the St. Lawrence Valley was *not* rural Crete. For a moment, I was tempted to wonder if the North Country might provide a way for exiled Cretans from Upstate New York to feel at home.

❈ ❈ ❈

My thoughts are spinning.
Nonsense looks like clarity.
This time, I'm dreaming.

* 14 *

Kitchen Apprentice

Sofia's younger sister Katherine is visiting us from California this week, together with her husband Afrim and their almost-three-year-old daughter Melissa. I live for a visit like this—no matter how tired out I get—because it's so darn comfortable, especially when it comes to the food.

In the United States, I have a hard time finding family or friends who really love eating good homemade food, and who like eating the kinds of homemade dishes that Sofia and I make. Put aside for a moment all the totally understandable allergies and intolerances. Most of my non-Greek friends in the academic world turn out to be vegetarians or won't eat red meat. My relatives—except for my brother, father, and Ben—are usually reluctant to eat such supposedly exotic foods as goat or rabbit or dandelions, no matter how Sofia and I prepare them. Even when they do, it's always with lots of trepidation, not an eager appetite. Such-and-such cousin won't eat broccoli. So-and-so uncle won't eat fish. Their kids will only eat this brand of chicken nuggets or that brand of macaroni and cheese. Even most of my friends from *Greece* living in the United States are some the fussiest eaters that country has ever produced.

It's not like this with Sofia's family. I swear that Afrim had tears in his eyes when I roasted lamb's heads especially for him—a food he said he hadn't eaten in the many years since he left Albania for university studies. Neither is it this way with Melissa. So far. Last summer, she was already sucking the marrow out of bones with a straw with a look of delight on her face so radiant that it would make kids sipping from a juice box or a soda can look melancholic.

Sofia's siblings also find the cooking process itself interesting. They aren't intimidated by a kitchen, and that makes cooking together a source of enjoyment. The last time Sofia's brother was here, I took out all the (lamb and goat) kidneys, livers, and hearts I'd been saving in the freezer not knowing what to do with them. He roasted them over a wood fire with rosemary, chopped them finely, added olive oil, lemon juice, a bit of soy sauce, and plenty of chopped green onions and garlic. It was *so* good.

When Katherine told us they were coming, my only disappointment was that March is the *worst* time of year for cooking. The earliest wild greens, not to mention Sofia's annual gardens, won't begin for about another month. The cold-hardy greens whose season we extended by using a cold frame don't last *this* late. All our pickles—naturally fermented and refrigerated, not canned—are used up. Sofia and I have already finished off the many bags of surplus greens, green beans, tomatoes, and such that we froze last summer. We still have shell beans, a fresh batch of beer, and a few other odds and ends, but compared to most of the rest of the year, there isn't much variety.

Tonight I'm making a lamb dish I first tasted when Afrim made it for us in Los Angeles a few years ago. It was a dish he was obviously proud of—he'd even called his mother back in Albania to ask how to make it. His mother's recipe called for using a pressure cooker. Katherine and Afrim had a pressure cooker but none of us knew how to use it, and we ended up doing an Internet search to learn how. The dish came out great, and I remembered that, although I'd never observed this dish in Crete, I'd seen a photograph of a similar one in my Cretan cookbook. I looked it up when we got back home and ever since I've been making my own version—something in between the Cretan cookbook's and Afrim's mother's recipe.

To make it even more different from Afrim's, I'm using goat instead of lamb. Sofia and I usually buy a few male kids from one of the local goat-cheese makers (who, only needing milk, has no use for all the males that are born). I'm the first to admit that the flavor in no way compares with that of the goats I used to eat in Crete, and I prefer lamb, but I feel like I just have to make goat, too.

The basic idea of this dish is to cook the meat until it's tender, to combine it with lots of strained yogurt, and let it roast in the oven. The braising of the meat can obviously be accomplished with or without a pressure cooker. (I'm using our new pressure cooker.) I usually brown pieces of meat in olive oil, add chopped garlic, and let everything sauté briefly before adding the juice of a lemon, maybe some white wine, and a little water. I don't add much water for braising the meat because I'll add the liquid to the yogurt later, and too much liquid will make the yogurt too thin. I'm using an entire hind quarter of a goat that I don't feel like sawing into pieces, so I forego browning the meat and just squeeze everything into the pressure cooker as best I can and cook it long enough for the meat to start falling off the bone.

While the meat is cooking, I dump between one and two pounds of strained yogurt into a large bowl. I whisk in a couple eggs and some salt and pepper. Since I'm craving more vegetables today, I also grate a celeriac we bought from the winter farmers' market and whisk it into the yogurt. I pour some uncooked brown rice—about as much as I'd need to cover the bottom of a large roasting pan with a thin layer—into a bowl, add some boiling hot water, and let it soak for a while. This head start will make it easier for the rice to cook later on.

The meat finishes cooking and I remove the bones. I spread the rice out on the roasting pan after dumping out the excess water that wasn't absorbed. I spread out pieces of meat over the rice. Onto each piece of meat I grind black pepper and grate a little nutmeg.

I ladle the hot braising liquid a little at a time into the yogurt mixture, all the while whisking so it won't cook pieces of eggs and yogurt but make a smooth blend. I add the liquid slowly so the eggs and yogurt won't coagulate. I gently pour the yogurt mixture over a chunk of meat near the center of the roasting pan so the flowing yogurt mixture won't overly disturb the evenly spread out rice and the evenly distributed pieces of meat.

I roast the whole thing in the oven at 400°F for about an hour, maybe more, until the top of the yogurt begins to brown. The rice absorbs much of the excess liquid from the yogurt and the rest evaporates. When it comes out right, the yogurt isn't watery at all.

We adults think it tastes pretty good. Melissa does, too. This pleases me to no end—even though I don't know anything about child development—because I'm hopeful it means that she's off to a good start in life, learning to like and crave a variety of real foods, in spite of so many efforts by the world to turn her into just another customer of big industrial food companies that care not one iota for her well-being.

The next morning I'm making a salad with dried shell beans for lunch. I usually make this cold salad in the summer, but Katherine wants to watch me make it so she can write down a recipe. Hopefully we'll get it done before Melissa wakes up.

Other people might make a salad like this one, but I came up with it on my own. It always consists of four main ingredients: boiled shell beans, a starch, a nut, and aromatic vegetables.

The first time I made it was to use up kidney beans I'd bought without knowing what for. (It was during a period of overenthusiasm for buying bulk beans.) Today I'm using the Boston's Favorite beans that Sofia and I grew at Aunt Patsy's. I already put them in a bowl of cold water to soak before I went to bed last night. Now I boil them in lightly salted water until they're just tender and gently rinse them in a colander under cold water.

I've used different starches over the years, including wild rice, white rice, brown rice, and hulled barley. Since we ate brown rice last night with the goat, today I'm using wild rice, which is only rice in name. I follow the instructions on the package for cooking the wild rice in water. When it's ready, I run some cold water through it in another colander rather than let it cool down slowly. Melissa could get up at any moment, so time is of the essence.

I think I've used almonds every time, but today I'm using pine nuts, which I toast in a dry frying pan. When I use almonds, I blanch them in hot water to remove the skins, toast them in the toaster oven, and chop them coarsely with a mortar and pestle or the food processor.

For the aromatics, I usually chop up one or more fresh herbs—dill, parsley, cilantro, fennel, or chervil—plus raw onion or garlic or both. Today I'm using dill from the supermarket and tiny heads of Chesnok garlic—the tail end of our last hardneck garlic harvest.

I put everything into our largest stainless-steel bowl—it's a big one—and drizzle on olive oil. Rather than stirring, which I fear could make the beans and starches mushy, I hold the bowl with both hands in front of me in the center of the kitchen and gently toss everything to get it coated with the oil. I add freshly squeezed lemon juice, Greek red wine vinegar, salt and pepper, and toss some more. I taste it to see if it needs more salt, vinegar, or lemon juice, which, as usual, it does. This salad needs plenty of acidity to really shine.

I tell Katherine that my mother, who usually won't eat shell beans, not only likes this salad, but even came over to watch me make it so she could learn how.

I transfer the salad to two large glass containers with lids and put them in the fridge to chill.

Melissa isn't up yet so we even have time for more tea.

Katherine is feeding Melissa her breakfast. I butcher the rabbit that I thawed out last night for tonight's dinner. I put it in a bowl to marinate with dry sherry, white wine, oregano, and cumin. I put it in the fridge for the day.

A few weeks ago, I ate restaurant-prepared rabbit for the first time. Sofia and I were asked to help wine-and-dine a candidate for an important administrative position at the college, and we ended up at one of those Saratoga restaurants that (supposedly) gives the impression that it's both fancy and Upstate-relaxed at the same time. Exactly the kind of place I'd never go on my own. Exactly the kind of place, I suppose, one takes a VIP when the company or the state is paying. The waiter sure looked surprised when I asked him if he knew what farm the rabbit came from. (I was genuinely curious—there's a rabbit farm nearby—and figured that there was no way I was gonna come off looking pretentious in a place like that.) The meal was a huge disappointment. The rabbit was braised in such an overpowering sauce, and there was so little meat to begin with, that I couldn't even taste rabbit. (Maybe that was the point.)

In Crete we ate rabbit all the time. I don't know why when I went to Greece I didn't hesitate to try it for the first time—the way I see most of my relatives hesitating whenever I offer it to them. Penny's family prepared rabbit in one of four ways: marinated in homemade wine then fried; roasted in the oven with potatoes; braised with lots of onions; or spit-roasted outdoors over charcoal. I liked all four ways but pan-fried was probably my favorite.

Back in the United States, I discovered fresh rabbit for sale in Ohio and started cooking it myself. Then, back in Upstate New York, I found frozen rabbit in an upscale supermarket. But it didn't taste like rabbit. It tasted of chemicals. So I swore off eating it. Later I found frozen rabbit for sale in a Chinese market—good not great—and started eating it again. Then a biologist acquaintance told me that you can catch "rabbit fever" just by *touching* infected raw meat, so I swore off eating it once again.

Then Sofia and I heard about a farmer nearby who sells rabbit. I read more about tularemia. I became convinced that just because a rabbit is raised by a conscientious small farmer was no guarantee that it didn't have rabbit fever, since it can apparently be spread by the bite of a deerfly. I also figured—since it can be spread by the bite of a deerfly—that an infected insect could bite *me*. As is often the case with food safety, it looked like it was a question of risk. Did I have any reason to believe it was riskier to touch a farm-raised rabbit than it was to do other everyday things that have a tiny but finite chance of exposing me to contagious diseases? From my reading I didn't get a sense that it was. In fact, most of the fuss over tularemia seemed related to concerns over its potential use as a biological weapon, not over food safety. And, the risk seemed limited to touching raw rabbit meat, not eating cooked rabbit.

Since I can't banish from my thinking the casual remarks of that biologist, now I wear latex gloves whenever I handle raw rabbit meat. I also inspect the color of the rabbit's liver—I read somewhere that white spots on the liver indicate rabbit fever. This gives me enough peace of mind to cook rabbit on a regular basis again. For all I know it's riskier to eat sushi or an undercooked hamburger or a raw salad at a restaurant. (The last two years I've been served undercooked chicken in restaurants twice!) It's just that I don't *know*.

For dinner, I panfry the rabbit in extra virgin olive oil. When the meat is cooked and starting to brown, I pour out most of the oil from the pan, add the dry-sherry marinade, bring it to a boil, and lower the heat to a simmer. I turn over the pieces of rabbit every so often so the juices of the marinade continue adding flavor to the fried meat.

When the water is all gone I add a small dose of sherry straight from the bottle and let it cook down for a couple more minutes. I dump the pieces of rabbit onto a plate and we're ready to dig in—using our hands, of course.

Katherine is interested in learning how to make spanakopita. For this I usually blend spinach with wild lamb's quarters, but, alas, we don't have any lamb's quarters left in the freezer. One of the farmers at our winter farmers' market sells spinach. It's expensive so normally we don't buy it, but since Sofia's family is visiting us we've got several bags of it in the fridge.

Sofia and I happen to have a rectangular roasting pan that is the same size as the sheets of phyllo that our local supermarket carries. Sometimes I make homemade phyllo that is thicker than the industrial kind, but I still can't resist the superthin—but preservative-filled—store-bought version every once in a while.

I take out the roasting pan and place it on the counter next to the (unopened) package of phyllo that should be thawed out by now. I fill up a small bowl with olive oil for brushing on the individual sheets. I've done it so many times that I know one bowlful is just how much I'll need.

I get to thinking: Why don't I just tell Katherine what to do and let her make it? That should make it even easier for her to learn. She agrees.

I sit down at the kitchen bar.

Katherine takes out a package of feta cheese, empties it into a small bowl, and mashes it with a fork so that it's good and crumbly. I preach my preferences regarding feta—something close to Greek feta, so it must at least be made from sheep's milk or from a mix of sheep's and goat's milk. I tell her that most of our local farmers who make feta don't use sheep's milk, and even when they do, their feta doesn't taste very good. (In the European Union, it wouldn't be allowed to call itself "feta" because feta is a protected designation of origin product: to bear the name, it must come from Greece—from certain *areas* of Greece.)

Katherine cleans and rinses the spinach. She chops an onion and lets it sauté in some oil in a large frying pan. Any *Allium* will do. I complain that we don't have any leeks left in our garden—I'd been digging them up from under the snow all winter to use in place of onions in dishes like this one. If only I knew earlier that Katherine was going to visit us, I'd've left some out there. I suppose I should've left some anyway, just in case.

Katherine coarsely chops the spinach. After the onions have cooked for a few minutes, she adds the spinach, some salt, some pepper, and a dash of cumin powder. She lets it cook for a few minutes. There's little excess water in farmers' market spinach compared with supermarket spinach. She takes the pan off the heat.

She turns on the oven to 375°F.

I get up and take out the paintbrush reserved for cooking and set it across the top of the bowl of olive oil for her. I explain that once she opens the phyllo she should be prepared to build the spanako-pita immediately so the phyllo won't dry out.

She begins building. She brushes the whole pan with oil. Then she puts the first sheet into the pan, brushes it with oil, then the second sheet, brushes it with oil, and so on. The bag of phyllo comes with about twenty sheets and she's counting as she puts down each sheet. After the tenth one she dumps on the cooked spinach mixture and gently spreads it out with a rubber spatula. She spreads the crumbled feta evenly over the spinach. Then she continues with the rest of the layers of phyllo, brushing each time with oil.

I show her how to use the paintbrush to go around the perimeter of the pan to sort of push the edges down so that the whole pie looks neat and trim.

All this is really easy to do, especially if you've seen somebody else do it once before. For a split second, though, I wonder: If Katherine hadn't worked as an apprentice in a French pastry shop to support herself while she was in graduate school, would she find it this easy? Why can't I picture my mother or Ben's wife or Aunt Patsy picking it up this easily, without tons of questions and lots of needless anxiety? Or am I being like Leonidas, who acts exaggeratedly surprised whenever Americans say they're impressed that he knows how to make such *difficult* things as baklava and spanakopita?

I tell Katherine to turn on the faucet and get her hands wet. I tell her to flick drops of water onto the surface of the pie to keep the phyllo from curling up as it bakes. Of course, since I've yet to forget this step—as Leonidas had drilled it into my head long before I ever attempted to make anything with phyllo myself—I can't testify from experience whether failing to do so is indeed detrimental. According to Leonidas it is, because his own spanakopita never came out right until after he happened to notice his mother doing this, a step that wasn't written down (because it was taken for granted) in the family recipe he'd always followed.

I tell Katherine to take a knife and gently cut the pie into pieces of whatever size she wants before baking.

She puts the pan into the oven and sets the timer for 50 minutes. I explain to her that the important thing is that the spanakopita puffs up and starts turning golden brown on top but not too dark.

I tell Katherine that, for years, Sofia had been trying to grow spinach from seedlings begun indoors, but it was only last spring that she was really successful. She bought the seeds from a different company, I probably did a better job of preparing the soil, and we made sure to plant it in the coolest location of the garden. Last year's weather might've helped, too.

I realize that it's almost time for Sofia to start this year's seedlings. I get a little rush.

The spanakopita finishes cooking. Katherine takes it out and lets it cool briefly before we dig in. It tastes somewhat bitter to me but no one else thinks it does. Spinach should be sweet, not bitter. I figure my taste is just off, or the spinach is a little different than usual.

Later in the evening I drink some milk and it tastes unpalatably bitter. I worry that something is seriously wrong with me and my mind starts racing, wondering what it could be. I consider looking online for information, knowing that sometimes this leads me to get overly anxious about unlikely worst-case scenarios. I look and I'm glad because the combination of words I search for brings up a bunch of websites talking about pine nuts causing some people to taste everything bitter for a brief period of time. I remember eating a handful of raw pine nuts yesterday when I was making the bean salad. (Thankfully no one else did.) I try to remember how long we've had the pine nuts in the fridge—why not the freezer?—and I'm pretty sure it's been almost a year, maybe longer. And who knows how fresh they were when we bought them. I decide that I must have the little-studied phenomenon of "pine mouth" that doesn't seem to be anything to worry about. I calm down.

Still, I'm disappointed, because it means I won't be able to enjoy eating all the wonderful things we'll be cooking for the last few days of Katherine's visit—including the angel food cake I love so much—a special request from Melissa to her favorite uncle.

* 15 *

Cooking Cretan in the United States

Easter will arrive at midnight. Sofia is away at an education conference, and my Athenian friend Thanasis is visiting from Queens. I met Thanasis in Ohio where we both attended graduate school.

I stand some concrete blocks on end at the corners of the square patch of lawn in the backyard where I usually build fires for grilling meat. In the middle, I scrunch up some newspaper and pour on spent olive oil. I place a bundle of last year's wild grapevine prunings over the paper and then a few logs from the woodpile over them. I light it. Thanasis and I go back inside so I can prepare the meat.

I know we only need to roast half of a kid goat but we both agree that I should roast two halves. Working in the kitchen sink, I poke the spit through one side, bend the meat back and weave it through once more. I get some wire and the wire cutters from the garage and tie the hind leg along the length of the spit and tucked into the ribs. Then I slide the spit forks onto either end of the spit, push the tongs into the meat, and tighten the screws to keep everything in place. I sprinkle plenty of salt over both sides of the meat. I carry the spit outside and hang it between two of the concrete blocks as the fire burns nearby.

This isn't just *ofto*—it's *ofto* the way they do it in Cretan mountain villages, except for the fact that I didn't slaughter and dress the goat myself, though I did purchase it from a local cheese maker.

I repeat the entire process with the other half of the goat and set it up on the opposite side of the flames.

Later today we'll be joined by one of Thanasis's old roommates from Ohio, Jason, and Jason's partner Jeff. It's fitting that this reunion is happening on a "Greek" holiday, because it was in Ohio that I began to cook and eat as purely and authentically Cretan as I possibly could.

As the day of my departure from New York's North Country—and from Emiko—approached, I thought more about how I'd be cooking and eating in Ohio, somewhat excited that for the first time in my life I'd be living alone with total control over the kitchen.

Emiko was becoming increasingly preoccupied with reforming our eating habits. She became a working member of the local food co-op and toyed with the idea of becoming a vegetarian, which, considering how many pounds of hot wings and General Tso's chicken we'd eaten that winter, was not a decision to be taken lightly. We shopped more often at the co-op, less often at the supermarket, and sought to eat a greater proportion of organic produce.

I took stock of my kitchen gear. When I'd packed up my things to ship back from Crete, I'd taken the few kitchen supplies that were already mine before I met Penny or that my parents had given us. Everything else I left behind. I had my trusty miniature Asian chef's knife and a cleaver I'd mistakenly bought thinking it was like a real Asian chef's knife. I had an old set of dishes and the flatware that my parents had given us as an engagement present when we were moving to Chicago, and a blender and a toaster oven that they'd given me as Christmas presents. I had a couple pots that Penny and I had bought in Chicago but that in Crete we'd retired because the worn-out bottoms were unfit for the flat burners of the German stove Eirini and Manolis had bought for us. I also had my parents' old microwave from when I was in high school. I had other hand-me-down gadgets—left over from numerous generations of European graduate students who'd come and gone over the years—that Leonidas had given me when he was moving. My mother checked her kitchen for whatever she didn't need any more, including an old vegetable peeler and two glass pie plates. For storage containers I saved all the empty yogurt containers and instant coffee jars that Emiko and I had gone through. There were one or two items I deemed I'd have to purchase, such as a roasting pan for the oven.

Preparing for Ohio, I filled my empty yogurt and coffee containers with organic dried beans—lentils, chickpeas, black-eyed peas, split peas, and lima beans—from the co-op. I never cooked dried legumes before but decided that I'd start cooking one legume dish per week. Supplementing what I could remember of Eirini's usual dishes with ideas from Kochilas's cookbook and the occasional tip from Leonidas over the phone, I tried making Eirini's vinegary lentil soup, her lemony chickpea soup, and her black-eyed peas with greens. Then, with only written recipes to go on since I'd never seen these dishes when I was living in Crete, I also tried making *fava*—a purée of split peas—and *fasolada*—a lima-bean-and-vegetable soup very popular in other parts of Greece. The co-op didn't sell fava beans, also known as broad beans and not to be confused with the split pea dish by the same name. I was disappointed because I'd come to believe that *koukia*—fava beans boiled down and cooled to a paste then scooped onto a plate and dressed with plenty of olive oil, coarse sea salt, and, optionally, raw onion—were the most symbolically Cretan of all the Cretan legume dishes.

Before departing for Ohio, I reconnected with the grilling that Manolis and I used to do when Emiko and I went camping at Lake Eaton. She'd brought sandwiches to eat in her cooler, but I wanted to cook something on the fire. After setting up our tent we took a long walk in the woods and looked for kindling, the way I used to do in the woods behind our house when I was a child, before my parents switched to gas grills. Also, inspired by both the spit-grilling of lamb that we did in Crete and by souvlaki (which means "skewer"; literally, "little spit"), I got the idea of cooking something like an oversized souvlaki on a full-sized makeshift spit. So I also looked around for a small tree or a branch that I could make into a longer and sturdier version of what my grandparents would have had me looking for—in these very same woods some twenty years earlier—in order to toast marshmallows. I found a good piece, peeled off the bark, and whittled down one end to a sharp point. We drove into Long Lake and bought some onions, bell peppers, and a few cuts of pork. We went back, started a fire, cut up the ingredients, slid them onto the green-wood spit, and roasted our *souvlara.*

A week later I left. I was having second thoughts about going so far away from Emiko. The passion we shared for eating good food and our joint dedication to trying to better ourselves as home cooks and environmentally aware food-shoppers was bringing us closer together than ever. But the long road back to Greece and my quest to re-create a Cretan table in my everyday life were calling.

In an oversized SUV he borrowed from a coworker, my brother drove me and all my belongings down to Leonidas's apartment. From there, I rented a van for the weekend. Leonidas came along to help me and to drive the van back, since a van with roundtrip mileage was cheaper than renting a one-way moving truck. We left at the crack of dawn on a Saturday morning and, even with the stops for gas and fast food, we arrived with plenty of time to spare before the office at the apartment complex closed. It was just a short walk from a supermarket and immediately adjacent to public transportation to the university. I picked up the keys, Leonidas and I moved everything from the van into the efficiency, and I started unpacking the essentials.

The furniture I brought mostly consisted of old items from my parents—a card table and folding chairs for dining, a heavy-duty folding table for a desk, a folding cot for sleeping, two folding bookshelves, and an unassembled bookcase I'd made from leftover pieces of wood from the old deck around the above-ground swimming pool I grew up with. Putting the homemade bookcase together gave me trouble. I'd routed slots into two six-and-a-half-foot two-by-eights for the sides, but dumbly left them leaning against a wall at home until it was time to move, and they'd bowed just enough so that when I tried putting the rough-cut one-by-eights into the slots, the middle shelves kept falling out.

Between the eighty-something-degree heat and the fact that we got up so early that day, I was about ready to toss the pieces of wood into the dumpster when the phone rang. It was one of my new professors calling to see if I'd arrived and letting me know that he was at the annual Greek festival and that I should stop by if I had time. I thought to myself that a Greek festival was about the last place Leonidas and I would want to set foot, but I also thought it might be fun to catch a glimpse of the Greek-American scene in this place and for Leonidas to attach faces to the names of the scholars whose work I'd talked to him about. With Leonidas's help I finally got the bookcase together, and we headed to the festival for a break.

We ran into my new professors, and they directed us to the exhibit about Greek Americans that a graduate student had created for the festival. Leonidas and I weren't interested but out of politeness tried disguising our lack of academic sophistication in the humanities and social sciences, strolled along looking at the display panels, and nodded our heads feigning enthusiasm as we listened to him explain what we were seeing. What *did* interest me about the festival was the fact that one of the faculty mentioned to us the existence a Greek-owned shop up the street selling Greek food products. In under an hour, Leonidas and I were out of the festival. We visited the Greek shop and headed back to my apartment, starving.

I dug through a few boxes and found the one-page "menu" I'd typed up before the move. Intent on cooking Cretan once I got to Ohio, I'd taken lists of dishes and ingredients I remembered from Crete and organized them into a restaurant-like menu, figuring it would help me to remember what my options were. I handed it to Leonidas and asked him to find something he was in the mood for, and hopefully possible to make amid my half-unpacked mess. *Yiouvetsi* caught his eye—a dish he liked but that for some reason he seldom made. We walked over to the supermarket and bought garlic, orzo, tomatoes, and their cheapest cut of beef. I was amazed to see that supermarkets in Ohio sold wine. Leonidas pointed out some "ridiculously inexpensive" reds from South America that he speculated were probably quite better than one might expect from the price alone.

Back at the apartment, I began preparing the first of countless Greek and Cretan meals that would follow there. Leonidas reminded me that he didn't like the texture of pieces of cooked tomatoes, so—not without disappointment, because it wasn't how Eirini did it—I put them in the blender instead of chopping them. I browned the meat on all sides in hot olive oil, added a head's worth of chopped garlic, some salt and pepper, and just enough water to cover the meat, and let it simmer for an hour. Then I added the puréed tomatoes and let it simmer for another hour. Next, I cut the tender beef up into smaller pieces and moved it to the roasting pan, poured in all the liquid with the tomato and garlic, and let it cook at 400°F for almost another hour, at which point I added the orzo, and stirred frequently until the pasta had absorbed all the liquid. When it finished cooking I added even more salt and pepper. We opened a bottle of Chilean red wine, sat down at the card table, and dug in.

That night I slept on the floor and Leonidas slept on the cot. In the yellow pages, we managed to find a mattress store in the suburbs that was open Sunday morning, got directions, and drove out there with the van. I bought the cheapest full-size mattress they had for sale and put it on the floor of the sleeping area. I gave Leonidas the cot to take back with him. We ate leftover *yiouvetsi* for lunch and Leonidas headed back home.

During my first term as a grad student again, I was doing at least as well with my cooking as I was with my formal studies.

On Saturday mornings, I'd wake up, put on a cassette I'd recorded in Crete of a liturgy at St. Minas, light one of the incense sticks Emiko had given me, and make two simple round loaves of bread following a recipe in the Kochilas cookbook. I'd also make one legume dish to last for much of the week. On weekdays, I'd eat simple lunches of beans and bread, or just bread, cheese, and olives, washed down with wine, which often made me feel like I was inhabiting the part of a Cretan farmer pausing from vineyard chores for a little sustenance, except that my vineyard was the academy and my chores were reading, thinking, and writing. A couple of times a week I'd also make a more elaborate dish of Eirini's—*yiouvarlakia* (meatball soup), *spanakorizo* (spinach rice), or *kokkinisto* (meat and tomato stew)—that would last me for several days as well.

My Greek colleagues told me about another potentially useful shop carrying Greek and other Mediterranean goods owned by Middle Easterners. I headed out on foot one Saturday to check it out—it was only a couple miles away. At last, a shop that carried many of the goods I needed to *really* make Cretan food! As the scent of sheep's cheeses and brined olives entered my nose and diffused throughout my body, I was careful not to show on the outside how elated I was. The last thing I wanted to do was look like the overly naive Middle American who goes happily touristing in shops like these for exotic new ingredients. I coached myself, thinking things like: "If you buy cheese, make sure you ask lots of questions, look skeptical, and ask for a sample first." I grabbed a hand-basket and checked every aisle. Broad beans, giant lima beans, grape leaves preserved in brine, orzo from Greece, Greek and Cretan brands of thyme honey, several kinds of green and black Greek olives, Greek sheep's- and goat's-milk cheeses, "Greek" varieties of zucchini and eggplant, and strained yogurt. They even carried barley rusks (dried bread slices) from Crete and Greek Nescafé—the spray-dried kind that dissolves and foams better in cold water for *frape*. I gathered together as much as I thought I could carry back to my apartment on foot.

My quest to cook Cretan was off to a great start. I was eating legumes several times a week, including puréed fava beans. I was drinking two or three small glasses of red wine with every meal. I made *frape* every morning and afternoon. Between the potently scented dried oregano, thyme, savory, sage, rosemary, mint, and bay leaves I'd brought from Crete and all the new finds at the Middle

Eastern shop, my kitchen was well stocked with the "specialty" items I needed.

I had several new colleagues from Greece whose company I enjoyed a great deal. I began inviting them over to my apartment "to drink a glass of wine." Most often, I invited Thanasis, an Athenian linguistics student with Cretan connections who also just began his studies, lived alone, and was downright passionate about eating Greek food. Our frequent and long discussions and debates about everything from language and science to religion—always over food and wine—made me feel a lot like I was back in Crete, except that he didn't smoke and hardly tolerated it when I or anyone else around him did. I enjoyed how Thanasis commented on the food I'd prepare. In compliments and criticisms, he evaluated the accuracy of my dishes in terms of his own memories of them from Greece, further inspiring me to try getting them just right.

Since Thanasis had a car, sometimes we'd go to a Cretan-owned restaurant and bar on the nights they had live Greek music. There we'd meet up with other undergraduate and graduate students from Greece and Cyprus, and I'd almost forget that we were in Ohio. After the first couple of visits, when I complained about the wineglasses, our regular waiter usually remembered without my saying anything to take away the stemware and replace it with small Greek-style wineglasses.

As the end of my first term at the university drew near, I remembered the existence of a *Cretan* cookbook, so I called up the bookseller in Athens who I was using for my courses and ordered one. The box from UPS was waiting for me outside my apartment door just as the holiday break was about to start. I was ecstatic. I was planning to hang out there during the break and had already checked out other books from the library to read, but now I held in my hands the single greatest tool I knew of for improving my Cretan cooking. I read it cover to cover as if it contained the secrets of the universe.

The first recipe I actually used in the kitchen was for *melomak-arouna*, honey-syrup-soaked cookies covered with chopped walnuts, one of the two Christmas cookies I remembered Eirini making. I already had her recipe for *kourabiedes*, rose-water-and-brandy-flavored butter cookies dusted with confectioner's sugar—because Leonidas had gotten it from Penny years ago. Thanasis stopped by the night I baked, watching me cream the butter and sugar with a fork since I didn't have a mixer, and seeing me bake them on my large glass roasting pan turned upside down since I didn't have a cookie sheet. We sat at the card table talking and drinking wine as each batch baked, and occasionally I'd go sit for a smoke at the kitchen windowsill with the window cracked, communing with my memories of Eirini sitting in her apron taking a cigarette break on the balcony.

❋　❋　❋

As the goat is roasting outside, Thanasis and I hang out in the kitchen sipping shots of grappa and munching the Greek cheese and Moroccan olives he brought from Astoria. We catch up on recent developments in his job-related travels and love life. We argue about politics and science and the philosophy of religion. We reminisce about good food and our favorite television shows. Except for the fact that we seem to have more than usual to agree than to disagree about, it's like we've picked up right where we left off the last time we were in touch about a year ago.

We both realize we should sober up some before Jason and Jeff arrive for dinner. I realize it's almost time to put the potatoes in to roast. I peel about twelve and cut them up in my hands directly into a large roasting pan the way Eirini always did. I pour on plenty of olive oil, squeeze on the juice of three lemons, and sprinkle on salt, pepper, and lots of last summer's dried oregano. I put them into the oven.

It's been just the two of us all day, so I'm remembering how I used to cook for us in my little apartment in Ohio almost ten years ago. I'm also feeling a little weird because this is the first time since moving here from Ohio—actually the first time since Sofia and I got married during my third year in Ohio—that I'm cooking for visitors without Sofia around.

Sofia and I met the first week of my second term in Ohio in a seminar on folk art and material culture. Hsiao-ju went by the "American" name Sophie that her mother had given her when she first came to the United States from Taiwan for college, but I promptly rebaptized her Sofia, the ancient Greek word for wisdom, transliterated in the modern way with an *f*. She didn't mind my renaming her but she *was* taken aback by my asking her out the first time, because I invited her to my apartment for homemade food instead of to a restaurant. But was she ever proud a couple months later when her graduate school colleagues were visibly impressed by the success of my moussaka when they stopped by to drop her off as they were arriving back in town after a conference.

When we weren't reading and writing, Sofia and I spent much of our time together cooking and eating. She soon discovered that many of the foods she thought she didn't like, such as olives and bread, she did like after all—it was just that up until then she'd eaten them only in their more processed versions. She realized that she liked salt, too, once she was exposed to the kosher salt I was using.

It wasn't long before we moved into an apartment together and our kitchen hardware mingled. We bought a piece of four-foot-square plywood to put on top of my card table for a larger and taller dining table. We spent many late evenings in used bookstores drinking complimentary coffee and thumbing through books about food. I introduced her to the Mediterranean and Middle Eastern food stores, and she introduced me to the city's Asian markets and Wild Oats. We spent many summer weekends driving around the suburbs scouting out farm markets and other stores where we could buy better, or at least less-expensive, palatable fruits and vegetables. Together, we explored the city's notable North Market and became members of a local food co-op. She got me into sashimi and Taiwanese oolongs and I got her into green salads, olive oil, and *frape.*

Sofia also took an interest in my desire to cook Cretan food. Well, she may not have cared about eating Cretan per se, but she liked the taste of the foods I made so much that she came to desire many Greek and Cretan ingredients, dishes, and cooking styles. When I made *dolmades* (stuffed grape leaves)—often at her behest—she helped stuff the leaves. At Christmas, she insisted that I make *kourabiedes* and *melomakarouna*, and at Easter, *tsourekakia* and *kallitsounia*—even though these weren't holidays that she celebrated.

She eventually got into certain aspects of Mediterranean food even more than I did. Though never one to eat raw salads, she soon fell in love with my green salads dressed with olive oil, red wine vinegar, and salt. And, after a few visits to an Italian restaurant, she also enjoyed eating bread dipped in a plate of olive oil and vinegar and started doing it at home. When she went to visit her brother, who was living in Flushing, Queens at the time, and having heard from me about the Greeks in nearby Astoria, she took him and their mother to scout out Greek markets. She ended up coming back with a whole case of Greek wine vinegar. To my delight, even after tasting some other similarly potent wine vinegars imported from Italy, she still preferred the Greek brands. Upon seeing pictures in my Greek cookbooks of spoon sweets—fruit preserves served in small quantities as a treat for visitors or dessert—she coaxed me to make some. Even though I'd never seen, let alone eaten, any homemade spoon sweets in Greece, we followed the recipes in my book and ended up making orange peel, pomelo peel, cherry, quince, and pear.

With Sofia by my side, and often as my accomplice, figuring out further ways to prepare Cretan and Greek foods in the United States—more accurately, more extensively, and at ever higher levels of quality—became as important to me as my formal studies. In time I was learning far more than I ever imagined I would.

I figured out that I could get an appropriately thick strained yogurt for the cucumber and garlic dip tzatziki by draining out the whey from good-quality plain whole milk yogurt. Upon studying the bulk grains for sale at Wild Oats, I figured out that cracked wheat was what I needed to make *hondros*, the wheat and tomato dish with snails. (But, since I couldn't figure out how to get wild snails comparable with those of Crete's mountains, I substituted mussels.) I also discovered sheep's-milk cheeses from Spain that were a fair-enough approximation of certain Cretan cheeses. Reading academic books by an anthropologist who did his fieldwork in Crete, I noticed that he translated *tsikoudia* as *grappa*. Once I realized that grappa was simply the Italian version of essentially the same thing, and that grappa was widely available in U.S. liquor stores, I had a decent substitute. I also learned how to make several Greek *taverna* foods: fried calamari, octopus with garlic and vinegar, garlic-fried shrimp, and garlic-potato dip (*skordalia*) to accompany cod dipped in batter and fried.

I replicated much of the Greek kitchenware I remembered. I was increasingly bothered by our [brand name] dishware. I grew up on that brand but I wanted dishes like the ones we had in Crete. I'd never paid much attention to the visual aspects of food presentation but Sofia did, and she made me realize that we should look for solid white dishware. It was easy to find the kinds of dishware we were looking for but it was always terribly expensive, especially considering that we needed lots of settings for when we had visitors. We kept searching department stores and factory outlets when we visited my parents during breaks. At last, on our way back to Ohio from one of these trips, when we stopped to see Leonidas for a couple days, we found several inexpensive boxes of exactly what we were looking for at a Big Lots: white ceramic dishware without flat bottoms that stick to the clear plastic I covered our tablecloth with (a trick I picked up from my mother) and with wide rims on the bowls. We bought them all, enough for sixteen settings. Thanasis brought me glasses from Greece for wine, and I purchased the tiny coffee cups that were appropriate for Greek coffee from the Arab-owned shop in Ohio. Sofia's Cypriot classmate bought me a large round oven pan on one of her trips back home for the summer.

I consulted my growing collection of dictionaries to learn the English names of the many unusual fruits I'd eaten in Crete. The *lotos* that Penny loved so much was the persimmon. My favorite citrus fruit, the *klimentini*, turned out to be the clementine. *Fragosyko* was the prickly pear. *Kydoni* was quince. *Frapa* was pomelo, a fruit Sofia knew well because of the Chinese moon festival. To my surprise these fruits turned out to be seasonally available at one of our supermarkets. I never really paid much attention to fruit in the supermarket before because in my experience most of it tasted awful and was a waste of money. Then I perused a really helpful book in a used-book store, written by an independent grocer. This book and others like it not only provided useful information about when various fruits were in season (depending on where they were grown), but also shared helpful hints for knowing when various fruits were ready to eat, and how to ripen certain fruits at home.

Fish turned into an even more elaborate project. Thanks to Manolis, I'd eaten plenty of fresh fish in Irakleio. As a child I'd gone through a phase of freshwater fishing of my own so I knew our local freshwater fish well. But since no one in my family ever bought fish (except for canned tuna or frozen fish sticks), I was largely ignorant of even the names of most saltwater fish, except the most widespread—tuna, salmon, and cod—and I wasn't aware to what extent saltwater fish differed from the freshwater fish I was familiar with.

In Crete I learned to recognize over a dozen Mediterranean fishes by their Greek names—sometimes by flavor and sometimes by how they looked—but I'd never given much thought as to what these species might be called in English. In fact, since one of them was called *perka* (which sounded to me like *perch*), and *tonos* was obviously *tuna*, I sort of just assumed that they were varieties whose names in English I'd probably recognize if I heard them. But in Ohio, not only was I hard pressed to find *any* whole fish for sale at the supermarket, I didn't have a clue where or what to look for if I wanted to make *synagrida, fagri, hannos, orfos, sfyrida, lithrini, gopa,* or *mayiatiko.*

Already in my personal library was a Greek book on the nation's fishes and an Audubon field guide. I then found a cookbook about Mediterranean fishes in a local bookstore. These books enabled me to put together an elaborate lexicon of fish organized according to scientific taxonomy. It may not have been perfect, especially by a scientist's standards, but it provided far more information about fish varieties than a home cook—or most professional chefs for that matter—would ever need. As it turned out, most of the fish I knew in Greece had names in English that I'd never heard of before.

Armed with my fish lexicon and Sofia's assistance, I soon discovered that several varieties or very closely related varieties were available (as whole fish!) once a week at a local Chinese supermarket. I pan-fried smaller fish in olive oil or baked them in the oven with potatoes, okra, tomato, and fresh-squeezed lemon. I roasted the largest porgies I could find with potatoes, lemon, oil, and oregano. I fried haddock or cod to go with *skordalia*. And, I was at long last able to make the fish soup that Eirini was renowned for among her family and friends.

Meats and poultry were in some respects easier than fish, in others more difficult. Cuts of lamb were readily available for most dishes. Rabbits and goat meat were both sold at North Market. I knew that if I wanted to boil *zygouri* for Cretan wedding pilaf I'd need mutton—although I successfully substituted a combination of lamb and (Chinese-market) ox-tail. I made do with beef instead of the younger *moschari* typically used in Crete. I wasn't (yet!) interested in roasting lamb's heads for the brains or obtaining the lamb entrails required for Easter *kokoretsi* or *mageiritsa* (a soup of lamb innards).

Something that eluded me for a long time was the *paseta*, the melt-in-your-mouth fatty cut of pork that Manolis and I had roasted over charcoal almost weekly. I never saw a similar cut of pork in the supermarket, and I couldn't find any information about the word *paseta* in any of my dictionaries. Little clues built up over time: I heard about *pancetta*—an Italian form of bacon—which, given the history of the Modern Greek language, seemed likely to be the etymological origin, or at least a cognate, of the word *paseta*. This eventually triggered another deeply buried memory: The very first time I'd eaten *pasetes* in Crete, Manolis had explained to me that it was *beikon* (bacon). This led me to think that the *paseta* was uncured bacon, but I didn't know where I could buy it.

Years earlier somebody had mentioned to me something about Americans butchering animals differently than Europeans and Asians, so I also kept an eye out at the Chinese markets. Then, on a spring break visit to Sofia's brother, we came upon packages of (uncured) pork belly in a market near his apartment. The meat looked familiar, but I remembered the *paseta* as having had some bone, which this pork belly didn't have. Once I learned to use the Internet as a tool for informational research, I looked more carefully at diagrams and pictures of the cuts of a butchered pig and realized that the *paseta* probably included at least some part of what usually goes into spare ribs, along with the pork belly, though I couldn't be quite sure, and none of the butchers I ever asked could tell me. I bought a rack of spare ribs and did the best I could to slice them up in the Cretan style—meaning that much of the time I was chopping through the ribs as well as the meat. It looked familiar—the sliced up spareribs looked like half of a *paseta*. I concluded that maybe if I had the entire side—with the spareribs and pork belly unseparated—I could slice it up to get the *paseta*. I didn't get too excited, though. Even if I could find such a cut of meat, I wasn't sure it would taste the same. It might be a different variety of pig or its feed might be completely different.

Drinking wine like Manolis's homemade wine was out of the question in Ohio, but at the local Greek shop I found a 1992 red wine from Sitia. It was expensive by my standards, but not unaffordable. The owner gave us a discount for buying a case and we rationed it, saving it for special occasions over the next couple years. It was a far cry from Manolis's amber nectar, but I was grateful that on a graduate teaching assistant's salary I had access to affordable red wines from South America, punctuated now and then by a bottle of wine from Crete made from specifically Cretan grape varieties.

I kept wondering how Manolis's wines ended up amber and tasted so different from anything else I'd ever had from a bottle, even wines from Crete. I'd read that leaving dark grape skins in the grape must during fermentation results in shades of pink or red, but not rich amber. I never saw or heard of a commercial wine that was amber. Was it just because Manolis stored it in a used barrel for so long, in the way that liquors like Cognac and whiskey gain color as they age in wood? With more detective work I learned of the fortified wines of Spain known as sherry. As I read about sherry, I noted some potential similarities with Manolis's wine: The sour flavor and amber colors (possibly from further oxidation of a white wine); the high alcohol content, at least 14 percent; the fact that Manolis usually added his newly fermented wines to the wooden barrels containing some of the older, aged wine—similar, it seemed, to the Solera method. So I went out and bought all the dry sherries I could find—a dry Oloroso, a dry Amontillado, and an extra dry Manzanilla. As soon as I opened the first bottle and took a whiff, it was entirely familiar. After drinking all three for a time, I decided that the closest approximation to my recollection of Manolis's wine was a mixture of equal parts Manzanilla and dry Amontillado, diluted with some white wine to bring the alcohol content back down to around 14 percent. Further Internet searches years later reinforced my conclusions when I found tourists reporting that they were caught off guard—unpleasantly, to my surprise—when they ordered local wine in Cretan restaurants only to be served something that tasted like sherry.

Even if it didn't become our standard wine for drinking, dry sherry became my standard wine for cooking Cretan dishes, such as when I marinated a rabbit for frying.

❋   ❋   ❋

The goat is still roasting. The potatoes are in the oven. Thanasis and I have sobered up. I want to make some kind of greens pie.

Slender nettles have been coming up in our backyard in larger quantities than ever this year. They're a kind of stinging nettle, whose sting comes from little hairs that have an acid that burns. There are supposedly other wild plants you can rub on the sting as a remedy—in Greece they recommend common mallow—but fortunately I've never ended up so badly stung as to need to test such a claim. Once the acid is neutralized through cooking or drying the leaves, stinging nettles make a terrific wild-green food, a favorite among many old-time Cretans and Greeks.

Thanasis is excited that I'm going to make *tsouknidopitakia*, a much older Greek greens-pie than the ubiquitous spanakopita made with spinach—one of the few greens in Greece that is, relative to the long history of foods there, practically a newcomer.

Using the stand mixer, I make a simple dough of oil, white flour, water, grappa, and salt. As the dough is resting, I briefly sauté the rinsed nettles and a little chopped onion in olive oil.

I roll out some of the dough on the large folding table resting on bricks in the bump-out area of the kitchen, where more conventional suburban families keep a kitchen table for everyday eating. I use an upside-down small bowl to cut circles out of the dough and reincorporate the excess back into the remainder. A spoonful of the nettles goes into the center of each circle before I fold it in half and seal it with a fork. I collect the finished half-moons onto baking sheets.

When the filling is used up I ask Thanasis, *"Na tsi tiganisoume?"*

"Vevaios," Thanasis agrees that we should fry them in olive oil.

It was in Ohio, not in Crete, that I learned almost everything I know about wild greens. In fact I didn't even *eat* all that many wild greens in Crete, though years of watching everyone around me eating them left me knowing many of their names and even what some of them looked like cooked and plated. But wild greens—and greens in general—comprised such a central and highly celebrated part of Cretan cooking that it was inevitable that I'd learn about them once I was back in the United States.

Perhaps because she grew up in Taiwan, Sofia was like a rabbit when it came to green vegetables. No matter how many greens I'd eat, she always ate more. She'd fight for the bottom of the salad bowl the way I'd fight for the last piece of grilled pork. So between my quest for eating Cretan and her missing the wide variety of distinctively flavored greens she grew up with—unavailable even in the Chinese markets—it's no surprise that foraging turned out to be our most extensive food-related project during our graduate school years in Ohio.

When I came back to the United States, I already owned a reference book on Cretan wildflowers because I liked to use nature metaphors when I came out with *mantinades.* I went through it page by page and used every relevant Greek dictionary and thesaurus I owned in an attempt to figure out more edible greens and what they'd be called in English. I also found references to a number of the most common wild edible greens in my Cretan cookbook. Another deeply buried memory eventually rose to the surface and

I remembered that I'd seen a new book written by a Cretan called *Ta Horta* (*Greens*) on display in several shop windows in Irakleio. I called my bookseller in Athens again, but, alas, it was out of print and he couldn't get me a copy. I got by with my other materials for another year until *Ta Horta* came back in print again. Sometimes I was able to figure out what these greens were in standard Greek, English, or scientific taxonomy, but not always, so I began taking advantage of Ohio State's extensive libraries and interlibrary loan privileges to obtain further lexicons and scientific books from Greece dealing with the nation's flora.

It wasn't long before Sofia and I realized that some of the greens sold by our Chinese supermarket were closely related, botanically speaking, to some of the greens I knew from Crete. For salads, the Chinese *da dou miaou* (large pea shoots) were what Cretans called *papoules*, and *tong hao* (crown marigold) was *mantilida*. For boiled greens there were *hsien cai* (red-tinged amaranth greens), a slightly different variety of ubiquitous Greek *vlita*, and several tender Chinese leafy mustard greens related to the wild mustards that Cretans called *vrouves*. On top of that, the Chinese market had the more flavorful variety of celery that was like the leafy celery I remembered from Crete.

When it came to *wild* greens I already knew how to spot wild grapevines, the leaves of which could be used for stuffing *dolma-dakia*. And, of course, I knew the dandelion, which at that point I'd been led to believe was the *radiki*. (Later I realized there was some terminological confusion among many Greeks when it came to dandelions and chicory.) When spring arrived my second year in Ohio, Sofia and I got in the car and explored our way out of the city through what seemed like endless suburbs, on the lookout for wild grapevines growing somewhere. We eventually found some good locations and filled a couple grocery bags with them so we could freeze an entire year's supply. It was the closest thing I'd had to a rural experience in quite a while, and I felt unusually contented and at peace the next day while Sofia and I stuffed the tomatoes, zucchini, eggplants, peppers, and grape leaves.

It wasn't until the next year when we moved to a new apartment that we gathered wild dandelions for *horta*—a side dish of boiled greens, usually dressed with oil and lemon. The lawn in the far back of the new apartment complex we moved to bordered on a small patch of woods, and I noticed that the lawn-chemical company didn't spray back there, so we decided to take our chances. We'd come home from the university after classes in the late afternoon, grab a knife and a bag, and go outside to put our hands in the soil and collect them. Even though the dandelions were much dirtier than store-bought greens, I felt exhilarated to stand at the sink washing them, and—judging from the eager smile on her face—Sofia seemed to love preparing and eating them at least as much as I did. I was in love just seeing the cleaned and rinsed foraged dandelions—green leaves descending into red stems leading to a white crown—glistening on a white plate ready to go into a pot of boiling water.

Grape leaves and dandelions inspired us forward into larger projects. Several nights a week over the course of a month or so we'd go to a bookstore near our apartment and peruse one book after another for potentially useful information about greens—from the lexicographic to the culinary, from the scientific taxonomic to the nutritional or folk medicinal. When we discovered that there were actually books describing how to forage for wild edible plants, we both knew right away that we had to buy them, along with some other field guides on wildflowers and weeds in general. After all, we knew there were poisonous greens out there too.

My first task was to take note of any greens that grew in Crete that also had entries in our new foraging books. Sofia and I took our books and notes and headed outdoors almost every afternoon upon returning from campus. We walked and studied the area behind our apartment and the field across from the nearby railroad tracks. We drove to unkempt areas surrounding local parks and to the less-manicured outskirts of campus. We'd each pick our own spot and sit there with several books trying to figure out what was growing. Whenever one of us thought we'd found a wild edible green we were looking for we'd call the other one over to help verify. In the evenings, back at the apartment, we kept reading and rereading the books and studying the pictures and diagrams so the next time we'd be outdoors and see a new plant we'd have a better chance of suspecting what it was, and of where to look it up.

We spent an entire Saturday on the outskirts of the park studying, identifying, and collecting several different greens. Then I called up Thanasis and another graduate student, Dionysis, to invite them for a dinner to be accompanied by wild green salads and wild *horta*. Thanasis hardly believed me when I told him what we'd be eating. He already had other plans that evening but couldn't resist stopping by briefly to try everything—to experience eating *agria horta* (wild greens) in Ohio.

After Thanasis left, Dionysis, Sofia, and I sat around the table chatting while I flipped through the pages of one of our foraging books, rereading about what we'd just eaten. As I read an extensive entry on perhaps the most unexpected find of the day—the sweet cecily that Sofia had discovered—I took note of the elaborate warning about its being easy to confuse with water hemlock, probably the most poisonous green in eastern North America, and one that was almost certain to cause a violent and painful death. As I read this I quickly grew hot and began perspiring. I felt my heart racing. The happy sounds of Sofia and Dionysis chatting sounded muffled as if my ears were closing up. I read and reread. I got up and grabbed our other books and looked at them for more information. I sat down and read the first entry again. I was convinced that there was a chance that we'd erred.

I interrupted Sofia and Dionysis and told them my concern. They just laughed, entirely confident that there was nothing to worry about.

How can they be so confident, considering that none of us are experts on this stuff? I thought to myself. I tried again to convince them that it might *not* be okay.

Sofia insisted that she and I had independently confirmed that the sweet cecily had an aroma of anise—it smelled like ouzo—so there was nothing to worry about. Indeed, it was precisely the anise scent that made us so much more cavalier than usual about deciding that we knew what we'd found. Then I read aloud a section from a book explaining that poison water hemlock—as distinct from your run-of-the-mill Socrates-killing poison hemlock—has a *sweet* scent. I wasn't convinced that the indeterminately described sweet scent wasn't the sweet aroma that we believed was anise-like.

On top of that, I remembered that the place we found our plant was immediately adjacent to a small creek—a perfect habitat for *water* hemlock.

I tried calling Thanasis to let him know but there was no answer.

Then I called the poison control hotline. I explained our situation to the woman and she asked why in the world we were eating weeds. I explained how it was commonplace in Crete, and in a thick southern accent she replied, "Oh yeah. . . . I lived in Greece for a

while and I remember how they ate the wild greens." I told her
we didn't have any symptoms, but my book said it could take up
to a couple hours. She assured me that we probably didn't have
anything to worry about but that she'd call us back in an hour to
check on us.

I hung up the phone as desperate as ever to know for certain that
we hadn't eaten water hemlock. I couldn't wait out the test of time.
I analyzed and reanalyzed all pertinent information in the books,
struggling to find something that would give us absolute *proof* that
it wasn't water hemlock. The lack of certainty was unbearable. How
could I have allowed myself to do something so potentially life-
damaging?

I was also tormented by guilt: How could I have fed this to my
friends? They automatically trusted that we knew what we were
doing. What if they die? My anxiety grew so unbearable that I
ended up consoling myself with the thought that if it *was* water
hemlock, maybe we'd all be dead soon and at least *our* ordeal would
be over.

Still desperate for an immediate guarantee, I took Sofia and we
drove over to the park where we'd collected it to see if we could
find one more plant to compare every detail against the entries for
water hemlock in our books. It was completely dark so we parked
the car and left the headlights on pointing at the place we'd found
the plants. Somehow we managed to find another one and rushed
back to the apartment with it.

When we opened the door we found Dionysis lying on the floor
in front of the couch. It was precisely the kind of prank I was
expecting from this ostensibly mild-mannered Greek American from
out West. We studied and sniffed and compared with the pictures
and diagrams in the books and eventually were convinced that we
hadn't eaten water hemlock. It was indeed sweet cecily. By the time
the woman from poison control called back, my panic had subsided
and the world went back to normal.

We resolved to be even more careful and systematic when foraging
from then on.

By autumn we could readily identify dozens of species. After a
lifetime of seeing most of the green in the world as one big blur,
we began to appreciate all kinds of details and nuance. Wild lettuce
growing through a crack in the pavement; a little patch of purslane
in the grass between the library and University Hall; wood sorrel

here, clover there; wild carrots and chicory growing in the traffic island in the intersection. The seasons, once evident to us mostly through the weather and tree leaves, were now marked by the myriad activities of wild plants growing all around us: common blue violets ceasing to flower, lamb's quarters still low to the ground, purslane just barely poking out of the earth, chicory plants sending up their tall flower stalks.

The more we learned about the taxonomies of the Plant Kingdom, the more we realized that we also delighted in the very knowledge we were gaining. It wasn't only pragmatically useful to know—when making a salad, say—that chicory and lettuce are cousins, it also just felt good to know something like this about the plants we'd see around us every day.

Sofia and I began to associate locations around our apartment, the campus, and the city with the kinds of plants we observed growing there: the small patch of woods between the apartment buildings where wild leeks and toothwort grew; the trees nearby holding up poison ivy, while those adjacent were overgrown with wild grapes; the section in the park where the sweet cecily grows; the gravel near the bus stop full of chicory; the grass behind the tennis court of the apartments across the street with lady's smock. Our environs were looking ever more finely textured.

Sofia and I had almost a full year of foraging experience under our belt by the Saturday of Greek Orthodox Easter, the year that a new graduate student from Greece—Stavros, half-Cretan by descent—was around to join us. Having grown up in Athens, he was eager to learn to forage for the wild greens he not only missed from back home, but associated with his Greek or Cretan heritage. The three of us spent the whole morning and early afternoon gathering them. We took him to all our favorite spots, collecting every kind of edible we could find: dandelion (*pikralida*), goatsbeard (*skoulos*), seedlings of lamb's quarters (*klouvida*), curly dock (a kind of *lapatho*), lady's thumb (a variety of *agriopipouria*), wood sorrel (*xinida*), garlic mustard (a kind of *vrouva*), winter cress, peppergrass, shepherd's purse (*agriokardamida*), toothwort, wild leek, lady's smock, wild garlic, and common blue violet.

Then we took our bags of treasure back to Sofia's and my apartment. For hours we trimmed and cleaned, washed and rinsed. I made phyllo dough and Sofia chopped the wild leeks and sweated them in some olive oil in a huge stockpot. We added the rest of the greens to the pot, a little salt, and let them cook. Stavros began rolling out the first batch of dough, eventually covering almost the entire four-by-four-foot plywood top on the card table. We cut the dough into circles using upside-down bowls and filled each circle with the cooked greens. Sofia fried the *hortopitakia* a few at a time while Stavros and I continued with the rolling, cutting, and stuffing of dough. By about ten o'clock that evening we'd made between seventy and eighty wild-greens pies.

I called Thanasis, told him we were going to eat just after midnight, and asked if he wanted to join us. Every year since we'd arrived in Ohio, he and I went together to the Greek church just before midnight for *Anastasi* (the Resurrection)—Easter being the biggest holiday of the year in Greece, even for those Greeks who say they feel *culturally* Orthodox despite not believing in a god or anything else supernatural. And every year Thanasis was disappointed with how different from in Greece the whole experience was. As for myself, not only did it lack the aesthetic aspects that I'd enjoyed at a place like St. Minas in Irakleio—from the architecture and iconography to the chanting and overall mood, not to mention the language—it also reminded me of the Americanized Catholic church I was made to attend every Sunday as a child. So every Easter Thanasis and I would swear that we wouldn't go again the following year. But the way time heals many wounds, the next Easter would find Thanasis hopeful again and we'd go, starting the cycle of hope and disappointment all over again.

I was determined not to go, but Thanasis was wavering. He thought he should go, meaning that he'd also end up going out to celebrate with other Greek and Cypriot friends and colleagues he'd run into there. I reminded him of his regret in years past but he wasn't convinced, and said he'd call me again later.

Sofia and I went to work on the lamb. She cut up the meat into large chunks while I peeled and sliced the potatoes. We squeezed some lemons, and mixed everything together in a large bowl with olive oil, salt, pepper, and plenty of Cretan dried oregano. By the time we got it into the oven, Stavros and I had already finished off the first bottle of wine.

Thanasis called back and asked what we were planning to eat. "I'm not going to tell you," I teased him. "You know that since *we* made it, you're going to like it. Come on, now, make up your mind," I urged. He hemmed and hawed but finally decided that he'd head over to the church.

By midnight, the lamb and potatoes came out of the oven, there were wild-greens pies piled high in the center of the table, and Stavros and I were well into the second bottle of wine. "*Hristos Anesti*" ("Christ is risen"). "*Alithos Anesti*" ("Truly he is risen"), we called, holding up and clinking our glasses.

But I was the one who felt resurrected that night, mostly because Sofia and I had managed to bring to life so many of the foods I remembered from Crete.

※　※　※

Just as Thanasis and I are checking the goat to see if it's well cooked, Jason and Jeff arrive. They've brought a dozen eggs from their own chickens, and a few bottles of hard cider they made from apples on old trees on their property, once part of a farm. Our Easter celebration is shaping up beautifully.

"We can eat any time after five o'clock," Thanasis declares, and I concur, "because when it's five o'clock here it will already be Easter in Greece."

16

Kitchen Apprentice Redux

Ben's ready with his pad and pen. He's also got his bowl of one cup of flour and one cup of water that—three days ago by e-mail—I instructed him to mix, leave out at room temperature, stir once a day, and bring with him when he came. I've got my bowl of the same kind of mix.

"We're gonna make three versions of the same recipe for white bread . . . a very simple white bread," I explain. "You'll see how simple it is. It's just the tip of the iceberg, but at least you'll start learning some of the basic principles. Once you see how easy it is you'll probably make it all the time instead of buying bread.

"Of course I don't recommend this particular bread as your staple bread. Tomorrow I'll show you how to make a whole-grain loaf that has hardly any white flour, and the white flour is lacto-fermented before you use it anyway. Who knows if it really makes any difference. It can't hurt, and some people seem to think it's better in terms of the glycemic index, or whatever it's called."

The last time Ben and Catherine visited us, I mentioned to Ben—reminded him?—that if he wanted I could teach him how to make things like bread and yogurt sometime while they're staying with us. I know they have to make an appearance at the marathon dance at the high school, but I think the main reason they're here for the whole weekend is for the fermentation lessons: bread, yogurt, lacto-fermented pickles, and beer. We've got enough time to make them all!

"Here's three bowls. We'll make one with commercial yeast, one with the wild yeast that you ended up with in your flour-and-water mixture, and one with the wild yeast that I ended up with in my flour-and-water mixture. Then you'll be able to compare the commercial one with the 'Rockland County' one and the 'Saratoga County' one.

"Put a quarter teaspoon of this yeast in the first bowl, and a cup of flour and a cup of water."

Ben follows my instructions. He writes down what he did on his pad.

"There. Now we've got three mixtures that are the same except for the yeasts. I take that back: the *water* is different in yours, too, but anyway . . .

"Now add a teaspoon of salt to each bowl, and mix it in so it starts dissolving.

"And another half cup of water.

"And two more cups of flour. Easy, right? Twice as much flour as water. One-and-a-half cups of water so three cups of flour

"Now just mix them. The way we're doing this you'll have a really wet dough and you won't even knead it. Tomorrow I'll show you how to make bread that you have to knead.

"Here. Put these shower caps over the bowls. We're already half done."

I think to myself how different this is from when I first learned to make bread from Grandma. Scald the milk. Dissolve the yeast. Knead the dough *x* number of times. For the longest time, the only breads I knew how to make were Grandma's delicate and yeasty white bread and the simpler but mediocre recipe from my Kochilas cookbook.

During my first months in Ohio, I eventually remembered the *prozymi* that Eirini made on a few occasions. *Prozymi* was one of those super-traditional, going-all-out elements of Cretan cuisine that was mentioned in Penny's house with tremendous pride and excitement, almost reverence, especially when it was for her version of the Easter breads called *koulouria*. The way the whole family talked, I got the impression that adding yeast to bread was almost like cheating, and that the outcome could never be expected to be as good as with *prozymi*—though I could never understand how it worked. How could you get bread to rise without yeast?

In Ohio, I had Kochilas's supplemental instructions for making *prozymi*—a wild yeast sourdough starter—as I discovered it was called in English.

One day, following Kochilas, I mixed flour and water in a bowl and left it covered with a towel for several days on top of the refrigerator for the warmth, vaguely recalling that Eirini kept hers on the fridge. A couple times a day I lifted the towel and smelled the mixture, eager to experience the new scent that was destined to develop. It felt like I was about to become privy to one of nature's great mysteries—and to one more secret for making true Cretan food in the United States. As far as I can remember, I'd never actually looked at Eirini's *prozymi*, and I certainly had no idea what it had smelled like.

My mixture indeed soured, and I used it one weekday morning in place of commercial yeast to prepare the same basic Kochilas bread recipe I'd been making on the weekends. When I got back from class a few hours later, excited as could be, I lifted the towel from the large plastic bowl only to discover that it hadn't risen at all. I threw it out.

A few months later I tried again to no avail. I was still out of my league.

After I met Sofia and we began hanging out in bookstores to study and drink coffee, every so often I'd get up and browse books in the food section just for fun. In time, I discovered useful books on bread making that helped me acquire a fuller understanding of the art and science of it all. Up until then, I knew that yeast eats flour, giving off the carbon dioxide that makes the bubbles that cause the dough to rise. I also knew that the yeast contributes flavor to the bread, and that if the yeast gets too hot, it dies. That's about all I knew.

Through my reading I learned that the longer and more slowly you let the dough rise, the more fully pleasurable flavors and textures can develop; that a great deal of the nice flavor in good bread comes not from the yeast, but from other microorganisms that grow alongside the yeasts; that some of these bacteria contribute flavor more slowly than commercial yeasts; and that there's a relationship between their activity and the chemical makeup of the dough—which has to do in part with the particular *kinds* of yeast that are present.

In short, it was helpful to think about bread dough as a little habitat for various useful microorganisms, a habitat whose particular characteristics have important effects on the flavor of the baked bread. Such effects can be manipulated by the bread maker by adjusting the basic parameters of temperature, time, and quantity and types of yeast.

Since I was learning all this from baker's literature, I couldn't be certain that I had the science quite right, but however cartoonish my understanding might have been, it was a vast improvement over what I knew before, and a more-than-reasonable-enough first approximation for my purposes in the kitchen. I could always correct any oversimplifications and misunderstandings by digging deeper later on if need be.

I was startled to realize how much I'd misunderstood bread making for so many years. Even after I stopped relying on conventional written recipes for most foods, bread remained one of the few things I still religiously followed written recipes for. I thought it was one of those fussy foods like cake or cookies that needs a great deal of precision in order to succeed. But there I was—learning that bread is actually one of the most flexible and unfussy of all foods, provided one keeps in mind how manipulating the basic parameters of time, temperature, and yeast affects things.

Before, in my ignorance, I thought the dough needed to rise in a warm location. Now I was experimenting with putting it in the refrigerator overnight! Before, I was measuring out precise quantities of yeast for the dough. Now, I was just tossing a little yeast into a bowl with some flour and water and leaving it out for a few days, then adding a little salt and as much flour as it happened to take in order to become dough that wouldn't stick to my hands. Before, I used exactly whatever flour a recipe called for. Now, I was adding a little barley flour here and some whole wheat flour there.

The more I did these things, the more intuitive bread making became. I quickly gained a sense of approximately how much salt to add to approximately how much dough, how much to knead it, and so on. Instead of cups and teaspoons, minutes and hours, my new recipe was comprised of knowledge of the interrelationship of the time, temperature, and yeast. It was comprised of knowing that gluten formation in wet flour provides architecture for the dough. It was comprised of an experientially gained tactile understanding of when enough flour has been added to the dough, and of visual apprehension of when dough has risen long enough for whatever bread is being aimed for.

When it came to the question of the kind of yeast, I read that the wild yeasts that end up in a wild yeast sourdough starter could vary unpredictably by geographical location and probably other factors. You couldn't just assume that letting any old local yeasts act upon a mixture of flour and water would result in a flavorful bread starter, let alone one potent enough to ensure even and effective rising of the dough. One book I looked at provided a number of different recipes for harvesting wild yeasts from sources other than the air—such as from grape skins by soaking dried grapes (i.e., raisins) in water, and using the soaking water in the starter.

I realized another mistake I'd made in my first attempts at wild sourdough bread. A purely wild sourdough loaf needs a lot more time to rise, usually overnight, not just a couple hours like a loaf full of commercial yeast. Also, it's a lot fussier about temperature. I ended up converting the top shelf of a closet with an incandescent light into a warm space for letting my wild sourdough breads rise. Most importantly, I learned to let the rise times be decided by whatever was going on with any particular dough, instead of expecting the dough to conform to the predetermined times indicated in written recipes

Learning to bake bread in this roundabout way, through fragmented reading and occasional experimentation, had its benefits. For one thing, it meant that in seeking out one piece of information, I had to wade through other related information, some of which inevitably piqued my curiosity, leading me to end up learning more than I'd originally intended, and enriching my understanding of the underlying logic of a recipe. It also frequently brought me into contact with conflicting accounts of things, leaving questions in the back of my mind that needed further exploration: Does a sourdough starter kept in the refrigerator, begun from the yeasts on raisin skins, eventually come to be dominated by local yeasts from the air? Does a starter really need to be fed as often as everyone says? Asking questions spurred me on to consider what I'd need to do in order to confirm one account or another. Is there an explanation that I can test myself? Is there a more reliably expert source that I should consult? Is there any evident logical or scientific flaw in what has been asserted? I learned, therefore, to be increasingly cautious and critical about whatever I was reading about food.

Besides, learning in this way—driven by desires to unearth certain information or to address particular questions, doing so with Sofia and occasionally with other friends—made the learning process more enjoyable.

My success with the raisin skin sourdough starter eventually gave me another idea: Why use California raisins coated with the spores of California yeasts if I could get raisins from Crete hosting spores from the island instead? I asked Thanasis to bring me back raisins from Crete the next time he went home to Greece for summer break. Then I made two wild-yeast sourdough starters at the same time, one with California raisins from the supermarket, and one with the Cretan raisins Thanasis brought me. When the new starters were bubbly and ready for making bread, Sofia and I invited Thanasis and other Greek and Taiwanese friends over for a bread tasting party, and I proceeded to make simple white loaves from both. As the gathering got underway and the first loaves that came out of the oven had cooled, I cut a slice from each. I called everybody over to watch as Thanasis did a blind taste test. He immediately pointed to the Cretan-yeasted bread and said, "That's definitely the Cretan one." Granted he had a fifty-fifty chance, and he usually spoke with inflated self-assurance for rhetorical effect, but even so, I wanted to believe he knew.

❊   ❊   ❊

"Okay, Ben, now I gotta tell you more about how bread works. The more yeast you have in the dough, the faster it'll rise. Also, the warmer the dough is, the faster it'll rise . . . unless it's too hot, which'll kill the yeast altogether. But, the slower the dough rises, the more time you're giving to the other bacteria to develop flavors in the dough.

"We'll just leave these out here on the table at room temperature and bake them tonight. But if you realized later that you didn't have time to bake them tonight, you could always just put the dough in the fridge.

Then I quiz him: "Putting it in the fridge would do *what*?"

Four or five hours later, I call Ben over to the table where all the doughs are. "What do you notice?"

Ben points to the dough with the commercial yeast. "This one has risen a lot more than the other ones."

"Right. Now take off the shower caps and smell them."

"Oh wow! What a difference!" He keeps smelling them. "Hey Catherine, come smell our 'Rockland County' sourdough."

"You'd never guess they were the 'same' recipes from the smell, would you?" I ask.

"Definitely not. The regular yeast smells a lot different than the sourdoughs."

"Even so, we've only put a small amount of commercial yeast, which is why it'll take all day to rise enough. That way we're giving it more time to develop flavor."

"Okay, so time for another quiz: The sourdoughs aren't rising as much as the commercial yeast dough. So what can we do to help speed them up?"

"Add more yeast?"

"Well, uh, yeah . . . that's right. In fact, okay, why don't we do that for one of them. We don't have any more wild-yeast starter, though, so we'll cheat and use commercial yeast. It's not really cheating, there's already so much flavor developed in there from the wild yeast, you'll see. It just won't be a purely wild-yeast bread. Which one do you wanna keep purely wild?"

"Ummm . . . purely wild? Let's keep the 'Rockland County' one."

"Okay. Here, sprinkle a quarter teaspoon of yeast over the 'Saratoga County' one and let it sit for a couple minutes, then mix it up again. It won't distribute perfectly but it should work well enough.

"So, as long as we we're waiting, let me ask you: What *else* can we do to speed up the 'Rockland County' wild dough besides adding more yeast?"

Ben thinks for a moment but comes up empty.

"Do you remember what I said about temperature?"

"If it's warmer it'll rise faster."

"Right. So why don't we try keeping that dough somewhere warmer than the other ones. We can put it in the oven with the oven light on."

I put the bowl into the oven and Ben sits down to write more notes.

"Hey!" I suddenly interrupt him. "Did I ever show you or give you a copy of the recipe book I wrote when I was in Ohio?"

Even though for the longest time I hated it when people would ask me for a recipe, I eventually thought I should try writing down recipes for most of the Greek dishes I made. I'd realized that the food Sofia and I cooked as graduate students had developed into something that was on the whole quite unique. We were able to cook "more Greek" and "more Cretan" than even our friends from Greece living in the United States. On the other hand, even when we cooked foods that were close to the dishes I knew from Crete, we did so using different kitchen equipment, sometimes slightly different ingredients, different culinary techniques, and certainly different shopping schemes. Our knowledge about the same dishes differed, as we learned a lot from books and not from our Greek mothers. Even the way we ate the same food could vary subtly, as when we began using chopsticks to eat *dolmadakia* made from North American *wild* grapevine leaves. There were obvious influences on our cooking from my American and Sofia's Taiwanese past.

I liked the idea of sharing my knowledge of home cooking as others had done with me. I liked the idea that more home cooks in the United States might cook in the Mediterranean styles that I found so delicious. And, just like when I made a "menu" of Greek and Cretan dishes upon moving to Ohio, I was also experiencing a vague desire to *collect*—to bring together into a single entity the many dishes that defined traditional Cretan food in the United States in the manner that Sofia and I were making them. It was probably the same urge to collect that I felt when I was researching fruits, fishes, and greens, compiling lexicons far more extensive than I'd ever need for kitchen purposes, taking pleasure from merely possessing the names and information. Or maybe the pleasure wasn't so much a matter of possessing them, but from imagining that I'd possess them *all* once I completed my research.

I had a hunch that such an impulse to collect was a telltale sign of some kind of spiritual unrest or psychological malaise. I couldn't help but wonder if it had to do with living in a consumerist society. I recounted some of the ways that my upbringing had encouraged it—rock collecting being one of my earliest childhood hobbies, then baseball cards, then postage stamps, then dictionaries of the Cretan dialect, and so on. I fretted over the possibility that this desire was no different from what I saw in so many other people I knew—from Aunt Patsy's collections of Elvis-related trinkets to Sofia's collection of owls.

When I found myself with a chunk of extra time on my hands, even though I was on the fence about writing down recipes, I decided to take a stab. But I didn't know what the recipes should look like. I thought that what goes into a recipe depends on the way you view the making of a dish: Is it the *quantity* or the *flavor* of a contributing ingredient that gets emphasized? Is the way an ingredient is *grown* as important as the kitchen techniques applied to it? Or how the *people* who grow an ingredient are treated as workers? Where does shopping fit in?

I also thought that it depends on how a recipe is likely to be read and interpreted. The same written recipe may be many different recipes depending on who's reading it. Even the most conventional written recipes can be read in unconventional ways, but my worry was that the potential virtues of the conventional written recipe were too frequently undermined by the way the people *I* knew—especially people in my family—were reading them, the way they were *taught* to read them. The way they read recipes meant it was unlikely that they'd try to understand more fully *why* something is made the way it is, or how it could be made differently. Preoccupied with whether or not they had a teaspoon of cinnamon left in the jar, they never paused to consider the role of cinnamon in the recipe, and whether it might also work to use a little nutmeg, allspice, clove, or cardamom instead. Then, maybe anxious about their own culinary inflexibility, they'd join in the romantic celebration of so-called traditional recipes and cuisines. Catching a glimpse of a traditional cook making something delicious without a written recipe, caught up in their written-recipe worldview, they'd nostalgically proclaim traditional cooking more *authentic*. Wearing modernity's shock absorbers against the unpredictable fluctuations of nature and culture—which in less-industrial circumstances affect the availability and consistency of ingredients—they wouldn't see the traditional home cook's *process*: the ingenuity, the sensible substitutions, and the clever reinterpretations of past knowledge in light of present circumstances. In turn, they'd fail to recognize their *own* creative potential and feel discouraged about seizing unexplored opportunities for creativity that depend on a different kind of understanding of a dish.

I knew conventional written recipes are not to be blamed for all this, but I also thought that the way they're written did little to *challenge* my relatives to interpret them in other ways.

I started by writing down whatever explicit knowledge I had in my head for all the dishes I usually made. For example:

FISH AND OKRA IN THE OVEN

Marinate okra in freshly squeezed lemon. Add peeled and chopped potatoes, chopped onions, and okra to a roasting pan. Add chopped tomatoes, several fish [e.g., snapper, trout, parrotfish], olive oil, salt, and pepper. Bake at 350–400°F until the fish and potatoes are cooked.

This kind of recipe provided an accurate representation of what I consciously thought about when making it, but it left out all the tacit knowledge that came into play—from the possible ranges of ingredient quantities and marinating and cooking times to possible cooking hardware and if and when and how to combine the ingredients. I gave a copy of this collection to my mother and a few others. But its recipes were far too succinct to be of much use to most of the people who asked me for them because they didn't include my tacit knowledge.

Eventually, I thought I should teach my relatives "how to cook," but in ways that would develop the particular kinds of knowledge and skills I thought would be helpful for home-cooking Cretan and Greek cuisine. I thought about a graduated approach, starting from just a few carefully chosen simple recipes written in elaborate detail. Not so much the kind of detail found in conventional written recipes, but about the kinds of principles and variations that I took to be integral to the recipes as I understood them. I wrote things like this:

SIMPLE BREAD

[. . .]

The next morning, the "starter" dough should be bubbly and have a distinctive yeasty aroma. Smell it. Learn to recognize and appreciate the many different delicious smells that result from various kinds of fermentation. Add about a teaspoon of salt. If the starter is really bubbly, it would be okay to add another half or full cup of water if you wanted to make a larger quantity of bread.

[. . .]

The idea was to proceed from simpler to more complex recipes in a deliberate fashion to help wean my relatives off the kind of cooking that blindly follows conventional recipes to the letter. They could start with a simple white bread with commercial yeast and gradually work their way toward wild sourdoughs, examples of how to vary the starches and other ingredients in the dough, ways to shape the loaves, a variety of cooking temperatures, and so on. They'd learn to make a basic romaine lettuce salad—in order to get down the washing, the drying, the cutting, and the dressing of the greens—and later, gradually, they'd get into the family trees of the Plant Kingdom and the characteristic flavors and textures of different families, to learn how to combine and substitute a wide range of greens for infinitely different green salads. They'd first learn to make a simple Greek-style salad of tomatoes and cucumbers, and then to use anything from fennel tops to nasturtium buds and sheep sorrel.

As I continued working on this new draft I faced new problems. For one thing, there was a vast amount of tacit knowledge that was potentially relevant to any given dish. It seemed clear to me that my goal shouldn't be to try supplying all of it, so much as to offer a start. I should encourage my relatives to develop the habit of seeking out such information on their own, as needed or desired, as Sofia and I had done and were continuing to do. And I should share a few ideas about how to go about doing so in case they'd never developed such habits in other contexts—as I happened to have done in college and in graduate school. In other words, I realized that my hopes for this new collection of recipes had at least as much to do with encouraging critical information literacy related to food as it did with teaching Cretan food in an American context.

Things quickly got complicated. It was no longer just a matter of writing about flour—where it comes from, how it's manufactured (e.g., the significance of bleaching), different varieties of flour and their characteristics—but also of writing about *shopping* for flour, about how to find out what stores are available nearby to shop at in the first place, about how to read an ingredient label, about how to do the appropriate research necessary for understanding the regulations governing labeling so as not to be confused by labels, and so on. I thought about providing a sample list of useful references to consult for more information—encyclopedias of fruits and vegetables, say—but no such list of references would be perfect or readily accessible, and so I'd also need to help them understand how to find and select references on their own and to make judgments about their quality and reliability. As with the dishes themselves, teaching these others kinds of skills would need to happen in a graduated way.

I was in way over my head. I was on the verge—as an amateur home cook—of trying to write my own version of a full-blown "home economics" textbook for people living in a complex, capitalist, industrial food culture!

Would my relatives feel motivated enough to learn such things in this manner, however well I might organize them? If I could somehow miraculously write such a thing, was their desire to eat healthier or to be able to cook more delicious foods so strong that they'd actually work patiently through the kind of textbook I was imagining?

Reflecting on how I myself had come to learn so much about food, I realized that it was my obsession with eating Cretan cuisine in the United States, on top of being somewhat favorably predisposed toward cooking ever since childhood, that made the patient and unwavering pursuit of so much culinary knowledge so incredibly inviting to me. I realized that much of the delight and downright ease of learning resulted from the fact that I was free to learn about bread when I was in the mood to learn about bread, and to learn about wine when I was excited to learn about wine. While my acquisition of new information and knowledge may have happened gradually, it certainly was not because I pursued it in a meticulously organized, strenuously self-disciplined, and graduated manner—as I had calculus or even the Greek language for that matter. There was no pedagogical "recipe" that I followed in order to learn the nonconventional food and drink dishes I ended up caring about—and even if there had been, I'm quite certain that I wouldn't have followed it, unless I'd been required to. I figured that if my relatives were motivated enough to work their way through anything I'd write, they probably would've been doing a lot more to learn about cooking *already*, considering how many opportunities—including some convenient and relatively inexpensive ones—are out there.

I gave up.

❅   ❅   ❅

Somewhere around seven o'clock in the evening I notice that the two breads on the table look ready to bake. I summon Ben back into the kitchen. I have him take out the third dough that's been rising in the light-warmed oven so we can turn it on for preheating.

"Turn the oven to four-fifty, and while it warms up we'll prepare the loaves.

"Take this tin of flour and spread a bunch of it all over the middle of the breadboard. Put lots of it. We'll end up putting most of it back into the tin anyway, so it won't go to waste."

Ben follows my instructions.

"There's different ways to do this but let me just show you the simplest way I know so you can get started at home."

I take out three baking sheets and three pieces of parchment paper I've used before. I lay the parchment paper on the baking sheets.

"I don't know how to explain this next step, so I'll just show you with the first one and then you can do the other two. It's easy once you see it.

"Scrape the dough out of the bowl . . . there, see how I'm doing it? . . . I try to keep it as more-or-less one big blob . . . Then put some flour on your fingers and start working it up from around the edges like this, where there's more flour, turning it over as you go. There, that looks good."

I set the loaf onto the parchment paper on one of the baking sheets.

"Okay, you do the other two."

Ben scoops out the first one but has a little trouble because he hasn't gotten used to the motions yet, and the dough sticks to his fingers.

"That's alright. Just get it more or less into shape. It'll still come out just fine."

He finishes the first dough and scoops out the second. This time he's doing better.

"What?" says Ben.

"Oh, nothing. You're doing fine. I was just mumbling to myself."

I just realized that the best-written recipes that come from me are whatever Ben and Katherine and anyone else who cooks with me here happen to write down for themselves.

☀ 17 ☀

Love of Hosting Others

Andy and Dafne—on their way back home from the farmers' market where they sell their cheeses on Saturdays—have stopped to visit us for lunch. It's their first time here. I'm trying to live up to the unwritten tenets of Cretan hospitality.

Our invitation to them was, of course, open-ended. We've dispensed with most conventional formalities and etiquette insofar as these could potentially interfere with their carefree pleasure.

Sofia and I have made lots of food and have plenty of wine on hand. When either of them stops eating I prod them to eat more in case they're too shy or polite to do so on their own. I keep my eyes on certain dishes in case there isn't enough of something for us all to get our fill, and I need to put the brakes on my own voracious appetite.

Sofia and I don't hurry to pick up the table but leave everything out as we continue sipping wine and talking. When Andy starts gathering some plates, I insist that he sit down as I jump up and remove the plates myself. We only let visitors like Andy and Dafne help out when we think that it'll bring them enjoyment—but not in the sense of merely alleviating guilt. For example, some visitors relish harvesting the vegetables we're about to eat from our garden. And there's such a growing fascination with food in the United States these days that some of our visitors take pleasure in watching us prepare food—as entertainment, I suppose, but sometimes as an enjoyable way learn more about cooking. So we make exceptions for visitors whose help is aimed at satisfying their own desires to learn or to create. Even Leonidas—who won't let other visitors lift a finger—lets us cook at his house when he knows it won't feel like a chore to us.

I try to remain diligent about not letting Andy and Dafne see anything in my behavior that might make them wonder whether their visit has become burdensome, which, of course, it hasn't, but that's beside the point. I try to strike a balance between doing things that need to be done—like opening the next bottle of wine and monitoring their spirits—and just relaxing and enjoying myself, too, which has the fringe benefit of making them even less likely to feel self-conscious about their visit.

I watch for opportunities to help nudge the collective mood in directions that are more likely to lead to the eruption of more intellectually complex discussions, more emotionally complex high-spiritedness, or both.

All this brings me immediate pleasure. It also makes me feel good about staying determined to uphold Cretan hospitality while living in the United States.

Filoxenia is the Greek word usually translated as *hospitality* in English, derived from the well-known prefix *filo-* (often transliterated as *philo-*) signifying friendship or love, and *xenos* meaning "stranger," "outsider," "foreigner," "other," or "the other." The verb *host* is *filoxeno* and the word for "houseguest"—whether *xenos* or not—is the participle *filoxenoumenos*, "the hosted one." So *filoxenia* could also be translated as "love of hosting others," much like *philosophy* sometimes gets translated as "love of wisdom."

When I was living in Crete, I often saw people discuss the importance of *filoxenia* explicitly, which isn't surprising since Greece is one of those places that has been associated with hospitality to the point of a stereotype.

More than once did I see Manolis assert that *filoxenia* was of central importance to Cretans throughout history, explaining that it obligated a host to treat even his enemies well for as long as they were under his roof. He also emphasized that his most noteworthy experiences with *filoxenia* usually involved the simplest food and drink, often a matter of just scrounging up whatever there was, like some bread or olives. When money was tight, it involved coming up with a little something quickly and discreetly without letting visitors catch on to their hosts' predicament.

He told a story about a Cretan mountain village renowned for its *filoxenia*. (I have no idea if it was apocryphal, or whether he knew.) Several men stopped by the house of one of their fellow villagers, a widow, who didn't have anything she could offer them. So she filled shot glasses with water and served them to the men saying that she didn't have quite enough *tsikoudia* for them all and so she had to fill one of the glasses with water, but that whoever got the water shouldn't say anything so as not to spoil their drink together. Supposedly the men all kept their word, each believing that he alone was dutifully doing his part to uphold the ritual clinking of glasses, while in fact they were all collectively—and, except for the widow, unknowingly—maintaining the widow's honor and the sanctity of *filoxenia*.

During high-spirited gatherings over food and wine, I often saw Manolis go into a trance-like state as he sang along with the most widely revered Cretan folk song dealing with *filoxenia*:

> Mother, if my friends should come, and our relatives too,
> don't make their hearts heavy by telling them that I died.
> Set the table so they can eat, make the bed so they can sleep,
> prepare the divan for them to put down their arms,
> and when they wake up at dawn and are saying goodbye
> tell them that I died.

It might as well have been this song that inspired Nikos Kazantzakis's literary accounts of Cretan *filoxenia*. For instance, in the chapter "Crete" of his quasi-autobiographical *Report to Greco*, Kazantzakis recounts several vignettes that supposedly occurred during one of his trips back to the island to recover from his spiritually and intellectually challenging travels and adventures. In one of these vignettes, he finds himself tired and hungry at dusk near a village unknown to him, but also at ease knowing that in Crete he'd be taken care of: "I knew that in a Cretan village any door you knocked on would open, the table would be set in your honor, and you would sleep on the best sheets of the house. The *xenos* is still the unknown god in Crete, and all doors and hearts open for him."[1] With the help of an old woman, he finds his way to the village priest's house and the priest welcomes him in, "'Welcome,' he told me, 'You're *xenos*? Come inside.'"[2] The priest says that his wife is under the weather and so he himself cooks for his visitor and prepares the bed for him to spend the night. In the morning, Kazantzakis enjoys the bread, cheese, and milk that the priest brings him. Then as he's leaving the village he encounters an old man. When the old man learns that Kazantzakis spent the night at the priest's house he tells Kazantzakis that the priest's only son had died the morning before. Then he adds that the wake was even being held right there in one of the rooms of the house, and that the mourners must have kept their dirges hushed lest Kazantzakis hear them and discover how burdensome his visit was.

When Kazantzakis wrote that the *xenos* is *still* the unknown god in Crete, he was probably referring to the ancient Greek custom of hospitality, called *xenia*. Zeus, the Cretan-born Greek god was known as *xenios Zeus*, protector of the rights of hospitality. Textual evidence from Homer's *Odyssey* to Ovid's *Metamorphoses* suggests an old belief that the gods sometimes roamed the world among humans, which meant that a stranger at one's door could be a god in disguise—a god who might punish a host who didn't live up to the expectations of *xenia*.

Or maybe Kazantzakis meant to suggest that traditional Cretan culture was *still* characterized by the kind of hospitality that treats strangers as though they were gods, and that such a tradition somehow managed to persevere—at least up until the time he was describing—in spite of Greece's modernization.

When Sofia and I moved into our first apartment together in Ohio, she was always on board with—even impressed by—how often I invited friends over to share the homemade foods we made. By living together, splitting the rent and utilities, and scavenging roadsides and dollar stores for our furniture, we usually had money left over from our graduate stipends to prepare meals for our Greek, Cypriot, and Taiwanese friends, sometimes weekly.

But soon enough we discovered that our being together meant having to confront certain differences between us. For example, it was just as unacceptable to Sofia to allow visitors to wear shoes in our apartment as it was for me to ask them not to. I always detested having to take off my shoes at someone else's house, and asking other people to do so was a serious offense to my Cretan sensibilities.

As I thought about the shoe issue, one particular example from Crete kept turning over in my mind. It occurred on May Day of my first year living there. After spit-roasting a lamb and eating it for lunch with lots of Manolis's wine, Manolis, Eirini, Penny, and I spent the rest of the day going from one relative's house to another, ritualistically continuing to eat and drink (all of us), playing the mandolin (me), and singing *mantinades* (primarily Manolis). By dusk we ended up at Uncle "Bigshot's" house, still going strong, and

I felt my first urge to break a glass on the floor. Not quite fully accustomed to expressing myself so freely, knowing that his wife would have to pick up the mess, and in spite of her repeatedly encouraging me to do so anyway, I relented. Eirini commended me for being so considerate. Bigshot, sitting on the couch next to her—visibly annoyed that his sister had approved of my prudent suppression of a spontaneous desire—proceeded to flip over the entire coffee table full of drinks and food, smashing everything all over the mosaic stone floor of their living room. For those of us who'd been drinking wine all day, Bigshot sent our spirits soaring even higher. I got up and stood on a chair as I continued playing the mandolin. A little later, Bigshot stepped out onto the front steps, pointed his pistol up in the air, and shot off a round.

With this kind of experience as my inspiration and guide, how could I possibly consider telling my Greek and Cypriot visitors that they should take off their shoes just to enter our apartment? For many years I'd been mostly interacting with Greeks, so I never felt the need to impose a Greek model of hosting on anyone around me. And even the idea of imposing it on Americans didn't much bother me. Fed up with the United States' military, economic, and cultural imperialism, I wasn't about to feel any more guilty about adopting a defensive posture of Greek ethnocentrism against offensive American ethnocentrism than quite a few Greeks I knew, who, if pressed on the matter, ultimately disapproved of *all* forms of ethnocentrism.

I told Sofia that I refused to give in when it came to hosting visitors.

Sofia also refused to give in.

As much as I wanted to believe that the Cretan way was objectively superior, I knew it wasn't true. I mean, I knew that the superiority of one way over another ultimately had to be argued relative to some set of shared assumptions about values or goals. This left me full of intuition but short on argument. I also felt uneasy about buying into the point of view on intercultural marriage that an American woman married to a Greek man had told me once at a picnic in Chicago many years earlier: "The stronger *culture* always wins," meaning that Greek trumps American.

(Still, I couldn't resist wondering which culture would win in such a match: Cretan/Greek or Taiwanese/Chinese?)

I was forced to confront my "defensive" ethnocentrism, which began to feel like a suspiciously convenient posture to have adopted. In other words, like a cop-out. Since Sofia wasn't an American, I could hardly justify imposing my views on her with such a rationale. On the contrary, I couldn't help but remind myself that she was an immigrant woman of color living in the United States, who rarely insisted on having things her way, and that I was a white male American who frequently so insisted. If I stubbornly imposed my way, how could I be sure that *I* wasn't committing a shameful act of cultural, racial, and gender domination? In the end, wouldn't that also leave me feeling horribly guilty?

I eventually decided that the cultural labels and narratives of victimization weren't getting me anywhere. There simply were no hard-and-fast rules justifying the adoption of Cretan, Taiwanese, American, male, female, or any other prepackaged-and-labeled model of hosting visitors in our apartment. Nor did it seem likely that we'd discover a general rule that we could apply whenever we had to decide between such personal differences that were clearly rooted in our differing social and cultural backgrounds. We'd just have to deal with these disagreements as theoretical and practical issues on a case-by-case basis.

In this particular situation, we settled on my writing a humorous sign to hang outside our apartment door:

ΚΑΤΑ ΠΑΡΑΒΑΣΙΝ ΤΩΝ ΙΕΡΩΝ ΦΙΛΟΞΕΝΙΑΣ ΚΑΝΟΝΩΝ, ΠΑΡΑΚΑΛΟΥΝΤΑΙ ΟΙ Κ.Κ. ΕΠΙΠΣΚΕΠΤΑΙ ΟΠΩΣ, ΑΜΑ ΤΗ ΕΙΣΟΔΩ ΤΩΝ, ΑΠΑΛΛΑΓΩΣΙΝ ΤΩΝ ΥΠΟΔΗΜΑΤΩΝ ΤΩΝ, ΣΥΜΦΩΝΩΣ ΤΑΙΣ ΑΠΑΙΤΗΣΕΣΙ ΤΩΝ ΙΕΡΩΝ ΚΑΝΟΝΩΝ ΤΗΣ ΤΑΪΒΑΝΗΣ ΟΙΚΟΔΕΣΠΟΙΝΗΣ.

In an exaggerated purist Greek bureaucratese, the sign asked visitors to pardon the violation of the sacred rules of hospitality but to kindly remove their shoes out of respect for the Taiwanese hostess's own sacred rules. Sometimes the sign convinced my Greek friends to take off their shoes. Sometimes it didn't. Whenever Thanasis visited, he'd diligently wipe his feet five or six times on our welcome mat, clearly uncomfortable about taking off his shoes. Sofia compromised by letting it go, especially since I couldn't muster up the courage to ask him to remove his shoes after the sign hadn't convinced him.

In time, Sofia became less adamant about having visitors remove their shoes, and I became less distressed about visitors feeling inconvenienced if they happened to do so, thinking that it was our desire.

It wasn't so much that we learned the importance of compromise to a successful relationship. It's more like we learned that the business of everyday living—when approached with both heart and mind—requires you to revisit your assumptions about social and cultural norms every now and then, and to consider how these norms influence, and are potentially influenced by, the decisions and habits of particular individuals in everyday life situations.

Meanwhile, I began seeing *filoxenia* from new angles as a result of the reading I was doing as a graduate student. I soon realized that when I was leaving Crete and had vowed to myself to uphold *filoxenia* in the United States, no matter how difficult it might prove, I'd been naive—if not about my resolve, then about *filoxenia* being merely a matter of an individual's ethics. I learned that it isn't only a matter of people's psychologies, sentiments, attitudes, or consciously held beliefs, norms, and ideals. *Filoxenia* is also—and maybe more significantly—an indivisible part of the particular social, economic, and political circumstances where it prevails.

In antiquity, travel was long and slow. Without hotels, travelers needed a place to stay. To the extent that such travel was integral to ancient societies, providing food and shelter to a stranger addressed certain broader societal expectations or needs. It would seem a little naive to claim that the *xenia* of antiquity—wherein people were obliged to put up strangers for the night—was primarily a matter of caring about visitors or of divine decree enforced by the likes of Zeus or some other deity. And even if it was, maybe one reason it was widely *believed* to be so caring or divinely imperative was because of the societal needs that it also addressed.

I realized that this line of thinking was just the tip of the iceberg once I came across the ethnographic texts of Harvard anthropologist Michael Herzfeld, who'd analyzed *filoxenia* in several of its recent Cretan and Greek incarnations. His research brought to my attention aspects of contemporary *filoxenia* that I'd never thought about.

For example, Cretan *filoxenia* can provide a vehicle for Cretan men to prove their masculinity. According to Herzfeld, certain highland rural Cretans believe that an essential aspect of masculinity involves a host dispensing "hospitality at every possible opportunity, deprecating the poverty of his table whilst plying his guests with meat and wine."[3] Therefore, a host's act of extreme *filoxenia* in this social context also sends certain messages about his manhood to other Cretans who witness it. In doing so, it reinforces or challenges everyone's taken-for-granted ideas about what it means to be a man. Since ideas about what it means to be a man arguably play a significant role in the goings-on in Cretan society in general, this means *filoxenia* is something more than a mere ingredient of Cretan culture: it also functions to shape widespread beliefs about gender in Cretan culture. *Filoxenia* may be a virtue that many individual Cretans choose to uphold, but it's not *merely* a virtue. Like it or not, it's also a practice that contributes to Cretans subscribing to certain beliefs about masculinity (and, by extension, femininity) and acting upon those beliefs—consciously and unconsciously—in particular ways.

Herzfeld also writes that the rural Cretan social world is organized symbolically in terms of nested insider-outsider dichotomies, like a series of concentric circles: kin/nonkin, covillager/non-covillager, Cretan from the same region/Cretan from a different region, Cretan/non-Cretan, Greek/non-Greek, and European/non-European. But, he argues, it's also usual that Cretans avoid mentioning these *specific* dichotomies explicitly. Instead, they tend to use the more ambiguous language of "insider" versus "outsider" (*xenos*). Such ambiguity, in turn, enables utterances and other forms of social interaction to allude purposefully and poetically to more than one of these identities at the same time.[4] Thus, he argues, an act of *filoxenia* can function to demonstrate not only "manliness," but also a host's identity as a Greek, as a Cretan, as an inhabitant of a certain village, or all of the above. Consequently, it can work to reinforce—or to challenge—local convictions about what it means to be an authentic Greek, a true Cretan, or a model inhabitant of a particular village.

There's also an element of competition involved. Conventionally, such Cretans seek to demonstrate that they (or their family or their village or their region) are *more* hospitable than others. This has implications for hospitality that is extended to strangers. The more of an outsider that an outsider is—the farther from the center of Herzfeld's concentric circles that he or she is—the fewer the mutual obligations between host and guest, which means the more *voluntary* the hospitality will appear, and the more hospitable the host will be viewed to be.[5] The same goes for impromptu hospitality:

> A possible crisis arises whenever unexpected visitors show up at a house where there is no meat at hand. [. . .] But even when large amounts of meat cannot be found quickly enough, the host may be able to emphasize his generosity, and above all his manhood, in

another way. He may apologize for the poverty of his table, pointing out that the guests would have to be content with "whatever can be found." This phrase invokes a crucial principle. Ability to improvise, to make the most of whatever chance offers, is the mark of the true man. It is unthinkable for a [Cretan of a certain village] to refuse to entertain extra guests; on the contrary, he is expected to make the most of what he has, announcing that "food for nine people also *defeats* ten!" Note the agonistic quality, the claim to moral victory, that this attributes to his hospitality. It is a quality that combines well with the ability to improvise a meal out of nothing, and that attests to his control over the female household members who actually do the work of preparing and serving the repast.[6]

The "extreme" hospitality of the rural highland Cretan who provides food and shelter to a complete stranger, or who manages to make the most of what he has at a moment's notice through improvisation, also demonstrates how very manly and competently Cretan (and Greek, etc.) he is.

Building on these and other arguments, Herzfeld avers that Mediterranean hospitality functions symbolically to enact "the moral and conceptual *subordination* of the guest to the host."[7] "Hospitality does not mark acceptance of the stranger so much as the moral superiority of the host."[8] "[T]he presence of lavish hospitality in Greek villages is an expression both of the moral superiority of the host and of the political potential of the guest."[9]

For instance, in the case of "the extreme hospitality that forces a man to shelter his bitterest foe, even though he may slay the visitor as soon as the latter leaves the house," Herzfeld says that it conventionally applied only to guests who were *strangers*, not to covillagers, "because, by definition, a co-villager never depends on one to any meaningful degree. The very clemency shown to the stranger is the mark of his total subordination."[10]

This subordination of guest to host can also be seen in village coffeehouse practices:

A visiting *ksenokhorianos* ("stranger from another village") will reciprocate the drink he is offered when he first steps into a coffeehouse by then treating the entire clientele. Here, the ritual is more complex because the stranger must prove himself to be a true Cretan, and so a *virtual* co-villager. The true foreigner is not allowed to reciprocate at all until a strong bond of familiarity can be established, although the local host acknowledges an entirely theoretical obligation on the part of the guest through the formula that "one day I may turn up in your place." Since, however, both parties usually know that such a development is in practice unlikely to occur, the possible irony—once again!—of the host's phrase reduces the foreign visitor to a state of still deeper moral indebtedness.[11]

Finally, subordination can also be seen at the level of Greece versus those Western nations (England, Germany, the U.S., etc.) that have exercised—for better and for worse—significant influence over the course of Modern Greek history. The lavish unreciprocated hospitality that many Greeks have been known to heap upon Western visitors can be viewed as accomplishing the symbolic subordination of the latter by the former: "As unilateral givers, then, the Greeks are enabled to use the moral implications of reciprocity to reverse the historical and political dependence of their country upon the West. Hospitality is the social format that permits Greeks to englobe the dominant cultures of Europe."[12]

After reading analyses like these, I began to see Cretan *filoxenia* as something of a mixed blessing. I still believed it was usually extended by Cretan individuals and families who sincerely intended to please their guests—*not* to subordinate them—at least not consciously. I continued to believe that many Cretans conceived of *filoxenia* primarily as a timeless ethical virtue of humanity more than as a means for showing off their manhood or their Cretanness. I also remained convinced that many visitors experienced genuine pleasure in the hands of their hosts, and not necessarily as, or only as, a masochistic pleasure derived from having been subordinated.

But my convictions didn't contradict, let alone negate, Herzfeld's interpretations. After all, the most heartfelt *filoxenia* at the level of individual people could *also* have the *social* effects he describes, even unintentionally, even unconsciously. This is so because the social meanings and identities generated by such acts can have more to do with whatever beliefs about gender and local and national identities are already in play in society than with any particular host's or guest's feelings or intentions. A host might aim to do nothing more than please a guest, but if acts of generous *filoxenia* are already widely viewed by the people around him as indicative of a competitive and subordinating Cretan masculinity, there might be little he can do, at least in the moment, to prevent people from interpreting them as such.

I saw for the first time that *filoxenia*'s acts of extreme human kindness and generosity might be to some extent part and parcel of the very ethnocentrism and male-dominating patriarchy I thought I was against! It wasn't *necessary* that Cretan *filoxenia* had these kinds of social effects, but it seemed to be the case in the particular Cretan contexts that Herzfeld researched. Maybe things had changed since he'd conducted his research. Maybe things weren't like this *everywhere* on the island even back then. My sense was that they didn't work quite this way in the middle-class Irakleio that I was mostly familiar with, but maybe I just couldn't see through to what Herzfeld was so good at seeing. At any rate: just because *filoxenia* might not be all good didn't necessarily mean it's all bad either.

I began to wonder more about the symbolic meanings and social effects of *filoxenia*. For instance, I became curious about the relationship between a given culture's model of hospitality and how that culture defined someone as an "outsider." In the vignette from Kazantzakis's novel, Kazantzakis was an outsider to the village that took him in, but he was a Greek. In fact, he was a Cretan! How would a Cretan *woman* traveling alone like that have been treated? And surely one would not have expected Cretan villagers in the 1990s to put up the countless waves of foreign tourists who crash onto the island's shores each year! What about Penny's parents hosting me? I could have been viewed both as an outsider (not local, not Cretan, not Greek, not European) *and* as an insider (married into the family, modernly educated, from another "civilized" nation, of European descent, a fluent speaker of Greek with a Cretan accent, a competent performer of Cretan folk music, a fledgling creator of Cretan *mantinades*). What about when Leonidas hosted me in *his* home as a foreign student living in the country *I* was a citizen of? Going back further to my childhood: At a close relative's house, I was less likely to volunteer to help with the dishes than if I visited a schoolmate's house—did this have anything to do with how my family—or northern New Yorkers? or European Americans?—define insiders and outsiders?

I also became increasingly wary of labeling things like hospitality as *Greek*, *Cretan*, and *American* hospitality. Reading about some of the nuanced ways that the conventions of *filoxenia* or their associated meanings and ideological functions varied from one village in Crete to the next, from one region to the next, and from one historical moment to the next (as with the advent of mass tourism), I began to appreciate that Cretan *filoxenia* isn't necessarily a single identifiable—let alone unchanging—thing. Moreover, thanks to Herzfeld's analysis of the role played by *filoxenia* in reinforcing or challenging what it means "to be Cretan," I recognized that labels like "Cretan" and "Greek" are anything but neutral: The meaning of the very label is itself caught up in debates, struggles, and contests over beliefs and values among the people to whom the label is applied! I continued to use such labels to try making sense out of things, but remembered to bear in mind that the labels are wrapped in scare quotes: Cretan *filoxenia* is really "Cretan" *filoxenia*, and it's Cretan *"filoxenia."*

I gained an argument against the conventional wisdom of "When in Rome . . ." Why should we think that any given social or cultural context can be so neatly reduced to a single, identifiable sociocultural entity ("Rome")? Why should we think that the plethora of actual practices in that context ("what Romans do") is uniform and known, when in fact there may be "Romans" who do not do what the Romans supposedly do, and perhaps with good reason? It's as if people who rely on "When in Rome . . ." as their sole rationale for how to act in a given situation wind up responding to their sensibly modest and thoughtful reservations about imposing on others the ethical assumptions to which they're accustomed by simply washing their hands of all further ethical engagement.

And at last I understood that I wasn't interested in trying to maintain Cretan *filoxenia purely* or *authentically* or *exactly*, and that such a project would have been impossible anyway since even at a conceptual level it presupposed an erroneous, oversimplified view of complex social practices. To the extent that I *did* want to live according to a Cretan model of *filoxenia* (i.e., to a "Cretan" model of *"filoxenia"*), I realized that practicing it in a different cultural context like the United States, would for better or worse, entail different social meanings and effects than practicing it among Cretans. The "same" virtue in a different context is ultimately a "different" virtue.

❄   ❄   ❄

Andy and Dafne have just driven off. Sofia and I are picking up the dishes, and I ask her how she thought the day went. She reminds me that "I'm still doing it," referring to when I asked her to get up and bring chocolates to the table for Andy and Dafne. It's an annoying habit of mine that Sofia has pointed out recently—that once we sit down at the table with visitors, I usually ask her to get things so I don't have to get up again.

This time I make the connection: This is almost exactly the behavior of one of Penny's cousins that Penny was always disgusted by, and that I also found offensive! Granted, he did it *all* the time, but still . . . How the heck did I get into this habit whenever we have visitors and we've been sitting at the table for a while?

I initially suspect—and I readily admit it to Sofia—that in the back of my mind I've decided that I'm already doing disproportionately too much of the work of hosting visitors. Actually, it's not that I think I'm doing too much, it's more like I think she's not doing enough, and this makes me feel like it's okay for me to keep asking her to get up and do certain things.

But why have I been thinking she's not doing enough?

I reflect some more on how I see our roles as hosts. I realize that even if I've rationalized Cretan *filoxenia* ("Cretan" "*filoxenia*") by articulating its supposed tenets, in practice I've mostly just tried to imitate certain behaviors of my best role models for Cretan *filoxenia*: Eirini and Manolis. When Sofia and I have company, I'm too preoccupied with everything else going on to be thinking about tenets and rules, let alone monitoring whether I'm actually following them. Instead, like an actor on stage, I'm trying to inhabit the parts of Eirini and Manolis.

But how can one host possibly play the parts of *two* competent Cretan hosts, especially when those two hosts are observing a conventional sharing of responsibilities (think: division of labor)? Obviously he can't.

And here's the thing: Eirini and Manolis shared their hosting responsibilities according to traditional gender divisions of labor, almost to the letter. So when I emulate Eirini, I take on aspects of the traditional female-Cretan role—which in some respects isn't difficult, considering my facility with food-shopping, cooking, and menu planning. When I emulate Manolis, I take on aspects of the traditional male-Cretan role—buying and grilling meat, trying to remember to refill visitors' wineglasses, and encouraging various discussions and debates.

While living in Crete, Penny and I rarely hosted visitors ourselves, because whenever we weren't working, we usually hung out at her parents' house. At most, we gave a hand to her parents when they had visitors at their house. But now that I think about it, I rarely helped out *Eirini* with the traditionally female tasks, the way Penny did. I helped out Manolis.

It was returning to the United States that filled me with a determination to uphold Cretan *filoxenia* in its *totality*. I realize for the first time—how did I miss this for so many years?—that I've never tried to work out with Sofia a hosting role for myself that is actually doable.

Instead, I start out trying to do everything I can picture Eirini and Manolis doing. Then as the meal goes on, I tend to settle back into the "male-host" role and completely lose my sense of when I should be performing other "female-host" tasks: getting up to clear dishes, bringing more food, or persuading people to keep eating. (No wonder I forgot on so many occasions that I'd made a dessert to serve!) Then I expect Sofia to automatically recognize her supposed responsibility as cohost to step in and perform these "female" tasks that I'm not attending to. She, in turn, resents being assigned default responsibility for them—precisely because they're traditionally considered female tasks, which she finds sexist.

After all these years living in the United States, knowing full well that household divisions of responsibility need not be assigned according to traditional gender roles, how come I keep expecting Sofia to assimilate automatically to certain aspects of the female-host role?

Damn! It's the whole story of trying to make Eirini's stew all over again. No matter how carefully I think I'm observing something, there may be obvious or important things about it that completely escape my attention.

✳ 18 ✳

The Vine, More than One Way

Sofia and I are getting ready to sit down to our dinner. I turn on the television and flip through a bunch of channels to find something to watch while we're eating. There's news, sitcoms, a movie, a nature documentary, and a local station.

"*Family Guy* or *Third Rock* [*from the Sun*]?" I ask Sofia.

"*Third Rock*."

"You want wine?"

"Okay."

I put two stem glasses on the table.

"Should I put out chopsticks?" Sofia asks.

I take the pan of stuffed grape leaves out of the oven and deliver it to the table.

By the very end of May or early June, we always have plenty of large-enough leaves to collect for cooking, and it continues this way for about a month. Then, even before the invasive Japanese beetles start munching away, the nymphs of the aphid-like insect known as phylloxera spoil many of the leaves with their galls, and it becomes much more difficult, often impossible, to collect a decent quantity of perfect large leaves. The North American native phylloxera is well known to wine connoisseurs because of the havoc it wreaked on European vineyards, leading to their replanting with phylloxera-resistant rootstock. My reading tells me that this happened primarily during the late 1800s, but I suppose the insect reached Crete much later, because Manolis had only just dug up and replanted his vineyard with phylloxera-resistant vines the year before my first visit to the island in the early nineties. So, between phylloxera and beetles, June has become *the* time of year when Sofia and I thoroughly enjoy stuffed grape leaves, using our beautiful leaves, absent chemicals

225

and sprays, grown and maintained with very little effort, and picked just hours before the food lands on the dining room table.

Back when Sofia and I began restricting the fruits and vegetables we bought at the supermarket to those that were in season (where they were grown), we probably thought that all we were doing was figuring out another trick for ensuring that whatever we ate was tastier—and first and foremost that is what we were doing. But as it turned out, we were also taking the first of many steps toward cultivating an awareness of connections between food and the seasons that resulted in our *feeling* those connections, not just knowing them. It unwittingly marked the start of our seduction by the rhythms and cycles of growing seasons. Within a few years we began to experience those cycles viscerally, as a new kind of pleasure that dismantled any dichotomies between the refined and the primordial, for it was a pleasure that felt as much like sipping an exquisite Armagnac as it did like jumping into a pile of freshly raked autumn leaves.

Every year, every week for about four weeks, I make a large pan of stuffed vegetables and vine leaves, each of which lasts for days, unless we have company.

I collect extra leaves for freezing, too, for the occasional out-of-season version when we're running low on other frozen greens. I find that I prefer to brush off the leaves one at a time under good light, but sometimes I don't bother if while collecting them they look especially clean. Then I put piles of leaves directly into freezer bags—*without* blanching, contrary to most of the recommendations I've seen.

(It's true. If it's just Sofia and me, we usually watch sitcoms while we're eating. I prefer to see the news and check the weather online. I find many nature documentaries too uninteresting to watch while we're eating. Sofia does too, I think.)

I first learned to make stuffed grape leaves from Eirini. By the end of my first visit to Crete, Eirini's dolmades—stuffed grape leaves, tomatoes, zucchinis, eggplants, and bell peppers—took the place of Grandma's lasagna as my favorite food. Eirini's take on this dish was so delicious that as soon as my Greek was sufficient, I tried writing a humorous *mantinada* in tribute:

Μπορώ να πιάσω το χαρτί να γράψω μαντινάδες,
μα προτιμώ καλύτερα τσ' ωραίους σου ντολμάδες.

I can get some paper to write *mantinades*,
but I'd really prefer your nice dolmades.

Dolmades landed me in the kitchen with Eirini on many occasions, and I was more inclined to help than just observe. It was a lot of work to open up the tomatoes, zucchinis, and eggplants. It took serious effort to chop the onions and parsley in one's hand with a little knife. (Eirini never used cutting boards or chef's knives.) It was time-consuming to stuff piles of blanched grape leaves into bite-sized *dolmadakia* with the intention of having leftovers and enough extra for any visitors who might happen to drop by unexpectedly. So Eirini was glad to have some assistance and happy that I wanted to learn to make this dish for which she was so widely revered by family and friends.

For Eirini this was clearly not a dish with a fixed recipe. It was a somewhat improvisational process with a range of acceptable possible outcomes. So I learned to make them through repetition. The two of us spent hours together in the kitchen during my earliest summer visit, which also gave my budding Greek language skills a healthy workout. "Should we try it without meat for a change?" "Let's leave out the spearmint this time . . . Well, should we add just a little?" "What do you think? The rest of the parsley?" she'd ask me, in Greek, as we worked.

Mostly, though, we talked about other things. If Manolis wasn't around she'd take a cigarette break, sitting just outside the balcony door in her apron, trying to persuade me to eat another piece of her staple lemon cake. She had endless curiosity about what it was like in northern New York and in Chicago. I'd tell her about windy-city skyscrapers and growing up around the Adirondacks. "You mean to tell me that in your place you go fishing in the *mountains*?" she'd say with a great laugh, since in Crete—where the sea is for fishing and the largely arid mountains are for hunting— "going fishing in the mountains" is an expression akin to "having a screw loose." She'd tell me stories about Penny as a child. She'd describe her and Manolis's courtship, their secret meetings and letters sent through vineyards and olive groves in the valley separating their respective villages. As my vocabulary improved, she also told me stories about how she advocated for the interests of the island's shepherds and agriculturalists, and about her role in helping a communist family friend—a fellow as idealistic and kindhearted as they come—put together a farmer-owned cooperative for exporting Cretan produce to other countries.

I can't remember exactly when during a normal year Eirini would make stuffed grape leaves, but I'm pretty sure that it was throughout the long southern Mediterranean grape-growing season. Sometimes when Manolis knew Eirini was planning to head out to their village vineyard to collect leaves, especially if she was taking along a friend or relative or two, he'd scold her about previous such outings when they stripped away too many leaves from a single *kormoula*—something that causes problems for the development of the actual fruit. Eirini would deny ever having done such a thing, a ritual spousal spat would play out, and before you knew it there was a pile of lush vine leaves in the kitchen ready to be cooked.

(To be honest, I haven't actually watched a nature documentary on television in decades.)

In northern New York you usually see more cornfields than vineyards, and, increasingly, more housing developments than cornfields. But, as I learned very early on from Leonidas when I'd moved from Crete back to the United States, wild grape vines are almost ubiquitous and relatively easy to identify. (I found out later with more systematic study, there are *some* poisonous sort-of-look-alikes that amateurs should beware.) Unlike with a tended vineyard, wild leaves are very much hit-and-miss. Depending on location and how late in the summer it is, there might be lots of holes from insects, galls on the undersides of the leaves, or other suspect imperfections.

Before we moved here, Sofia and I would find places with plentiful vines and fill plastic grocery bags with leaves every spring, enough to freeze for use throughout the entire year. There were a couple times when we were driving or walking around our neighborhood in Ohio and Sofia noticed old women collecting them. We assumed they must be Greek and I'd feel an unspoken connection with them in our shared New World retooling of this Old World practice.

As the years went by, Sofia and I became more cautious about where we collected leaves. That's because we became increasingly aware of how frequently people applied chemicals to the air and the ground for who-knows-how-many different reasons. So it was a great relief when we bought a house and could grow our own wild grape vines.

(Now that I'm thinking about it, I vaguely remember watching *Wild Kingdom* when I was a kid. I forgot all about it. Did I actually *like* watching it back then? I think probably I did.)

Sometimes I leave out the meat. Sometimes I make only stuffed grape leaves—no stuffed tomatoes or other vegetables—and cook them on the stove in a pot. For a few years I thought my favorite version might turn out to be the meatless one, cooked on the stove, eaten cold from the refrigerator starting the next day, accompanied by tzatziki (cucumber, garlic, strained-yogurt dip). That conviction passed and now I make them without meat infrequently, just for a change. The last few years, since we've been striving to eat mostly our home-grown vegetables—and our garden tomatoes and zucchini won't ripen until long after the June window for the vine leaves closes—I've been mostly foregoing the other stuffed vegetables. Later in summer I can make stuffed tomatoes and throw in some stuffed grape leaves using frozen leaves if I want.

(I wouldn't necessarily count this as a nature documentary, but I enjoyed the PBS special on Michael Pollan's *Botany of Desire*. Especially the part where they showed those guys who have an apple orchard with about a zillion different varieties of apple. That was really attractive. When I try thinking about the actual details of it, I don't think I can imagine myself enjoying doing that kind of work, at least not for long, but—I don't know—there's something about it that I find enticing.)

At Eirini's, a roasting pan full of dolmades usually included stuffed tomatoes, stuffed zucchinis (the small, light-green variety), stuffed smaller-than-your-typical-American-sized eggplants, stuffed green bell peppers, and stuffed grape leaves. Since the stuffing also includes whatever comes out of the hollowed-out tomatoes, zucchini, and so on, part of the idea is to stuff the grape leaves to use up whatever stuffing is left over after filling up the other vegetables. Peppers, being already more-or-less hollow, also function this way. I always tell my relatives that if you make this dish enough times, somehow you manage to end up with very close to the right amount of leftover stuffing for the number of leaves you have prepared. Not that it matters very much. If I end up with too many leaves, into the compost they go. So what? They were free. If I'm short on leaves, I can go out back and pick a few more.

When I do include other vegetables, tomatoes and zucchinis are musts. Whether or not I include eggplants or peppers depends on the quality of what's available, my mood, and whimsy. I usually use our largest rectangular roasting pan, but if I want to make a lot, I use two. I've even tried using my really large round roasting pan, but I guess because the sides are so tall the tops of the vegetables don't seem to brown, and the excess water seems not to cook off in time. Regardless of which pan I'm using, I always lay out the tomatoes, zucchinis, and so forth first, to get a sense of how many will fit, taking into account that I need to leave some empty space for the stuffed vine leaves, too. Stuffed leaves will also fit in the nooks in and around the larger vegetables. (The idea is to fill up space in the pan as much as possible.) Sofia and I also have a small round casserole dish, so if in the end I discover that I don't have enough space for all the stuffed grape leaves, I put the extras in there and cook them alongside the large pan.

When using fresh leaves, one thing that's good to do in advance is to blanch them in boiling water for a couple minutes, but sometimes I skip this step when I'm using frozen leaves. If I do it at the last minute I rinse them under cold water so they're not too hot to handle. For blanching, I choose one of my largest pots, fill it up with water, and bring it to a boil. Having kept the leaves in somewhat neat piles as I collected them—and even if I've rinsed them lazily in a bowl of water, or meticulously one at a time under running water—I can very easily blanch them without getting them all folded and intertwined. We happen to have two large slotted spoons, one substantially larger than the other. So, I put a handful of leaves—still neatly piled—into the deeper slotted spoon and then put the smaller slotted spoon on top to hold them in place. Then I dip them into the boiling water and hold them there for about a minute or so. I usually loosen my grip somewhat so more water can get in and around the leaves, but not enough so that the leaves break free from the pile pressed between the spoons. Then I lift them out and plunk them down into a colander with a bowl underneath to catch any water that drips off.

The next big job is preparing the stuffing, starting with hollowing out the vegetables. I use a small knife to slice the top off the tomato—not quite all the way off, though, so the lid that results remains attached. Then, I use a spoon to hollow out the inside of the tomato. With the tomato's lid open and just sort of hanging there—if it breaks off, it doesn't matter—I take the spoon, back-side facing the tomato wall to match the convexity of the tomato, and push it down just inside the tomato wall. Then I scoop around the perimeter, turning the tomato one way and the spoon the opposite way. Whenever necessary, I then scoop down deeper toward the bottom of the tomato to free its insides completely and plop them out into a large bowl. The hollowed out tomato goes into its approximate location in the roasting pan. After I've done all the tomatoes, I chop up the tomatoes' innards. I find an easy way to do this is to leave them in the bowl and use a pastry scraper to chop them right there. Of course, that's because our large bowls have wide, flat bottoms. Otherwise I'd just use a knife on a cutting board to do the job.

Hollowing out zucchinis can be a little more delicate, but not too bad. I cut off the tip (and save it), then I grip the zucchini in one hand, take a butter knife in the other hand, and rotate it into the cut-end of the zucchini—carefully. Gripping the zucchini prevents me from tearing through it too easily—a minor tear isn't really an issue, except maybe in terms of appearance. The more I rotate, the deeper into the zucchini I can go, and after a while I'm able to take out the knife and shake out some of the insides. Since zucchini is soft, the butter knife does a fine job cutting into it and turns easily, and won't stab me in the other hand if I accidentally poke it all the way through. I plop all the zucchini innards onto a cutting board and chop them up a bit more before tossing them into the bowl with the chopped tomato. I put the hollowed-out zucchinis and their tips back into the roasting pan in their approximate cooking locations.

I find the eggplants are the trickiest and I don't think they've ever worked quite like the ones I helped Eirini with in Crete, where they were also the most difficult of the vegetables to work with. The idea is to squeeze the eggplant to loosen the insides from the walls before you even cut it open. You need to squeeze hard all around, but not so hard that you end up breaking the skin. It's difficult to get started, but then as the eggplant softens it becomes easier. Then you roll them back and forth between the palms of your hand. When it works well you can just cut the tip and pull out all the insides. I've never once managed to do it so easily here. Maybe it's the varieties of eggplant I've tried. Or maybe I just don't remember how to do it right. At any rate, I can usually poke a knife down into the squished-and-rolled-between-my-palms eggplant and scrape out the insides that are somewhat loosened and ready to come out. Then I chop them up and add them to the tomatoes and zucchini.

When I use peppers, I cut off the top so it becomes a lid, and shake or rinse out the seeds.

(Okay, so maybe I like nature documentaries more than I think, especially when they have something to do with food or drink. I loved *The Real Dirt on Farmer John* and *The Future of Food* and *Flow* and *Tapped* and *Sharkwater*. And my all-time favorite is *Mondovino*.[1] The first few times I watched it I laughed out loud at the way the filmmaker kept showing clips of everybody's dogs, and, at the end, of one dog humping another out in the streets.)

Continuing with the stuffing: In theory, I could add various ingredients. My standard approach is this: I add one or two finely chopped onions, a bunch of finely chopped parsley and a good-sized bunch of finely chopped dill, and a few finely chopped fresh spearmint leaves. If I'm making only leaves and not stuffing other vegetables, I make sure to use *plenty* of parsley and dill.

Then, I add some ground beef, and a few handfuls of (usually medium grain) rice. Lately I've been trying brown rice. The more stuffing I have, the more rice I add—always intuitively. Then plenty of salt and pepper, the juice of two or three lemons, and some olive oil, like one or two tablespoons. I mix it all up and am ready to stuff. This is when I usually turn on the oven for preheating to 400°F.

It only takes a couple minutes to stuff the tomatoes and such. When I stuff the zucchinis, I close them with their tips reversed (i.e., with the stem inserted into the zucchini) or with a stuffed vine leaf.

The time-consuming work is stuffing the individual vine leaves. (There are plenty of Greek cookbooks and recipes on the Internet with diagrams, pictures, or videos of how to do this.) Sometimes I arrange the bowl of stuffing, the roasting pan, and the colander in a convenient way at the table so I can sit while I do them. I make them small, like Eirini did. I put the stuffed leaves directly into the pan as I work.

The leaves I collect are not all one size, so for really large ones I might use a little more stuffing than for smaller ones. I've found that when I prune wild grapes in late winter or early spring—as though they were part of a cultivated vineyard—the vines produce much larger leaves than when I just let them grow unfettered. If I have some really small leaves—which sometimes happens when it's slim-pickings—I do what Eirini did: I use two leaves as though they were one, overlapping them somewhat, one below the other. Another thing that affects how much stuffing I put in my leaves is my intuition about how much stuffing I have relative to how many leaves I've collected or how much space for leaves I have in my roasting pan. If I think I'm running out of stuffing too fast, I put less in each one. If I think I'm short on leaves, I use more stuffing.

Once everything is stuffed, I generously drizzle olive oil over the top of everything, as well as the juice of another lemon or two. For a while I was hesitant about adding too much lemon juice to the stuffing and found the quality went down. The flavor of the leaves and the lemon really seem to complement each other so now I'm careful not to skimp on the lemon juice in the stuffing. I lay leftover leaves, and any leaves that tore while I was handling them, over the top of the section of the pan with the bulk of the stuffed grape leaves. That way the top parts of the stuffed leaves that otherwise would've been exposed don't burn and become crumbly.

(It seems like whenever I show my copy of the documentary *Mondovino* to anyone who likes wine, they pretty much just take it as an exposé on how the business world has corrupted the romantic world of wine they'd like to keep believing in. Or as a critique of how big business and globalization have corrupted the wine industry. Corrupted the wine *industry*? I don't buy it.

I actually find that the filmmaker shows most of the film's *characters* in a critical, usually a negative, light—even if he also implies that at some level he can respect their ingenuity or brilliance or skill.

Apart from the various employee-laborers he interviews or shows in the background, the only characters who the filmmaker sort of makes look like they should be thought of as the good guys, and are in charge of something, are a peasant winemaker in Brazil, an old couple in Italy trying to keep alive the tradition of Malvasia, a winemaker father on an estate in Bourgogne (France), and his stubbornly committed-to-certain-preglobalization-winemaking-principles daughter. It's probably no coincidence that these are the people who Nossiter, the filmmaker, shows again at the very end of the film. What do these people have in common? It's not that they're all necessarily pro- or antibusiness or pro- or antitradition, or even from the same socioeconomic class. I think there's something else going on, and I suspect the key lies in the emphasis of the Burgundy father's insistence that the real problem nowadays is "monolithic thinking."

The film doesn't exactly explain what monolithic thinking is, but it hints that most of the interviewees who are in charge of something are living, breathing examples of it, whether they're manically in favor of big business and globalization—like the globetrotting wine consultant Roland—or caught up in communist or socialist or populist movements against globalization in the name of justice and the common good—like Guibert, who's initially portrayed as a likable romantic fighting the good fight for traditional wine until, at last, the inclusion of another interview clip gives the impression that maybe his romantic rhetoric has been covering for some other self-interested motive.[2]

It's not that the effects of modern business on traditional wine are all good or all bad. The section of the film on wine critic Robert Parker shows this best: On the one hand, the state capitalist market provides mechanisms—in this case, wine critics—to push back against traditionally entrenched interests and tastes in the name of the consumer. On the other hand, these very mechanisms can quickly turn into entrenched interests in their own right—as when a handful of critics and the largest winemakers seem to exercise too much influence over nearly the entire world wine market at the expense of smaller winemakers and the desires and preferences of consumers who don't conform to that market.

This is where the dogs come in as a crucial symbol. It is suggested that most of the characters shown in the film—representative of people in general who possess significant power in the world of global capitalism—are *like* dogs in the sense that they're just sort of mindlessly going about their instinctual business . . . whether that business is a matter of narrowly self-interested "corrupt" local politics or narrowly self-interested "savvy" market dealings. But whereas a dog supposedly acts according to its natural *genetic* instincts, these humans are acting according to the *social* or *cultural* "instincts" that a largely *monolithic* socioeconomic system—namely the present system of global capitalism—conditions, in part by encouraging everyone to think that the practices of global capitalism are the logical consequence of embracing the ideal of freedom and the inevitable culmination of the spread of democracy.

But through his emphasis on these few other good-guy characters, Nossiter also implies that there's hope that this instinct hasn't completely taken us over. There's the possibility that some of us might find ways to avoid the allure of monolithic thinking in any and all its forms, and that this might somehow help usher in change. We humans are not, in the end, mere dogs. (No offense to dogs.) Even if most humans will always act more-or-less "instinctually" in response to the predominant expectations of whatever socioeconomic system we inhabit, there are always exceptions. There are always cracks and contradictions in the system. Though there are no guarantees, there's the possibility of a better kind of socioeconomic system, one that encourages more people to think nonmonolithically, and where even the most humdrum instances of individual cleverness, savvy, and creativity are not so antagonistic to the greater good.

Nossiter doesn't seem to get around to suggesting what such a system might look like, but Michael Moore's documentary, *Capitalism: A Love Story*, gives a moment of attention to companies that are worker cooperatives, reminding viewers that the word *market* doesn't have to mean *capitalist* market.)

It generally takes about an hour to cook dolmades, sometimes a little longer: The rice cooks but doesn't dry out, most excess water evaporates or is absorbed as everything cools down leaving mostly oil (yum!) in the bottom of the pan, and the tops of the vegetables brown a little.

❀   ❀   ❀

I peel away part of the thin layer of leaves covering the dolmades. Sofia brings the salad she made.

We sit down—eager to enjoy our meal of homemade stuffed grape leaves and global capitalist industrial French wine.

* 19 *

The End of Nostalgia

Sofia and I are picking blueberries at a nearby you-pick orchard, the same one that Grandma took me to when I was a little kid. I overhear a little girl a few rows over picking berries with her grandmother.

"Gramma, do you think we're doin' 'em a favor if we pick off the bad ones?"

"Well, if *we* don't pick them they'll fall off eventually."

"Wow, this bush doesn't have a bad berry on it! [. . .] Oops, there's one."

"You *had* to go and open your mouth, didn't ya?"

"Most people are prob'ly polite and go around, but I'm gonna go *right through* like *this*. [. . .] Ah! There's a beetle on this one. Oh boy!"

I realize that some thirty years ago I could have been here saying everything the little girl is saying, with the same enthusiasm, using just the same words, and with the same local pronunciation and intonation. I'm transported back in time as though I just caught a whiff of a long-lost scent. A flicker of ecstasy as I relive the naive joyfulness of my childhood is followed by racing thoughts.

"My old northern New York self and my later Cretan self are so incredibly different!"

"You can never go back to being either one."

"*Xenos* here, *xenos* there, and wherever I go [I'm] *xenos* . . ." [a standard first line in some *mantinades*]

"Act upon these significant moments of nostalgia if you must—just don't act upon them by deceiving yourself into thinking that you can return to, recover, or rebuild any past, no matter how beautiful or comforting. Don't kid yourself that you *remember* the past in all its significant complexity."

"Let your memories of the past *in*form how you're living in the present, but don't try *con*forming to those memories."

"Instead of weeping, eat and drink!"

Then it hits me that we're picking *blueberries*—a fruit I never saw in Crete. I'm picking them to freeze for pies—a very *American* food. Especially for pies at Thanksgiving—the quintessential American holiday. Yet, I know my motivation for doing all this work instead of just buying berries from the store derives almost entirely from having been influenced by Manolis's tireless efforts to produce and to procure local, safer, and more sustainably produced foods for his family and friends.

(For crying out loud! Why can't I just make my peace, once and for all, with the fact that I can never return to the self of my childhood or to the self of my years in Crete?

Why in the world am I *still* coaching myself not to conform to past memories? By now I should be well past something like this. After everything I've been through? It's been *years* since I was trying to transform my food life into one that was as authentically Cretan as possible.

What's *wrong* with me?)

(I guess for now I'll just take a deep breath and count to ten so I can continue writing this thing.)

The better I got at preparing Cretan foods in the United States, the closer I got to the very information, ideas, and questions that caused me to relax my obsession with trying to reproduce Cretan cuisine in the United States.

During my years as a graduate student in Ohio, teaching myself extensively about species of fish, varieties of fruit, and wild greens did more than just help me find what I needed for my Cretan table. It also made me realize that there were foods that I considered quintessentially Cretan—fish like the dentex bream (*sinagrida*) and greens like wild coast (or spiny) chicory (*stamnagathi*)—that were simply unavailable in the United States, whether at market or in the wild. The unexamined vague hope that was growing in the back of my mind that I'd someday reach a quintessential Cretan diet in the United States became increasingly evident as this realization began making appearances in conscious thought.

My research into the scientific taxonomies and Greek, Cretan, and English names of greens and grains, fruits, and fish led me into books on the history of food in Greece and the Mediterranean, and of agriculture worldwide. This, in turn, helped me develop a view of the Cretan diet that was less static and more historically accurate. I began differentiating between ingredients that had been used on the island for thousands of years and those that had only been brought there in the last several hundred years or even more recently. I became more aware of regional variations in food across the island. I read about the various cultures in the region influencing one another's eating habits as populations interacted or conquered one another.

All this got me wondering exactly which version of Cretan food I was trying to replicate. As a first approximation, it seemed like I was trying to re-create the foods I remembered from Manolis and Eirini's house. But did that mean I wouldn't make other Cretan or Greek dishes? Clearly not. So why limit myself to re-creating just Cretan, or just Greek, or even just Mediterranean recipes?

My growing collection of Cretan and Greek cookbooks struck another blow at my determination. I realized I should confront the fact that several of the most frequent Cretan commentators on Cretan cuisine and wine—whose enthusiasm for the island's food and drink and personal sociability I thoroughly shared—were coming from a perspective that also made me uneasy, especially the more I learned about the role of cultural nationalism in the history of Modern Greece from such scholars as those of the so-called Ohio School of Modern Greek Studies. Reading their work made me think more carefully about nationalism as a cultural phenomenon, not merely as a political one.[1]

This led me to take a closer and more critical look at Greek cookbooks during a class I was taking with faculty in Folklore Studies. I hunted for every Greek cookbook I could get my hands on through interlibrary loan, and I ordered additional books from Greece. I quickly discovered that one could discern much of the history of Greek modernization that I was learning about in my Greek literature classes—including some of the subsequent reactions against certain aspects of modernization—within the pages of these cookbooks.[2]

Until the nineteenth century, Modern Greeks had just one book on food, written in the early seventeenth century by a monk in Crete named Agapios, containing information about medicine, dietetics, and agronomics.[3] Agapios was rurally oriented, describing how to identify and forage for wild greens and supporting his claims about nutrition and health with examples of deer and Cretan wild goats that instinctively recognize and use herbal remedies such as the Cretan mint *diktamo*.

Then attempts to modernize and Westernize Greek food began, starting with what seems to be the first modern Greek cookbook in 1828, *Cooking, translated from Italian*.[4] Though translated from Italian, it was an international collection of the most well-known Western dishes from all over Europe, with primarily meat-based main courses utilizing butter, not olive oil. In a short prologue, the anonymous translator justifies his efforts by appealing to the importance of proper nutrition for good health, questioning outright prevailing wisdom that esteemed the "monotonous" rural diet, and arguing that eating many different foods is healthy—provided they are prepared in a healthful manner.[5] He also suggests the need for women to learn home economics. The cosmopolitan and urban perspective of this book is quite a departure from Agapios's, and wasn't well received in its time. At the end of the nineteenth century, something like this was widely thought to contribute to the corruption of the Greek ethnos, clashing with the accepted wisdom of rural and indigenous culinary practices, contradicting the view that such indigenous practices were integral to Greek national identity.[6]

But the modernizers eventually began to win out. Tselementes's modern *Cooking Guide*, initially published in 1920, was expanded and reprinted throughout most of the twentieth century.[7] Many Greeks today even use the word *tselementes*—the author's last name—as the generic word for "cookbook." (They may not even *know* that it's a last name.) Tselementes went to great lengths to provide the most up-to-date information about food preparation that the modern Western culinary and nutritional sciences had to offer, not to mention modern directives about proper domestic customs more generally.

His cookbooks include charts that systematize nutrition data and the measurement of ingredients, weekly menus, descriptions of how to serve wine properly, and detailed guides to etiquette. There's a defense of modern canned foods that chastises Greeks for viewing them as "a way for the Americans to send their products to different countries," and thereby impeding them from understanding their "beneficial impact and usefulness."[8] In some of the earlier editions, there's a "technical study" celebrating good-quality butters and margarine, and criticizing the majority of Greek olive oils with their "high acidity" for being "too-strongly scented and difficult-to-digest."[9] Readers are persuaded to use industrially canned ingredients like tomato sauce, beer, and powdered eggs.

Informed by modern nutritional science and emphasizing systematization and codification, Tselementes elaborated on the modernizing project of the unsuccessful cookbook translated from Italian. But Tselementes took the additional step of addressing explicitly the issue of Greek national identity. In addition to including recipes taken or adapted from European cuisine, Tselementes took traditional Greek foods and adapted them in the spirit of modern Western culinary practices and scientific standards. He also addressed at length any anxieties his readers might have had about Greek ways being spoiled by foreign influences from either East or West.

Tselementes's essay on "The History of Greek Cooking" (included in the cookbook) seeks to put to rest any questions about the authenticity of his version of Modern Greek cuisine. This is accomplished through an interpretation of European culinary history. Tselementes argues that the art of cooking first appeared in the world during the golden age of Greece and from there spread to the rest of Europe. Progress in the art was halted by the "invasion of the barbaric peoples of the North into lower Europe," causing cooks to retreat to the monasteries until the Renaissance when all the arts were resuscitated.[10] It was then that the renowned tradition of French cooking began, a tradition founded on Greek cooking. In Tselementes's view, the modernization of Greek cuisine should not be interpreted as importing Western culinary practices, because Western cooking *is* Greek cooking: "Beginning in Homeric times (when the art of cooking in today's sense did not exist), up until the Renaissance, without exception, all the culinary preparations of all the Nations carry the stamp of Greek culinary art."[11] The modernization of Greek food also serves to "purify" it of any Turkish and Eastern contamination:

It is difficult to come up with the name of a food of purely Greek cuisine because it will appear under the mask of what is mistakenly called Turkish or Eastern cuisine. [. . .] Most of today's meals that appear to be examples of Turkish or Eastern cooking are nothing other than the products of Greek cooking, and simply need to recover their original Greek name, as well as to be reworked by cooks of the highest learning to remove from them the influence and corruption of the tastes and preferences of various Eastern peoples.[12]

Tselementes's cookbook helped pave the way for many more modern cookbooks that generally left behind such topics as agriculture and foraging and paid little attention to regional variations in ingredients or dishes. The Greek modernizers succeeded in describing an urban national cuisine by ignoring local differences, making it possible to identify particular foods like moussaka with the entire nation. Cultural, economic, technological and political modernization in Greece were intertwined, so by focusing on issues of cultural identity in texts about the culture of food preparation, Tselementes's project resonated with the broadest intentions and developments of the modernization of Greece. Its success was facilitated by his meticulous treatment of cooking, but also by the careful attention he paid to issues of national identity in relation to Western and Eastern cultures.

Since the 1980s, Greek cookbooks have been taking the notion of national cuisine in new directions, and often include such phrases as "traditional Greek food" or "authentic Greek recipes" in their titles. Consistent with an ideology that believes authentic Greece resides in its traditional rural regions, many of these cookbooks emphasize regional variations, pointing out that "every corner of Greece, from north to south and from east to west, has a unique surprise of its own."[13]

Since the 1990s, countless cookbooks have been published in Greece—often by local publishers—focusing on a single regional cuisine, such as Cretan cuisine. The first Cretan cookbook I ordered from Greece while I was living in Ohio is one of the best examples of these. Indeed, for many Cretans, Maria and Nikos Psilakis's bestselling *Cretan Traditional Cuisine*, published in Irakleio, remains *the* Cretan cookbook.[14]

The authors include a series of prologues arguing that changes in everyday culinary practices and consciousness are imperative for health reasons. In contrast to modernizers like Tselementes, these authors claim that modernization is actually to blame for many of the island's—and the nation's—current health problems. In the book's first preface, Nikos Skoulas discusses a paradox:

> I became convinced that we in Greece are tending to abandon our nutritional habits which go back centuries. Bowing to the rage of homogenization and fast food imposed upon us by the fast pace of modern life and imported habits, we, the nation which authenticated "the good life" and harmony, are giving in like crazy to processed and pre-manufactured foods, all for the sake of easy profit.[15]

He then points out how ironic it is that this is happening just as urban Europeans and Americans are increasingly looking to Mediterranean flavors and cuisines. Skoulas proposes a partial explanation for how Cretans have arrived at this paradoxical historical moment: it's the result of "the almost complete lack of knowledge among modern Greeks about our rich gastronomic heritage."[16] He illustrates this ignorance further by echoing Tselementes's arguments about French and Turkish cuisine:

> The inconceivable becomes infuriating when the savory creations of Atheneus's deipnosophists that were passed by the Byzantines into the food of the nomadic people of the Ottoman Empire, thereby helping it acquire flavor, appear today in our vocabulary as Eastern delights with Turkish names. [. . .] With the same ease, we consider the sweet and sweet-and-sour sauces which predominated in Ancient Greece and Byzantium as inventions of French high cuisine.[17]

The problem is no longer simply ignorance of correct nutrition, but ignorance of Greek culinary history. This diagnosis immediately suggests a possible remedy: educate the public about its "unbroken historical continuity from classical Greece of the fourth century BCE, through the Hellenistic period, Byzantium, and up until the grandmother in Crete, in Smyrna, in Epirus, in Macedonia, and in Thrace."[18] Like Tselementes before him, Skoulas would like to see Greek cuisine purified and preserved, but unlike him, contends that it's found in its most authentic form at the hands of regional grandmothers, not big-city professional chefs.

It's a fitting prologue for a cookbook that emphasizes Cretan *regional* cultural continuity, drawing on the techniques of early

Greek *nation*-centered folklorists working to establish and maintain the modern Greeks' position as "quintessential Europeans."[19] Generally speaking, the collection of folklore has played a major role in cultural politics in Greece (and elsewhere) by serving as a repository of evidence of cultural continuity.[20] Many Greek folklorists assume the existence of an identifiable (and largely unproblematized) entity called "Greek tradition," then dig into the history of the rural Greeks (whose past was virtually undocumented for centuries) in order to identify cultural links from classical Greece, through Byzantium, to the Modern Greek nation-state. They tend to downplay certain complexities in this history. The result is that history is reduced to little more than a chain of periods linking one era of Greek tradition to the next.

This is the principle that organizes the historical narratives of the Psilakis cookbook. Each section of recipes leads with background discussions that generally begin with references to Minoan Crete and ancient Greek civilization, continue on through Byzantium and the period of Venetian rule (1204–1669), only touch briefly on the period of Ottoman rule (1669–1898), and end with discussions of the modern period up to the present.

These discussions treat periods of non-Greek rule according to the norms of Greek nation-centered histories. For example, The Venetian period, much like the Minoan period, occupies a relatively unique position in the perception of cultural continuity in Crete as compared to the rest of Greece. Crete was one of the few areas of Greece to fall under Venetian rule, a presence that wasn't welcome by many Cretan Greeks of the period. Nevertheless, today's popular perception of the Venetian period of Cretan history is rather positive, no doubt in part because of the flowering of a Cretan vernacular literature during the so-called Cretan Renaissance. Maria and Nikos Psilakis include numerous excerpts from the works of Cretan Renaissance literature scattered throughout the text that provide information about the foodways of the time. Their emphasis isn't on Venetian *influences*, but on the continuity of Cretan foodways:

> The names of various kinds of preserved meat which come up in medieval texts are not unknown to today's inhabitants of Crete, especially in agricultural areas. They have been preserved in such an amazing way, proving that the gastronomic tradition of a place can survive, even when that place undergoes successive conquests.[21]

When they mention Venetian influence they make a point of down-playing it:

> Many of the names indicate the influence of Venetian cuisine on Cretan cuisine, since the Venetians controlled Crete from 1211 until 1669. But even if there was influence, it must not have been very important, since on the island Byzantine customs and tastes survived for so many centuries (and survive even today).[22]

The authors associate the Ottoman period with the Cretans' love of freedom, struggle for independence, and acts of undaunted heroism under the most brutal of circumstances,[23] arguing that "Cretan cuisine does not appear to have been influenced at all during the following centuries of Turkish domination."[24] Reflecting the prestige generally accorded to Minoan Crete in the history of Greece and Crete, the authors invariably refer to this pre-Greek ancient period in a positive light. Here, for example, they link the modern Cretan with the ancient Minoan inhabitant of the island by means of a shared reverence for the land:

> Cretan flora, so rich in variety, always made it possible to have inexpensive foodstuffs in the Cretan household. Minoan frescos clearly show the particular relationship which these old Cretans had with nature and her crops, since they depict many plants which play a very important role in everyday life and worship [. . .] The Cretan sacred trees transmit throughout the centuries amazing testimony about the relationship between the Cretan-Minoan and nature. And it is not at all by accident that dozens of such holy trees, which play a role in folk worship, still exist today in Crete.[25]

Going through analysis like this really opened my eyes about Greek and Cretan cuisine. Not that I had any reason to question any of the *facts*—I was sure that Psilakis and Psilakis knew far more about food history than I did. What concerned me was how their *interpretation* of those facts amounted to little more than a matter of the endurance of an identifiably Cretan tradition. How could it be that the food-related *vocabularies* of conquerors were locally influential but not their foods? If Greek and non-Greek (Minoan) inhabitants count as "Cretans" in their view of history, why wouldn't second- or third-generation Venetian inhabitants of the island, say, also count?

Considering that experts on agricultural history[26] have written about the use of wheat and barley in the broader region predating their use in Crete by Minoans, why didn't the authors contextualize these original Cretan foodways in terms of broader agricultural developments? And, when it came to those historical periods *without* rule by foreign conquerors, why didn't they ask how Cretan food practices evolved because of—or stayed the same in spite of—the ways various *Greek* elites ruled over the peasant masses?

I became frustrated with the ambiguity of statements like, "Pure traditional ingredients which come from local production, and authentic flavors combined with beautiful local customs and local culture are what characterize the traditional cooking of Crete."[27] What are "pure traditional ingredients"? Ingredients that conform to merely aesthetic criteria like "color" and "taste"? Those that are grown without the use of industrially produced pesticides and fertilizers? Are the flavors "authentic" when they come from produce grown from genetically modified seeds? What makes these local customs "beautiful"? Just the fact that they're local?

I began noticing this kind of ambiguity showing up in other places. For instance, a Greek national newspaper supplement focusing on ecotourism in rural Crete has this to say about the mint family herb *diktamo* that grows in Crete:

> Few plants in Greece have come to be identified so much with a place as *diktamo* has been identified with Crete. *Diktamo (Origanum dictamus)* is a native plant of Crete and grows wild on virtually every mountain of the island. [. . .] The persistent popularity of *Diktamo* was, in addition, the reason why its populations today have been significantly reduced. In the *Red Book of Plants of Greece* it is characterized as "rare." Today it is grown commercially, primarily in the village of Ebaro, thereby providing an opportunity for its natural populations to recover and allowing *Diktamo* to continue to remain the symbol of Cretan nature.[28]

In the last sentence, the preservation of a species serves as a means for reproducing a symbol of local cultural identity. It also provides a context for interpreting the *mantinada* included at the beginning of the article:

Δυο φυλλαράκια Δίχταμο από τον Ψηλορείτη,
Βάνω στο μπέτι και γροικώ την μυρωδιά σου Κρήτη.[29]

> I put two little leaves of *Diktamo* from Psiloreitis
> on my chest and I can smell your scent, Crete.

Read in the context of the article, this *mantinada* promotes ecologically minded nature conservation and tradition-minded cultural preservation simultaneously. The *mantinada* (as a genre of folk poetry) is a cultural vehicle analogous to the *diktamo* that is nature's vehicle for keeping alive the distinctive nature and culture—the scent—of Crete.[30]

To be fair, I realized that the Psilakis cookbook probably intended to push contemporary Cretans toward agricultural practices that are more ecologically sound—the way traditional agriculture in Crete likely used to be, albeit under very different circumstances. But I also worried that it risked encouraging readers to think romantically about Cretan agriculture instead of pressing them to confront the disagreement, conflict, deception, and struggle over important environmental issues ongoing today. Much food and wine in Crete is locally produced and seasonally consumed but much is not. According to the stories Manolis told, synthetic pesticides and other environmentally questionable practices have long been widespread all over the island. Indeed, for Manolis's family, eating foraged wild greens, planting gardens, raising snails, and making homemade wine were responses to long-term ecological and short-term human-health concerns. Sure, the reason they knew *how* to forage was because it was traditional knowledge, and the fact that they grew up eating these greens during leaner times might help explain why they loved their flavors so much. They certainly felt proud that there were scientific studies confirming that some of *their* food and drink traditions were healthful and environmentally friendly, especially in comparison with those of nations like the United States or Germany, say, against whose governments and economies there were (and still are) political grudges. But their struggle to keep up these particular traditions, selectively, seemed to me like it was driven more by a reasoned response to what they were learning through various media about human and planetary health and well-being, not so much by a desire to maintain tradition for tradition's sake, or out of a sense of regional patriotic duty.

I finally figured out why the extensive references to Cretan culinary history in the Psilakis cookbook left me so uneasy: It was because they struck me as primarily reinforcing a sense of collective belonging among Cretans while simplifying the treatment of the island's food history—and most of the economics and politics of this history—to a mere cataloging of certain culinary characteristics that persist through the ages. I saw Psilakis and Psilakis invoking Cretan history as a way to tidy up the meanings of "Crete" and "Cretan" and "Cretan food," making it that much harder for the general reader from Crete to discern the complex, sometimes mysterious, and ever-changing forces that make the world—including Crete—what it is. My sense was that knowledge of history should first and foremost help people reckon—comfortably or uncomfortably as the case may be—with the complexity of the present through improving their understanding of the past. I worried that such understanding is diminished when reinforcing a sense of collective belonging becomes a higher priority than seeking the best possible empirical interpretation of things.

Not that reinforcing a sense of collective belonging is in itself so terrible. I understand that history can legitimately supply groups of people with good reasons to identify with one another. Faced with a moral dilemma or a difficult challenge, knowing you're a Cretan sometimes helps you understand what the right thing to do is, and gives you the extra resolve you need to do the right thing when the right thing is the harder choice. It's a double-edged sword, though. Sometimes knowing you're a Cretan can *interfere* with knowing what the right thing to do is, especially when it leaves you so preoccupied with "being Cretan" that you forget to inquire with all your intellectual might into the history of what "being Cretan" means in the first place. It can leave you so focused on preserving Cretan tradition for tradition's sake that you stop grappling with the question of which aspects of tradition are worth upholding, which are not, and why.

Even worse: Sometimes it can lead you to believe that doing the right thing is doing the Right Thing.

It was as though Psilakis and Psilakis were presenting arguments about cultural continuity dating back to the Minoans (whose "civilisation is surely the greatest achievement of Crete, and the most important of the Bronze Age cultures within the Greek world as a whole"[31]), together with modern scientific evidence for the nutritional superiority of traditional Cretan cuisine, so that readers would be compelled to conclude that Cretan tradition is *the* superior Greek regional tradition.

I began to notice arguments for Cretan cultural superiority more frequently. In a promotional booklet, *Cretan Wine: The Nectar of the Gods for 5,000 Years*, whose rhetoric largely parallels that of Psilakis and Psilakis, the author talks about the practice of blending water and wine.[32] In antiquity, Greeks would often dilute their wine with water before drinking it. Indeed, this practice led to the replacement of the ancient word for wine, *οίνος*, with the word *κρασί* that is derived from the word *κράσις*, which means "mix" or "blend." After citing an ancient Greek text that mentions that in Crete men would drink their wine *without* diluting it with water, the author states that, "the tradition remained intact . . . *Cretans, unlike other Greeks, refuse now and have refused for many centuries, to put water in their wine*."[33] The full import of this statement is evident when you know the common idiomatic expression in Greek for compromising: "I put water in my wine." The author's literal statement of a fact also winds up signifying that real Cretans are even more uncompromising than other Greeks, and, consequently, have better equipped themselves to resist the inroads of modernization's problems.

As I discerned regionalist and nationalist tendencies in the cookbooks, I wondered: To what extent was I, too, guilty of letting my enthusiasm for Cretan food slide into a regionalistic or nationalistic stance? Was my interest in cooking Cretan food in the United States not also a reflection of the fact that I hadn't really paused to examine my own everyday participation in a conventional tendency to divide the world up into overly neat categories of Us and Them using as my litmus test some of the most conventional categories of social and cultural identity?

And what about my beliefs regarding the environment? I'd always been sympathetic to Manolis's ever-expanding experiments with producing safer and more sustainable food and drink for his family and friends. Why had I become so preoccupied with figuring out how to cook foods only in terms of their Cretan flavors, ingredients, textures, and recipes, and not in terms of their sustainability and safety? I began to question why I was so interested in drinking wines merely because they were from Crete or resembled Manolis's homemade wine. Why didn't I prefer buying wine that was *organic*? Why didn't I prefer making homemade wine without added chemicals, even when the grape varieties were "wrong" (i.e., not Cretan) and the wine tasted altogether different?

I knew I wasn't in a position to get good grapes, let alone good wine grapes, and let alone good wine grapes that weren't sprayed. To make matters worse, once I began perusing books about homemade winemaking, I found that they all insisted that making wine the old-fashioned way as we'd done in Crete simply wouldn't work in a place like Ohio. Even with good grapes the local wild yeasts on the skins or in the air would supposedly be the wrong ones for turning the grape juice into a drinkable wine. Somewhere I saw it argued that the only reason wine could be made successfully the old-fashioned way in the Old World was because winemaking had gone on there for centuries or millennia, and had significantly altered the local ecological balance of wild yeasts in such a way as to favor strains that indeed made good wild wine.

I decided to try anyway. If I was going to commit myself to more environmentally sound food and drink, I had to start somewhere. I remembered that Manolis had said that his oenologist acquaintance told him *off the record* that making wine the old-fashioned way would usually work. I decided that I wouldn't take the books I read at their word. How could they be so sure that it was impossible to make wine this way *everywhere* else in the world? Had anyone ever tried? How could they know what yeasts were in the air in my apartment, or in the air where all the grapes for sale were grown?

So I went to the supermarket and bought several bags of red grapes and black grapes that I thought tasted sweet enough, pressed them by hand, and left the juice to ferment in a large stock pot. After fermentation, I transferred the pinkish liquid to a large glass jar, covered it with a piece of plastic wrap, and screwed on the lid. The cloudiness eventually subsided and Sofia and I opened it up to try after about a month. It didn't resemble any wine we'd ever tasted before. Also, when left exposed to the air for even a short time, it began to develop a film on top. It was clearly not a success.

A year later, I got up the courage to try again. This time I decided to try something a little different. First, after destemming the grapes, I rinsed them under hot water from the kitchen faucet. Then, inspired by my wild sourdough bread-making, I soaked some of the Cretan raisins from Thanasis in a little dish of warm water with a spoonful of Cretan honey, and then I added the strained liquid to the grape must. I also paid more attention to sanitation by boiling water in the stock pot I was planning to use for fermentation, and running everything else through the dishwasher. After fermentation, I carefully transferred the new wine to the large glass jar one ladle at a time, sealed it, and put it inside a picnic cooler in the closet and left it there undisturbed for several months.

·One evening, when fellow grad students Stavros and Dimitra were visiting Sofia and me at our apartment, Stavros and I decided that the time had come to see what had become of my experiment. When I unscrewed the lid of the jar, there was a puff of air and the wine started bubbling. It had continued fermenting in the jar and had actually become a slightly sparkling wine. I ladled some out into our four Greek-style wineglasses and we tried it. It was substantially better in flavor than my first attempt, if rather unusual. We left the jar open for a while to see if we could get rid of the carbonation, then portioned the wine into several empty bottles, and closed them with those rubber corks that let you pump some of the air out of the bottle. We decided we'd drink it in small quantities every now and then on special occasions.

The next time Stavros came back from spending a break in Greece, he brought me a gift—a bottle of his Cretan grandfather's homemade wine. It was the first time in over five years that I'd tasted homemade Cretan wine, and its flavor resembled Manolis's wine just enough to make me instantly euphoric. Rather than finish off the entire bottle, I saved the last glass or so and added it to the single remaining bottle of my homemade wine, imagining that the microorganisms present in the Cretan wine might improve and Cretanize mine. A couple months later we opened it again. Sofia and I believed that the flavor had improved in the direction of the wine from Crete, but it was hard to know for sure, since wishful thinking sometimes affects our experience of flavors and aromas.

When it came to greens, I began to think along the same lines as with wine. I decided it was more important to re-create a practice I valued in Crete (foraging for wild greens) for the reasons we valued it (pleasures of taste *and* social and environmental well-being) than just trying to obtain the same varieties that grow in Crete and preparing them only in ways Cretans prepared them.

My desire to eat Cretan foods in the United States didn't go away, but it relaxed. And, because I'd been addressing that desire in such a sustained manner, I found myself well prepared for putting a wide variety of tasty food and drink on our table. I'd already acquired a wealth of practical knowledge about food, shopping, and cooking. I'd already developed habits that would enable me to continue learning more about food and drink in general.

For instance, the more I learned about bread making, the more I experimented—first by including barley flour in my recipe, inspired by Crete, then by adding such "un-Cretan" ingredients as oatmeal, corn grits, maple syrup, and ground flaxseed. I also began expanding my bread-making know-how to homemade pizza doughs. Making phyllo dough from scratch eventually led me to making homemade ravioli, lasagna, and gnocchi. My love for *spanakorizo* (spinach risotto) turned out to be a prelude to the many stirred spring risottos I'd improvise—including one with sunchokes, carrots, pine nuts, and Greek *retsina* wine. My growing appreciation for various mustard-family greens inspired me to stir-fry them with garlic in Taiwanese fashion at least as often as I'd make them into boiled *horta* served with lemon and olive oil.

I started making some of my old Greek recipes in new ways. That I was disappointed—but no longer resentful—that most Americans who claimed to know about Greek food actually knew little about what people in Greece actually ate no longer prevented me from being as creative as I wanted to be with Greek-inspired recipes at home. I switched to making a lighter version of moussaka with broiled instead of fried vegetables, and with a béchamel made from whole wheat flour and olive oil instead of white flour and butter. If Sofia and I happened to be visiting my parents, I'd make stuffed tomatoes and grape leaves using whatever fresh herbs were growing in their backyard instead of trotting off to the supermarket for the standard parsley and dill that I'd learned to use in Crete.

My obsession with Cretan food turned into an obsession with food and cooking in general as I began adding new cooking techniques and styles to my repertory that were not directly inspired by my knowledge of Greek cooking. My urge to collect didn't go away but turned in new directions. I sought to try every bulk grain sold at our local Wild Oats—wheat berries, pearled barley, wild rice, quinoa. I sought to try every new fruit I could get my hands on—kumquats, star fruit, currants, mangos. A Penzeys Spices store opened up only a block away from our apartment, and I bought samples of spices like star anise that I'd never tried before. I researched the many different spices for sale at Chinese markets and, once I knew where they fell taxonomically, I tried them out too. Sofia and I kept our eyes open for any greens or other vegetables—parsley root, celeriac, Belgian endive, watercress—that one or both of us hadn't tried before. And, of course, we continued studying wild greens and foraging, learning to recognize for the first time several new species with each passing year.

Careful exploration of supermarkets, ethnic and specialty food stores, restaurant supply retailers, and the cooking section of bookstores became a regular pastime. It became usual for us to spend Saturdays going around to every farm market and farmers' market that we could find, on the lookout for good fruit, especially apricots, watermelons, honeydews, cantaloupes, and plums. We began to use farmers' markets for our salad greens. It was shocking—but then again no it wasn't—to realize just how much better flavor and texture these greens had compared with those from the supermarket.

Instead of coffee I'd drink Taiwanese tea nearly every day. I spent time learning about oolongs, and Sofia's brother took care to find really good ones to bring back to me whenever he went home to Taiwan. His father would take him up to the mountains to an actual tea farmer, from whom they'd buy tea. I no longer had the nectar that was Manolis's wine, but to my pleasant surprise, the many Taiwanese oolongs I now had access to were nectars in their own right.

I took out books about cooking from the libraries on campus. I photocopied excerpts from both volumes of Julia Child's *Mastering the Art of French Cooking*. After recalling having heard about Laura Esquivel's *Like Water for Chocolate*, I devoured all the novels-with-recipes and culinary memoirs I could get my hands on. Sofia and I watched every food-related film we could find at the video store or library.

As my obsession with Cretan foodstuffs eased up and gave way to acknowledging the inescapable transformation of cultural products and practices in new contexts, I was finally in a position to start appreciating how someone like that graduate student in the Greek festival the day I first arrived in Ohio could become so interested in the experiences of Greek *Americans*. Who knew that someday I'd actually *enjoy* reading a book like Anagnostou's *Contours of White Ethnicity* about "the making of usable pasts in Greek America"?[34]

*   *   *

I continue picking blueberries with both hands as quickly as I can, filling and refilling the recycled yogurt container hanging around my neck, emptying it each time into the larger box I keep nearby on the ground in the shade of one of the blueberry bushes. I hope it won't take much longer. It's getting hot. After we get home we'll have to rinse them all, and then to freeze them in 4-cup batches—4 cups being the amount needed for one pie.

I wonder how many Sofia has picked so far? Not as many as me, I'll bet, because she always takes her time, aiming to pick out the largest, sweetest ones. Those will be the ones we save to eat fresh. Sometimes I wish I had her patience.

A pickup without a muffler charges down the road adjacent to where I'm picking. It vanishes in the distance and I notice for the first time just how quiet it's been here today at the orchard.

I think to myself: No, I no longer need to coach myself out of trying to conform to any particular past. I just need to remind myself that, like it or not, the heart will continue thrusting upon me moments of intense nostalgia. And so what? There are plenty of good ways to enjoy and act upon such moments. It just takes care and thought.

※ 20 ※

Birthdays, Inc.

It's just after lunchtime—1:20 p.m., to be exact. Sofia and I arrive at my brother's house for my nephew's birthday party, which is scheduled to end, according to the Incredible Hulk invitation we received in the mail two weeks ago, at 4:00 p.m.

We're all out back. Numerous folding tables have been temporarily set up under tarps.

The first is a card table and it's covered with wrapped birthday gifts.

On the second table there are three plastic trays containing snacks. The first tray contains festive tortilla chips—festive because they seem to be of as many different colors as the gift-wrapping on the presents—and a bowl of half-homemade/half-store-bought black-bean-and-corn salsa. The second tray contains a big bowl of run-of-the-mill potato chips of the unruffled variety. The third tray looks like it came directly from the store with the food already in it—raw baby carrots and other assorted vegetables, surrounding a centerpiece of off-white veggie dip with specks of something or another in it. Let's hope they're parsley flakes.

The third table, which looks like it's part of a high-end plastic patio furniture set, is empty. If my calculations are correct, it's destined to be used for the cake and ice cream a little later.

There are two large picnic coolers sitting on the ground near the tables but they don't quite fit under the tarps.

It's a hot August day but like half the Cretan professional musicians I know, I'm wearing my usual black shirt, blue jeans with a black leather belt, and black leather shoes. My relatives and my brother's in-laws are mostly wearing shorts, T-shirts, and sneakers.

My brother comes up and tells me that in the cooler on the right there's beer, but that if I want to I can just go into garage into the left-hand fridge and grab one of his homemade brews, and that I should remember that there's a bottle opener affixed to the wall next to the fridge.

Until I moved back here, I'd gone some fifteen years without attending any birthday parties like this.

As a kid I loved the way birthdays served as occasions for fun family get-togethers. But I also decided long ago that the birthday cons outweighed the birthday pros, even when I was the recipient of all the gifts and attention. *Because* I was the recipient. I certainly wasn't the only teenager in America who sensed that most birthday and holiday cards of the prewritten variety are a waste of paper, and that the business interests of card companies make it that much easier for people to stay hooked on this poor substitute for other kinds of ritualized communication. I was at an age when it was impossible for most of my relatives to anticipate what gifts I'd like, and it made me feel really guilty that they were spending their hard-earned money on stuff I had no use for, and which would end up as that much more garbage. As excited as I was to receive the occasional ten- or twenty-dollar bill, accepting it also made me feel like I was greedy and maybe a little vulgar.

Plus, ritual demanded that I stand there showing joy and appreciation as I opened the cards and gifts in front of everyone, without letting on how troubled I felt. After all, it was the *thought* that counted. Whenever my father opened presents on his birthday, he set the bar for present-opening as high as could be—patiently reading aloud each card, slowly unwrapping each gift with frequent pauses to make a humorous comment or to engage in repartee with the gift-giver, building suspense, and convincingly showing how happy and appreciative he was. It looked like an effortless performance. I don't even think it *was* a performance in that sense. I think he really felt this way with all his heart.

❀   ❀   ❀

Wearing sunglasses is making it easier for me to observe what's going on around me at today's party. My observations help pass the time but also make me more anxious.

Like when I notice how all the girls have been dressed up by their parents like little dolls whereas all the boys—like most of their fathers—are dressed simply and comfortably.

Like when I see how freaked out the fathers get if one of their boys picks up a "girl's toy" to play with.

Like when it hits me just how much of the time the kids are playing with some version or another of a gun.

(Why, though? I grew up playing with toy guns. Really, why the heck am I more bothered by seeing these kids playing with toy guns than by seeing Cretans shooting off *real* guns during celebrations?)

Like when I overhear my relatives talking—saying *heck* instead of *hell* and *darn* instead of *damn* and *shoot* instead of *shit* and *jeepers* instead of *Jesus*.

(Yes, I *know* I just wrote *heck* two or three sentences ago.)

Out comes the cake. It's an impressive-looking Hulk. I overhear my brother's mother-in-law telling my mother and my mother's sister the story of the cake. Homemade by a girlfriend of my brother's wife, I think. Chocolate and *something*. (Either I didn't hear the word right or it's something I've never heard of before.) All I know for sure is that if my grandfather was still alive, he wouldn't touch it with a ten-foot pole—because of all the supersweet *green* frosting.

The candles are lit, everybody sings "Happy Birthday," and Thomas makes a cut.

Thomas is turning four. It reminds me that I can still remember when my brother turned four—which means I was almost seven at the time—and how I was standing alone looking out our dining room window thinking to myself, "Wow, he's four already!" Now he's all grown up and raising kids of his own.

I notice my sister-in-law ask my cousin Rachel if her (Rachel's) son Tyler can have ice cream, because of his really bad allergies.

"No, he can't."

"I also have sherbert [*sic*]."

"Yes, he can have sherbert [*sic*]."

I know my brother and sister-in-law well-enough to know that they probably didn't check the sherbet to make sure that it doesn't have an ingredient list that runs all the way down to *here*. How can Rachel be sure that Tyler's fine with it? I recently gave Rachel a list of industrial ingredients that are manufactured from soy and that turn up in the darnedest places, so I know she knows you can't take this kind of thing for granted. And I certainly know she *cares*—she's been taking poor Tyler to specialists all over the northeast because he's got so many allergies. Maybe she hasn't developed the habit of checking every single label in a situation like this? Maybe she feels she can't risk saying no to everything at a birthday party?

My sister-in-law asks me if I want cake and ice cream, adding apologetically, "I know it's not as gourmet as what you guys are used to."

"No thanks. I'm good."

I feel bad about saying no, but I have to say no. I'm still not sure what "homemade" means in this case—whether it means made from scratch or just that it didn't come from something like a supermarket bakery. I don't dare ask. I'm even more skeptical about the frosting, and I'm simply not the kind of person who can scrape off all the frosting and eat just the cake. Thoughts about diabetes epidemics, food-coloring intolerances, and unpronounceable chemical additives race through my mind. But mostly I just can't stop wondering why no one else here seems to be concerned about any of this when it comes to all these kids.

Anyway, it's one more uncomfortable moment over with. Everybody knows I'm obsessed with food and that I'm critical of much of what they like to eat. So even when I'm just trying to be nice and get along, turning down a piece of birthday cake probably makes me look . . . mean? . . . weird? . . . I don't know, exactly. Whatever it makes me look like, and even though I'm pretty sure I don't like how it makes me look, I still don't take the cake.

As hosts, Sofia and I work hard to keep most of the food we serve at least as nonindustrially processed and homemade for visitors as we do for ourselves, while also taking into account, as best we can, the restrictions that visitors themselves observe. Trying to do this in the contemporary United States is something of a tall order and it makes us look like extremists—maybe like snobs—to most of my relatives, even though from a historical perspective it's really all the advanced science and engineering behind today's most common foods that is the extreme. I'm sure my family thinks we're strange for having a drawer full of organic lemons in the fridge but no bottled ketchup.

The really tough thing is knowing how to behave when somebody else in this industrial food culture hosts *you*.

Sometimes it's pretty easy. Like the time a stranger living across the hall from Sofia and me in Ohio invited us over for dinner. She did it to thank us. We'd noticed she'd left her keys in the door of her apartment one night, and she didn't hear us knock because she was asleep, so we took the keys out of the lock and put them on the floor just inside her door with a little note. She ended up preparing a full meal for us. An extraordinary gesture. But it was also incredibly unnerving in that most of the food was thoroughly industrial, from the distilled vinegar for the salad to the dessert of colored gelatin with suspended canned fruit. It wasn't the unassuming character of her table that I found disturbing. Hell, she could've served us boiled rice and an apple and I'd've been just as moved. And by many Americans' standards it was probably a pretty nice spread. I was mostly bothered because in a very tangible way it woke me up to the fact that industrial food inventions have so successfully managed to displace other foods in this country that visitors are regularly expected to eat who-knows-what ingredients and additives from who-knows-what factories.

I ate it, though. It *was* challenging taste-wise, yes. But between my thoughts about love of hosting others and my having felt genuinely moved by her offer, I managed to muster up the wherewithal to take it in stride.

I know well that visitors from one cultural context are frequently subject to the experience of being offered foods that—while perfectly conventional, customary, and normal to the host—seem unusual, unacceptable, unpalatable, or downright disgusting to the visitor. I had my share of such offers the first couple years I visited Crete. I wouldn't be surprised if vegetarians struggle with the generous offer of exclusively meat-based dishes, celiacs of a meal with gluten in everything from the beer to the batter on the fish, observant Jews of a piece of pork. Wherever there are people with diverse beliefs about what is safe to eat, diverse beliefs about what is fair and just when it comes to food production, diverse concepts of edibility and palatability, diverse health issues, diverse views on food safety, and so on, it's hard to imagine how food can remain central to hosting visitors.

It seems unlikely that anyone could deduce universally agreed upon rules for dealing with such differences. I guess there's a politics of accepting and not accepting food, just as there's a politics of offering it.

From one point of view, I'm very open and easygoing. Sofia and

I both are. Neither of us is driven by any food taboos in the sense of religious beliefs or principles like vegetarianism. We don't have significant food allergies or other immediate food-related health problems we have to worry about. Sofia has even become lactose tolerant. Sure there's some perfectly natural ingredients we either don't like or would never likely try, though most of these would fall outside the realm of edibility or palatability for all the people we know.

But when it comes to my increasingly powerful aversion to industrially manufactured and processed foods, I'm reaching the point where it's becoming difficult to eat almost *anything* that people in my family have to offer. Yet, because I don't think that my own relative food safety and my opposition to much of the modern industrial food system ought always to trump *everything* else I value—such as getting along with my relatives—I find myself grappling with the question of when to give in and when to stick to my principled food preferences.

Typically, if someone doesn't know that I have these kinds of principles, then depending on the situation I might find a way to bring it up, find other unrelated excuses (to avoid eating something) that they'd likely find perfectly legitimate, or just give in and eat. If they *do* know about my principles but aren't really in a position to know how to deal with them—especially if they seem to be *trying* to deal with them—I think I'm much more likely to give in and eat.

But, if they know about my preferences and they have—or could very easily get—the kind of knowledge that would enable them to respond to these preferences, but they continue serving me the industrial stuff anyway, I tend to refuse the offer. Maybe I sense that they don't really care that much about me so I won't allow myself to care enough about them to subject myself to who-knows-what newfangled substances. Or maybe I sense that they *do* care about me but that responding to my preference would require them to compromise their sense of self ("these are the foods of *my* world"), in which case I'd say: just as they care more about protecting their identity than they do about protecting me from possible physical harm, so shall I care more about protecting myself from potential harm than about offending their identity. Or maybe I sense that they believe I've grossly exaggerated the risks of many industrial foods and they simply won't go to the extra trouble of trying to address my preferences, in which case—knowing that they've probably never even looked into the matter with any diligence—I stand my ground that these are not exaggerations and that *my* expectations are ultimately not the extreme ones.

This isn't to say that I'm not troubled by my choice to do so. Apart from the emotional discomfort that can come from standing one's ground in an otherwise conflict-free situation, I worry that in some way I'm behaving a lot like other people who sometimes get on my nerves with their own food-related insistences. For example, my Asian mother-in-law who, although she eats potatoes and bread and pasta, when you offer her any of these things, *preferring* rice for her starch, feels justified in asking somebody to make her some rice. Or my Albanian brother-in-law who, although he eats rice, complains when there isn't any bread.

(Why should this annoy me? Why not bread and rice for everyone! Isn't that usually how I think? I guess I don't like it when people choose to travel to other cultural contexts while expecting people in those other contexts to accommodate their home expectations. I expect them to show a little more willingness to adapt to the contexts in which they've chosen to visit.)

I worry that some people will find my expectations no less stubborn or idiosyncratic or selfish, which leaves me having to choose between maintaining the pleasantness of the moment and protecting myself and others from industrial-food risks.

❄ ❄ ❄

Aunt Juliette: "You're not eating any cake?"

"Not today."

My mother: "It's *real* good."

I decide it's time to take a walk.

I wander around the perimeter of my brother's backyard to observe what's growing. I notice the oregano that my brother asked me for so he could transplant it at his house. It's not doing well. Of course not—it's planted in the shade.

I'm behind the swing set. A little boy comes up to me—not a relative. He must be one of my brother's friend's kids. I'm surprised that he's so comfortable with strangers. "Bang!" He shoots me with the toy gun he's carrying.

I'm dying to say, "That killed me."

Instead I say, "You got me."

The little boy turns around and walks away.

(Wait: My mother-in-law didn't *choose* to have her daughter marry an American, and my Albanian brother-in-law didn't *choose* to desire marrying an Asian. Maybe I'm not being understanding enough about the ways that rice or bread can go a long way to make them feel more comfortable when they're outside their comfort zone.)

I finish making my round and take a seat in a lawn chair near Uncle Rich, my parents, and a few of my cousins. They're talking about who might be the next superintendent of our school district. Uncle Rich ends up recounting the story of when he met one of the teachers at the high school: "I say, 'Nice to meet you, William,' and he says, 'I'd prefer it if you called me Doctor Moore.'" Everybody responds as expected: "Oh [. . .] my [. . .] god." "Ugh, how arrogant!"

Everybody except me: "Don't you all call the priest *Father Aurelia?*"

"That's different," counters another aunt.

"Why's it different? If you're willing to call the priest 'Father' why aren't you willing to call a teacher with a doctorate 'Doctor'?"

Uncle Rich explains that Doctor Moore truly *was* arrogant. I say that I didn't know the guy, and that he may very well have been arrogant, but that I still didn't think expecting to be addressed by his title was necessarily evidence of it. Then Uncle Rich adds that Moore had actually said to him, "Nice to meet you, *Rich,*" first, so he (Uncle Rich) ended up telling him, "I'd prefer it if you called me Mr. Potter." I agreed that if this was the case, maybe this Moore guy *was* messed up—he should've said "Mr. Potter"—but there was still nothing wrong with a teacher with a doctorate expecting to be addressed that way in a professional setting, at least by anyone who freely addressed other people by their professional titles.

I can tell from the look on my cousins' faces—even the ones who are (nondoctorate) teachers—that they don't agree.

"I know—I must've come from the milkman."

Time to make another round of the backyard.

Driving home about an hour later, I've got a Cretan CD playing in the car. I sing out a new *"mantinada"* I've just come out with in *English:*

"It's better to have loved and lost," they say as consolation,
But never knowing how much pain can come from separation.

A few minutes later, I come out with yet another, again in English:

> I wish I was a red-tailed hawk gliding around the sky,
> Never bothered by other birds because I fly so high.

I decide it's okay to allow the words *sky* and *high* to count as two syllables because they end on long vowels, and because in Greek this sound is literally pronounced as two syllables (the sound *ah* followed by *ee*, with the stress falling on the *ah*).

Back home, I evaluate a few student papers.

I'm getting hungry, but Sofia and I haven't given a thought to dinner yet.

I get up and open the fridge, glance quickly from top to bottom, and close the door.

I walk to the back door of the house and look out. I see a squirrel make parabolas across the grass and disappear behind an oak tree. I turn around, march through the kitchen and dining-room-turned-den, sidle up to the front window, put my face in the blinds and look out left, right, then left again. Nothing much to see.

I head back toward the fridge and repeat the whole process.

Again.

Again.

Once more.

I finally realize what I'm doing and freeze: "Think!" I admonish myself, out loud, in Greek. I strain to imagine something to eat for dinner but come up empty.

The hungrier I get, the less averse I become toward eating out.

Sofia comes down the stairs. I ask her if she wants to go somewhere to eat.

"Huggy Bear!" she smilingly scolds me. "You know we shouldn't eat out again!"

Of course, I agree, but sometimes when my mind has been preoccupied with other things, I have a hard time deciding what to eat. It's not that preparing the food is taxing. It's trying to figure out *what* to prepare, and reminding myself that preparing it will be easy, done and over with before I know it.

It's not like it's much easier for me to decide what to eat in a restaurant. Even when we go to restaurants that serve food that's more like actual homemade food, I can sit there for the longest time going in circles over the menu, finding something I don't like about most everything I might otherwise like to eat: I assume the salmon is farm-raised, the deli meats are cured with nitrites, the meat isn't from a local small farm, the pasta isn't whole grain, the salad isn't freshly washed, the salad dressing contains artificial ingredients or the salad oil isn't extra virgin olive oil. It seems like almost every dish that looks good to me has at least one ingredient or component that makes room for sneaking in some industrial-food tricks to make it taste better or cut costs. So half the time I just end up suggesting we go for sandwiches or chicken wings or pizza, figuring if we're going to eat out, we might as well have something that tastes good and doesn't cost much.

"Can't we *cook* something?" Sofia pleads.

"I guess . . . You sure you don't wanna go somewhere?"

"I can stir-fry green beans."

I don't say anything as I try beating back my craving for all the industrial temptations.

"You don't want beans?"

"Here's an idea: What if we make something like what we'd get in a restaurant, even if we have to use ingredients from the supermarket? It'll be better than what we would've gotten if we went out. At least I'll know what's in the hot sauce, so to speak. . . . You want chicken wings? I hate the idea of using chicken from the store, but it can't be any worse than whatever we'd end up getting in a restaurant, right?"

"Okay, so you'll make chicken wings and I'll make beans?"

✳ 21 ✳

Food and Health

Leonidas, Sofia, and I are in Ithaca, NY to shop for food. For Sofia and me it's primarily about olive oil.

While we were living in Ohio, Sofia and I would buy tasty Greek extra-virgin olive oil—five or more gallons at a time—every time we visited Leonidas, at a store in Binghamton that had by far the best price we'd ever seen for it. They stopped carrying it after a few years. Then, Leonidas found it for sale in Ithaca, in the store where he buys good Greek feta, also at a decent price. The price of Greek oil isn't nearly as low as it used to be, but it's several dollars cheaper per gallon here than everywhere else we've looked, and we've looked in a lot of places. Since we usually buy around thirty or forty gallons at a time—some of which are for my parents, my brother, and my cousin Ben, who all like us to pick up some for them—the money we save more than compensates us for the expense of the trip. Otherwise, we'd just buy it locally.

We fill up the trunk of the car with oil and feta and head to several other food stores Leonidas knows. We stop at a supermarket to pick up a few things Leonidas needs for making dinner. As has been our habit for years, whenever we visit Leonidas, we spend time wandering up and down the supermarket aisles checking out what's available and interesting, keeping our eyes peeled for good deals.

Much of the food Sofia and I eat at home comes from our own garden and neighboring farms, but a lot of our nonlocal food doesn't even come from local shops or local supermarkets. Sofia's brother brings us oolong teas from Taiwan. Her sister brings us Japanese gyokuro tea from LA. The last time Sofia and I visited LA, we filled up a suitcase with seaweeds and a brand of soy sauce that we couldn't find locally. Greek olive oil, vinegar, Cretan honey, and the like come from the shop in Ithaca. Thanasis brings us vinegar and honey from Astoria when he visits. We buy Greek coffees from an Italian-American store in Albany. We get peaches from my cousins' business in Oneonta.

Walking the aisles, I remember that Sofia and I want to get into the habit of eating more canned fish, especially smaller fish like anchovies and sardines.

Ideally, I'd like us to take up fishing. Fishing was one of my favorite summer pastimes while I was growing up. When I was only three or four years old I'd hold a stick with a string tied to the end in Brown Tract Pond and tell everyone I was fishing, believing I really was. Later my parents gave me a children's fishing pole—the kind you can't really cast—and then when I was eleven or twelve they gave my brother and me real rods and tackle boxes. Nothing fancy—just inexpensive closed-cast fishing poles from the local department store, which had an entire aisle dedicated to fishing gear. I used it straight through my first two years of college, right up to the second-to-last time I went fishing. I never tried fly fishing or ice fishing. Mostly I fished with earthworms that I found in the yard or woods or out in the road during rain. Now and then I'd use artificial lures, especially when I was allowed to borrow Grandpa Leclaire's rowboat with the electric trolling motor. There was a summer on Schroon Lake when it seemed like I spent all my waking hours either fishing or preparing hooks and sinkers.

I had no idea at that time that some kinds of fish were actually stocked in the rivers and lakes by New York State. I also had no idea that so many anglers came to the Adirondacks from faraway big cities and suburbs to fish for sport. I thought most of the other people fishing were small-town or country people like my relatives and me.

After my sophomore year in college, when my best friend Joe and I were stationed at a Department of Transportation job along the west branch of the Ausable River, we'd go fishing after work before heading back to the hotel. There we caught trout. Mostly rainbow trout, I think, but I guess there might've been some brown or speckled. During the week we'd save up our daily catch in the refrigerator in the DOT field office. Then we'd take the fish with us in a cooler when we went back home for the weekend and have Joe's father cook them for us on the grill with butter and fresh lemon. I discovered I liked trout even better than perch.

That was right around the time Joe and I joined the "philosophy discussion group" at college. Discussions there inevitably put us in contact with moral questions and ideas we hadn't considered before and for the first time in our lives we became self-conscious—even a bit squeamish—about such things as sticking live nightcrawlers on hooks, pounding bullheads over the head with the butt of a knife, and cleaning trout while they were alive. After a while I just sort of gradually lost interest in fishing. By the time I joined Manolis and his friends for a half-day of longline fishing in a boat off the southeast coast of Crete six years later, it was as though fishing was something I only knew from some distant previous life.

Nowadays, the idea of fishing around home scares me in ways that it didn't when I was a kid, because of polluted waters. I vaguely recall that New York State publishes information about how much they recommend eating.

※ ※ ※

Sofia and I end up filling our basket with cans of anchovies, some sardines, some mackerel, and some albacore tuna—since they have a brand that is packed in olive oil instead of mystery broth—and the price is better than in our supermarket back home. The cashier doesn't notice that we have six cans of light tuna and six cans of more costly white tuna, and he charges us for twelve cans of light tuna. I'm watching carefully but I don't say a word because it's an error in our favor, and this is a large supermarket chain. This is my way of trying to redress the errors that these stores make at our expense. I just take advantage of the fact that it's customary for them to use cashiers who know little or nothing about food. When I have the energy, I watch for errors in their favor and make sure the cashier corrects them. But when the cashier makes them in our favor, I keep my mouth shut.

Sometimes it gets even more subtle. Cashiers are constantly asking us what various fruits and vegetables are because they don't know—and probably aren't trained to know—what they are. I don't lie, but say technically true things that can lead a cashier to make errors in our favor. For example, Belgian endive costs more than another kind of endive. When the cashier asks me what it is, I just say "endive," and most of the time they put in the code for the less expensive endive, not Belgian. If I have a bag of shitake mushrooms, say, and they ask me what kind of mushrooms they are, I just feign ignorance. Sometimes they take the time to find out. Other times they just put in the code for button mushrooms.

I don't always do this. Sometimes I get a sense that a cashier, especially a young cashier, is genuinely curious. The teacher inside me kicks in, and I end up telling them more than they're probably bargaining for—especially when they ask me follow-up questions about cooking.

We return to Binghamton.

Leonidas gets to work on cooking dinner while I open up a couple cans of fish for us to snack on. It's not that I'm crazy about canned fish, especially after all the years of eating fresh fish at Manolis and Eirini's, but I'm determined to make our diet healthier, and I avoid eating farm-raised fish because of what I've read about the feed. I've also read that methylmercury levels in wild-caught fish can vary depending on the size and type of fish and what they eat, and that some of these canned fish tend to have less methylmercury than some others. It's hard for me to pinpoint when I came to think so much about food in terms of my physical health. Sure, we learned about the four basic food groups in elementary school, and Grandma always said something about eating various colors of vegetables every day, but when did I actually start thinking about things like this on my own? Maybe it started when I was an undergrad working summers up in the Adirondack Mountains, when my friend Joe and I decided to drink water instead of soda with our meals.

Later, when I found myself in a position to eat foods made from scratch, I suppose I stopped giving much thought to the question of food and personal health. I must've thought that by eating a variety of mostly homemade foods, there wasn't much to worry about and that I was probably doing myself more good than people like Aunt Patsy and Aunt Juliette who paid attention to the latest reports on television or in the newspaper about which particular food was supposedly discovered that week to be really good or bad for you.

When it came to good health I was usually more preoccupied with the question of exercise than food. Growing up, I got lots of exercise without even thinking about it—playing hockey on the backyard pond in the winter, basketball in the driveway turnaround in the spring and summer, and football in the backyard in autumn. We rode our bikes a lot, went hiking, ran around the yard playing games, did yard work, played in the snow building forts and going sledding. Sometimes, being the superskinny kid that I was, I'd impose calisthenics and weightlifting regimens on myself, drawing up charts to keep track of my daily activities, imagining that I'd finally become like the muscular cool kids in school, though I never stuck with these ambitions for more than a week or two at a time. After I went off to college and my so-called life of the mind took off, I found that I was spending a lot more time studying and sitting around with friends having discussions. Realizing how sedentary I'd become, I'd push myself to go to the gym to shoot hoops or play racquetball or run laps. I always felt better afterward but it wasn't like I felt so bad without doing it that I *felt* the desire to exercise. I just *thought* I should, given the prevailing wisdom about exercise and good health.

During grad school in Chicago I exercised even less, though Penny and I did walk almost everywhere. Sure, I occasionally tried to discipline myself with a regimen of sit-ups and push-ups in the apartment, but I never enjoyed that kind of exercise and it never lasted more than a few weeks. It was the same thing when I moved to Crete. I walked almost everywhere in Irakleio and danced Cretan dances at family gatherings, but whenever I tried to impose on myself an exercise routine in the apartment it never lasted. As my belly grew, I'd tell Penny's mother—whenever she was persuading me to eat more, and I hadn't eaten *little*—"I'm on a diet," which always got a good laugh.

I thought it was kind of funny how my body provided evidence supporting the claim that—at least as I've heard it expressed in Crete—a person shows his true colors only after he's tied his donkey (i.e., hitched his mule). The only time I'd ever stuck to a self-imposed exercise regimen for months, and a somewhat intensive regimen at that, was when I was in the process of pursuing Penny. But that's just it: sooner or later my distaste for exercising for the sake of exercise ended up trumping any other preoccupation I might've had for good health, muscular strength and stamina, or a particular physique. If exercise wasn't the coincidental byproduct of doing something else that I wanted to do—like getting from here to there, digging a hole, or shooting hoops with my friends—I could only stick with it for so long.

That is, until about a year before I finished my graduate studies in Ohio, after Sofia persuaded me to go to the doctor's for the first time in years and I discovered that my "bad" cholesterol was high and my "good" cholesterol was low. I was shocked. Given how Cretan I thought I was eating, and given the Mediterranean diet's fame in the world for being heart-healthy, I thought this was the last health issue in the world I'd ever have to worry about. And it never occurred to me that sometimes cholesterol is a matter of heredity.

The doctor told me I was young enough to try modifying my diet and exercise to see what happened before making any pharmaceutical moves. He sent me to a nutritionist to educate me about food and cholesterol. Because of all the reading I'd done about heart-healthy diets as part of my research into cookbooks and the politics of the Cretan diet, and because of all my reading about food in general, I was pretty sure I'd know more about these things than a run-of-the-mill student health–center nutritionist, but I went anyway. I didn't want the MD to think I was arrogantly ignoring his advice. Sure enough, the nutritionist didn't tell me anything I didn't already know. In fact, all the info and advice seemed totally dumbed down, framed as though every cholesterol patient was a stereotypically scientifically subliterate, culinarily challenged, white, middle-class American. By the end of our chat, I ended up teaching the nutritionist two or three new things.

As I thought more about my situation, I became aware that Sofia and I were eating industrial foods out at corporate restaurant chains, sometimes as often as two or three times a week. And I knew that even when we ate at home we didn't usually eat greens and salads in the same quantities that I remembered everyone eating in Crete. And I certainly didn't keep up with eating legumes *every* week like Eirini always insisted we should. My shock began to turn into fear, and, to some extent, embarrassment and shame: How could I, Mr. Cretan-diet-in-America, have set myself up to die young of a heart attack when none of my donuts-and-macaroni-and-cheese-eating relatives ever has?

I resolved to give my diet and lifestyle another overhaul.

Even before the test results were in, the doctor told me that I ought to lose some weight, stirring up the peace I'd only just made with myself—standing in front of the bathroom mirror a few weeks earlier—about the aging process and the fact that I was no longer, and never again would be, my thin young self. So much for that! I declared war on my weight. I started exercising every day. I began walking instead of driving to and from the university—about five miles each way. I went cold turkey on caffeine and cut way back on wine. Sofia and I switched to eating only whole grain breads, pastas, rice, and other cereals. We tripled or quadrupled the amount of green vegetables we'd eat and cut out meat almost entirely. I converted a bunch of my recipes into what I took to be heart-healthy versions—pie dough made with olive oil, puréed vegetable soups without any cream.

Within a few months I went down thirty pounds. My blood pressure was normal. For the first time in years I felt great and—if I may say so myself—I looked good. I could take the stairs to my fourth-floor department without getting out of breath. Grocery store clerks were ID'ing me again whenever I bought wine. Students in the classes I taught were flirting with me again. Anyway, I don't want to get into the whole question of how I *looked*. The point is that my cholesterol levels improved significantly, even if they remained slightly out of medical science's approved bounds.

Coincidentally, my parents were going through some health issues around that time. So, whenever Sofia and I visited them during one of our breaks, I'd cook lots of homemade food, introduce my mother to all kinds of vegetables and whole grains, and generally educate them more about nutrition. I'd trick my mother into eating ingredients like spinach or legumes that she claimed she couldn't stand. She'd discover she liked them after all—at least in the dishes I was making—expanding further the range of vegetable-rich homemade dishes she could make.

I was too embarrassed to tell my parents that it was my cholesterol tests that scared me into becoming such a nutrition freak, and that the reason I was cooking all the meals when we visited them wasn't only because I was bored and there wasn't anything else to do, but also because I didn't want to compromise my new obsessively heart-healthy eating habits. I don't think they even noticed how much I'd suddenly changed my own cooking and eating habits, since for many years most of the foods they saw me preparing were . . . ahem . . . Greek to them.

Back in Ohio, my Greek friends must've thought I'd lost my mind over the summer. No coffee? No meat? Seemingly overnight, I'd turned into a low-cholesterol fanatic, heart-healthy fundamentalist, and born-again quasi-vegetarian. I weighed myself several times a day, and used the body mass index to figure out what my ideal weight should be, aiming for the lower end of the specified range, given my small-bone build. I never counted calories or anything like that. I just made sure that I kept eating wholesome, mostly vegetarian, homemade foods. Every time I walked by a mirror or a reflecting storefront window I'd check myself out, especially my shrinking belly—a constant source of vane self-congratulation.

After Sofia and I finished our doctorates and moved here, the greater extremes of my fanaticism subsided. With the move to Upstate New York and a new job came changes in lifestyle. There was so much work to do and there were so many things to cope with at my new job that I *needed* coffee to keep up with the pace—and wine to unwind—and I had little time or mental space to think carefully about food on an everyday basis. Sofia's cigarette-smoking, beer-chugging brother was living just a half-hour away, meaning that the temptation to party was back again. I was eating more meat and refined starches, although not in nearly the same quantities I did before.

On the whole, I managed to keep up a good diet, but exercise fell by the wayside. It was only a five-minute walk to the office and, anyway, the sidewalks were all covered with ice during winter. I'd been hoping to drop five more pounds but by midwinter I was back up five or ten pounds from my record low. I increasingly felt ashamed and embarrassed. Despite all my knowledge of good nutrition and cooking, my own body shape was getting away from me again. The size of my stomach had increasingly become the touchstone of my personal identity. The less flat it became, the more I felt I wasn't *objectively* attractive. I'd look at my stomach every time I walked by a mirror, sighing in despair.

Spring arrived and I resolved to get my weight back down again. Almost every afternoon I walked laps around the perimeter of the park by our apartment for an hour or ninety minutes. I had to stop, though, because I'd been wearing my usual leather shoes and ended up with severe pain in my shins and feet. Then Sofia and I moved into our house and I did a lot of yard work, took lots of walks on nearby trails, and occasionally swam in the pool. All winter I kept up my exercise with a treadmill and dumbbells. I kept checking how I looked in front of the mirror. I found my groove again and was looking better than ever.

For the first time in my life I became interested in shopping for fashionable clothing. I'd follow Sofia, Sofia's brother, and his girlfriend to outlet stores and shopping malls on weekends and buy tight-fitting jeans and shirts, designer sports coats, and new kinds of leather jackets. No more loose-fitting clothes. I had nothing to hide. I loved it when Sofia's brother's girlfriend would walk behind me at the outlets, whistling and saying loudly how hot I looked.

Then I'd slip and eat a little more than usual, or not keep up with all my exercise routines, and gain a few pounds. I'd lament my predicament every time I walked by a mirror. I'd hold the stomach fat in my hands and sigh to Sofia, complaining about how stressful it was to find the mood and energy to do exercise or to prevent myself from eating the foods I desired. But by the time I gained five pounds or so I'd somehow manage to get back with the program.

The stress of trying to maintain a desired weight started to get to me, and it wasn't clear that any of this had much to do with cholesterol or blood pressure or good health anymore. I wondered whether my *mental* well-being was at stake. I didn't think I had an eating disorder, although I did feel like I recognized *some* of what I'd read about anorexics. I never considered for a moment depriving myself of my regular meals nor did I ever contemplate making myself throw up after eating. The worst thing I ever caught myself doing was, after I'd eat a little more than I thought I should, I'd immediately go walk extra miles on the treadmill to compensate. Or I'd become obsessed with walking to and from our favorite coffee shop, instead of driving, so I could burn off many of the calories I'd eat there.

I thought again about nutrition, but not for any academic projects, just for myself.

I had no patience for food and health claims—however comforting, fun, or spiritually satisfying they might feel—made by people whose ideas and methods don't even begin to stand up to well-reasoned analytical appraisal of observable evidence. I was only interested in what various experts had learned about food and health through rigorous study. But, this led me to more than one *kind* of expert. It led me, first of all, to nutritional scientists whose work deals directly with food and health. It also led me to *social* scientists and *philosophers of* science who study how a scientific field like nutritional science operates in the first place—how its experts function as professionals, how the entire field works as a profession that constructs information, knowledge, and provisional truths about food as nutrition.

All those years I'd been working in math and science, I'd noticed that no empirical science—not even physics—makes *discoveries* about the world out there unless it also makes certain *assumptions* about that world. Depending on the viability of the assumptions being made, the *significance* of any particular scientific discovery is then diminished or magnified. Consequently, the more awareness there is of assumptions being made and the better understood are such assumptions, the more hope there is to understand any given discovery's relevance and implications for the world.

I knew firsthand that one assumption informing virtually all modern scientific research—especially in the applied sciences—is that scientists are skillful at deciding which questions to focus on and which methodologies to employ even though such decisions are frequently made not for strictly scientific reasons but in response to who's paying for the research, how much, and why. I'd grown pretty wary of the viability of this assumption, especially wherever lots of money was at stake. This didn't mean that scientists' actual studies are untrue. It meant that the literal findings—once considered in light of the various stated and unstated assumptions upon which they're predicated—might be far less relevant to the broader concerns their work is meant to address than they're apt to acknowledge, especially in front of funders and a scientifically subliterate public.

When I'd walked away from applied math, I'd left with an interesting lesson about just how complicated "simple" things could be. The example often given by University of Chicago faculty was that of water dripping from a faucet. The nonscientist might suspect that compared with the behavior of celestial bodies or of elements or molecules, a drop of water is a no-brainer. Not the case. Significant research—really difficult research—had been done on modeling the formation of a drop of water. One of my professors liked to point out that modeling the behavior of superhuge things (like planets) or supersmall things (like molecules) is, from the scientist's perspective, relatively "simple." It's the stuff going on all around us at scales we're accustomed to in everyday life that are really hard to get a handle on, even when many simplifying assumptions are made for the purpose of trying to achieve good-enough approximations.

I was already predisposed, then, to a lot of skepticism about a field like nutrition. I recalled various media reports I'd heard over the years, and how frequently it seemed as though promising discoveries about food and health had been later overturned or greatly qualified by subsequent research. It wasn't surprising to me. Intuition told me that nutrition and health involve *many* variables, most of which don't look like they can be treated as negligible. I couldn't imagine—especially given the nature of the media reports about the latest discoveries, focused as they were on this particular ingredient or that particular nutrient—that nutritional scientists had developed supersophisticated ways of taking all the important variables into account, or even of figuring out which variables are the important variables. I would have been very surprised if the apparent complexities of diet and health could be well understood by what I assumed had to be the relatively "simple" methods employed by nutritional scientists. Sure, they might lead to "simple" albeit crucial discoveries (such as the connection between vitamin C and scurvy), but not to a whole lot of "complex" discoveries regarding the relationship between food and chronic illness.

A little research into the matter only reinforced my hunches. A 2001 commentary in the *Journal of Nutrition* states that "In the last twenty years, powerful new molecular techniques were introduced that made it possible to advance knowledge in human biology using a reductionist approach. Now, the need for scientists to deal with complexity should drive a movement toward an integrationist approach to science. We propose that nutritional science is one of the best reservoirs for this approach."[1] A 2001 commentary in the *Journal of the American Dietetic Association* declares, "It is time to pay more attention to overall dietary patterns."[2] A 1995 article in the magazine *Science* asserts that "Epidemiology faces its limits."[3]

I was also quite sure that most of the information that the public receives about food and health comes from nutrition counselors, medical doctors, medical associations, government dietary recommendations, journalists, advertisers, and various other modes of popular culture. But as far as I could gather, such groups who assess, summarize, and transmit nutritional research to the public do so without paying much attention to such caveats, and therefore risk massively inflating the significance of that research. Even worse, not only do they further simplify, if not totally misunderstand, the scientists' (frequently speculative) statements about the significance of their own research, they often transmit and translate these "truths" while under the spell of the same underlying assumptions as many of the scientists. At least many of the scientists, if pressed on the matter, can probably acknowledge the kinds of assumptions they find themselves needing to operate under in order to arrive at their results. Many of these transmitters and translators, on the other hand, seem completely ignorant of the fact that the scientists are making any such assumptions. As a result, they transmit and translate scientific findings as though they're Truths—without acknowledging that such truths are only as sturdy as the assumptions upon which they're built, let alone calling into question the viability of those assumptions.

I wanted eating advice carefully distilled from the vast store of empirical knowledge on hand, including empirical knowledge of modern nutritional science's working assumptions, accomplishments, and missteps. But there was no way I was about to try going through all the research myself in order to draw my own conclusions. I wanted translators of nutritional science who consulted the findings of the nutritional scientific research *and* who tempered the implications of those findings through a critical awareness of the many stated and unstated assumptions behind them, and of any other relevant empirical knowledge—such as that of history, evolution, and ecology. And, because of the financial stakes involved in this topic, I wanted translators who were not likely to be overly swayed by special interests, fears about their financial well-being, or temptations to pursue career success at the expense of rigor.

About a year later, journalism professor Michael Pollan offered himself as just such a translator with his book, *In Defense of Food: An Eater's Manifesto.*[4]

Pollan takes into account knowledge produced by nutritional science as well as inherent limitations of such knowledge that are attributable to the field's largely nutrient-centered methodological assumptions. His assessment of the evidence leads him to argue that eaters interested in good health should abandon the modern Western industrialized diet. He argues that such a diet poses a high risk for human health, at least in terms of chronic diseases and overall life expectancy.

The problem, though, is that he just *assumes* that *diet* is the thing. He rightly points out that nutritional scientists are unwarranted for being nutrient-centered in their assumptions—for assuming that individual nutrients matter more than the *interaction* of nutrients, more than the *foods* that happen to contain them, more than the *diets* that contain those foods, and more than the broader *lifestyle patterns* that include particular dietary patterns. But then he turns around and is *diet*-centered in his, even while he admits that "the precise causal mechanisms [of Western diseases] were (and remain) uncertain."[5] He seems too eager to agree with experts who believe that, "the chronic diseases that now kill most of us can be traced directly to the industrialization of our food,"[6] and that "food" in this context is best thought of in terms of "diet" rather than "nutrients."

I didn't get it. Why stop at the level of *diet*? What about the industrialization of our environment and of our lifestyles more generally? What about physical activity? What about relative exposure to various industrially generated pollutants in the air or water? What about stress? How about daytime naps? What if it's the *interaction* of diet and other modern nondietary environmental factors that matters most for good health? Even if it can be shown that industrialization is a major cause of these chronic illnesses, absent convincing empirical evidence about which scales matter most—from the tiny scale of the nutrient to the large scale of whole-lifestyle-in-a-particular-environment—do we really know which effects of industrialization (effects on diet? effects on lifestyle? effects on environmental conditions? all of the above?) have the most impact on personal health? Where's the conclusive research showing that diet is really the most important?

Obviously I had to take Pollan's interpretation of the empirical evidence with a huge grain of salt, but I wasn't about to throw out his diet-centered reading of things quite yet. Besides, he did indicate that, "*How* a culture eats may have just as much bearing on health as *what* a culture eats."[7] So maybe he wasn't being completely diet-centered, at least not always.

Pollan's overall argument recognizes the potential value of both traditional knowledge about eating and modern scientific knowledge about food and health. He may be critical of the effects of industrialization on diet but he never suggests that we return to some golden age of traditional eating that never existed. If we want to undo some of the awful effects of industrialization on our health, we can benefit from both reliable modern scientific knowledge and traditional eating knowledge. It's all a matter of trying to be informed by both kinds of knowledge in reasonable ways. Traditional eating knowledge, in particular, might help rescue us from any poor or wrongheaded eating advice sponsored by nutrient-centered scientists and their translators.

Just knowing that traditional diets like that of mid-twentieth-century Crete correlate with a low risk for modern Western diseases, we can wager that we probably know a lot about more or less healthy eating already. Pollan states it more poetically: "You don't need to fathom a carrot's complexity in order to reap its benefits."[8] We can fall back on certain traditional eating knowledge, supplemented with a few basics discovered by nutrient-centered nutritional science (we really do need vitamin C!), and then come up with some decent guidelines for healthy eating.

Pollan offers such guidelines in the form of simple rules whose simplicity derives not from dumbing-down what the empirical evidence says but from taking into account *more* of the empirical evidence in various fields: "Eat food. Not too much. Mostly plants."[9] For each of these general rules, Pollan elaborates with more specific rules of thumb. Only twenty-something things to keep in mind when eating for good health.

"Eat food," means eat whatever used to be traditionally considered food and avoid industrially processed "foods" that just *resemble* traditional foods. It's hard to put into practice, though, because, as Pollan himself acknowledges, "industrial processes have by now invaded many whole foods too."[10] Can meat from factory-farmed animals that have been fed industrially manipulated diets be considered the same as meat in a traditional sense? Is today's wild-caught fish the same as traditional wild-caught fish? Just because a chicken is called "free-range," that doesn't guarantee that it's been outside walking around, never mind its having eaten what a traditional chicken eats. You can't even assume, as it were, that a carrot is always the same as a traditional carrot. What if it's been sprayed with a modern chemical? And just because it's USDA organic, that doesn't necessarily mean that it's exactly the same as a traditional carrot either—what if it was grown on one of those intensive industrial-organic farms?[11] There are exceptions and loopholes in USDA organic regulations that allow for plenty of nontraditional growing practices.

Actually, unless you grow all your own ingredients, trying to "eat food" while living in the United States seems likely to aggravate, not combat, this nation's problem with orthorexia—the "unhealthy obsession with healthy eating"—that Pollan cites.[12] In order to avoid modern industrial foodstuffs that resemble traditional foods, you might find yourself obsessing constantly—like I do—about the invisible contamination or processing of foods which, at first glance, look perfectly traditional. You might find yourself trying to keep up religiously with all the changing rules and regulations about labeling, the exceptions and the loopholes regarding agricultural practices, and the less widely publicized information about things like genetically modified seed supplies. Even if you *do* grow your own food, you might find yourself eventually worrying about what could be in the cow manure or compost you're fertilizing with.

"Mostly plants" seems like a pretty good principle, especially the emphasis on leaves. Still, many of the plants people consume today are refined grains (white rice, white wheat flour, etc.) whereas nonindustrialized traditional diets after the Paleolithic Era rely more heavily on whole grains. Maybe this is the point: a diet rich in white wheat flour or white rice is good on the "mostly plants" side but bad on the "eat food" side?

"Have a glass of wine with dinner."[13] Maybe. But isn't most of the wine available to Americans *industrial*—from the pesticides and synthetic fertilizers used for the grapes to the addition of things like citric acid, which, as Pollan himself might like to point out, could be made from industrially raised, and possibly genetically modified, corn?

"Eat more like the French, or the Italians, or the Japanese, or the Indians, or the Greeks."[14] Okay, but which French? Which Greeks? Last time I checked, many French, Italians, and Greeks have been eating their own versions of the Western industrialized diet. As someone familiar with the Greek case, I don't know of many reliable sources that Americans can consult for knowing what "Greeks eat." Anyway, the point isn't to eat like contemporary Greeks but the way Greeks, especially Cretans, used to eat—the ones who'd first been discovered to be unusually healthy in mid-twentieth-century studies. But *which* of those Cretans? Having looked at some studies, I'm not sure I can tell which Cretans were the remarkably healthy ones. For instance, seafood is mentioned a lot, but does this mean that traditional Cretan mountain-dwellers who consumed more meat and whole-milk dairy (much more?) by comparison were not also very healthy?

Also, thinking more carefully about *how* traditional Cretans ate—following the fasting rules of the Orthodox Church, eating on a schedule punctuated by daytime siestas, getting lots of physical activity outdoors throughout the year—not to mention much of *what* they ate—including lots of foraged greens most people here don't have access to, homemade nonindustrial wines, foraged snails, wild game, freshly caught fish from less-polluted waters, etc.—convinces me that most people in the United States *can't* much eat like traditional Cretans ate—unless, of course, we ignore the Cretans' actual diet and focus only on a subset of the nutrient and nutrient-combinations that can be readily replicated in the United States—a move that would go against the whole spirit of Pollan's counter-nutrient-centered approach.

Pollan's second rule of thumb, "[Eat] [n]ot too much," is problematic. It's consistent with his emphasis throughout the book on being overweight or obese as an illness in itself. Of all the cause-and-effect relationships between diet and health, this seems to be his favorite. But is it true?

After questioning my own aversion to gaining weight, I decided I ought to look more carefully into the issue of fat. I knew, after all, that in the contemporary United States and other modern societies, many of us are conditioned to dislike fat human bodies—a prejudice about appearance.

I was also convinced that ever since *eating* fat (as opposed to eating protein, say) became associated with bad health, dislike for fat human bodies has been reinforced, to say the least. I figured it probably works the other way around, too: Already biased against fat human bodies, people are increasingly predisposed to believe that eating fat is unhealthy. One version of "fat is bad" reinforces the other.

I suspected that historical and cultural factors encourage many Americans to associate fat human bodies with shameful self-indulgence and a lack of appropriate self-restraint, as evidence of the moral shortcomings or inferior character of the people who inhabit fat bodies, further reinforcing the dislike and disgust. Not that I thought the size of one's body is entirely beyond a person's control, that it's determined wholly by one's genetics, those aspects of one's environment that are beyond one's immediate control, or some combination thereof. I just thought that many Americans tend to ignore the possible role of genetic or environmental conditioning in making a body fat. Many Americans also seem to ignore the possibility that what some people view as an indulgence others might interpret as living the good life.

As I read about eating disorders, I also came to believe that many Americans fail to pick up on the possible connection between the psychological drive for self-*control*—such as control over one's appetite and weight—and problems like anorexia nervosa and bulimia, and how this relationship might further complicate the association of morality with bodily self-restraint and self-imposed eating asceticism.

I reasoned that maybe what's wrong with getting fat is that recent developments in food economies have made some eaters gain weight despite their reasonably good, sometimes downright heroic, efforts to remain thin, and in spite of the fact that they probably would not have gained that extra weight in the first place if they weren't being so cleverly manipulated by these newfangled food economies. I realized, of course, that humans' food economies have always been changing and that many of the intended and unintended effects of such change—sometimes including mass hunger and starvation—have always been beyond the control of most of the individual eaters who lived in those economies. But my sense was that there's something about the contemporary food economy—where ingredients and substances can be produced and manipulated in extremely complex ways through the application of modern research science and engineering, where people's food preferences can be manipulated in subtle and complex ways (through empirical testing, through understanding human genetic predispositions regarding various nutrients, etc.), and where information about foods is disseminated and regulated in complicated ways (through advertising, through various government bodies, through nongovernmental agencies)—which has the potential to persuade all but the luckiest or most vigilant consumers (who depend on advanced degrees and plenty of time and reliable informational resources in order to decipher critically what goes into all these foods and their potential risks) to eat in ways that cause unwanted weight gain.

Even so, I knew this doesn't mean there's anything wrong with getting fat per se. It just means that sometimes getting fat could be the result of *other* things that are wrong—including the everyday modern eater's relative lack of ability to control the healthfulness of his or her diet while living in a toxic world, combined with the illusion that he or she actually *has* such control.

The only plausible sensible reason I could find for remaining averse to being fat is that it's simply bad for personal health and, by extension, for public health—and thus for taxpayers.

I wondered if the empirical research agreed.

So I purchased several provocative minority-view books on the subject to see what they had to say.

University of Colorado law professor Paul Campos reviews the scientific literature on weight and health and concludes that, "the health risks associated with higher-than-average weight have been greatly exaggerated, while all sorts of related but far graver risks have been ignored. In particular, [. . .] poverty, poor nutrition, and a culture that makes it easy for Americans to be sedentary are impor- tant public health issues in America today. [. . .] [T]here is very little evidence that attempts to achieve weight loss will improve the health of most people who undertake them, and a great deal of evidence that such attempts do more harm than good."[15] (Barry Glassner's *The Gospel of Food* describes attempts to get a Harvard professor of nutri- tion to provide counterarguments to Campos's position.[16])

University of Chicago political science professor J. Eric Oliver argues that "While Americans do face many health challenges, few of these arise from our increasing weight. Our growing weight is merely a symptom of some fundamental changes in our diet and exercise patterns that may (or may not) affect our health. There is, however, very little evidence that obesity itself is a primary *cause* of our health woes."[17] He goes on to write that "While heart disease, cancer, stroke, asthma, and diabetes are undoubtedly serious and costly health concerns, there is no convincing evidence that such ailments arise from our growing weight."[18]

As Campos and Oliver reassess the broader body of scientific evidence in terms of the implications of weight, they both conclude that focusing on weight and obesity per se does more harm than good: "Whether it is from a failed diet, a botched gastric-bypass surgery, complications from an eating disorder, or heart damage from diet drugs, every year thousands of Americans are literally dying to be thin."[19] "There is no good evidence that significant long- term weight loss is beneficial to health, and a great deal of evidence that short-term weight loss followed by weight gain (the pattern followed by almost all dieters) is medically harmful."[20]

I developed some hypotheses—well, more like suspicions that I was in no position test—of my own: Maybe when certain people in a modern industrialized nation are getting fat it *is* a sign that they're living unhealthy lifestyles in unhealthy environments, predisposing them for chronic illnesses like heart disease and diabetes. But it may not be the *weight* that's causing these diseases, but rather the unhealthy lifestyles and environments. So it might be that living a (generally unhealthy) modern industrial lifestyle on fewer calories (so as to avoid getting fat) *is* healthier than getting fat while living a modern industrial lifestyle. In other words, if you are living on too much white bread and white rice, factory-farmed chicken, artificial sweeteners, highly processed snack foods, and all manner of unpronounceable food additives then—yes—maybe you'd better not eat "too much." Though, if you do happen to get fat, you'd still better think twice about trying to lose weight, because the evidence suggests that in most cases, you won't be able to keep it off, thereby increasing your risk for chronic illnesses *and* other new dieting-related problems. The question of trying to lose weight isn't, after all, the same as trying never to gain it the first time.

But what if you are *not* eating a modern industrial diet? Where are the studies of people eating nonmodern Western diets that show how, all other things being equal, it's primarily the overweight and obese ones who end up with chronic diseases, whether weight is a cause or just a symptom? Maybe I just didn't know where to look for them.

I wondered if maybe instead of an obesity epidemic we should be talking about a modern or industrial food epidemic as contributing to the slew of chronic modern Western diseases, and which also just "happens" to make many of its adherents fat, which in itself wouldn't be a big deal except that the glorification of thinness (maybe also a matter of modernization?) drives many people who happen to be fat—whether or not they're consuming the dangerous modern Western diet—to try losing weight instead of addressing real causes (overall diet quality and lifestyle, increasingly toxic environments), all with a stamp of approval from their doctor and nutritionist . . . and even if they do lose weight, they'll most likely gain it back (leading to more anxiety; oh God!—*another* risk factor?) and either way place themselves at higher risk for chronic diseases or a shorter life expectancy, since risk apparently only decreases, except in the most extreme cases, for those who never gained too much weight in the first place, not for those who lose it.

The practical upshot of all this for me was that I decided that if I wasn't a couch potato, if I was "eating food," and if this food was "mostly plants"—with lots of leafy greens from a wide range of botanical families, fruits, and more whole grains than refined grains—I wasn't going to worry about eating "too much."

※   ※   ※

I've got no qualms about trying out the canned fishes before eating dinner tonight. If it's indeed true that the canned fish was wild caught and is only minimally contaminated by environmental pollutants, it mostly qualifies as food. Our dinner later will include, among other things, a lettuce salad and boiled chicory in olive oil and lemon. (I don't know anything about how these plants were grown, though.) And lately I've been getting plenty of physical activity with all the garden chores. I've been sweating my ass off, actually. So if anything, I should just be worried about how I'm going to persuade myself to keep up the exercise once the weather turns cold.

☀ 22 ☀

Thanks, but No Thanks

It's the Tuesday before Thanksgiving. Sofia and I are driving to a nearby farm to pick up our Thanksgiving turkey and some chickens, ducks, and rabbits to put into the chest freezer for winter.

The bridge over the Hudson that I usually take is temporarily closed so I'm taking a detour. I'm squeezing my brain as hard as I can in order to remember how this drive looked back when I was in high school and we'd come to visit Grandma Leclaire in the adult home. For some reason I'm having difficulty conjuring up images of the exact route.

In Ohio, Sofia and I were buying most of our meat from the supermarket, and we were never very keen on cooking turkey anyway, not even for Thanksgiving. But the year before we left, we happened upon a flyer for Thanksgiving turkeys from a local farm. We put in an order and showed up to a parking lot near campus where the birds were distributed to customers from the back of a pickup truck.

Once we moved here, and before so many local meats were widely available, we ordered "Amish" or "free-range" turkeys from the butcher shop at the local supermarket. Recalling our local bird in Ohio, Sofia asked around at the farmers' market. She soon learned about Justin's farm and put in an order that summer.

As Thanksgiving approached, Aunt Patsy called me to ask me if I'd seen the article in the paper about our cousin who sells turkeys, chickens, ducks, and rabbits, and how he and his wife were home-schooling their eight (and counting) kids. I hadn't seen the article, but when she mentioned the name of Justin's farm it sounded vaguely familiar. When Sofia and I drove out to pick up our turkey, I tried explaining to Justin how we're related, but it's so complicated that after we went back home I had to look it up again on the family tree Grandma had been working on up until she died.

Arriving at Justin and Lynne's farm for the first time, seeing the various signs painted with quotes from the Bible, and how Lynne was dressed—to my ignorant eyes reminiscent of Mennonites or Amish—I concluded that they must be born-again Christians. What I couldn't know was whether they were trying to coax all the mistaken and misguided people around them to adopt their particular faith, or if they were just enthusiastically trying to share their faith with anyone and everyone else who might need something to believe in. So far, all the evidence I have, which only comes from stopping by on poultry runs, suggests the latter. This pleases me, because just as I've never come up with a good argument for why a person who believes in God shouldn't, neither have I encountered a good reason why a person who believes in God should try persuading someone who doesn't that they should.

Nevertheless, as we're approaching their farm, I'm as anxious as ever, and it's perfectly clear to me why: I associate such outward demonstrations with Christianity at its best and worst. I continue to believe that Justin and Lynne are an example of Christianity at its best—of embracing those who've been rejected by others and "do unto others" and "turn the other cheek" and "let he who is without sin." Maybe it's because I secretly want them to know that I, too, am dismayed by much that gets celebrated in this dollar-driven world; I, too, feel an affinity for something like the born-again experience; I, too, despite my teaching in a public university system, appreciate the efforts of many parents to homeschool their kids in the face of disappointment with the conventional educational system.

Yet, I don't want to let on that no God or Jesus or Bible figure into any of my explanations, beliefs, faith in, or reasons for anything, except maybe insofar as such things are admitted to be synonyms—though no-longer-adequate synonyms—for certain significant ideas, feelings, and experiences. I don't really want them to know this about me, because I fear it could lead them to believe that I'm thinking this way because I've been corrupted by a secular view of the world. I'm certainly not going to lie to them about my beliefs, but I'm not going to volunteer them either. I only know Justin and Lynne superficially, so I can't be confident that they won't pigeonhole me as a heathen, the same way many of the people in my circles would pigeonhole them—in about three seconds flat—as

Bible Thumpers. I'm still guarding against the possibility, however remote, that holier-than-thou-Christianity is somewhere down there at the bottom of a slippery slope where you sometimes least expect it. Overall, I'm frustrated knowing how what likely divides us in one way may be precluding our ever learning much about, or from, each other in other ways—including ideas and feelings that for all intents and purposes we could very well share.

Aw, who am I kidding? Maybe I'm just anxious because I tend to feel extremely guilty whenever I'm around Americans who I suspect could be living a more ethical life than I am, even if it's not necessarily in accord with my own views on ethics but with those I was brought up on and have partially rejected.

Sofia and I turn into the driveway, and I continue fretting about all this. Then it hits me: Why in the world am I thinking about this so much? I'm just one of who-knows-how-many people who buys poultry from them, and they only see me a few times a year, for ten or fifteen minutes each time. So what if we're distantly related? What makes me think they'd ever stop for even a moment to wonder, let alone to care about, what *my* beliefs are? Maybe my anxiety isn't so much about us and them and belief systems but about my avoiding grappling with the fact that I continue feeling anxious in what otherwise appear to be pretty mundane situations.

We park the car. We buy our meat. We barely talk much with Justin and Lynne, because on turkey pick-up day they're busy with lots of customers.

Sofia and I head home with a cooler full of meat, and I know I won't think about any of this again until our next trip there sometime next spring.

Thanksgiving morning. I put the eighteen-pound turkey into a huge oval roasting pan on top of the rack that came with it. I throw a couple sprigs of rosemary and thyme and a few cloves of garlic into the cavity of the bird. I fill the bottom of the pan with about a quarter of an inch of water and put on the cover. (It barely fits.) I put it over two burners on the stove turned to medium, and then I duct-tape a piece of aluminum foil over the steam vent in the cover for a better seal. What a blessing that I've figured out how to steam a turkey, and finish it off in a high oven to crisp the skin. It's essentially the same method I learned for duck from various Chinese websites. And how lucky that we'd bought this huge roasting pan in Ohio, when one of the major department stores was going out of business and they reduced the prices by 75 percent. I don't have to get up that early to cook the turkey. I can be perfectly confident that it's well cooked but not dried out. By the time I move it to the oven, keeping it on the same rack but placed over a baking sheet, I'll have an extremely flavorful broth left over from the steaming and with which I can prepare the gravy.

As if this doesn't make Thanksgiving preparations easy enough already, I'm trying something else this year. When I got up, I started a wood fire in the remnants of the gas grill left behind by the previous owners of the house. I'm putting all our garden vegetables—potatoes, beets, kohlrabi, brussels sprouts, celeriac—with a little oil and salt in separate pieces of aluminum foil so they can slowly roast over the coals until it's time to eat.

The last few years, Sofia and I have been experimenting with nontraditional Thanksgiving dishes with traditional ingredients. Last year we came up with an idea for a light, tricolor salad to counterbalance the other heavy Thanksgiving dishes. The salad was simple: grated raw beet, grated raw turnip, and grated raw carrot served on a plate with or without oil, lemon juice, and a pinch of salt. Of course, with such experimentation come unpredictable responses from my family. Even though I'm pretty sure my mother had only ever eaten cooked supermarket beets before, and I'd made up her salad plate without beets, she audibly declared, "I *hate* beets," when my father tried to get her to try some of his, thinking she might actually like them prepared this way.

This year we're just putting a few small dishes around the table with whey-pickled carrots, beets, and turnips for whoever wants to try. I fermented them for about a month during late summer and they've continued maturing in the refrigerator.

Right on time, my parents and Aunt Patsy arrive.

When Sofia and I moved to here, one of the things we were looking forward to was the opportunity to have relatives over to our house. During our first few years here, Thanksgiving provided an especially good excuse for such get-togethers. Sofia's brother was still in Albany, and there were my parents, Aunt Patsy, my brother, and his wife, and eventually their two kids. I also had several old colleagues and friends living just a few hours away. Nowadays, my brother-in-law is back in Taiwan and most of my friends have moved far away, so these gatherings have dwindled down to my immediate family.

Honestly though? I'm seriously reconsidering this holiday as an appropriate occasion for gathering together with them. I want to get together like this and we don't find many chances to do so, but it's getting to the point where there's nothing I can talk about with them. When my friends or Sofia's brother were still around I could mostly talk with them while my relatives mostly talked with each other. The family could be together and everyone could enjoy the afternoon. But lately, I just can't pretend to be interested in what's being said. I can't go along with my father's sentimentalism. (God, this sounds mean.) I can no longer ignore my mother's sour comments about the food, even though I know that over the years she's endured hours of my critical commentary about industrial foods at her house. I can't think of anything interesting I might say that they'd also find entertaining. I can't pick on Aunt Patsy's absurdity anymore, only meet it with a blank stare, especially since it comes in part from a place of caring. Like, when I called and invited her and she said—as she often does—that she'd come if she felt good enough, but that lately she hasn't been doing good at all, then asked me if she could bring anything. (Of course, I said no, as usual.) Like how she then told me she doesn't even have money to buy Christmas cards this year, and called me back again five minutes later to see if I *really* didn't want her to bring anything. When she was coming in the door today, I heard her telling Sofia that she felt bad about not bringing anything. She already knew that I didn't need her to bring anything, but why in the world would she think that even if I *did* want her to bring something that I'd tell her so after she said she didn't have money even for Christmas cards, didn't feel well, and wasn't even sure she was coming? Can't she just accept that she isn't bringing anything and keep quiet, or, if she really feels that strongly about it, bring some little anything for the mere symbolism of it? Oh yeah, and she called while I was making gravy to ask me where I wanted her to park, since my brother might be coming, too. Seriously? Sofia and I have a large driveway, my parents have an even bigger one next door, and the street is always empty on both sides as far as the eye can see—not to mention that she's been here before during family picnics with ten or fifteen cars parked outside. Couldn't she just park *wherever* and if for some reason there was a problem later on we could just move her car? Why would she call to ask me something so silly at a time when she should know from experience that I'm busy cooking?

(Wow, I'm really getting nasty.)

Then there are all the other little absurd annoyances that shouldn't matter but somehow they do on a day like this. Like, when I'm setting the table and I can't decide what to do about wine-glasses. Okay, I know that Aunt Patsy—being on my father's side of the family—is a teetotaler and I shouldn't put a glass out for her even just as a polite gesture. Except that I never know for sure where she'll feel comfortable sitting. Okay, so we just move some glasses around once we sit down. But then what about my father? He drinks wine now, and normally drinks it with a meal like this, but I'm not sure if he does so in front of Aunt Patsy. And I'm not sure if I should even *imply* that he does by putting out a glass for him. But not putting out the glasses goes against my core being when it comes to being a host. Having grown up in such a strong anti-alcohol family, I know in my gut that these are no small matters. (Jesus, in spite of all my chemistry classes and my love affair with Cretan wine—even just the word *alcohol* has negative connotations for me when I'm typing it!) I'm able to put myself in the shoes of those who equate alcohol with sin and the devil and sort of see how things look from their side, though on our first Thanksgiving here I did manage somehow to persuade myself that it was okay for *me* to drink wine in front of Aunt Patsy without feeling the least bit bad. But I can't bring myself to talk about it explicitly with any of them. I could've called my father up ahead of time to ask him if I should put out a wineglass for him, but the thought of my doing something like this so deeply disturbs my sense of who *I* am—the part of me that, alongside so many Cretans I've known, looks upon wine with reverence, respect, and awe—that I just can't bring myself to do it.

(I feel bad. I probably shouldn't be writing all this.)

We eat. I drink plenty of wine to keep my mood up. Sofia and I finally manage to get up from the table and put the leftover food in the refrigerator.

My brother and his family arrive. Lately I can't get a straight answer out of my brother about whether they're coming or not, at least not until the last minute. He hadn't responded to my invitation until two days ago, saying they'd come. When he asked me about the time I said it didn't really matter to me, but since everyone else had already been asking me I'd told them we'd eat around one. He said they couldn't come at one because the kids would be taking a nap then, so they'd just come whenever they could. I told him that if he'd gotten back to us earlier I'd've been glad to have arranged the time around *their* schedule—since they arrange their schedule around their kids, and the rest of my family wouldn't have cared what time I picked—but I think he thought he was doing us a favor by not having us plan things around them and by just showing up whenever they could. Without demands or expectations, of course, just to be together with family.

But expectations or no expectations, Sofia and I take everything back out of the fridge and set up the table again. My father goes back home to get ketchup for the kids. Sofia catches me in the kitchen and whispers to me, much to my surprise, "I can't believe they only eat here once a year, but they still say that the kids *have* to have ketchup."

When it's time for pie, I notice that my mother brought her own homemade apple pie, even though I always make one or two apple pies—knowing that my mother dislikes the berry pies and pumpkin pie that the rest of us love. She doesn't say anything but I know based on previous years' comments that she brought it because there's something about my apple pie that isn't quite to her liking, even though I essentially follow the longtime family recipe for it, except that I use olive oil instead of shortening in the crust and instead of butter in the crumb topping—a substitution she supposedly likes, so go figure. She takes one bite of her own pie and immediately declares to my father that it isn't good. It wasn't cooked long enough. The apples are cut the wrong size. (Things he was responsible for?) She eats it, though, and doesn't try mine. At some point I notice her glancing over at Aunt Patsy's plate to see what pie she's eating. When she sees it's blueberry she turns away. Hey, at least she doesn't say anything out loud. And the verbal complaints about the apple pie this year are about the pie *they* brought.

(I'm feeling *really* bad now, but—what can I say?—Thanksgiving is some kind of, like—what would Woody Allen say?—a *neurotic's jackpot*. I mean, I could *totally* crash my word processor just trying to analyze whether it's really them or just me.)

Thanksgiving evening. Everyone's gone back home. Ben and Catherine, who are staying with us for the long weekend but who went to Ben's parents' for the Thanksgiving meal, come back. I tell them about the things that have been annoying me about our Thanksgivings and that I'm wondering if maybe Thanksgiving isn't the best day of the year to invite my family over for a meal.

The holiday's primary meaning to Sofia and me seems to have evolved into something like an opportunity to give our proverbial thanks for all the good food we have in spite of the industrialized food culture we live in. And, it's a good chance to celebrate—with a once-a-year, over-the-top meal—the end of the growing season and the start of a life mostly indoors until the following spring. Even though for years I didn't celebrate Thanksgiving at all, and when I did I rarely cooked traditional American foods, I've been back into the swing of the once-a-year turkey for a while now. Since this is the time of year a good turkey is readily available, why not? I'm using the typical Thanksgiving ingredients, though I still opt not to prepare the traditional table I grew up with. I make turkey sandwiches, but use olive oil and garlic instead of mayonnaise, arugula, capers, and goat cheese instead of lettuce, and toasted homemade bread instead of supermarket sandwich bread.

Sure, I'd prefer to enjoy this celebration with loved ones, but if people in my family aren't into the same kind of celebration that we are, why not just leave them to their own celebrations and us to ours? Why shouldn't Sofia and I just invite people (like Ben and Catherine) who are more likely to revel in the ingredients and flavors that we work so hard and enthusiastically to obtain and prepare? Do I really believe that Thanksgiving is ultimately about being together with family just for the sake of being together with family? We all live near each other now and can get together for a family meal many other days of the year if we really want to, and it would be that much easier to make accommodations to everyone's tastes and preferences on the other 364 days of the year that we're not cooking a turkey and other Thanksgiving-related ingredients.

The idea of not inviting my immediate family makes me feel bad. I always loved Thanksgiving growing up, and for so many years we were apart. But I also wonder: Maybe the nuclear family isn't what it used to be? Maybe as patterns of social relationships in and out of family contexts evolve during the times we're living in, so should our assumptions about who should get together for a holiday like Thanksgiving. Have I been too eager to treat the association of Thanksgiving with family as a natural law instead of as an evolving social phenomenon?

I really want to propose the idea to Ben and Catherine of our having Thanksgiving together the following year. But I hesitate because I figure while they'll probably like the idea from the point of view of the food, it'll be too awkward for them to drive all the way up here and then not get together with Ben's immediate family on such an important holiday.

I finally throw out the idea. It sounds like they'll seriously consider it.

Saturday morning. I thought Ben and Catherine would enjoy meeting Andy and Dafne, seeing their farm, seeing the sheep, seeing the cheeses ripening in the cheese house, and seeing the cheese-making facilities. Plus, Ben and Catherine could buy cheese to take back home if they wanted. But late last night before we went to bed I checked my e-mail and found a message from Dafne saying there was a last-minute change in plans and that Andy would be joining her at the Saturday farmers' market and wouldn't be able to meet us at the farm after all.

I remember another cheese farm Sofia and I have visited in Vermont, and I look it up on the Internet. It says they're open Saturdays at noon so we decide to go. I know that Ben and Catherine will like at least two or three of their cheeses, and maybe they'll get to see some goats. We call to confirm that the farm will be open to the public but we get an answering machine. Ben leaves a message using his cell phone and we think maybe they'll call us while we're in the car driving there.

We arrive and they aren't open. We luck out, though, because they made an appointment during a short window of time between two different farmers' markets to sell some animals to someone, and we happen to catch them while they're there. They let us sample a wide range of cheeses and check out their aging rooms. We all buy a few chunks of cheese and declare our trip a success.

As we're driving back, Catherine wonders if the tasting room is open at the self-pick farm where Sofia and I pick many of our summer fruits. Why not drive over and see? Sure enough, it's open. We taste four ciders—including a sparkling cider and two "ice wine" ciders. We buy a few bottles as well as some cider donuts for the road. Then we head to Hudson Falls for hot dogs.

Ben and Catherine know Glens Falls's famous hot dog joint, but they aren't familiar with the also locally renowned Dog Shack in Hudson Falls. I ironically declare that it's unacceptable for someone who grew up around here not to know both establishments. It seems that Catherine, as a curious downstater, is also game for chomping down a few hot dogs in the car on this unseasonably cold afternoon. So we go.

After the hot dogs, we head down the road to Fort Edward because it also turns out that Ben and Catherine only know finger rolls from Mandy's, and not the ones from the bakery on Broadway. Unfortunately the bakery is closed. We turn around and head back toward Glens Falls, because I'm pretty sure I'd seen those finger rolls for sale a few days earlier at the place where we buy our milk.

Alas, they're sold out.

As we get closer to Glens Falls we're craving more hot dogs and head over to New Way Lunch—taking as our excuse that we couldn't possibly make objective comparisons of the two establishments if we didn't eat their hot dogs close together. By the time we finish, we've eaten four or five hot dogs apiece.

We go back home.

Ben and Catherine leave to visit Ben's sister's family for a few hours. I take a quick nap and then hop on the treadmill for a little while to get my blood moving again. I wonder about dinner. I know that after all the hot dogs (and the donuts, and the cheese, and break-fast) no one is likely to be hungry for a big meal, and I figure Ben and Catherine might eat something at his sister's. I get the idea of making a version of Grandpa Leclaire's soup using some of the huge pot of broth that Sofia spent a lot of time making yesterday from the leftover turkey bones. Apart from being a light dinner, it's the soup that Ben, Catherine, Sofia, and I have discussed many times, and which I have a hunch Ben might especially enjoy as symbolically fitting for this family holiday.

Ben calls Grandpa's soup "pepper soup." Grandpa Leclaire was notorious for his liberal use of black pepper, but since I've always loved lots of black pepper in my food I never noticed anything remarkable about how much he used. I always knew that there was a "spice"—actually an herb, but in our house we called all herbs and spices *spices*—that I really loved that gave the soup its extra special flavor. I eventually found out that it was savory, one of the herbs my mother didn't have at our house. If anything, I associated Grandpa's soup with savory, not pepper. I associated *Grandpa* with savory just like everyone else associated him with his meat pie, both things—the savory and the tourtière—that I now know are pretty much typical or stereotypical among French Canadians in general.

I decide to make Grandpa Leclaire's soup but with the turkey broth instead of chicken broth. And what a broth it is! Sofia trimmed off most of the remaining meat (for sandwiches) and then made a huge pot of broth with the bones. We recently collected, cleaned, and refrigerated a bunch of wild carrots from the backyard that she threw into the broth, too. Actually, it was Sofia who collected them this time because I remember helping her double check them one by one for the scent of the root and for the little hairs on the green tops, lest we end up with one of the carrot family's many poisonous—sometimes deadly poisonous—look-alike species. Not that we had much doubt. There aren't any other wild plants from the carrot family growing anywhere in or near our yard. Still, we weren't about to take any chances. Sofia also included the fresh celery that, just before the first hard frost, I'd transplanted from the garden to some pots that we've been keeping in the kitchen by the sliding glass doors. The onions were from the farmers' market, as was the single habanero pepper that she decided to throw in on a whim. She let the broth simmer slowly all evening and the result was outstanding.

The thing about Grandpa Leclaire's soup, at least the way Grandma taught me how to make it, is that it's made from a large can of chicken broth, another can's worth of water (or is it two?), a can of whole tomatoes run through the blender, and the kind of rice that has been precooked and only needs a minute or two to reconstitute. Using any of these ingredients would now go against my principles. Last year, after I dried Sofia's first-ever harvest of savory from our garden—perennial winter savory, the "wrong" kind of savory; the next year she added annual summer savory, which is the "right" kind of savory—I decided to make Grandpa's soup for the first time in many years. The problem was that we didn't have any broth, and when I checked the local grocery store I couldn't find a single brand—not even in the "natural food" section—that didn't contain ingredients we'd never put in homemade broth, though in some cases this was almost disguised by the FDA-approved language. So I boiled a chicken and used that. As I neglected to add any vegetables or herbs, it wasn't as flavorful as it should've been. So, a few months later, when Grandma Leclaire passed away, I boiled a chicken together with some carrot, celery, and onion, and made Grandpa's soup to bring to the postfuneral gathering at Ben's mother and father's house. That batch didn't come out half bad, even though I used canned tomatoes—after checking the ingredients on the label for the one that just said "tomatoes"—because that was the year I neglected to buy inexpensive seconds from the farmers' market to freeze for winter.

Now I've got this terrific turkey broth that Sofia made, a freezer shelf full of bags of frozen tomato, and—it goes without saying— noninstant rice. I fill a three-quart saucepan just over two-thirds of the way with the broth, figuring that at most each of us would want a smallish bowl or two. I plop in a frozen cube of the already-cooked-down-and-puréed farmers' market tomato, turn the heat to high, and add some salt. Then I grind in a lot of black pepper, even though Grandpa used pepper that was already ground. I add some of our dried winter savory, dried summer savory, and even a little of our dried thyme. This is because we didn't grow enough summer savory and I have to stretch it to make it last for a few more winter dishes. Once the tomato cube melts, I turn down the heat so the soup just simmers, and toss in a couple of handfuls of medium-grain rice. Luckily I've made soups like this enough times that my intuition about how much rice to add is pretty good. Too much rice and you end up with a juicy pilaf; not enough and, well, it's not enough, though I suppose you can always add some more and wait a little longer. The thing about the rice is that it never seems to puff up and become the way I like it in soups until after you turn the heat off and let it sit for a while. I don't know if this has to do with the temperature, the time, or both. Anyway, it's good to let the soup cool for a little while because then it's easier to taste it in order to adjust the salt and pepper.

The soup is ready. Ben and Catherine return. Sure enough, they've already eaten dinner at Ben's sister's. Everyone except Ben tries some soup. It hits the spot. The spiciness of the habanero pepper in the broth strikes me as more noticeable than the use of turkey instead of chicken, soothing on a cold November night, and warming us up for the cheese and cider and DVD of *Big Night* that are to follow.

☀ *23* ☀

Personal, Political, Environmental

It's moments like these when I think about Manolis the most—when I'm alone out back but I feel his presence so strongly that it's almost like he's somehow here watching over me. It's moments like these when I imagine how much I've become like him as I'm pruning vines, harvesting oregano, or—on a day like today—shoveling compost and sheep manure onto garden rows.

Sofia and I were overjoyed when, owning our own house, we could stop throwing out much of our trash. For the first month we lived here, I'd take our collected kitchen scraps, dig a little hole out back, and bury them. Then I spent an afternoon reading online about making compost. I learned some of the basic principles—"greens" and "browns" and moisture—and various techniques people use. My priority was to do something easy, nothing high maintenance. So for about two years we'd just throw everything onto a big pile located off our back deck. In addition to kitchen scraps, I'd add fallen leaves, miscellaneous plant trimmings, and sod I'd dug up from the yard when making new garden beds. At the end of winter, I started a new pile and turned over the old one—meaning that I shoveled it from where it was into a new pile immediately adjacent—and covered it with an old tarp that the previous owners had left behind.

The following spring, when I went to turn over the new pile and I discovered what I think were voles that had taken up residence there, I considered trying something different.

Eventually I settled on a slow method of composting with earthworms added for some extra oomph. (I don't know why I didn't think of the worms earlier, considering that I'd read about composting with worms back when Sofia and I lived in an apartment.) I took a plastic garbage barrel we'd gotten for free with a hardware-store coupon that came in the mail, cut out the bottom, punched some air-holes in the sides, dug a hole, and buried it up to the lid. I found six or seven worms in our old compost pile and tossed them in. As I'd hoped, once I'd added food scraps, the worms multiplied like crazy. I added a second barrel the following autumn. I can pop off the lid and toss in kitchen scraps or the occasional batch of paper or cardboard. The lid keeps large critters out and unpleasant odors in, and it provides me with easy access during the winter, provided I keep the snow brushed off. Since it's outdoors and I'm not in a hurry for the compost, I don't worry much about the green-to-brown ratio or the population of worms, so it's essentially maintenance free.

The barrels fill up more quickly during winter, presumably because decomposition slows down when it's cold. That's why I'm emptying them today, before the weather turns too cold. I use a pitchfork to scoop out everything into a wheelbarrow, dump it into a trench I've raked into a garden row, and rake the trenched-out soil back over it.

We can't make nearly enough compost for our whole garden, so we do other things to fertilize as well. We leave about a third of the garden fallow every year. I plant annual winter rye (a grass) whenever the food plants have finished for the summer in an area that we'll leave fallow the following season. In the spring, once the danger of frost has passed, I mow down the rye with a battery-operated weed whacker, till it in with an electric garden tiller, and follow it with two plantings of buckwheat (mowed and tilled in the same way) and a planting of oats (another grass), that gets killed off by the extreme cold of the following winter. I also use oats as a cover crop on any garden rows that finish early in the season but won't be fallow the following year. Sofia and I rake leaves in the fall that we can incorporate into the soil or use as mulch. Sometimes I cover the ground with broken down cardboard boxes, then cover the cardboard with grass clippings from my father's lawn mower.

This year I'm also trying sheep manure. Andy and Dafne have a small mountain of it behind the barn. Sometimes when Sofia and I visit them, Andy and I shovel some of the aged manure into bags that Sofia and I take home in our trunk. Today I'm adding some of it to an especially infertile row out front.

I'm reminded of the pile of sheep manure for fertilizing the vegetable garden that Manolis kept behind . . .

Crap! I wasn't going to say anything, but it's been driving me nuts: I hate writing *Manolis* and *Eirini* over and over like this.

I *never* talked about them in the third person using their proper names, except for maybe the first year or two when we met—I can't remember. On the *rare* occasion that I needed to refer to them while talking with someone who didn't really know them, I'd say "my father-in-law" or "my mother-in-law," and if I was talking to someone like my mother on the phone, I'd say, "Penny's father" or "Penny's mother," but 99 percent of the time I'd refer to them—just as Penny did—as "*o babas*" and "*i mama.*" The problem is English, because in English the definite article is awkward—you can't say, "The pile of sheep manure that *the dad* kept"—just like in English you can't say "the Leonidas" or "the Sofia," the way we do in Greek.

So, putting aside for a moment the issue of ambiguity, and the fact that there's no good way to work in an "ex-" prefix, why don't I just follow the usual method of translating Greek to English—"The pile of sheep manure that *Dad* kept . . ."? Easy: Because I *never* addressed them as "Mom" (*mama*) and "Dad" (*baba*), using the vocative case, which is *not* preceded by a definite article, because it would've felt yucky and unnatural; it's not like they were *literally* my parents. Thus, by extension, it would be totally awkward and misleading to refer to them with the normal English translation of "Mom" and "Dad," which leaves out the definite article.

I *know* it sounds like I'm contradicting myself, since it feels perfectly natural to me to say "the Sofia" in Greek and just as natural to say plain old "Sofia" in English. But here's the thing: We *do* say things like "the doctor" and "the teacher" and "the boss" in both English *and* Greek. So referring to Eirini and Manolis as "the mom" and "the dad" in the third person felt somehow like referring to them by the *titles* of their roles in our (Penny's and my) lives—close, personal, familial titles. "The dad" struck me as a more intimate and appropriate title than "the father-in-law" or "my father-in-law" (literally, in Greek, "the father-in-law my"), but *not* the same thing as just plain "dad." It also struck me, given their roles in my life, as more appropriate than referring to them in the third person—or the second person, for that matter—as "Manolis" and "Eirini." Luckily I was usually able to avoid calling them *anything* when I spoke to them, since neither "Dad/Mom" nor "Manolis/Eirini" felt quite right.

There, I said it.

I just thought I should put it out there.

Now, where was I . . . ?

I'm reminded of the pile of sheep manure for fertilizing the vegetable garden that Manolis kept behind the house in the village. It gets me thinking again about how my admiration for Manolis's efforts have inspired so much about how I'm living today. When we met, Manolis and I were already somewhat likeminded about the environment. Though neither of us was particularly prone to taking every pronouncement by a supposed expert at face value, we both took seriously the reported claims of scientists that humans are increasingly being put at risk by the unintended ecological consequences of so many of the achievements of modern progress. If Manolis's firsthand experience with agriculture and fishing sensitized him to such claims, my formal education and other miscellaneous experiences thus sensitized me.

As early as in elementary school, some of my teachers were directing my attention to environmental issues. In Junior High, I especially enjoyed earth science class. Instead of in parks or on playgrounds, my brother and I grew up playing in the woods behind our house, which also attuned me to many of nature's rhythms and flows, and my own relative inability to control them, try as I might. (Remember those ferns I kept cutting down when I was a kid?) By the time I was in college, surrounded by scientists and engineers, I was noticing how many of my colleagues and I conveniently left off our radar screens the possibility of our work having hazardous environmental consequences. And, when I considered our myriad short-term interests, and those of the organizations for which we typically labored, I realized that too frequently there were few immediate incentives to do otherwise.

I therefore came to understand that in the activities that many of us engage in, there's an unstated and therefore unexamined and unsupported implicit claim—namely that, on the whole, the predicted and unpredicted environmental consequences of whatever we're doing on this planet will be absorbed by the earth and incorporated into its ecosystems without having ill effects on ourselves or other people, present or future—at least not ill enough to outweigh the risks of *not* doing such things.

It's this unsubstantiated claim that the empirical research of so many scientists who study the earth's ecology or human health ends up calling into question. There's mounting evidence that continuing to live and act as though this claim were true is having significant ill effects on the health and well-being of many people, possibly to our species as a whole. And, while such research offers no *guarantees* that doing things one way or another will be safer, its findings, though provisional, put us in a position where we can think them through, discuss, and argue about them, instead of just flipping a coin, going with the flow, or blindly trusting that we'll always find ways to solve all the new problems we create.

My reading in recent years has given me more reasons than ever to fret about the erosion of topsoil, the effects of certain industrial pesticides on human health (including indirectly through effects on other species), the loss of edible biodiversity, and the unintended consequences of genetically modified organisms in the food supply, the seed supply, and the environment in general. It's bad enough that while for the first time in history we're producing enough food to feed the entire human population, more than 10 or 15 percent of the human population isn't getting enough food; that even if we continue producing enough food, many people in the future are still not likely to get enough to eat; that many of us who *are* getting enough food are also unwillingly, and often unwittingly, getting foods, ingredients, additives, and pesticide residues that may be damaging our health and well-being.

But on top of all this, environmental degradation through our current food practices is happening with little regard for how it's likely to affect the next generation, and other generations to follow. The most widespread practices of food production, while frequently lucrative for those who profit from them the most in the short term, also increasingly risk the destruction of the very preconditions— sufficient topsoil, sufficient clean water, sufficient biodiversity, and so forth—that are likely necessary for future production of enough relatively safe food for the people of tomorrow. Not only have we been unable to solve many of the social injustices regarding food for the people of our own generations, we also seem to be in the process of making it difficult if not impossible for future generations to feed themselves, even if they could otherwise manage to address adequately the social, political, and economic injustices that we haven't.

This makes it difficult for me to stand idly by waiting for things to get better. But trying to figure out how one might best help bring about significant improvements can also be incredibly unnerving. Especially when you believe that neither state capitalist market forces nor national and international food policies are sufficient to the task, except if it turns out that they wind up playing out—and petering out—in such a way that they help usher in a different kind of more truly free market society, one with an invisible hand that *can* ensure human well-being.[1] Especially when you believe that the social, economic, political, and legal systems in place today—however good they might be compared to other systems in the past or in certain other places in the present—remain predicated on a system of defining property that ensures that the few will constantly boss around and control the many, even in otherwise democratic nations.

Wendell Berry, in his essay "The Pleasures of Eating," suggests that a responsible eater in the modern world doesn't take it for granted that market forces or governmental regulations ensure that his or her available food options are fair and just when it comes to how they might affect others. He argues explicitly that a responsible eater actively seeks to understand the potential effects of his or her decisions about what to eat on agriculture, and therefore, ultimately, on "how the world is used."[2]

What is interesting about Berry's argument is that he connects this conviction not so much to moral imperatives but to a discussion of pleasure. He maintains that as long as I remain ignorant of how my eating habits affect the world at large (which, among other things, means I remain ignorant of the connections between my own eating and how agriculture works), I endure *displeasure*—namely, the experience of "exile from biological reality," "[estrangement] from the lives of domestic plants and animals (except for flowers and dogs and cats) [and] wild ones," and "a kind of solitude, unprecedented in human experience."[3] Exile. Estrangement. Solitude. Even worse, even if I overcome this ignorance, chances are I'll experience "great *dis*pleasure in knowing about a food economy that degrades and abuses those arts and those plants and animals and the soil from which they come."[4] In Berry's view, in order for me to truly experience pleasure when I eat, first, there needs to be a food economy that is well, and, second, I need to be aware of the connections between that food economy and what I'm eating.

Like Berry, I happen to take much pleasure in exactly these kinds of connections. Ever since I've experienced this pleasure in so many ways, I've sensed that to become disconnected now would indeed feel like exile, estrangement, and unhappy solitude. But I hesitate to claim that this is the *normal* experience of all human beings. Even if I were to grant, for instance, that evolution may have somehow conditioned *Homo sapiens* to experience these connections as pleasurable, it isn't clear to me that *not* experiencing them entails displeasure for everyone everywhere at any time in history. Is the *need* for this particular kind of pleasure really so universal?

I also wonder: What if someday there's a postcapitalist free market with democratic governance (among the worker-owners of each business) or some other as yet unimagined way of organizing food systems such that individual consumers could reasonably assume that available food choices are, on the whole and to the best of humans' collective ability, fair and just in their effects on others? Berry seems to be suggesting that even *then* we'd still experience the displeasure of exile, estrangement, and solitude, since "[a] significant part of the pleasure of eating is in one's accurate consciousness of the lives and the world from which food comes."[5] This strikes me as extreme.

Or, is his point that if each of us as individuals doesn't have this accurate consciousness, we simply *can't* be in a position to know that the food system is fair and just in the first place, regardless of the form of social and economic organization? Is he saying that a necessary condition for ensuring that any given food economy is reasonably safe and fair is that the individual eaters who are part of that economy possess this accurate consciousness? That absent such firsthand knowledge, our trust in (capitalist or noncapitalist) market forces, elected officials, or appointed regulators will inevitably lead to these mechanisms' failure, and then to a loss in our grounds for trusting them? That our firsthand knowledge as individual eaters is necessary (and pleasurable!) insurance against the likely shortcomings of *every* collective strategy we humans might develop to protect ourselves and each other as we go about feeding? Maybe he's right. But I guess because I've experienced so many of the positive consequences of even state capitalist markets, I'm holding out hope that if we're someday lucky enough to find ourselves living in a better world, such firsthand knowledge will be available to all who seek it, but not something that most everyone *has* to know in order to keep things from falling apart again.

Many writers have written in the wake of Berry's essay trying to persuade readers how to prioritize food choices in terms of sensitivity to others who we feel deserve our loyalty—from the global south and the urban poor to future generations and other animal species. (Peter Singer and Jim Mason's *The Way We Eat* comes to mind.[6]) It all gets really complicated, especially the more you dig into the arguments with a critical eye. I welcome all the information I can get from reliable sources but so far I find myself quibbling with certain assumptions of every writer who's tried to offer a set of rules for eating sensitively to others. So when it comes to thinking about what I myself count as sensitive eating, instead of getting mired in an impossibly difficult calculus—as much as I'd love to have access to the conclusions reached by such a calculus provided it started from assumptions I could share—I mostly just try to withhold as much immediate and direct support for the grossest concentrations of state capitalist power in the food world as I can, and to provide direct and immediate support to various alternative experiments as they arise, just in case keeping such alternatives going helps foster more extensive and systemic changes further down the road.

I'm not even sure I know quite what I mean by saying grossest concentrations of power. I guess it has something to do with the *amount* of power but also the *use* of such power for what I consider some of the highest-risk food-related activities, based on whatever I've read over the years.

Though it's difficult for me to envision how it would work, I remain open to the possibility that future generations could discover environmentally sustainable and socially just ways to produce and distribute lots of food nonlocally and on a large scale, especially if less polluting, more renewable forms of energy can be devised and operationalized, and if it can all be institutionalized in a fair and just way—possibly through large-scale worker-owned co-ops. Meanwhile, I recognize that the carbon footprint of small-scale local food production and distribution in the current configuration of things may be worse than that of large-scale agribusiness, so that it's not even reasonable to "feel good" about polluting less *today* when we buy local. I also worry about making a fetish out of local foods, which can run the risk of contributing to the commoditization of particular locales at the expense of the people who live there; of nostalgically associating food production with traditional patriarchal family farms; of making locale-specific foods and drinks (think: famous French appellation wines) affordable only to the very classes of people who support and benefit most from industrial agribusiness; of supporting oppressive institutionalized efforts to protect the individuality of a place's food products, in the face of industrial corporate food interests to be sure, but also at the expense of unjustly compromising the freedom of people living there to grow, distribute, and consume the kinds of foods they may have good reason to value; of reinforcing the myth that just because "the personal is political," the only viable political options left for most of us are local and personal, thereby taking away potential energy and support from other potentially valuable larger-than-local efforts and struggles to transform unjust and unsustainable food systems.

Still, I remain convinced that it's important to provide much greater support for small-scale, more sustainable, and—when and where reasonably possible—local ingredients. Not only because it might help serve as a good ally to other ambitious work being done to combat the most egregious aspects of the dominant food system, but also because it could help generate and support varied practical experimentation and other projects on the ground that could gradually help pave the way for lower-risk food systems in the future.

It's impossible to predict with much confidence just how likely it is that these or many other strategies will work. To my mind, there's not a lot of reason for optimism: We have increasing evidence of the complexity and unintended consequences of our interactions with the physical world at the same time that these interactions seem to be operating on a much larger scale than ever before in history—the stakes are much higher. Sure, there's opportunity for high-stakes potential payoffs—of new technologies, say—but also a greater possibility for precipitating great catastrophe, especially when things don't go the ways we intend them to. As if that's not reason enough to become pessimistic about the long-term environmental effects of our current food practices, there's also this: Taking the high-risk approach to interacting with the natural world seems to be overwhelmingly supported by very powerful individuals and groups who can afford to take those risks—and who also have great incentives to take them, given the way regulated and unregulated capitalist markets operate.

And as long as we're living under state capitalism, I don't think the problem with the food system can be more than slightly improved by consumers voting with their dollars or by politicians responding to their voters or by farmers fighting for their rights. It would take unprecedented organized collaboration among so many of us, and I just don't see this happening except maybe once it's already too late. How could the evidence be amassed to convince us that this is what it takes? And even if it could be, how could it reach enough of us? And even if it could reach and persuade us, how could we manage to agree upon a strategy for doing something about it? It just seems highly unlikely to me. Except through totalitarian strategies that, however well intentioned initially, will inevitably cause more harm than good—probably *much* more harm than good. Anyway, it hardly seems worth overinvesting in this idea when there's a chance that the state capitalist system has reached a (temporary, I hope) state such that the very workings of the system ensure that most of the people living in it will remain undesirous of or unwilling to plan moving beyond it in such an organized way. Maybe we just have to wait until an end to this system emerges on its own, maybe mostly unintended, and largely as a consequence of the system's own *systemic* problems and failures. I just hope that in this case we'll be lucky and that arriving at such an end can sidestep the many great social and environmental catastrophes that could accompany it. If there are enough worker-owned cooperative businesses already up and running by then, maybe everyone's most basic needs will be provided for and catastrophe can be avoided. Come to think of it, maybe faster growth in the area of worker-owned, democratically managed co-ops could help bring about an end to the current system before we reach a point where such catastrophes appear imminent.

In the meantime, which could be a long time, I think it makes sense that, alongside the radical experimentation that seeks to get us beyond the current system someday, many well-intentioned people are pushing for mere reforms—such as protecting and making more space for agricultural alternatives that support lower-risk approaches to food production. Who knows? Modest reforms, apart from alleviating certain immediate injustices, might also help accelerate the current system's eventual exhaustion.

I find it unsettling to ponder these things. I've often wished I could decide once and for all that doing the kinds of things Sofia and I are doing with food are the best we can do—from growing our own wild chicory greens to debating ethics and politics at a dinner table where such talk is usually considered taboo. But I can't decide this, and the questions persist. I continue to wonder what else I might be doing differently or more effectively.

This means wondering when I should focus my efforts on reducing my own immediate contributions to the world's problems versus when I should focus on trying to alter the social and economic structures, the cultural conventions and societal values, the institutions and normative principles that tend to lead so many of us to create and to contribute to so many problems in the first place. Will I spend that extra hour tonight trying to reduce how much *I* pollute (by researching the carbon footprint of the next car we might buy, say), or allowing myself to continue polluting more for the time being (by driving long distances to buy honey, say), provided I'm also trying to support large-scale initiatives (e.g., policy changes, legal moves, civil disobedience) aimed at reducing how much humans are polluting *in general*?

It also means wondering when I should say the heck with all these efforts and just give myself a break and take pleasure in doing things—perfectly acceptable things from most currently conventional perspectives—that I nevertheless know are not so innocent. If only the best-tasting, most healthy, readily available foods and drinks were always inexpensive, enjoyable to make, prepared from ecologically sound ingredients, grown and made with tools and equipment produced by free and fairly treated workers, and consumed in the best of all possible company! Maybe someday. For now I'm not going to let the unlikelihood of such a perfect situation deter me from accepting and dealing with the reality of my contradictory desires. If nonorganic, nonenvironmentally sustainable industrial ingredients are so cheap because they're subsidized, I'm not about to pay both the taxes supporting the subsidies *and* full retail price for organic or local foods every single time. If large-scale political action is ultimately necessary to take away the unfair advantages of subsidized unsustainable special interests, I'm not going to kid myself that as an "enlightened consumer" I'm contributing significantly to reforming the system through how I spend my dollars. I try not to become too complacent about the environment, but neither do I risk letting my idealism burn me out and make me give up all the small everyday joys that I need to compensate for the other anxieties, struggles, trials, and experiences of alienation I experience in this life.

I can never be *content* with my efforts, however great or small. I can only be resolved that for the time being I'm doing what I'm *prepared* to do, but that there's always something more I could consider doing, something that I can't preclude from consideration once and for all. *Resolved*, not content. And without regrets that something that began consciously motivated by immediate self-gratification has somehow evolved into something motivated by care for others as well, and for the most part without even having to sacrifice my epicurean desires: Without spending quite as much money or time or physical exertion as one might suppose, Sofia and I eat an incredibly wide variety of foods we love, which usually taste better than the would-be alternatives from supermarkets, and—between the lack of chemicals, and the fact that many of them are grown in soils that aren't industrially fertilized—which are probably more nutritious and less damaging to the well-being of ourselves, our immediate environment, and those who will live in it in the future. And who knows, maybe we're helping to keep in business a small farmer who pays a living wage to laborers and supports a small but ambitious and environmentally sensitive seed company. Or maybe the existence of these alternatives—in addition to feeding a niche of the population—will provide insight into, and starting points for achieving, a better socioeconomic system in the future as the time grows ripe for it. Nevertheless, I see so many other things that are needed that I'm really doing nothing to support—like the unionization of farm laborers, changes in legislation that remove barriers to more sustainable agricultural and business experiments, and changes in legislation that provide incentives for things like worker-owned cooperatives in all food sectors.

I do whatever I think I can do, but strive to remain vigilant about what "can" means—actively striving to resist easy complacence about what I deem for myself to be sufficient effort, and just as actively striving to resist giving into guilt that I'm not doing enough—dancing on a ledge between insensitively cynical or defeatist self-indulgence, on one side, and naively or self-righteously heroic self-abnegation on the other. In a world where many of us crave to be free, where the mind appreciates and justifies the value of freedom, where hearts can increase their circle of loyalty to include all of humanity, I know that the best ethical and political commitments are much more than knee-jerk reactions that aim to reduce guilt over our immediate forms of complicity in the injustices we observe. Our commitments, and the criteria we use to evaluate them, need to be reasoned out, without ever thinking that the reasoning process can *prove* they're right.

Responding to concerns about the environment and human oppression are complicated affairs. Ascertaining the potential effects of various food-related practices is anything but an exact science. There's the question of access to huge quantities of potentially relevant information. We frequently have to rely on direct or indirect access to the work of various scholars, scientists, and intellectuals. Even when the work of these specialists is largely trustworthy, there remain many reasons to be suspicious of the ways it gets interpreted or communicated to us—whether through corporate media or government-mandated labels and warnings. There's the question of synthesizing all the arguments and evidence we come upon. It takes effort to put all this together to make highly informed decisions, and not just decisions that we deceive ourselves into believing are informed because they somehow just *feel* informed because we refuse to examine them with a more critical eye.

So, in spite of frequent urges to do otherwise, I've been learning not to speculate too much about what will *really* change the world— what will bring about nonexploitative production and distribution of safe, nutritious, and hopefully pleasurable foods to all tables of earth's human inhabitants today and tomorrow. I'm trying to resist the social conditioning that tempts me to believe that if I try hard enough—alone or together with others—I might gain, and can *know* that I've gained, significant, predictable, and direct control over the future. I'm trying to accept the possibility that the large-scale and long-term efficacy of particular strategies aimed against a socially and ecologically unjust status quo are only knowable in hindsight, while I continue to believe in trying out particular strategies as we go along, and making our best efforts to ascertain the potential rewards and risks of such strategies.

Instead of letting my recognition of the probable nonlinearity and unpredictable complexity of history make me anxious that no matter what I do, I can't know if or how it might matter, I let it cheer me up whenever my best efforts feel like they *must* be futile. In striving for a better future whenever and wherever I'm resolved to do so, I only have faith that this overall strategy is the best we sort of know we can do, and remain wary of becoming overly self-confident about any *particular* strategies to which I remain provisionally committed.

And instead of lamenting the fact that I can't think of anything I do for the environment that doesn't also save me money or give me better-tasting or safer food—except for putting things in the recycle bin instead of in the trash—I remind myself how wonderful it is that most everything I'm doing for the environment also saves us money or gives us better tasting or safer food!

For what do any of us really *know* about the mechanisms by which significant social and ecological progress can be precipitated from our present predicament?

There's a saying in Crete that goes something like this:

Don't go often to the place you love;
and if you do go often, don't stay too long;
and if you do stay too long, don't talk too much;
and if you do talk too much, you better know what you're talking about!

I guess I've said too much.

✳ 24 ✳

Hot Tempers

I run next door to my parents' house to let them know Sofia and I will be away for a few days because we're going to visit Leonidas for New Year's.

My father unlocks and opens the door. I step inside, barely, and tell them. I stand there twirling my *koboloi* beads quickly between my fingers. My glance shifts up and down, left and right.

My mother is still sitting on the couch. "Before I forget, I wanted to ask you . . . Did you go to school with [I can't recall the name]?"

"I don't remember," I mumble.

"Maybe it was your brother who went to school with him. His wife's from Germany. He manages the furniture store in Queensbury where your father and I got our new chairs. They're supposed to be better for your back. I thought you went to school with him. I guess she's from . . . Hon', where'd she say she was from?"

"Somewhere in Germany."

"I know, but didn't she tell us the name of the city? I thought your son might know it."

"Why would I know it?"

"I don't know. I just thought you'd know. She's real nice. We must have talked to them for about fifteen minutes. They're both real nice. They met in Germany. I was telling them about you and Sophie, and about how you lived in Greece. You didn't go to school with him?"

"I don't remember that stuff."

"Maybe it was your brother, then."

My mother gets up and heads toward the kitchen. "Come here. I want you to try something."

313

I take a few steps farther into the living room. "What do you mean you want me to try something?"

"Do you know what ham hocks are?"

"I don't know . . . I guess . . . doesn't it have to do with pigs' feet or something like that?"

"We went to the church supper and had the *best* soup. Did you ever know [some woman's name I never heard of]? Her father made it. He used to work in a restaurant for years. Your father and I went crazy over it and I asked him about it. It's made with ham hocks. I never heard of them before. He gave me the rest of the soup to take home and I told your father you'll have to try some and see what you think."

"That's alright. We *just* ate. I'm stuffed." I take a few wandering steps closer to the bar separating the living room and the kitchen.

"You can just *try* it. We thought it was *so* good."

"But I'm not *interested* in that kinda thing. Why do you think I mostly cook my *own* food?"

I'm standing next to the bar. I glance down and notice a book sitting by the small pile of outgoing mail. Something or another about all-natural herbs and good health. While my mother is heating up a small plastic bowl of the soup in the microwave and taking out a dessert spoon, I flip the book over and scan the back cover. The author has listed three or four college degrees after his name. The book is published by some press I've never heard of. It definitely doesn't look like the kind of thing that goes through any kind of rigorous review process, at least not in terms of its health claims. In fact it looks like yet another book preying on the ill by putting forth some kind of specific program for good health. More magic bullets.

My mother sees me looking at it, opens the cupboard, and takes out a bottle of pills. "These are supplements the book recommends. It's supposed to be all natural and organic."

"How many times have I explained to you that the phrase 'all natural' doesn't mean what you think it means?"

"Marion swears by it. She's been feeling a lot better ever since she started it."

"That doesn't mean anything. It could be the placebo effect."

"You see . . . he writes all about how everything nowadays is full of chemicals and stuff, the way you've always said. Then he tells you all the natural foods you should eat to help you with different problems and diseases." She opens it up to the chapter on [a minor medical condition] to show me. She's got that chapter bookmarked with a piece of paper on which I see she's scribbled information.

[. . .]

She gives me the soup. I smell it. Now I'm positive it's not anything I'd particularly care for, but I quickly take a small spoonful and get it over with.

"Well?"

"It's alright."

She pulls a package out of one of the cupboards. "What do you think of this pasta I bought?"

I look at the ingredients. "Why would you get this? Didn't you read the ingredients?"

"But it says it's supposed to be healthier."

"What do you expect them to say? They'll say anything they can get away with if it helps them sell their product."

She puts the pasta back into the pantry.

"I don't understand how you can get a book like this and take it seriously after everything I've explained to you all these years."

"Well, Marion swears by it. Her [minor medical condition] was a lot worse than mine and now she's doing better."

My father interjects that they do a lot of the things I tell them, but that "they can't do everything perfect."

My mother is thankfully still upbeat. "Tell Leonidas we said hi. How's he doing?"

"Fine, I guess . . . Alright then . . ." I head in the direction of the door.

"Did he ever get his furnace fixed?"

"I guess. I mean, he must've."

"Didn't you ask him?"

"No."

"[My first name]!"

"What? We've got better things to talk about than that."

"Don't you think you should get yours checked too? Your father and I just had ours looked at. Hon', what was the name of that guy?"

"That's okay, don't worry about it."

"I'm not worried about it. But you don't want the same thing to happen to you that happened to Leonidas do you?"

"Anyway . . ."

"Hey, I'm just trying to help. Oh, before I forget, next summer, on June twenty-third, Aunt Juliette and I are planning to put on a family reunion for all our side of the family. Hopefully a lot of the cousins will be able to come down from Canada. And then Aunt Juliette's family and Uncle Lucas's. So that's forty-two grown-ups plus the eight kids. Unless Gilbert can make it after all. I guess they're in the process of moving. If they can make it there'll be forty-four. Wait, is that right?" She looks up and starts counting everyone on her fingers.

"Yes, forty-four. Anyway, I might need you to help your father to cook the [name of a typical picnic food] on the grill, and [name of another, less typical picnic food] for the kids because that's the only thing most of them will eat."

Fragments of thoughts race through my head as I stand, frozen, staring intensely at her.

Now she's upset. "After everything we do for you, you won't do this for us? Every time you need help with something your father drops whatever he's doing to come and help you, but if we ask you for something you always give us a hard time."

Now *I'm* getting upset.

"I *know* you don't like my food, but how do you think that makes *me* feel? You wouldn't even eat anything on your father's birthday."

"What do you mean? I ate."

"Yeah, right. *Barely.* You won't eat anything I make, or Aunt Patsy makes, or anybody else in your family. Unless it's Ben. And we're still *your* family, whether you like it or not."

"So? Why should you care what I eat or don't eat?"

"Don't give me that. You're always telling *us* what *we* should eat."

"Yeah, because I know something about food and I'm trying to *help* you. You're not trying to help me. You're just trying to make sure everybody conforms to your image of how a family is supposed to be."

"Oh yeah? Well I know better by now than to expect you or your brother to care about family. Everything's always gotta be *your* way. Anyway, if you don't wanna help with the family reunion . . ."

"I didn't say that."

"I know what your look means."

"You know I don't cook [name of the typical picnic food]. Now you're telling me I have to help poison our relatives just because that's what you've already decided?"

"Well that's what *our* family likes to eat at a picnic, so that's what we're gonna have. It doesn't always have to be *your* way. It's bad enough you wouldn't even let me cook the ham on Christmas!"

"What? You gotta be kidding me. *You* called *me* to ask me where to get an uncured ham, and when I told you, you said you didn't know if you could get there to buy it so I did you a favor and said *I'd* get it. Then you asked me twenty questions about how to cook it even though I already wrote down my recipe for you last year. Then you complained that you didn't have the right equipment to cook it, so I figured I'd just do us both a favor and offer to cook it myself!"

"That's not what happened. I just asked you the temperature and how long *you* would cook it. I was still going to cook it my own way."

"You asked me a lot more than that, *and* you implied that it was gonna be a burden to make from scratch."

"I most certainly did not."

"Yeah you did."

"You just didn't want *me* to cook it, your own mother! I don't know why I bother to try anymore. You never appreciate all the things I do. Someday you'll be sorry. You just better hope God forgives you."

"*What* God?"

My mother stands up. "I've had enough of this!" She points at the door, "Get out!"

I'm halfway out the door and my father is right behind me ready to close it. An unfamiliar emotion overcomes me, and before I know it I turn around, grab the door with my hand so it can't close, and yell: "You say everything you wanna say and then you think you can just kick me out. Well, this time you're gonna hear what *I* have to say whether you like it or not, and if you're not gonna let me in the door then the whole neighborhood's gonna hear it too!"

My father lets me back in. I immediately lower my voice and speak calmly, mostly in the direction of my father. "I know that from your point of view it's no big deal to expect me to cook [name of the typical picnic food] for other people. But for me it's a *really* big deal."

"We've seen you eating [name of the typical picnic food]."

"Not usually."

My mother interrupts. "Yes you do!"

My father motions her to stop and listen. She sits down.

"And even if I do, it's because there's so few alternatives around here and it takes so much effort to overcome the temptation a hundred percent of the time. But there's a big difference between that and cooking a whole bunch of them to feed to the whole family. It goes against everything I believe in."

"He always exaggerates everything! He's mentally unstable! Penny knew it, too!"

My father motions to her again. "Why couldn't you have said it like this before instead of accusing us of poisoning our relatives?"

"I didn't say *anything* at first. Mom's the one who blew up. *Then* I said it."

My mother jumps up again. "You didn't *have* to say anything. Your stare said it all."

"I was caught off guard. You think it's easy for me to know how to respond to these things when I'm surprised like this? Of course I don't wanna cook that stuff, but I don't want to say *no* either."

"Why not? Obviously you don't wanna do it! You never wanna do anything I ask you to do, and I don't ask for much."

"I know that's how it looks to you."

"It's not just how it looks to me. You ask anybody. You never want to do anything for me."

"You gotta be kidding me! So I never cooked for you when you were sick? I never found all that information about [a minor ailment] for you?"

"I'm *sorry* you had to do all those things for me."

"I didn't say you should be sorry I did them. *You* said I never wanna do anything for you and I'm just giving you examples to show you're not right."

"Well I don't know *why* you did them."

"Because you're my mother and I *love* you."

"Well you sure don't know how to show it." She turns to my father. "They never call to ask me how I'm feeling. All I ever cared about was my kids and this is the thanks I get."

"You see why I always feel trapped when you ask me to do things? Every time I come over here I'm scared to death because I don't know what I can talk about with you, and I never know when you're gonna blow up at me."

My mother sits back down again. "It doesn't matter what I do, everything I do is wrong. I won't ask you for anything ever again."

She starts crying. "If it's so hard to be around us, why did you move in next door?"

I don't say anything.

"Why? To kill me? Because that's what you're doing."

I turn to my father. "You see? How can I not be afraid of coming over here, or know how to respond when this is how she takes it?"

My mother gets up again and the shouting begins again. "Why don't you and Sophie just move!"

"Why don't *you* move?"

"We were here *first*! Get out of my house! And don't bring any more of your food over here!"

She runs toward the bedroom.

My father says there's no point in talking any further when my mother is so upset, and that he needs to go check on her.

I go back home.

I walk through our front door and see Sofia sitting at her desk. "Well, all hell broke out this time. Worse than ever before. Don't worry, though. It's not really affecting me this time, so I won't have to drive you crazy all night."

She looks up and gives me a blank stare.

I go into the kitchen, pour myself a snifter of Armagnac, and sit down at the bar. I hold up my glass as though toasting the icon of Euphrosynos, tap it on the bar, and take a sip.

A few minutes pass. Sofia comes in and makes herself a cup of tea. "So?"

I summarize the highlights.

"That's your pattern."

"What do you mean?"

"You and your mother always do that."

"Yes, but this time I reacted differently. In fact it's prob'ly because you made me see the pattern that I reacted differently."

"You still just tried to insist on having things your way."

"Come on, we talked about this before. They tried to impose their way on me. But this time I didn't let my mother just kick me out when she didn't agree with me, and then I stayed calm enough to be rational when we talked more. I even said that I did those things I did out of *love*. I never managed to just say it like *that* before.

"But you know how it is. I can see things from *their* point of view because I grew up in that family, but they can't see anything from *my* point of view. They've never lived in my world. So I'm always at a disadvantage because I can't be self-righteous about everything like they can. So then I have to . . ."

"You're both self-righteous."

"No. There's a difference between provisional conviction and self-righteousness. Self-righteous means that one person believes the other *can't* be right. No dialogue is necessary because the one person thinks they're absolutely right. They raised me. I grew up here. I more or less know where they're coming from, so there's not much reason to expect them to come up with an argument that I haven't already considered, it's true. *But*, I *still* discuss with them because I also know that I could be wrong, because *anybody* and *everybody* could be wrong . . . no one's infallible. I might think it's highly unlikely, but I'm not complacent in the conviction that it's impossible. But they—I mean, my mother—believes that it's *impossible* that she might not be right."

"Do you hear yourself?"

"What? They think they're right and I think I'm right. But they don't think they should have to persuade me that they're right. They think I should just see the light."

"You Westerners are always trying to prove you're right. Maybe it's not about right or wrong. You know your mother can't argue rationally with you. We all know we can't beat you with logic. So all you're doing is reminding her that you think she's inferior because she can't really argue with you."

"So it's pointless to try persuading them of anything if they think I'm just doing it to prove I'm right. If they don't think I'm doing it because I actually care about *them* . . . So basically what you're saying is that when I try to help them eat better they mostly don't see it as me *caring*, but as someone who just wants to put them down because I'm more educated or whatever? But then why do they ask me for advice so often?"

"They're parents."

"And . . . ?"

"They're still hoping."

"Hoping what?"

"That you care. That you don't look down on them."

"So once again my rhetoric's all wrong. I guess I just don't know how to get out of the pattern—the pattern you said. If there's all these congealed habits of communicating . . . on top of all the congealed habits of *feeling* that accompany them . . . and most of this is happening more-or-less unconsciously, there's no hope that I can find the appropriate rhetoric so they won't think I'm just looking down on them."

"Why do you always think you can fix everything?"

"Now I'm feeling guilty again."

"Why?"

"Because I always think I can fix things, but whether I'm trying to help them or just protecting myself from their demands—I mean, my mother's demands—I'm always just making them feel bad."

"So? I thought you don't have a romantic view of family? Who says families don't have a lot of conflict?"

I get up and pour myself a second glass of Armagnac. I sit down again.

Sofia continues. "They make you feel bad, too. That's the parents and kids."

"I know I'm not responsible for whatever suffering they go through just because I happen to follow different ethical criteria from them. And I know I'm not responsible for the fact that much about their world has conditioned them to believe that their ethical criteria are indisputably the absolute best. But I still feel their disappointment with me—or even their *potential* disappointment—like it's a powerful force. All the more so since I can *remember* what it feels like to believe the kinds of things they believe are true. Of course, not so powerful as to make me stop believing what I believe. But still . . ."

"Nobody can make you do anything. We all know that."

"Yes, I know. There's no *actual* force. It just *feels* like being forced, at least to me. They only have power over me to the extent that *I'm* afraid of disappointing them."

"You think they want to disappoint you?"

"Of course not. They can't help it . . . just like I can't help it."

I take a big sip.

"In fact, maybe when they act in certain ways that make me really feel that threat of disappointing them, *they're* acting the way they are because *they're* struggling with their *own* fear of disappointing me or my brother!"

I get up and pace back and forth in the middle of the kitchen.

"So once again it's about resolve. My father's always telling me, 'We don't want people to do things for us if they don't want to do them,' but it's not a matter of *wanting* or *not wanting*. It's about being *prepared* to do something or not. I might wanna do it and not wanna do it at the same time. The question is what am I *prepared* to do, and how can I stay *resolved* about it."

"That's what you always do."

"Yes, but what I'm saying is that I need to stay resolved without bouncing back and forth between the extremes of overwhelming guilt and overly arrogant self-satisfaction. Right now I might stick to my guns, but in a way that leaves both them and me feeling lousy most of the time . . . because over and over again I think I can just persuade them with a rational argument to stop trying to persuade *me*, and then after that doesn't work, I feel guilty because the argument itself makes them feel bad. And we just go in circles."

"I guess I don't know what *guilt* means."

"Guilt? What about when you do something that you know makes your mother feel bad? You don't think about it and get a sinking feeling inside you?"

"Yes."

"And then you feel regret because you're responsible for making her feel bad?"

"No."

"No? Then what's that sinking feeling?"

"I don't know. I guess I just feel sorry for her."

"And you don't feel regret?"

"Not usually."

"Well, I once read that anthropologists used to stereotype some cultures as *guilt* cultures and others as *shame* cultures. Maybe cultures characterized by lots of guilt tend to be more usual wherever capitalism's in full swing—where growing up in a modern nuclear family trains you to experience and respond to guilt in ways that prepare you for adult life as an employee and citizen who won't much question the authority of employers or governments, no matter how undemocratically they might behave.

"What about shame? You don't feel regret because of what other people will think of you, even your mother?"

"Not anymore."

"Because you left Taiwan?"

"Maybe."

"Then maybe you managed to avoid the whole guilt thing because you grew up in the midst of at least the residue of an extended family, and then to undo the whole shame thing because you moved here."

"Or because I overcome the feeling that I need to be responsible for my mother's feelings. I told my mother she needs to be emotionally independent from kids and not see me like I'm seventeen years old. But what can you do?"

"I don't know if I can do anything, especially if it's not mostly a matter of *me* but of the kind of world we live in. But at least I have something new to try. Maybe for the first time in my life. For one thing, I can try to be more aware of when I'm feeling guilty, and try to stop myself from doing things just to alleviate the guilt—since when I do they just end up making me feel more guilty anyway. Even if I can't make the guilt go away, at least knowing what's going on might enable me to endure my way through it better 'til it passes."

"You really think you can do that?"

"I said I can *try*. Maybe it's the wild-goat-dancing-on-a-ledge thing again . . . the ledge between guilt and self-righteousness. Maybe it's all related. Yes! What if the struggle for total freedom has to happen in many different contexts at the same time? In families and workplaces, in schools and churches, in governmental politics and therapies . . ."

"I thought we were talking about your family."

"We are. What if all these years I've been letting myself believe that my parents are trying to *force* me to do things—which obviously I don't think they should do—just because that's what it *feels* like to me? As long as I keep seeing it like this, there's no way I can see myself as negotiating between responding to my desires and their desires, and them as negotiating between responding to their desires and mine . . . even if that's not how *they* see it because of the whole family values thing."

I sit down at the bar again. Sofia keeps listening as I think aloud.

"So then I deceive myself into thinking I'm just sticking up for my freedom, and feeling bad in the process, when all I'm really doing is going around and around a vicious cycle of guilt that may itself have to do with the particular combination of freedom and lack-of-freedom we're living under . . . It's like the relative freedom we experience living in a capitalist democracy conditions us to be very passionate about sticking up for our individual freedom, but then the daily governmental, employer, parental, and other forms of coercion that we perpetrate and endure weaken our ability to distinguish between violations of freedom and other kinds of pressures that aren't strictly violations—like the most overwhelming pressures of guilt."

[. . .]

"Tomorrow I'll go over and tell them that they can still ask of me whatever they want, but that they have to accept the possibility that whenever they ask I'm allowed to say no."

[. . .]

"Aren't you gonna say anything?"

"You're always doing that, thinking you can fix things the right way. I think you shouldn't say anything else to them for now."

I don't say anything for a while. I am thinking.

Epilogue:
"Happy Name Day, Euphrosynos"

I continue to find myself wavering between the joys of living in a beautiful world and despair over what might have been or could be but isn't. Belonging to two continents still leaves me feeling torn. I eat and drink to celebrate. I eat and drink to mourn. But I usually don't make apologies to saints, especially about what, where, why, how, and with whom I eat and drink. Not least of all because I don't know of any saints with whom I could share a worldview or set of ideals—not even you as I imagine you.

But when I'm alone in the kitchen, thinking about things as I'm doing whatever else I happen to be doing, the photocopy of your icon on the wall reminds me that even my most private thoughts, for better or worse, feel like they're under some kind of moral surveillance. Call it conscience, Socratic daemon, Freudian superego, fear of the boss, intimidation by the teacher, a moral sense, the omnipresence of God, the specter of role models, social intuition, or the psychological residue of a kid who grew up being told there was a Santa Claus. All I know is that lately my brain allocates a decent proportion of my caloric expenditure for critical reflection on how I'm living day to day.

Don't get me wrong, it's not like I'm trying to follow elaborate moral codes or that I desire the imposition of lots of ethical conventions and restrictions. Live and let live, I say.

But what does the phrase "let live" mean? How do we ascertain whether one person's living interferes inappropriately or unjustly, even unwittingly, with the potential course of someone else's "living"?

For that matter, what does it even mean to "live"? After all, it could be that there are individuals, groups, or institutions unjustly interfering with the potential course of *my* life, even to the extent that I remain unaware that I could be living otherwise—because they've taken a better choice away from me, ensured that I don't even realize I should have such a choice, or deceived me about how my choices will affect me. And there's no point relishing the notion that ignorance is bliss, because the bliss of ignorance rarely outweighs the suffering you secretly endure later on when you come to understand that your bliss was only made possible by your prior ignorance. Ignorance is bliss only for those who somehow remain ignorant through to the end.

Near as I can tell, then, "live and let live" isn't so much an ethical precept as it is the ultimate dare: a dare to question, analyze, wonder, feel, and make judgments about what it means to "live" and what it means to "let live," all the while one is attempting to do so—total freedom on the condition of total responsibility, every move susceptible in principle to interrogation by the questions *How is this living?* and *How is this letting live?*

The particular ways I've been responding to this dare in my own life have been immeasurably influenced by my having landed in a particular family in Crete, my leaving the island when I didn't much want to, my pursuit of advanced studies in the humanities and social sciences, and my choice to live where I grew up—a place that sometimes leaves me feeling disappointed and disturbed, but where I nonetheless wish I could appreciate more heartily who and what I *do* have. It *still* puzzles me that I did such an about-face and decided to move back here. Maybe there was an unconscious change of heart, catalyzed by the events on your first Name Day in a new-but-not-(yet?)-improved millennium, when for many Americans the world suddenly got a lot smaller but loved ones never felt farther away.

Along the way, I've learned that if we want to steer the course of history toward greater living and letting live, we cannot rely solely on the escape from the mind that the rebel heart offers up, nor should we put too much hope on the taming of emotion by the mind and all its rational inventions. How best to nurture the development and collaboration of a rigorous mind and a generous heart remains an open question. An *important* open question.

I've come to recognize the potential significance of pleasure derived from believing or doing the same things as a group of people with whom you identify. In other words, from the pleasures of belonging. And I've realized how difficult it can be to gauge the extent to which liking something—anything at all—has to do with the fact that liking it gives us the satisfaction of knowing we belong to some family, place, club, team, religion, culture, cult, institution, or organization. (To what extent do I find the taste of chicory greens pleasant because it awakens in me feelings of connection to Crete?)

In the phrase "live and let live," it turns out the word *live* is also about love.

Love is a word I rarely use, at least in English. But I don't know how else to name that form of attachment that, even if you usually don't much notice it, is so strong that it provides an anchor for meaning in your life—for the day-to-day conviction that the universe isn't meaningless, at least not for humans. I mean the kind of attachment that you only truly understand exists when in a moment of just waking you have the half-conscious, split-second experience of apprehending your life exactly as it is, except with whoever you love most forever gone—and you feel unexpectedly terrified to your core. A moment that, if you're like me, is followed by trembling at the thought that maybe you've ended up in this predicament because you've made life-altering mistakes you could have readily avoided if only you'd been more attentive to the possible consequences of certain decisions before making them.

Throughout my first visit to Crete, whenever the wine was flowing and hearts were rebelling against minds, Manolis would proclaim calmly and with self-assurance: "*This* is [what] Crete [is]." I took him to mean that, of the many things one might experience in Crete, the frequent and widespread triumph of the heart in many Cretans' lives is what really matters. He also made clear the contrast to some other places, like the United States, where "business" and calculating self-interest too frequently seem to triumph over heart. His pronouncement not only promoted resistance to marginalization of spirit and emotion by the modern calculating mind of Western—and especially American—capitalism, but also claimed that Cretan culture is particularly well versed in this particular kind of resistance.

Manolis's Crete—or, more precisely, my ongoing interpretation of Manolis's Crete—is the Crete that continues to inspire much about how I try to live my life, and it's the one I feel connected to when I'm brought to ecstasy by a *lyra* player singing at the top of his lungs to the drumming, heavy-metal-like rhythm of a climactic *syrtos*:

Ένα πουλάκι τραγουδεί πάνω στον Ψηλορείτη,
Άλλο νησί δε βρίσκεται στον κόσμο σαν την Κρήτη! [1]

A little bird is singing on top of Psiloreitis [Crete's tallest mountain],
There's no other island in the world like Crete!

Yet, identifying particular values with a particular group of people,
even if it makes possible joys of belonging, also risks excluding
others who might share similar values. The potential political progress—the further advancement of "letting live"—that such an act of
identification might help bring about needs to be measured against
the potential damage caused by the exclusions it entails, especially
when it comes to all the many nasty *isms* (racism, ethnocentrism,
sexism, etc.) that might be engendered. The rebel heart has to be
vigilant about not turning into the reactionary heart.

Having moved to this half-acre in New York knowing that I'll
never again live in Crete, or as part of a Cretan family, I've been
reckoning with certain memories of childhood, family, and place that
I might otherwise never have needed to—and probably wouldn't
have been able to. That wasn't a conscious motive for moving here,
but it turned out to be useful for observing and unraveling certain
patterns in my life that I hadn't noticed before. Useful? Does better
understanding of these patterns necessarily translate into living
better? I suppose it does if living well involves making better sense
of chronic disappointment or moments of extreme dismay instead
of just burying your head in the sand in order not to.

Maybe engaging in so many food-related activities is a way Sofia
and I attempt a provisional solution to the problem of meaning-
making in the particular world we currently inhabit, where we keep
rediscovering that we rarely share categories of meaning or criteria
of meaningfulness with the families who we love and who love us.
Maybe my having taken the time to write about these activities is
another part of this attempt.

Maybe, though, food is also a way for me to avoid directing my
energies more fruitfully toward dealing with the fact that *this is
where I am*. If I'm really constantly in danger of falling off the cliff
into the abyss of meaninglessness, isn't it possible that all these
obsessions with food and eating right have been distracting me
from more adequately recognizing the complexity of my relationships with those around me? That cultivating so much garlic in the

suburbs has also become a strategy for avoiding cultivating more openness to direct forms of dialogue with other people? That food brings into the foreground Manolis's and Eirini's many influences on my life at the expense of my coming to terms with whatever happened between Penny and me? I increasingly suspect that Sofia not only understands more than I do about many of the plants she grows, but also about the patterns of interaction that occur between me and other people, and yet that she also believes that it's usually futile to intervene unless or until I'm prepared to welcome such intervention. Why does so much of my desire point toward her cabbages and cucumbers instead of toward her understanding of these patterns?

As an academic cultural critic, I enjoy using reason to question many commonsense conclusions about how one should live, and I have limited patience for dogmatic opposition to reasoned critique of the very categories and terms in which such questions are usually raised and addressed. For me, responding to the dare to "live and let live" means trying to unstrap myself from unwavering faith in any of the formulaic moral doctrines or tidy philosophical systems on offer, and from unquestioning adherence to the beliefs and conventions of this or that society, religion, country, or culture—including any that claim to have already fully worked out the necessary concepts, principles, rules, and institutions for bringing a live-and-let-live worldview to fruition. It means denying ultimate authority to ancestry, family, deity, mystical revelation, emotional insight, or the self, and persuading myself that the better I can understand ancestral, familial, religious, and emotional phenomena, the better equipped I might become to deal with the question of *living*. The upshot is that I'm too critical of many American norms for the tastes of most of my American family but too connected with my family for many other cultural critics. I'm far too "Cretan" for most of the Americans around me but probably too "American" for many Cretans.

As a corollary, I not only believe that everything people do is political in the sense that it has political effects and is informed by political assumptions, but that politicizing and negotiating issues can be relevant and important in some of the very spaces where many people around me think it should be taboo: such as in domestic gatherings of family and friends. This gets me thinking about Manolis's use of the *mantinada*—of a succinct poetic genre deeply meaningful to other people sitting at the table—in order to persuade them. Unlike Manolis, I grew up and live in a place without such a lively, widely shared, and explicitly revered succinct literary form that could readily be deployed to engage friends, families, neighbors, and others in the community in such discussions and debates. (We do have bumper stickers and T-shirts.) I think I get the taboo: joyful gatherings in a domestic space can provide a useful *escape* from many of life's burdens—including the burdens of politics and disagreements. But such gatherings can also provide a safe space for grappling with the very issues that put burdens on our lives in the first place.

I guess that's another reason why I enjoy leisurely open-ended gatherings over good food and drink, especially when they evolve into hours-long discussions, sustained inquiries, and all-out debates.

Our last such gathering was with Andy and Dafne at their farm almost two months ago. As we sat at the table and continued drinking wine after the meal, we deliberated on the viability of their importing Italian farm wines as part of their business. Then they tried coaxing us into visiting them in Italy later in the summer or the following winter. This got me talking about Crete.

"The other day I got an invitation in the mail for a wedding in Crete, from another professor I know who's originally from there. I know I won't go, but I haven't been able to stop looking at it, which is why I've left it sitting out on the table.

"It's the first time since I left the island that someone there sent me something like this in the mail . . . like I'm suddenly back in Crete . . . part of run-of-the-mill social life there all over again. I keep staring at the *mantinades* that the invitation's written in, and the little map they put on it that shows how to get to her village. I keep sorta picturing myself showing up there. And this reminds me that my *other* friends Stavros and Dimitra are getting married in a few weeks. I wish I could surprise them and just show up for their wedding out of the blue. 'Til last fall we hadn't even talken [sic] to each other for years . . . Not that we're invited. Well, anyway, that doesn't necessarily mean anything."

Then Dafne asked me, "Is that thing around your neck from Crete? What is it?"

"Yeah. It's a kind of traditional headband. A shepherd I used to know gave it to me—which is why I decided to wear it tonight. But this is the first time I'm wearing it around my neck instead of on my head. This is the way *other* people of *my* generation in the city would usually wear it, like if they were dancing to Cretan music at a wedding—"

Andy jumped in, "Come on! I think you should go!"

"Yeah, right. Of course, with the terrible economic situation there now who knows how many of their friends *in* Greece'll manage to get to their weddings. It's really not good. The banks and big businesses are taking over big-time now and it's at the point where the government can't even pretend that there's much national sovereignty. Then again, the other day when I asked my friend Thanasis what he thought, he said, 'Eh, everybody's exaggerating. This is nothing compared to the Turks. We've survived a lot worse.' Of course, maybe that's easy for him to say, since he's living here in the U.S."

Andy continued to insist that I should go to at least one of the weddings. "Tell me again why you won't go back to Crete? I still don't get it."

I tried deflecting the question but Andy insisted on trying to understand. He pressed me to explain precisely what my reasons were. He poured us both some Italian grappa.

At first, like a reflex, I reached into the back of my head for a handful of the litany of reasons: I don't want to see up close what I lost and can never have again. I don't want to be there as a "tourist." Now that Greece has moved to the Euro I'll feel like an incompetent stranger in my own home, constantly fumbling to figure out which coins are which when everyone else has already gotten used to them. Since I managed to reconcile with living here and I'm getting by fairly well, I don't want to mess with the balance. If I ever reopen even the theoretical possibility of living there again—which visiting could do—I'll have trouble knowing what the right thing to do is vis-à-vis my ex-in-laws. I'm afraid to experience Crete as an "orphan." I at least owe it to Penny's family not to subject them to the possibility of catching a glimpse of me—a much-too-tangible reminder of the past—on their home ground. Now that so many years have gone by, once I'm there I might deeply regret not having gone earlier and more often. And so on.

But before I could get out even one of these reasons, my heart told me in a flash—for the first time in more than a decade—that these and twenty other reasons I'd thought of over the years no longer comprised a viable argument. And in an instant I knew my heart was right. I knew Andy had me with his question.

I broke out in an embarrassed grin, but decided I had to try to make my case against going to see if it might hold up. I tried explaining things this way and that as Andy kept interrogating my assumptions and forcing me to support my assertions. Even *I* wasn't buying any of the arguments I was trying to make, the moment I was making them.

The next day Sofia and I reserved our tickets.

We leave the day after tomorrow.

Is it any wonder that I've remained so enamored of the ancient Greek etymological significance of the word *symposium*—when the mere *get-together* happens to turn into just such a *drink-together* and the kitchen is eclipsed by the dining area?

Sofia and I made our dining area in the living room. You and the other "kitchen gods" can't see it from where you are, but hanging on the living room wall is a piece of cardboard that I found in a dumpster in Ohio, onto which I painted the sun and sea and sky around the silhouette, unpainted, of a Cretan wild goat dancing on a ledge.

Acknowledgments

The text itself must stand in for the bulk of my deepest acknowledgments, which I direct with all my heart at its central characters.

I should also point out that I might not have written this kind of book had I not been immersed as a faculty member in a particular kind of mentoring community at Empire State College. I especially want to acknowledge my gratitude to Alan Mandell and Lee Herman, whose written articulations and daily practices of mentoring help me to make sense of this immersion.

This book bears traces of my having pursued advanced studies in literary and cultural criticism, and I want to acknowledge my formal training at Ohio State, especially in Modern Greek Literature by Gregory Jusdanis and Yiorgos Anagnostou; in folk literature by Patrick B. Mullen; in Environmental Literature by H. Lewis Ulman; and in literary and cultural theory by Eugene Holland.

It also bears specific traces of intellectual stimulation and moral support that I gratefully received from Bill Vitek during multiple periods of my life.

Finally, I want to acknowledge my high school English teacher, the late Robert J. Porter. As a senior, increasingly contemptuous of compulsory education in the humanities, I gave him as much trouble as I could get away with. But he—teaching at a time when public school teachers were still somewhat free to teach—responded so intelligently and supportively, planted so many viable seeds, that he made it impossible for me not to remember later, time and time again, how lucky a kid like me was to have received such a high-quality public education. I mean, the guy showed us a *Bergman* film, for chrissakes! I bet he knew all along that someday I'd pay the price for trying my best to avoid reading the books he assigned, when I'd wake up and find it impossible not to try writing one of my own.

Notes

Prologue
1. Nikos Kazantzakis, *Αναφορά στον Γκρέκο* [*Report to Greco*] (Athens, Greece: Εκδόσεις Ελένης Ν. Καζαντζάκη, 1982 [1961]).

Chapter 1
1. Virginia Scott Jenkins, *The Lawn: A History of an American Obsession* (Washington, DC: Smithsonian Institution Press, 1994).

Chapter 3
1. Joel Salatin, *Everything I Want to Do Is Illegal: War Stories from the Local Food Front* (Swoope, VA: Polyface, Inc, 2007).

2. Michael Pollan, *The Omnivore's Dilemma: A Natural History of Four Meals* (New York: Penguin Books, 2006), 125.

Chapter 4
1. Nathaniel Sylvester, *History of Saratoga County* (Philadelphia: Everts and Ensign,1878; Bill Carr and the Heritage Hunters of Saratoga County, 1999), http://www.rootsweb.ancestry.com/~nysarato/Sylvester/contents. html. Retrieved April 1, 2008.

Chapter 11
1. See also Eric L. Ball, "Guarding the Wild: Place, Tradition, Literature and the Environment in the Work of a Cretan Folk Poet," *Journal of American Folklore* 119 (43) (2006): 275, 282, and Eric L. Ball, "Negotiating Regional Identity in the 'Literature' of Everyday Life: The Case of a Cretan *Mandinadhologos*," *Journal of the Hellenic Diaspora* 26 (2) (2000): 81–82.
2. Nikos Kazantzakis, Ασκητική [*Spiritual Exercises*]. (Athens, Greece: Εκδόσεις Ελένης Ν. Καζαντάκη, [1927] 1983).
3. Nikos Kazantzakis, *Ο βίος και πολιτεία του Αλέξη Ζορμπά* [*Zorba the Greek*]. (Athens, Greece: Εκδόσεις Ελένης Ν. Καζαντζάκη, [1946] 1981).

Chapter 12
1. Alexandros Droudakis [Αλέξανδρος Δρουδάκης], *10,000 Μαντινάδες της Κρήτης* [*10,000 Mantinades of Crete*] (Hania, Greece: A. Κ. Δρουδάκης,

1982), 339. This also appears in Yiannis Pavlakis [Γιάννης Παυλάκης], *Κρητική Δημοτική Ποίηση: Οι Μαντινάδες* [*Cretan Folk Poetry: Mantinades*] (Athens, Greece: Βιβλιοεκδοτική Αναστασάκη, 1994), 129. As the *mantinada* is considered a form of "traditional" or "folk" poetry in Greece, the authorship (in the conventional modern sense) of most *mantinades* remains unknown. Even recently composed *mantinades* can quickly pass into general circulation among the people of Crete (as well as in Cretan musical performances and recordings) and are considered "traditional." Also, in Crete, originality frequently has more to do with using a *mantinada* in an appropriate and original context than with having devised the actual words. In my own writing, then, any references I provide with *mantinades* are meant to point to at least one accessible place I've encountered them. Since it's impossible in many cases to say where these *mantinades*—these texts "of the people"—first originated, or whether any evidence of their original authorship even exists, these attributions are not meant in themselves to imply anything one way or the other about authorship in the conventional modern sense.

2. Droudakis, *10,000 Mantinades of Crete*, 365.

3. For an earlier version of the following interpretation, see also Eric L. Ball, "Guarding the Wild: Place, Tradition, Literature and the Environment in the Work of a Cretan Folk Poet," *Journal of American Folklore* 119 (43) (2006): 288–289, and Eric L. Ball, "Negotiating Regional Identity in the 'Literature' of Everyday Life: The Case of a Cretan *Mandinadhologos*," *Journal of the Hellenic Diaspora* 26, (2) (2000): 80.

4. Maria Lioudaki [Μαρία Λιουδάκη], *Λαογραφικά Κρήτης Τόμος Α', Μαντινάδες* [*Cretan Folklore Volume 1, Mantinades*] (Athens, Greece: Εκδοτικός Οίκος Ελευθερουδάκης, 1936), 142.

5. Droudakis, *10,000 Mantinades of Crete*, 363. Also appears in Pavlakis, *Cretan Folk Poetry*, 344.

6. Droudakis, *10,000 Mantinades of Crete*, 274. Also appears in Pavlakis, *Cretan Folk Poetry*, 235.

Chapter 13

1. Droudakis, *10,000 Mantinades of Crete*, 502.
2. Droudakis, *10,000 Mantinades of Crete*, 494.
3. Pavlakis, *Cretan Folk Poetry*, 242.
4. Kazantzakis, *Report to Greco*, 23.

Chapter 17

1. Kazantzakis, *Report to Greco*, 307.
2. Kazantzakis, *Report to Greco*, 308.
3. Michael Herzfeld, *The Poetics of Manhood: Contest and Identity in a Cretan Mountain Village* (Princeton: Princeton University Press, 1985), 124.
4. Herzfeld, *The Poetics of Manhood*, 16.
5. Herzfeld, *The Poetics of Manhood*, 36.
6. Herzfeld, *The Poetics of Manhood*, 135.
7. Michael Herzfeld, "'As in Your Own House': Hospitality, Ethnography, and the Stereotype of Mediterranean Society," in D. D. Gilmore, *Honor and Shame and the Unity of the Mediterranean*, ed. D. D. Gilmore (Washington, DC: American Anthropological Association, 1987), 77.

8. Michael Herzfeld, *A Place in History: Monumental and Social Time in a Cretan Town* (Princeton: Princeton University Press, 1991), 81.

9. Michael Herzfeld, *The Body Impolitic: Artisans and Artiface in the Global Hierarchy of Value* (Chicago: University of Chicago Press, 2004), 86.

10. Herzfeld, "'As in Your Own House,'" 77.

11. Herzfeld, "'As in Your Own House,'" 78.

12. Herzfeld, "'As in Your Own House,'" 86.

Chapter 18

1. *Mondovino*. DVD. 2005. Directed by Jonathan Nossiter. [n.p.]: Think-Film.

2. The following paper makes me think that such an interpretation might not be me just reading too much into the film: Diane Barthel-Bouchier and Lauretta Clough, "From Mondavi to Depardieu: The Global/Local Politics of Wine," *French Politics, Culture & Society* 23 (2) (2005): 71–90.

Chapter 19

1. Books like: Vassilis Lambropoulos, *Literature as National Institution: Studies in the Politics of Modern Greek Criticism* (Princeton: Princeton University Press, 1988); Gregory Jusdanis, *Belated Modernity and Aesthetic Culture: Inventing National Literature* (Minneapolis: University of Minnesota Press, 1991); and Artemis Leontis, *Topographies of Hellenism: Mapping the Homeland* (Ithaca, NY: Cornell University Press, 1995).

2. The writing here about Greek cookbooks is reworked from parts of the previously published paper: Eric L. Ball, "Greek Food After *Mousaka*: Cookbooks, 'Local' Culture, and the Cretan Diet," *Journal of Modern Greek Studies* 21 (1) (2003): 1–36.

3. Agapios, *Γεωπονικόν Αγαπίου Μοναχού του Κρητός* [*Geoponikon*] (Athens, Greece: Εκδόσεις Κουλτούρα, 1979 [Reprint of 1850 edition printed in Venice]).

4. Anna Matthaiou, *Η Μαγειρική: Ανώνυμη μετάφραση του 1828* [*Cookbook, Anonymous Translation of 1828*] (Athens, Greece: Βιβλιολογικό Εργαστήρι [Reprint of 1828 edition printed in Syros], 1992).

5. Matthaiou, *Cookbook*, 3.

6. Matthaiou, *Cookbook*, viii.

7. Nikolaos Tselementes, *Οδηγός Μαγειρικής και Ζαχαροπλαστικής*, 15th ed. [*Cooking and Pastry-Making Guide*] (Athens, Greece: Φυτράκης, 1970).

8. Tselementes, *Cooking and Pastry-Making Guide*, 15th ed. xxxviii.

9. Nikolaos Tselementes, *Οδηγός Μαγειρικής*, 10th ed. [*Cooking Guide*]. (Athens, Greece: Οίκος Σαλιβέρου, 1951), 51.

10. Tselementes, *Cooking and Pastry-Making Guide*, xlv.

11. Tselementes, *Cooking and Pastry-Making Guide*, xliv.

12. Tselementes, *Cooking and Pastry-Making Guide*, xlv.

13. Sofia Souli, *222 Συνταγές Ελληνικής Μαγειρικής* [*222 Recipes of Greek Cooking*] (Athens, Greece: Εκδόσεις Μιχάλης Τουμπής, 1989), 5.

14. Maria Psilakis and Nikos Psilakis, *Το Κρητικόν Εδεσματολόγιον: Κρητική Παραδοσιακή Κουζίνα*, 5th ed. [*Cretan Traditional Cooking*] (Irakleio, Greece: *Καρμάνωρ*, 1997 [1995]).

15. Psilakis and Psilakis, *Cretan Traditional Cooking*, 7.

16. Psilakis and Psilakis, *Cretan Traditional Cooking*, 7.

17. Psilakis and Psilakis, *Cretan Traditional Cooking*, 7.

18. Psilakis and Psilakis, *Cretan Traditional Cooking*, 7.

19. Michael Herzfeld, *Ours Once More: Folklore, Ideology, and the Making of Modern Greece* (New York: Pella, 1986), 13.

20. For example, see William A. Wilson, "Herder, Folklore and Romantic Nationalism," in *Folk Groups and Folklore Genres: A Reader*, ed. Elliott Oring (Logan: Utah State University Press, 1989), 21–37. See also Roger D. Abrahams, "Phantoms of Romantic Nationalism," *Journal of American Folklore* 106 (419) (1993): 3–37.

21. Psilakis and Psilakis, *Cretan Traditional Cooking*, 30.

22. Psilakis and Psilakis, *Cretan Traditional Cooking*, 35.

23. Psilakis and Psilakis, *Cretan Traditional Cooking*, 116.

24. Psilakis and Psilakis, *Cretan Traditional Cooking*, 36.

25. Psilakis and Psilakis, *Cretan Traditional Cooking*, 170.

26. Daniel Zohary and Maria Hopf, *Domestication of Plants in the Old World: The origin and Spread of Cultivated Plants in West Asia, Europe and the Nile Valley* (Oxford: Oxford University Press, 2000).

27. Psilakis and Psilakis, *Cretan Traditional Cooking*, 11.

28. Manolis Avramakis [Μανώλης Αβραμάκης], "Δίκταμος ο θεραπευτικός [Therapeutic *Diktamos*]," in *Εφτά Ημέρες Κρήτη: Οδοιπορικό στον Ψηλορείτη* [*Seven Days in Crete: Traveling Across Psiloreitis*], ed. Eleftheria Traiou. (Insert in newspaper *Η Καθημερινή*, July 30, 2000), 31.

29. Avramakis, "Therapeutic *Diktamos*," 31. See also Pavlakis, *Cretan Folk Poetry*, 372.

30. See Eric L. Ball, "Toward a Greek Ecocriticism: Place Awareness and Cultural Identity in Pandelis Prevelakis's *Οι δρόμοι της δημιουργίας*," *Journal of Modern Greek Studies* 23 (1) (2005): 7–8.

31. Theocharis E. Detorakis, *History of Crete* (Trans. by John C. Davis) (Iraklion: n.p., 1994), 4.

32. Manolis Doulgerakis, *Οίνος Κρητικός: 5000 χρόνια το νέκταρ των θεών* [*Cretan Wine: Nectar of the Gods for 5000 Years*] (Irakleio, Greece: Ένωση Ξενοδόχων Ν. Ηρακλείου, 1997).

33. Doulgerakis, *Cretan Wine*, 2.

34. Yiorgos Anagnostou, *Contours of White Ethnicity: Popular Ethnography and the Making of Usable Pasts in Greek America* (Athens: Ohio University Press, 2009).

Chapter 21

1. S. H. Zeisel, L. H. Allen, S. P. Coburn, J. W. Erdman, M. L. Failla, H. C. Freake, J. C. King, and J. Storch, "Nutrition: A Reservoir for Integrative Science," *Journal of Nutrition* 131, (4) (2000): 1319.

2. Mark Messina, Johanna W. Lampe, Diane F. Birt, Lawrence J. Appel, Elizabeth Pivonka, Barbara Berry, and David R. Jacobs, "Reductionism and the Narrowing Nutrition Perspective," *Journal of the American Dietetic Association* 101 (2) (2001), 1419.

3. Gary Taubes, "Epidemiology Faces Its Limits," *Science* 269 (5221) (1995), 164.

4. Michael Pollan, *In Defense of Food: An Eater's Manifesto* (New York: The Penguin Press, 2008).

5. Pollan, *In Defense of Food*, 11.

6. Pollan, *In Defense of Food*, 10.

7. Pollan, *In Defense of Food*, 182.

8. Pollan, *In Defense of Food*, 66.

9. Pollan, *In Defense of Food*, 1.

10. Pollan, *In Defense of Food*, 143.

11. An excellent read: Julie Guthman, *Agrarian Dreams: The Paradox of Organic Farming in California* (Berkeley: University of California Press, 2004).

12. Pollan, *In Defense of Food*, 9.

13. Pollan, *In Defense of Food*, 181.

14. Pollan, *In Defense of Food*, 173.

15. Paul Campos, *The Obesity Myth: Why America's Obsession with Weight Is Hazardous to Your Health* (New York: Gotham, 2004), xxv.

16. Barry Glassner, *The Gospel of Food: Why We Should Stop Worrying and Enjoy What We Eat* (New York: Harper, 2007), 193–197.

17. Eric J. Oliver, *Fat Politics: The Real Story Behind America's Obesity Epidemic* (Oxford: Oxford University Press, 2006), 2.

18. Oliver, *Fat Politics*, 5.

19. Oliver, *Fat Politics*, 11.

20. Campos, *The Obesity Myth*, xxii.

Chapter 23

1. For more on truly free markets, see Eugene W. Holland, *Nomad Citizenship: Free-Market Communism and the Slow-Motion General Strike* (Minneapolis: University of Minnesota Press, 2011).

2. Wendell Berry, *What Are People For?* (New York: North Point Press, 1990), 149.

3. Berry, *What Are People For?* 148, 150, 148, respectively.

4. Berry, *What Are People For?* 151.

5. Berry, *What Are People For?* 151.

6. Peter Singer and Jim Mason, *The Way We Eat: Why Our Food Choices Matter* (USA: Rodale, 2006).

Epilogue

1. Frederick Ragovin, *Cretan Mantinades: Song Poems, Collected and Translated into English Verse* (Athens, Greece: Cnossos, 1974), 31. (The English translation, however, is my own.) Also appears in Droudakis, *10,000 Mantinades of Crete*, 411.